WOMEN IN RUSSIAN THEATRE

Women in Russian Theatre: The Actress in the Silver Age, the first study of Russian actresses to be published in English, is a fascinating feminist intervention into the field of Russian theatre history. With unprecedented access to newly opened files in Russia, Catherine A. Schuler examines how actresses, as a class of working women with common experiences and objectives, had an impact upon Russian modernist theatre.

Women in Russian Theatre offers case studies of the popular actresses and actress-entrepeneurs of the age of Stanislavski, the Moscow Art Theatre and Vsevolod Meierhold. It examines the circumstances within which performers, such as Mariia Savina, Mariia Ermolova, Glikeriia Fedotova, Polina Strepetova, Anna Brenko, Lidia Iavorskaia and Vera Kommissarzhevskaia, dominated the provincial, state and arts theatres of the period. It is with clarity and insight that Schuler considers how the social, political and aesthetic context contributed to the "apogee of the actress" at this time.

Women in Russian Theatre is an engrossing and unrivalled document of a neglected side of this dynamic era of theatre history. It makes invaluable reading for academics and graduate students of theatre studies, Russian studies, women's studies and comparative literature.

Catherine A. Schuler is Associate Professor of Theatre History at the University of Maryland. She is co-editor of *Theatre and Feminist Aesthetics* and has published widely in the areas of Russian theatre and feminist performance.

GENDER IN PERFORMANCE
General editors: Susan Bassnett and Tracy C. Davis

The *Gender in Performance* series reflects the dynamic and innovative work by feminists across the disciplines. Exploring both historical and contemporary theatre the series seeks to understand performance both as a cultural and a political phenomenon.

Also available:
CONTEMPORARY FEMINIST THEATRES
To each her own
Lizbeth Goodman

ACTRESSES AS WORKING WOMEN
Their social identity in Victorian culture
Tracy C. Davis

AS SHE LIKES IT
Shakespeare's unruly women
Penny Gay

FEMINIST THEATERS IN THE U.S.A.
Staging women's experience
Charlotte Canning

GETTING INTO THE ACT
Women playwrights in London 1776–1829
Eileen Donkin

WOMEN IN RUSSIAN THEATRE

The Actress in the Silver Age

Catherine A. Schuler

London and New York

First published 1996
by Routledge
11 New Fetter Lane, London EC4P 4EE
29 West 35th Street, New York, NY 10001

Typeset in Garamond by
Ponting–Green Publishing Services, Chesham, Bucks

Printed and bound in Great Britain by
Biddles Ltd, Guildford and King's Lynn

British Library Cataloguing in Publication Data
A catalogue record for this book is available from the
British Library

Library of Congress Cataloging in Publication Data
Schuler, Catherine A.
Women in Russian theatre: The actress in the silver age /
Catherine A. Schuler.
p. cm. – (Gender in performance)
Includes bibliographical references and index.
1. Actresses–Russia–Biography. 2. Women in the theater–
Russia–History–19th century 3.Women in the theater–
Russia–History–20th century.
I. Title. II. Series.
IN PROCESS
792'.028'092247–dc20 99–3695

ISBN 0–415–11105–6 (hbk)
ISBN 0–415–14397–7 (pbk)

PN
2727
.S38
1996

*To Nancy and Bill Schuler
whose forty-three years of
love, patience, and support
made this book possible.*

CONTENTS

ILLUSTRATIONS

ACKNOWLEDGEMENTS

Many individuals and institutions contributed to the realization of this project.

I would like to thank the National Endowment for the Humanities for a travel grant which supported my first tentative sallies into the subject of women in Russian theatre. I am also deeply indebted to the Graduate Research Board at the University of Maryland for two substantial summer research grants as well as a grant for materials. My deepest appreciation is reserved for the Russian and East European Center at the University of Illinois, Urbana-Champaign. I could not have researched or written this book without continuous financial and technical support from this extraordinary institution. Long may its banner wave!

I owe much gratitude to librarians and staff at the following libraries: Widener Library and the Theatre Collection at Harvard University; the Library of Congress in Washington, D.C.; the Slavic Library at the University of Illinois at Urbana-Champaign; the Slavic Library in Helsinki; the Lenin Library in Moscow; and the Saltykov-Shchedrin Public Library in St. Petersburg. Although all of the Slavic librarians at the University of Illinois are extraordinary, I want to extend special thanks to Helen Sullivan for her support and advice over six years. In addition, the librarians and staff at the St. Petersburg Theatre Library went far beyond the call of duty in assisting me to find and photocopy large amounts of material in very short periods of time. I am especially grateful to the Director, Raisa Andreeva Mikhaliova, for smoothing my way, and to the Associate Director, Galina Nikolaevna Rodomanova, for her personal kindness to me during moments of research panic. My archival research in Russia was assisted by the following institutions: The Bakhrushin Theatre Museum and the Central State Archive of Art and Literature in Moscow, and the Theatre Museum in St. Petersburg.

Many friends and colleagues here and abroad contributed to this project. Among my British and Finnish colleagues, I want especially to thank Linda Edmondson, Melanie Ilic, Catriona Kelly, and Liisa Byckling for helping me to sort through and clarify ideas about, and connections between Russian culture, theatrical conventions, actresses, and feminism. As a long-time member of the "Women in Slavic Culture and Literature" discussion group at the University of Illinois' Summer Research Laboratory, I must express my appreciation to the many colleagues in that group who have listened patiently while I droned on about Russian actresses over six summers. Daria Krizhanskaia was my saint in St. Petersburg and I could not have negotiated Moscow without the help of Ludmilla Selivanova. I want to thank Patti Gillespie, Harry Elam and Jane Donawerth, colleagues at the University of Maryland who read and offered valuable advice on the first draft of the manuscript. I owe much gratitude to Tracy Davis for encouraging me to pursue this project and for her patient perusal of multiple drafts. I suspect she has had her fill of Russian actresses for the time being. Although they are blissfully ignorant of Russian culture and theatre, I would also like to thank Susan Leonardi and Rebecca Pope for helping me to maintain a sense of humor during difficult moments – especially when those moments involved any sort of air travel.

Finally, what can I say about Mary Zirin? Without her encouragment, support, and guidance, this book would not have been written. I am fortunate that such a model of personal and scholarly integrity has been my friend and mentor for the last six years. Thank you, Mary. May we have many more years of working together – and I promise not to yell at you again in front of the Moscow Pizza Hut.

Parts of this book have appeared elsewhere in somewhat altered form. Chapter 6 appeared as "Anna Brenko and the Pushkin Theatre: Moscow's First Art Theatre?," *Theatre Survey*, May 1992, vol. 33, pp. 85–105; Chapter appeared as "The Silver Age Actress as Unruly Woman Starring Lidia Iavorskaia as Madonna," *Theatre Survey*, November 1993, vol. 34, pp. 55–76; parts of Chapters 6 and 8 appeared as "Female Theatrical Entrepreneurs in the Silver Age: A Prerevolutionary Revolution", *Theatre History Studies*, 1993, vol. 13, pp. 79–94.

NOTE ON TRANSLITERATION

For the most part, I have used the Library of Congress system of trans-
literation. With respect to proper names, however, I have tried to use more
familiar transliterations. For that reason, the reader will find "Meierhold"
rather than "Meierkhol'd," "Stanislavski" rather than "Stanislavskii," and so
on. In addition, although the Russian soft sign (') appears in the notes, for the
benefit of non-Russianist readers, on the whole I have dropped it from the
text. Unless otherwise indicated, all translations are my own.

NOTE ON PROPER NAMES

Russians traditionally identify themselves using some combination of three
different names, a practice that often leaves non-Russian readers in abject
despair and confusion. Throughout this study, I have followed Russian
practice by freely using first names, patronymics, and surnames to refer to
the actresses. To assist the general reader's comprehension and pleasure,
therefore, a list of the full names of the major figures is provided below.

Mariia Gavrilovna Savina
Glikeriia Nikolaevna Fedotova
Mariia Nikolaevna Ermolova
Polina Antipevna Strepetova
Anna Alekseevna Brenko
Lidia Borisovna Iavorskaia
Vera Fedorovna Kommissarzhevskaia (Kommissarzhevskaia's last name was
    spelled with two 'm's during her lifetime and one after the Revolution.
    Except where the author of a book or article prefers the later spelling, I
    have used the pre-revolutionary form.)

1

THE APOGEE OF
THE ACTRESS
Rhetoric or reality

In spite of the influence of Russian drama and theatre on Western practice, only a few canonized figures are widely recognized outside Russia, and most of their activities are confined to a single period: the Silver Age (c. 1898–1917). Men like Konstantin Stanislavski, Anton Chekhov, and Vsevolod Meierhold are rightfully perceived as major theatrical innovators. For that reason, scholarship in Russia and the West has tended to focus on their accomplishments, often at the expense of equally remarkable events, people, and movements.

The period between 1870 and 1910, when starring actresses dominated the Russian stage in St. Petersburg, Moscow, and the provinces, is less familiar, but equally intriguing. This period, which does not correspond precisely to existing chronologies of Russian theatre, art, and literature, includes, but is not limited to the Silver Age. Described by John Bowlt as "a sudden and spectacular renaissance in art and literature,"[1] the Silver Age is familiar to theatre historians as the age of theatrical modernism when the giants of Russian theatre – Stanislavski, Chekhov, and Meierhold – led actors, directors, playwrights, and designers out of the dark ages of Imperial monopolies, obsolete production practices and conventions, starring actors, and cheap popular drama into a new era of progress and innovation. As a result, for the first time Russian theatre won respect in the West and prominent Russian practitioners and playwrights achieved recognition outside their own country.

That Russia became a center for progressive theatre and drama during the Silver Age is beyond doubt; that it was also a progressive era for women in theatre is less certain. Although there was much interest in the Woman Question (*zhenskii vopros*) during the period, Silver Age theatre was not particularly receptive to feminists or feminist ideology. Nonetheless, certain characteristics peculiar to the period were propitious for women in modernist literature and the arts. In 1899, *The World of Art* (*Mir iskusstva*) trumpeted the notion that by its very nature modernism embraced marginal artists, especially those who had been rejected for reasons of academic tradition or aesthetic propriety by established critics, publishing firms, museums, and galleries.[2] This constituted an open invitation for women, who surely

1

constituted one of the most marginalized groups in Russia, to engage in hitherto restricted activities. According to Charlotte Rosenthal, the modernists' elevation of art to the status of "secular religion" and concomitant emphasis on "individual creativity" encouraged women to step outside traditional roles.[3] Not only did the number of women authors and artists expand, they also profited from the trend toward professionalization in Russia during the post-reform era.[4]

Given the achievements of women in Silver Age literature and art, the period would seem ideal for a reconsideration of Russian actresses. It is tempting, therefore, to believe Isabella Grinevskaia, who, speaking before the first Russian Women's Congress in 1908, proclaimed to the assembled representatives of Russian feminism that the apogee of the actress had been achieved in their own era.[5] Unfortunately, despite the many remarkable advances in the art and practice of theatre during the Silver Age, it accommodates neither the rise of starring actresses and actress-entrepreneurs nor the corresponding popularization of "women's themes" on the Russian stage. Indeed, it might be argued that modernism and the attendant rise of the neo-Wagnerian master artist hastened the demise of starring actresses, displaced actress-entrepreneurs, and chased "women's themes" from the stage.

Assuming for a moment that Grinevskaia's "golden age" of Russian actresses can actually be located near the end of the nineteenth century and beginning of the twentieth, it began at least 20 years before the dawn of the Silver Age and was already fading before 1910. Facilitated by the ever increasing power of the mass-circulation press, the public preoccupation with actresses and "women's themes" was in large part a response to issues raised by the Russian women's movement after 1860 and to increased contact with the West. The effect of feminism and Western sex/gender ideology on the theatre was gradual. The first Russian actresses who could legitimately claim a sort of superstardom in their own country started their careers in the 1870s and reached the pinnacle of their popularity in the 1880s and 1890s; "women's themes" began to predominate in dramatic literature and on stage in the 1880s; and the first actress-entrepreneurs in St. Petersburg and Moscow did not appear until 1880. It is ironic – and perhaps not coincidental – that as both the real and symbolic power of women increased between 1870 and 1900, so, too, did attacks on both the business and art of theatre.

One question central to this study is whether the "Apogee of the Actress" in Russian theatre, like the "Year of the Woman"[6] in American politics, was more rhetoric than reality. It is a question without an easy answer. Certainly the number of actresses increased, which was part of a broader trend in female employment, and the most prominent of them enjoyed unprecedented notoriety and privilege. The influx of aspiring actresses into the theatre and the higher status enjoyed by a few of them clearly reflects the growing instability of Russian patriarchal autocracy. But even Grinevskaia, who enthusiastically proclaimed their ascendancy at the Women's Congress, understood perfectly the constraints that continued to hinder the development of actresses as independent artists. Although the situation of women in the theatre had improved over several decades, she was not naive enough to suppose that the fundamentally patriarchal infrastructure of the theatre had changed significantly. Regardless of the power of starring actresses and the independent achievements of actress-entrepreneurs, Russian theatre was, she complained, still controlled by men, and Russian audiences, which were as unruly as the mobs at Roman spectacles, still viewed actresses solely as commodities. "The reign of women on stage," she concluded pessimistically, "will last only as long as men want it and allow it to continue."[7] Plunged into momentary pessimism, Grinevskaia may have overstated the case. Certainly there was progress between 1870 and 1910, but the notion that it was a "golden age" for actresses must be approached with caution. It is the purpose of this study to consider the authentic achievements of actresses during the period and the changing social and political context that engendered them, but also to acknowledge the often unpleasant realities of life in the theatre for Russian women.

A BRIEF OVERVIEW

In order to appreciate the altered status of actresses between 1870 and 1910, it is necessary to have a fundamental grasp of conditions for women in theatre during the eighteenth and early nineteenth centuries. Grinevskaia, who prefaced her remarks on the ascendancy of the actress with a brief history of women in Russian theatre from its inception through the Silver Age, provided her audience with an overview of the situation as she saw it in 1908.[8] From the beginning, Russian theatre was distinguished from Western European theatre by the absence of a history of excluding women from the stage on moral and religious grounds or for reasons of social convention. By Grinevskaia's account, Russian theatre, as distinguished from folk entertainments, arose late in the seventeenth century when pastor Gregori founded an acting troupe consisting of young children (*molodye rebiata*). Gregori's enterprise lasted for only three years and there was no further attempt to initiate a Russian theatre (recognizable as such by the West) until 1703, when Peter the Great built the "*komediinaia khoromina*" in Moscow and invited a German troupe, which included actresses, to perform in it. The first Russian actress, Pagankova, the wife of Peter's court physician, was an amateur who performed with the Germans. The Imperial theatres, which were founded in the 1750s, included performers of both sexes, as did the estate theatres that flourished in the eighteenth and nineteenth centuries.

Grinevskaia suggests that actors and actresses enjoyed equal status during the eighteenth and much of the nineteenth century. Under the tsarist autocracy, she declared, neither men nor women enjoyed civil rights; for that reason, a certain uneasy gender equality existed in Russian society and, by extension, in Russian theatre. Echoing the assumptions of many Russians about pre-Soviet equality of oppression, Grinevskaia added that: "Women, in the epoch from the founding of the theatre to the abolition of serfdom, shared fully the position of their comrades, the position of slaves who entertained their masters."[9]

Russians, many of whom resist the assumptions of Western feminism about women's oppression, are fond of using this history of mutual social, political, and economic inequality as evidence that the separate issue of women's equality is largely irrelevant to an understanding of prerevolutionary culture. But in the theatre, though actors of both sexes may have felt the sting of the master's whip, their material conditions were hardly equivalent. As an example, Grinevskaia offered the discrepancy between the salaries and benefits received by Aleksei Iakovlev and Katerina Semenova, both leading actors in the Imperial theatres at the beginning of the nineteenth century: "In 1805," she wrote, "Semenova, who was the romantic female lead, received a salary of 1,600 roubles, 200 roubles for an apartment, and a benefit performance for which she bore the expenses, but during the same period, Iakovlev, who was the male lead, received a salary of 4,000 roubles, 500 roubles for an apartment, and the directorate bore the expenses for his benefit."[10]

Having sketched with broad strokes the history of women in Russian theatre, Grinevskaia proclaimed the ascendancy of the actress during the Silver Age – and in spite of the obstacles they still faced, she had good reason to think so. Unprecedented numbers of women began pouring into the theatre in the last decades of the nineteenth century. Between approximately 1870 and 1910, starring actresses dominated the Russian stage and for the first time, personality cults arose around the most prominent of them.[11] During this period, the hegemony of Mariia Savina, Glikeriia Fedotova, and Mariia Ermolova defined the repertoires of the Imperial theatres in St. Petersburg and Moscow and set the standards by which other actresses were measured. Spectators wept over the eternal oppression of Russian women as it was reflected in Polina Strepetova's anguished characterizations. Deeply touched by her soulful, modernist heroines, youthful idealists of both sexes idolized the Duse of the Russian stage, Vera Kommissarzhevskaia. Duse herself, along with Sarah Bernhardt, Rejane, and other Western touring stars, spawned a host of imitators, the most prominent of whom was Lidia Iavorskaia. Iavorskaia, about whom critics wryly observed that she could not play any role if she hadn't seen Bernhardt in it first, took imitation of Western European manners and fashion to its zenith. Inspired by the examples of Bernhardt, Duse, and Russia's own Anna Brenko, who established the first semi-legal private theatre in Moscow in 1880, at least fifteen Russian actresses opened their own theatres in the capital cities between 1880 and 1917. The sheer volume of gender-specific literature published about actresses attests to the public's obsession with them during this period. This material includes revelations about individual stars, articles about actresses as a generic category of theatre worker, about actresses and family life, about actresses and prostitution, poems dedicated to individual actresses, as well as fictional accounts of actresses' lives published as stories in thick journals and as books.

Changes in the theatre often reflect fundamental shifts in ideology and cultural values. The period between 1870 and 1917 was characterized by tremendous civil unrest in Russia culminating in the October Revolution. The disintegration of the tsarist autocracy, which began well before the Revolution, was enacted on many levels, including the sexual and theatrical. The predominance of "women's themes" during the period, the rise of starring actresses, and the inclination among several of the most prominent to independent entrepreneurship raise fundamental questions about the relationship between theatre, sexual ideology, and the interests of the state. Precipitated by a conflation of social, political, economic, and aesthetic factors, the phenomenal influx of women into the theatre and their temporary magnification was part of a larger trend which presaged a decline in the authority of the patriarchal family and, by implication, of the tsarist autocracy.

TRANSFORMING "*ZHENSTVENNOST*": ACTRESSES AND THE WOMAN QUESTION

In order to understand why so many enthusiastic, aspiring actresses poured into the theatre at the end of the century, it is necessary to consider the effects of the social reforms of the 1860s and the state's program of modernization on sexual ideology and gender identity. Although Russian women enjoyed certain privileges denied to women in the more progressive nations of Western Europe, at the dawn of the nineteenth century Russia was still a rigidly patriarchal, authoritarian autocracy, the laws and customs of which "subordinated Russian women to men more absolutely than was the case for their European sisters."[12] The maintenance of social and political order was contingent upon the subordination of women because, according to Barbara Engel, family stability, which was essential to that order, depended on the absolute authority of husbands over wives.[13] Confined to the private sphere, denied opportunities for education and employment, Russian women had little presence or representation in the public life of the nation. Those few who had the temerity to encroach upon the public domain of men risked severe censure.

Although occasional reforms in the laws governing women were initiated before the middle of the nineteenth century, until Aleksandr II came to power in 1855, few women outside the aristocracy accrued any benefits from them. The most famous of the so-called Great Reforms introduced by Aleksandr was the emancipation of the serfs in 1861, but his generally liberal regime launched a number of progressive projects. Aleksandr oversaw the reorganization of self-government and initiated judicial reforms. Censorship laws were relaxed, a process that stimulated the formation, expression, and dissemination of radical ideas and ideologies, many of which can be traced to post-Enlightenment Western Europe. The mass-circulation press, which developed in the second half of the century, made not only radical ideas, but also general information about national and international events and people widely available. The success of the mass-circulation press was contingent upon greater literacy in the general population.[14] Although Aleksandr continued to regard with suspicion the prospect of an educated populace, educational reforms were enacted, the most radical of which was higher education for women. Finally, the post-emancipation period also witnessed economic modernization and dramatically increased industrialization, which in turn brought large numbers of the rural population to work in urban factories. And although Russia did not have a standard Marxist bourgeois class, economic reform and industrialization speeded the the development of an entreprenurial class with bourgeois tastes and aspirations.[15]

If few of the reforms enacted by Aleksandr between 1855 and his assassination in 1881 were expressly intended to advance the cause of women in Russia, they inadvertently assisted the emancipation movement by calling into question, and ultimately undermining, the absolute authority of the autocracy. The effects of ideological instability, political unrest, and economic transformation on gender relations were apparent at all levels of society. Although peasant culture and village life resisted modernization, according to Laura Engelstein, the migration of country folk into the cities affected gender relations among the Russian "*narod.*"[16] "City living," she wrote, "undermined folk customs and weakened traditional family ties, releasing not only women but children too from the chastening bonds of patriarchal authority. The result was sexual as well as social chaos, the emergence of a new public space inhabited by female creatures with the independence and energy of men and by men who sought a way to exercise power, or to claim power of a new kind outside the frame of respectable family life."[17]

If the decay of patriarchal authority affected the psychology of, and conditions of life for, lower-class women, the effects of this disintegration were even more profound among women of the intelligentsia who could, after 1872, audit advanced university lecture courses, receive a medical education, or, by the end of the decade, enroll in a women's university.[18] As women moved into the public sphere during the 1850s, 1860s, and 1870s, the tendency among many was toward social activism. Women from the upper classes plunged enthusiastically into a variety of charitable organizations and reform movements, especially among the urban poor and in peasant communities. Rebelling against the restrictions of family and state, the more radically inclined educated women demonstrated their solidarity with nihilism by cropping their hair, simplifying conventional feminine attire, wearing blue glasses, and smoking in public. Many educated gentry and middle-class women joined violent liberation movements like the People's Will, which plotted the assassination of Aleksandr II. Others pursued revolutionary objectives by distributing propaganda and espousing the ideology of populism (*narodnichestvo*) among the peasant population.[19] Intoxicated by lofty ideals of suffering and self-sacrifice in the name of social justice, Russian women displayed a moral zealotry almost unknown in the West. So powerful was the imperative for selfless service to family and state that many emerging professional women, including actresses, used the rhetoric of social service to describe – and perhaps justify – their presence in the public sphere.

Industrialization and the wide range of educational and economic reforms enacted under Aleksandr II obliged men and women alike to reassess conventional gender assumptions and relations in both the public and private spheres. Among the women, some were forced unwillingly out of their traditional roles, while others escaped voluntarily. For a range of reasons, from the most selfless to the most self-serving, women of all classes increasingly resisted confinement to hearth, home, and husband, but it would be misleading to suggest that the changes that swept the country between the emancipation in 1861 and the second revolution in 1917 altered the fundamental ideological bases of Russian patriarchy. Demands for social reform were met with great resistance and women lagged behind men in gaining access to education and employment. Deeply influenced by the dogma of Church and State, closely bound to the very traditions and institutions that were the source of their oppression, and increasingly separated from each other by class, education, and economics, Russian women were often a reactionary rather than progressive force.[20] Nonetheless, there were some who recognized the desirability of solidarity among women and the need for a program of social action that addressed the specific needs of women. Although social and political instability, as well as swift suppression of subversive movements, hindered the development of an effective women's rights movement in Russia, inspired by Western European models, one did emerge, albeit tentatively, after 1861. If the Russian women's movement did not enjoy the authority of its British or American models, the questions it raised about the "natural" inclinations and capabilities of men and women and about equal rights posed a tangible threat to male privilege – which in turn helped to weaken that cornerstone of the autocracy, the patriarchal family.

The Woman Question, which arose in Russia in the 1850s and 1860s, was an inevitable product of both external and internal influences.[21] The theoretical framework was imported largely from the West, but the emancipation of the serfs was an equally important factor in the rise of the Russian women's movement. As Linda Edmondson pointed out, the parallel "between the subjection of the peasant to the serf-owner and that of a woman to her father or husband was quickly drawn and the emancipation of the serfs encouraged demands for female emancipation too."[22] In the 1860s and 1870s, supporters, who were primarily concerned with female unemployment and gaining access to higher education and professional status for women, made significant gains in at least one of those areas – education. After the assassination of Aleksandr II in 1881, his successor not only abrogated most of the earlier reforms, but also barred women from joining societies that did not have specifically philanthropic or educational objectives. In all of the major cities except St. Petersburg, women's higher education was dismantled. Although this and other equally repressive measures temporarily disrupted the forward progress of Russian women, they may actually have had a salutory effect on theatre. Tatiana Shchepkina-Kupernik suggested that during and after the 1880s, with their courses and universities closed, many bright women who might otherwise have gone into medicine or other helping professions turned to literature, art, and theatre.[23] The repression persisted until the end of Aleksandr III's reign in 1894 when, in spite of continued resistance to its agenda, Russian feminism was revitalized and educational and employment opportunities for women expanded once again.

The Woman Question in Russia was multifaceted, and the barrage of articles, feuilletons, and books published about it during the period focused on a number of related issues, including the proper role of women in public and private spheres, the role of biology and environment in the subordination of women, problems of deviant sexuality and prostitution, and proper relations between the sexes. Liberals, who tended to accept Enlightenment arguments about egalitarianism, supported expanded educational and employment opportunities for women. Endeavoring to counteract the alien ideology of sexual equality that threatened to undermine family and state, conservatives combed through the misogynist wisdom of the ages for evidence to support their contention that women were innately inferior and destined by nature to be subordinate and submissive to men. Persuaded of the moral and intellectual inferiority of women, conservatives argued that their behaviors and activities should be regulated more strictly than in the past. An important ideological "side effect" of the gender war that was sparked between feminists and their detractors was the destabilization of conventional femininity, or "*zhenstvennost*," a phenomenon that had tremendous resonance in the theatre.[24]

Today, the idea that gender is socially constructed and flexible has gained wide acceptance in the West, at least within academic communities. But during the nineteenth and early twentieth centuries, all but a few Russians accepted without question the notion that gender is determined by nature and therefore immutable. The leaders of the early women's emancipation movement were the first to challenge biologically based apologies for sex discrimination. Embracing Darwinian theory insofar as it sustained a constructionist point of view, they argued that environment, not biology, was the chief determinant of individual development. Inequality of opportunity was, from their point of view, the principal obstacle to equality between men and women because, as one anonymous author optimistically declared: "Women and men have exactly the same capabilities."[25] This basically benign liberal feminist demand for equal access to education and employment may seem naive to sophisticated practitioners of contemporary feminist theory, but sentiments like these threatened to undermine the very fabric of Russian patriarchy. Challenged by the advocates of equal opportunity to justify continued discrimination, defenders of male privilege offered "woman's nature" (*zhenskaia priroda*) as an excuse for maintaining constraints on female education and employment.[26]

In *Idols of Perversity*, Bram Dijkstra explained that, during the second half of the nineteenth century, the rhetoric of science, which declared that inequality between men and women was an "inexorable law of nature," was employed throughout Europe to wage war on women.[27] Though Dijkstra does not specifically identify Russia as a polestar of international misogyny, the "backlash" literature that appeared at the end of the nineteenth century provides evidence of the pervasiveness of "scientifically based" opposition to women's equality. Feminist demands for equal education and employment challenged existing sexual ideology, which accepted as gospel the idea that a "true woman" was incapable of "sustained intellectual endeavor, sound and rational judgement, or creativity in anything other than reproduction, self-adornment and a little drawing or needlework."[28] To suggest that women could compete on the male playing field was to defy nature. Opponents of the women's movement, therefore, expended tremendous energy shoring up an increasingly inadequate system of beliefs about "*zhenstvennost*" that required physical and intellectual inferiority as God-given attributes of the female sex.

Typical of the anti-woman genre was I. Astafev's essay on the psychological world of women.[29] The Woman Question turned, according to Astafev, on two central points: 1) should women's position in the family and the state be determined on the basis of their physical and psychological constitutionn? 2) are women and men fundamentally different and are these differences determined by nature? According to Astafev, in both sexes, the particulars of function determine both their psychological makeup and spiritual inclinations; the reproductive function, which is natural to the female sex, limits women's intellectual development, constrains their freedom, and confines them to domesticity. Nature provides women with a limited supply of energy which must be focused on bearing and raising children. Anticipating the objection that not all women bear and raise children, Astafev countered that menstruation consumes an equivalent amount of energy. Thus, from a "scientific" point of view, women's natural functions do not leave any surplus energy for pursuing occupations outside the family. Indeed, according to Astafev, the *raison d'être* for the Woman Question was the presence in Russia of too many unmarried, unnatural, barren women. Denouncing the pernicious influence of women who rejected conventional forms of "*zhenstvennost*" based on natural law, Astafev predicted that any challenge to existing relations between men and women would destroy the institution of the family and, by implication, the state itself. Thus his conclusion that the obvious physical and psychological differences between the sexes are natural, ordained by God, and proven by scientific method comes as no surprise.

Echoing Astafev, the anonymous author of an article entitled "Femininity and the Bluestockings" (*Zhenstvennost i sinie chulki*) argued that a truly feminine woman stood out in a crowd because she was always surrounded by male admirers. Expounding on the characteristics of "*zhenstvennost*" as prescribed by natural law, he described the ideal woman: she was of "moderate height, full breasted, with a wide pelvis, small hands and feet, and a weak musculature." The form of her body should be "soft, round, and undulating," yet willowy; her movements must be "light" and her face, "expressive."[30] Coquettishness, an organic weapon in her feminine arsenal, was a function of natural selection which guaranteed the reproduction of the species.[31] Though he argued that a reciprocal relationship existed between female erudition and debauchery and protested that educated, scribbling women were an outrage against nature, the author also suggested that certain types of art, especially the "imitative, expressive, and transient" forms (for example, acting), were more accessible to women because they did not require inventiveness or depth of analysis.[32] Responding to prescriptive, reactionary critiques like these, one Russian feminist protested that traditional "*zhenstvennost*" implied "something undefined, weak, limited, and narrow."[33] It is no wonder, then, that many looked elsewhere, especially to the West, for new ideals.

Among the many crises that rocked Russia at the end of the century, the crisis of gender identity precipitated by the women's movement was simultaneously the most elusive and global. The demand by feminists for higher education and nontraditional employment contained an implicit challenge to existing sex/gender ideology and, therefore, to long cherished platitudes about women's nature and proper "*zhenstvennost*." The woman described by Astafev and his sympathizers could not possibly hope to compete in the public marketplace, but the changing social, political, and economic context required one who could. The new models came primarily from the West. One independent, free spirited New Woman, who had tremendous resonance among women aspiring to escape domestic bondage, was Maria Bashkirtsev, whose rebellion against social, religious, and moral conventions, devotion to aesthetic endeavors, and freewheeling lifestyle prompted Bernard Shaw to use her as the prototype for his "unwomanly woman."[34] Though many Russians were puzzled by, and hostile to, Ibsen's New Woman when she first appeared on stage in 1884, by the 1890s actresses, critics, and spectators were beginning to take her seriously.[35] Another genre of New Woman came to Russia from the United States, and though Russian ambivalence toward American culture and values was widespread, the series of "letters from America" published in *The Northern Herald* (*Severnyi vestnik*) attests to the fascination of educated Russians with the American "New Woman."[36] Because the Western New Woman, or "third sex" (*tretii pol*) as one anonymous author called her in "Echoes from Abroad" (*inostrannye otgoloski*), was a bit too individualistic even for most Russian feminists, her advocates modified the image to suit their own context. For that reason, the image of the New Woman popularized in feminist literature was framed in the rhetoric of individualism tempered by modesty and dedication to serving society.[37]

Balancing precariously along the shifting ideological fault lines of post-emancipation Russia, the theatre was simultaneously a harbinger of change and a buttress of tradition. Challenges to hegemonic sex/gender ideology were reflected in both the content of the drama and in its realization in performance, but because any expression of political dissent was subject to severe censorship, the relationship between Russian feminism and the theatre was largely indirect. The suffrage theatres and women's collectives that flourished alongside the British and American feminist movements were absent from Russia and little specifically feminist dramaturgy was produced. Though many of the concerns expressed by actresses about conditions of employment in their profession echoed general concerns of the feminist movement, few dared to espouse feminism publicly. Nonetheless, Russian feminism was important to the theatre for the questions it raised about the role of women in society, questions which stimulated production of a tremendous amount of book, periodical, and newspaper literature, which in turn influenced the theatre. And because theatre was an increasingly powerful – albeit strictly regulated – tool of social control, the controversy over sex/gender ideology was often enacted within its walls.

It was the debate between feminists and their detractors over "woman's nature" that destabilized "*zhenstvennost*" as a fixed term of cultural discourse and it is the conceptual instability of the term that helps to explain the public fascination with actresses during this period. In "Private Parts in Public Places," Juliet Blair argued that actresses as a generic category of women are unique because they have socially sanctioned access to the public space.[38] This was particularly true in Russia. The debate over "*zhenstvennost*" focused public attention on actresses largely because in Russia they were the most visible, concrete embodiments of particular gender qualities and ideals. In a culture that still demanded silence, obedience, and invisibility from its women, actresses became highly visible representatives of, and concrete points of reference for both the preservation of old, and the construction of new models of "*zhenstvennost*."

Questions about masculinity (*muzhestvennost*) occasionally arose, but for the most part the concept itself was more stable. Anxiety about the disintegration of conventional gender roles was, therefore, focused primarily on women. Though one angry anti-feminist requested her readers to turn their attention to the "Man Question," most discussions of *"muzhestvennost"* were in reference to deviations by women from traditional feminine norms.[39] The relative conceptual stability of *"muzhestvennost"* and instability of *"zhenstvennost"* may help to explain why the theatre-going public was simultaneously preoccupied with actresses and largely indifferent to actors as personalities or as representatives of particular gender ideals and stereotypes.

Two companion articles, "Actresses" and "Actors," published in *A Survey of Theatres* (*Obozrenie teatrov*), offer particularly instructive examples of how gender was handled in theatre journals and magazines.[40] The first article is gender-specific; actresses are discussed as a subclassication within the larger female species. Readers might logically assume that the second would treat actors as a subclassification of the male species, but there is nothing gender-specific about the second article, which discusses professional problems common to any performer. The actor, then, was generic and the actress, particular. In a culture seeking to reconcile competing sex/gender ideologies, actresses more than actors bore the weight of excessive symbolic signification. For that reason, their offstage lives – romances, sexual escapades, political sympathies, and tastes in clothing, home furnishings, food, and other personal items – were as interesting to audiences as their onstage performances. Concerned critics complained that the uncritical worship of personalities had reached pathological proportions.[41] And although a general preoccupation with celebrity was characteristic of the period, for actresses, much more than for actors, personality rather than craft became central to professional success.

In a rare contemporary article on the significance of Russian actresses in nineteenth-century culture, G.A. Zhernovaia argued that, during the 1880s, "women's themes" occupied a prominent place on the Russian stage largely thanks to the influence of three starring actresses: Mariia Ermolova, Polina Strepetova, and Mariia Savina.[42] According to Zhernovaia, more so than any other actresses of the period, Ermolova, Strepetova, and Savina embodied contrasting ideals of *"zhenstvennost,"* thereby drawing attention to and helping to popularize women's issues and stories. Later, during the last decade of the nineteenth century and first decade of the twentieth, Vera Kommissar-zhevskaia, Lidia Iavorskaia, and several other popular actresses introduced new ideals and images appropriate to the changing social and aesthetic context. It is Zhernovaia's contention that the actresses themselves created the appetite for "women's themes," but the evidence suggests otherwise. The tremendous attention paid to actresses in this period and the fascination with them as personalities were products of the controversy in Russia over sex/gender ideology and the role of women in society. Thus, it was not the personal charisma of a few powerful individuals that stimulated the interest in "women's themes" and, by implication, sex/gender ideology; rather it was uncertainty about ideology and proper gender identity that created the appetite for particular actresses, roles, and themes.

THE WESTERN INVASION: SARAH
BERNHARDT AND ELEONORA DUSE

In spite of the tendency among some historians to deemphasize Western influences on Russia, even a cursory glance at patterns of development in theatre at the end of the nineteenth century reveals the degree to which Western sexual ideology and aesthetics framed debates about the role of women in theatre and the role of theatre in Silver Age culture. Given the influences pouring into Russia from the West during the period, it was, perhaps, inevitable that the first actress to galvanize interest in the sex/gender controversy was not Russian. Sarah Bernhardt made her Russian debut in 1881 and, having discovered that substantial amounts of money could be earned in that country, returned several times. Bernhardt's influence on Russian actresses is indisputable, but she was a problematic figure for Russians because she embodied so many qualities inappropriate for – at least by conservative Russian standards – a truly feminine woman. Bernhardt, a mistress of the public relations coup, who slept in a coffin, paraded around in male attire, had multiple, well-publicized sexual liaisons, owned her own theatre, enjoyed tremendous personal, professional, and financial autonomy, and who indulged in emotional excesses on stage and off, simultaneously provided Russian women with an alternative – and apparently very attractive – model of "*zhenstvennost*" and threw Russian critics into a fury.

Although Bernhardt drew large crowds in Russia, many critics concurred with Turgenev that she was simply a "grand poseur"[43] whose success lay in her mastery of the crass art of marketing (*reklama*). The views expressed by V. Khabkin were typical of the extreme reactions she provoked. "Nine-tenths of her 'genius,'" he wrote, "is the product of outrageous advertising foisted on the rest of the world by Paris; the other tenth gives an approximate representation of her real talent."[44] Charging that her success was the "success of scandal," he condemned French depravity as it was embodied in this "priestess of sensuality." One of the most articulate critics of the age, Aleksandr Kugel, was more equitable. While calling her a mistress of self-promotion and complaining about the type of fame produced by cunning marketing, he also acknowledged that Bernhardt was one of the most original, intoxicating, and complex figures of her age.[45] Nikolai Efros offered a clue to the hostility of many male critics to Bernhardt when he observed that Russians were repulsed by self-promotion and demanded "modest restraint," especially from actresses.[46]

Bernhardt did have defenders among male critics, but the excerpts cited above clearly demonstrate that many of them were not receptive to the image she presented – and, in the context of nineteenth-century Russian culture, rightly so.[47] The antithesis of traditional sex/gender ideology, Bernhardt was correctly perceived by conservative critics as a subversive influence. Traditional ideology demanded from Russian women that they maintain monogomous relationships with their husbands and that their lives be modeled on ideals of silence, subservience, obedience, humility, modesty in dress, devotion to children, and emotional restraint. Bernhardt offered them a model of rebellious individualism that contradicted the very essence of Russian "*zhenstvennost.*"[48] Although some critics preferred Bernhardt, it is, perhaps, not surprising that Eleonora Duse, who, at least superficially, embodied many of the sex/gender ideals dear to conservatives, was greeted much more warmly by the Russian critical establishment.

Although they occasionally complained about the monotony of Duse's characterizations, most Russian critics were mesmerized by her. The taste for angst was strong in Russia during the period. Perhaps for that reason, Duse's immense capacity for suffering and the apparent emotional authenticity of her mimesis resonated powerfully among Russian audiences. Kugel wrote of Duse: "In art, some raise the soul, others purify it. Duse belonged to the latter: through her suffering, she purified our souls."[49] Duse's emotionally lacerated heroines touched a chord in the Russian spirit that Bernhardt, with her callous calculations, Parisian cynicism, outrageous fashions, and scandalous escapades, could not. To grasp, therefore, those qualities of Duse's stage persona that resonated with Russian critics is to understand what type of "*zhenstvennost*" appealed to them most. The phrase "eternal femininity" (*vechnaia zhenstvennost*), the ambiguity of which was heightened by frequent application to a wide range of contrasting actresses, was often applied to Duse's characters. Also described by several critics as the "most feminine of all women," Duse projected particularly seductive qualities on stage.[50] A series of articles on Duse published in 1897 helps to clarify her special appeal for male critics. According to the author, Duse "devotes herself to men with the sincerity and heartfelt conviction of an intelligent woman, with the trembling, fearful conviction of her whole feminine essence, which is afraid of dry, empty solitude, which wants to merge with her beloved and find herself in him." He continues: "There is a kind of shyness about her, a mood ... largely free from tawdry accents; it is reflected not only in her acting, but also in her manner of dress. One rarely sees onstage such an elegantly modest wardrobe, one imbued with such personal taste."[51]

Critics found Duse so attractive and compelling that even Ibsen's Nora succeeded in her interpretation. With the possible exception of Vera Kommissarzhevskaia, Russian actresses who ventured to play *A Doll's House* generally received at best indifferent and at worst openly hostile responses. Reviews of Duse's performance suggest why she succeeded with this proto-feminist character where native actresses failed. Writing for *Artist*, Ivan Ivanov regarded favorably the emphasis placed by Duse on Nora's maternal qualities. Another critic, who also praised this aspect of her interpretation, observed that her interpolations improved Ibsen's play and character immeasurably.[52] Echoing his colleagues, Aleksandr Kugel wrote that Duse's was the only bearable production of *A Doll's House* because her Nora was not the author's Nora. The secret of her successful interpretation was that she replaced Nora's rational faculty with "feeling and the truth of the heart." Kugel added that he was not offended by Duse's feminism because it was not "George Sandism." She was not, he declared, interested in the pursuit of narrow civil freedoms; she was effective precisely because she understood that civil rights would not contribute significantly to women's happiness.[53] Duse spoke to a higher (albeit equally ideological) ideal: the liberation of the human spirit. Duse was less threatening than Bernhardt precisely because the qualities of "*zhenstvenennost*" she exhibited – modesty, restrained elegance, maternal feeling, devotion to her man, self-sacrifice, and elevated idealism – were familiar and acceptable in the Russian context.

That the ideal represented by Duse was both abstract and precarious is illustrated by an anecdote involving Kugel. Invited backstage between acts, Kugel trembled in anticipation of meeting Duse, the incarnation of perfect "*zhenstvennost*." When the friend who promised to introduce them led him behind the curtain, Duse was onstage inspecting the furniture and screaming at a "little Italian" in a disturbingly "sharp" and "vulgar" manner. Her face was "ugly and old" and her expression, "unpleasant and malicious." Forgetting his companion's invitation, Kugel moved quickly toward the exit and hurried back to his seat without ever having met his idol. When the actress emerged onstage for the next act, she was so charming that for a moment he could not accept the transformation. What lesson did Kugel draw from this experience? With respect to actresses, a remote, sublime fantasy is better than tangible, repugnant reality: "Let the constructed image be the one that stays in your memory," he cautioned.[54]

Though critics, especially the nationalists among them, were not universally receptive to the Western stars, those who were often preferred foreign actresses to their own.[55] For that reason, Bernhardt, whose "*zhenstvennost*" was more ambiguous than Duse's, but still transcendent, and Duse, who represented an ideal "*zhenstvennost*," became the standards against which many critics measured native actresses and by which actresses measured themselves. That Russian actresses and female spectators were strongly influenced by Western sex/gender ideology and foreign stars is clear from the large body of literature – feuilletons, reviews, and articles – published on the subject in journals and newspapers. But because male critics, many of whom had their own agendas in regard to actresses, authored so much of the literature, it tends to be tendentious.

Except as consumers, women had limited access to print media. Perhaps for that reason, the attitudes of actresses and female spectators toward influences from the West are more elusive. Their views must be inferred, therefore, from a few letters, scattered interviews, contemporary fiction, and memoir literature. What is clear from these sources is that Russian actresses were profoundly ambivalent about competition from the West. Though some grew weary of constant comparisons to Bernhardt and Duse, others admired, envied, and imitated their acting styles, personal affectations, and fashions. Having seen the positive response of audiences to their exotic foreign rivals, Russian actresses increasingly abandoned native traditions in favor of Western innovations, a process that produced several results. On the positive side, Russian actresses learned invaluable lessons about marketing and independent entrepreneurship from Bernhardt and Duse and to be compared favorably to either usually resulted in acquisition of a larger market share of the theatre-going public. On the negative side, actresses who imitated their Western counterparts, especially the French, were often accused of contributing to the demise of Russian drama and theatre (and indirectly to the destruction of the family) through frenzied pursuit of cheap notoriety, fashionable clothing, and large amounts of money – all of which were, according to their critics, antithetical to authentic art and traditional *"zhenstvennost."*

Conservative ideology continued to influence the stage until the turn of the century; for that reason, an actress like Polina Strepetova, who was virtually free from the taint of foreign stars and Western feminism, could enjoy substantial success even in that most Western of Russian cities, St. Petersburg. Nonetheless, those Russian actresses who achieved the greatest notoriety, prospered the most financially, and enjoyed personality cults of their own were the ones who could adapt and apply lessons learned from the West to the Russian context. Though imitation of Western stars reached its apotheosis with Lidia Iavorskaia, who enjoyed a brief vogue in the 1890s, simple-minded plagiarism was not generally well received. Actresses like Iavorskaia quickly became targets for obstreperous critics like Kugel, who predicted that these blatantly sensual, Frenchified horrors would be the ruin of proper Russian *"zhenstvennost."* Disturbed by the pernicious influence of Western, especially French, decadence and immorality on their cultural traditions, many Russians resisted the wholesale appropriation of their theatre by Western aesthetics and sex/gender ideology. If the continuing influence of European cultural developments helped to shape the outlook of both the intelligentsia and professional class, Russia, according to Laura Engelstein, "produced its own version of the Western tradition, in the sexual arena as well as other cultural domains."[56]

The need to temper Western sexual ideology with a more traditional Russian form of *"zhenstvennost"* is apparent from the response to actresses like Iavorskaia, whose open scorn for cherished Russian conventions angered many critics and spectators. Having misjudged Russian tolerance for a completely alien sex/gender ideology, she ruined a promising career by mindlessly imitating French stars, brazenly exhibiting sexuality on stage, and indulging her taste for excessive fashions. The public's response to Mariia Savina, Mariia Ermolova, and Vera Kommissarzhevskaia, the only Russians whose popularity in their own country rivalled Bernhardt's and Duse's, was both more positive and enduring. Ermolova's stage reputation was based primarily on spirited depictions of rebellious heroines from the classical

Western repertoire, but she took care to maintain a modest profile off stage and to avoid accusations of crass self-promotion that plagued many Western stars. Mariia Savina, who was often compared to Bernhardt, and Vera Kommissarzhevskaia, the "Russian Duse," had little in common except their extraordinary perspicacity with respect to audience tastes. Understanding that the public would not swallow Western sex/gender ideology in undiluted form, both constructed images of *"zhenstvennost"* that simultaneouly exploited Western sexual ideology while retaining native traditions.

Influences from the West helped to alter the relationship between actresses and their audience. One effect of the growing tension over sexual ideology and gender identity was the gradual disintegration of barriers between actresses and "respectable" women. Efforts to elevate theatre as an art and professionalize its practitioners intensified during the 1890s, and although actresses' personal morality and class affiliations were still suspect, their social status rose sufficiently for a relationship of mutual imitation to develop between actresses and women of the privileged classes – aristocratic, intelligentsia, and entrepreneurial. This was partly the result of changes in the theatre itself and partly because the mass-circulation press, which encouraged consumers to "select and crown their own royalty," shamelessly hyped its favorite actresses.[57] In addition, the most popular genre by the end of the century was the "drama of everyday life" (*bytovaia dramaturgiia*) which consisted of two subgenres: Ostrovskian depictions of traditional Russian life and Western society comedies and dramas adapted to the Russian context. The latter subgenre, which had largely displaced the former by the mid-1880s, required actresses to reflect the tastes and fantasies of their audience. But if actresses constructed various images of theatrical *"zhenstvennost"* based on the tastes and values of the privileged classes, women of all classes, especially those with aspirations to higher status, acquired their gender identities, at least in part, from models provided by actresses, the most popular of whom affected the latest Western fashions.

The degree to which actresses were implicated in the disruption of traditional sex/gender ideology and *"zhenstvennost"* is indicated not only by the influx of women into the acting profession and the veneration of certain actresses who embodied particularly desirable gender qualities, but also by the increased application of theatrical rhetoric to women outside the profession. So, the author of "Characteristics of the Fashionable Woman" (*Kharakteristika svetskoi zhenshchiny*) complained that the French manner of education popular among fashionable young women encouraged them to forget conventional Russian modesty and view their lives as theatrical presentations. Like actresses, fashionable women were, he argued, purely artificial creations whose stylish clothing and affectations were carefully crafted to produce the desired effect on an "audience" of admirers. When a fashionable woman set out for the theatre, he concluded, foremost in her mind was not the spectacle she was about to see onstage, but the spectacle she would create in the auditorium.[58]

There is no doubt that the process of social, political, economic, and aesthetic transformation that occurred in Russia toward the end of the nineteenth century affected women in the theatre. Challenges to traditional sex/gender ideology and the reactionary posturing that followed positioned actresses firmly in the center of a heated debate over the proper role of women in society. One effect was to demonize or deify actresses in response to the particular qualities of "*zhenstvennost*" they embodied. Another effect – perhaps the most troubling – was the conditions of life created by an oversupply of actresses.

In 1905, O. Dymov wrote: "From the farthest corners of Russia people (*liudi*) fly to the footlights like seabirds to a lighthouse."[59] Although Dymov uses the universal "*liudi*" to introduce his theme of supply and demand in the theatre, the discriminating reader quickly realizes that the topic is not gender-neutral. Dymov's specific concern is with the oversupply of actresses, a trend that became alarming in the 1890s. In 1897 Aleksandr Kugel was already railing against the large numbers of women flocking to the stage who, in his opinion, had little talent and for whom there were no jobs.[60] Although neither Dymov nor Kugel offers statistical evidence, implicit support for their position is found in the steady stream of articles appearing between 1890 and 1916 in major theatre journals about actresses dying from hunger, engaging in prostitution, or committing suicide because they could find no work at all or because the work they could find paid below subsistence wages.[61] Judging by the amount of fiction published about actresses in this period, tragical, pseudo-documentary tales of distressed young women filled with romantic illusions about service and sacrifice to art and nation were extraordinarily popular with the literate public. If life in the theatre was such an abyss of despair, why did so many women see it as a viable – even desirable – option? The following chapter, which considers the economic realities of female labor and quality of life for women in provincial, Imperial, and private theatres, suggests several answers.

2

THE NINA ZARECHNAIA EPIDEMIC
Economics and consequences

The abolition of the Imperial monopoly in 1882 encouraged the gradual expansion of a network of private commercial and art theatres in St. Petersburg, Moscow, and the provinces during the last two decades of the nineteenth century. Expanded employment opportunities had the equivocal effect of making theatre more attractive as a professional activity and of creating a surplus of aspiring actresses and actors. Although this surfeit affected employment opportunities for both sexes, critics and representatives of the theatre community were particularly alarmed by the growing number of women entering the acting profession. When Nina Zarechnaia, Chekhov's hapless seagull, appeared on the stage in 1896, she assumed a dual significance: for critics, she represented the unhappy consequences of romantic self-delusion; for young women eager for independence, adventure, and meaningful activity, she was an attractive symbol of self-sacrifice and devotion to a higher calling. Inspired by both fictional and real examples, aspiring actresses flocked to theatres thoughout Russia.

If romantic notions about art and self-sacrifice, desire for independent achievement and self-realization, and confusion over gender identity and sexual hierarchy were intangible factors in the oversupply of actresses, there were also more concrete causes. As the Russian economy changed during the second half of the century, larger numbers of women moved from the agricultural into the industrial labor force. But although more jobs were available in a variety of fields, many women still preferred the theatre. Indeed, in spite of its many liabilities, theatre remained one of the most attractive professions for ambitious, assertive women who aspired to autonomy.

The economic basis for the popularity of acting as a profession is easy to understand. A starring actress like Mariia Savina, whose salary in 1882 for an eight-month season was 12,000 roubles, earned more in a year than most women, even those with university educations or a skilled craft, could hope to earn in twenty.[1] Many employers did not recognize degrees granted by women's universities, and neither high school (*srednaia shkola*) nor university education guaranteed women a living wage.

An article on professional education and access to employment published in 1899 in *The Woman's Cause* (*Zhenskoe delo*), paints a bleak picture of the situation faced by educated women.[2] The author noted that in spite of tremendous demand for professional training for women, especially in agricultural fields, educated women had few opportunities for promotion and could not expect to make more than 20 or 25 roubles a month in jobs usually occupied by semi-literate men. She further suggested that a provincial teacher could expect to earn 12 roubles a month, that governesses were treated like servants and paid like maids, that a music tutor would be lucky to receive 25 kopeks an hour, and that even though low-level government jobs were now accessible to women, their salaries of between 30 and 40 roubles a month were far below those of men performing the same tasks. To make matters worse, the growing competition among women for these poorly paid positions lowered their value even more.

Five years later, the employment and salary situation had improved only slightly for a small number of women. Statistics published in the *First Woman's Calendar* (*Pervyi zhenskii kalendar*) in 1903 and 1904 offer a comparative study of women's wages in a variety of fields.[3] According to statistics gathered by the editor, many employers still categorically refused to hire women and those that did hire them paid embarrassingly low wages. For government jobs, salaries ranged from 25 to 120 roubles a month with an average salary of between 35 and 50 roubles. In educational fields, a headmistress might earn as much as 4,500 roubles a year, while a teacher's assistant received as little as 65 roubles a month and the school's female physician took home 55. A female journalist might earn as little as 25 and as much as 200 roubles a month at *The New Times* (*Novoe vremia*). Many women earned their livings by producing various kinds of handicrafts, and although a small number managed to penetrate skilled crafts traditionally dominated by men (e.g., bootmaking and metal engraving), most were in the sewing industry. At the highest level, a skilled dressmaker could earn between 15 and 18 roubles a month with room and board; at the lowest, seamstresses hired by the day received as little as 50 kopeks for a full day's labor. Those few women who worked in nontraditional crafts like metal engraving could make as little as 25 or as much as 60 roubles a month.

In many fields, women were not only poorly remunerated for their labor, but were also subjected to extraordinarily disagreeable, often physically injurious working conditions. In one factory that manufactured feathers and artificial flowers for women's hats, for example, women worked 12 or more hours a day and inhaled feather down, the odor of rotting fowl, and fumes from the rubber cement used to glue flowers and feathers to the hats. Even worse, women who worked in this factory were compelled to apprentice for between one and two years before they could receive a salary. In a crystal packing plant, women who worked 10-hour days without a single break were locked out of the factory if they were more than a minute late for work.[4]

To many women trapped in poorly paid, emotionally draining, physically exhausting jobs, the theatre must have seemed like an oasis of luxury and leisure. Publicists writing for newspapers and women's magazines painted alluring pictures of elegant stars surrounded by luxury and basking in the warmth of enthusiastic admirers. In the imaginations of many women, therefore, working conditions in the theatre were surely preferable to conditions in factories, mills, and even small businesses that hired skilled and unskilled female labor. By contrast, a typical working day in the theatre must have seemed very attractive. An actress rehearsed from 10 o'clock in the morning to 1 or 2 in the afternoon for the play being performed that evening; from 2 to 4, she worked on new plays; and, finally, the evening performance engaged her energies from 7 in the evening to midnight.[5] Given these conditions, would any reasonable woman choose life in a factory over life in the theatre? Apparently not, since so many were knocking at the stage door.

Although the larger number of theatres surely encouraged the oversupply of actresses during the last two decades of the nineteenth century, other factors were equally significant. Particularly important was the fact that, unlike most fields, professional acting in Russia already had an extensive history of female employment. When he spoke to the First Russian Women's Congress in 1908, A.N. Kremlev undoubtedly exaggerated the equality of men and women in the theatre and the role of theatre in the struggle for women's rights. But even if a secure utility position at an Imperial theatre paid little more than a teaching position in a provincial gymnasium and acting on the commercial stage exposed women to stern moral censure, his argument that theatre was in general more accessible and hospitable to them than other professions were is unassailable.[6] Russian theatre, which had no significant history of female impersonation, had, from the beginning, bowed to the necessity of hiring women. By the end of the nineteenth century, as the number of theatres grew and "women's themes" predominated, the demand for actresses increased proportionally, and a small number of starring actresses earned as much, if not more than, starring actors.

Salary and accessibility were surely important, but as a profession, theatre was also unique with respect to female employment. Acting was attractive to women because it not only allowed, but actually encouraged them to exploit traditional feminine skills and attributes: physical beauty, sensuality, coquettishness, and intuitive rather than intellectual reasoning were highly valued in the theatre. Neither high school nor university education was required for success and, before 1900, few actresses felt compelled to seek formal training in their own craft. Although, as Shchepkina-Kupernik suggested, when they were debarred from other fields, bright women were attracted to the stage, actresses with higher education were still exceptional. If a minority of women from the aristocracy and intelligentsia challenged patriarchal privilege by demanding access to nontraditional fields, many more were not so ambitious. Because it allowed women to transgress class barriers, gave them access to the public space and a voice in public affairs, and made it possible for the most fortunate to enjoy financial independence, acting was a potentially subversive activity for women. But because actresses required no special educational or employment privileges and because most maintained the outward marks of conventional femininity, they did not, for the most part, overtly threaten established gender ideology and sexual hierarchy. For women, then, accessibility, acceptability, working conditions, and the promise of financial independence were among the most seductive features of professional acting.

But was life in the theatre really as congenial as its impassioned, would-be acolytes imagined?

IMPERIAL AND PRIVATE THEATRES IN THE CAPITALS AND PROVINCES

Although critics, playwrights, and practitioners generally agreed that Russian theatre was in a state of crisis at the end of the nineteenth century and beginning of the twentieth, there was little unanimity within the theatre community itself on the Woman Question or the position of actresses. Speaking before the First All-Russian Congress of Representatives of the Stage in 1897, Iulia Tarlovskaia-Rastorgueva, a Russian actress working in Warsaw, addressed the situation of women in the theatre directly. Arguing that conditions of employment and quality of life for actresses had changed markedly for the worse over the past thirty years, Tarlovskaia asked the assembled representatives of Russian theatre whether any woman could prosper as an actress without risking her honor, respectability, and individuality.[7] Conditions continued to deteriorate to the point that, fourteen years later, an anonymous critic called the position of women on the stage "tragic" and declared that equality between women and men in the theatre was a dangerous myth. "Although there is plenty of interest in actresses," this commentator wrote, "there is no respect for women."[8]

Not everyone perceived the situation in such dismal terms, however. Following Tarlovskaia's report, several performers of both sexes defended the treatment of women in Russian theatre as it was presently constituted. Objecting to Tarlovskaia's characterization of actresses as morally depraved, one contended that there were many respectable women in the theatre who resisted temptation and would never sell themselves for a dress. Another argued that the position of women in the theatre was not only better than any other profession, but even very good.[9] Although A.N. Kremlev understood and was unusually sensitive to the plight of actresses, in 1897 he claimed that from the moment they began to take an active role in theatre, women had enjoyed full equality with men.[10]

In spite of the seemingly contradictory points of view expressed by representatives of the theatre community, there was an objective reality, but this reality was not the same for all actresses. A small minority of them enjoyed tremendous material advantages over their less fortunate sisters, but a wide range of experience was available to women in the theatre. In most cases, two factors determined conditions of employment and quality of life for Russian actresses: 1) the category of theatre in which they worked; 2) their position in an individual theatre's economic and artistic hierarchy.

The venerable Nadezhda Mikhailovna Medvedeva, who addressed the Congress in 1897, divided Russian theatre into two categories: Imperial and private. The first group was small and concentrated in Moscow and St. Petersburg; the second, which included theatrical enterprises in both the capitals and provinces, was much larger and spread throughout Russia. According to Medvedeva, ideally the provincial theatres functioned as "schools" in which actors could hone their craft, while the Imperial theatres remained the "temples of art" (*khram iskusstva*) to which all aspired.[11] Although certain vicissitudes of the profession affected all actresses regardless of the category of theatre in which they worked or their position in it, a wide gulf separated provincial actresses from Imperial. And within individual theatres, the typical walk-on (*vykhodnaia*) and so-called second-level (*na vtoriia roli*) actresses often had strained relations with first-level and starring actresses.

Until 1882, when their monopoly was abolished, the Imperial theatres dominated Russian theatre in Moscow and St. Petersburg. These included the Aleksandrinskii, Mariinskii, and Mikhailovskii theatres in St. Petersburg and the Malyi and Bolshoi theatres in Moscow.[12] To obtain a secure position at an Imperial theatre was, as one provincial actor observed in 1880, the principal objective of most Russian performers. "To have real security without worrying where the next piece of bread will come from, to have support in old age – that is why actors want to join the state theatres," he wrote.[13] Although not every actor found life in the Imperial theatres to her or his taste, it is generally true that the Imperials offered a security virtually unknown in private theatres, especially in the provinces.

Although salary had enormous significance for actresses, the money was often less important than the status a high salary conferred. A respectable salary raised an actress's value in both the entrepreneur's eyes and in her own: the more she was paid, the more she was able to demand and receive.[14] For the most part, salaries in the Imperial theatres exceeded those in private theatres. Although a small cluster of starring actresses received exorbitant remuneration for their services, there was a wide range of salaries and most were comparatively modest.

The *First Women's Calendar* for 1903 lists salaries for the lower categories of actresses at the Imperial theatres and, interestingly, they are not significantly higher than a typical low level government employee's monthly wage. Statistics from the calendar suggest that the average utility actress at an Imperial theatre earned little more – and in some cases less – than an average teacher. Keeping in mind that the Imperial theatres kept a significant number of unoccupied, supernumerary, and second-level performers on salary and that these statistics do not include the wages of the most prominent actresses or the inflated salaries of a few stars, the monthly wage for a dramatic actress was 53 roubles; for a member of the opera ensemble, 57 roubles; and for a ballet artist, 151 roubles.[15]

Competent, mid-level actresses enjoyed more substantial salaries. For example, when Elizaveta Goreva joined the Imperial stage for the 1895/96 season, she earned a salary of 1,140 roubles with "additional maintenance" (*dobavochnoe soderzhanie*) of 3,860 roubles. In 1894, after almost 50 years of service, Nadezhda Medvedeva received 8,000 roubles a year. In 1899, Vera Michurina-Samoilova received a salary of 5,500 roubles. And in 1901, Elizaveta Levkeeva received 3,000 roubles a year. In addition, Imperial actresses often received assistance with wardrobe costs. In 1901, for example, actresses at the Aleksandrinskii who received less than 2,000 roubles a year in straight salary were given additional money for costumes.[16]

The Imperial theatres were also attractive because they provided pensions upon retirement and often supported actresses during times of illness. When progressive paralysis forced Glikeriia Fedotova into early retirement, the Malyi Theatre reduced her salary to 4,000 roubles, but continued to maintain her on that amount for many years. When Mariia Savina, who was often plagued with anemia, "nervous attacks," and stomach ailments, took the waters at Carlsbad, the Aleksandrinskii kept her on salary and even helped pay for her treatments.

Starring actresses were, of course, envied for their salaries, for their annual benefit performances, and for the influence they were thought to enjoy both inside and outside the theatre. Glikeriia Fedotova was the first actress to earn a salary of 12,000 roubles. When Polina Strepetova signed her third contract at the Aleksandrinskii (1883–5), she received a salary of 6,000 roubles with additional maintenance of 4,860 roubles. In the 1895/96 season, Mariia Ermolova, who shared star status with Fedotova at the Malyi Theatre and who was at the pinnacle of her career in the the 1880s and 1890s, received a salary of 12,000 roubles a year. Vera Kommissarzhevskaia received 6,000 roubles during her first year at the Aleksandrinskii (1895/96), but by 1899, she was already taking home 9,000.

Mariia Savina's career provides the best case history of what an ambitious, pragmatic actress could achieve financially within the Imperial theatre system. Savina, who began her career in the provinces, was hired by the Aleksandrinskii Theatre in April, 1874 at a modest salary of 900 roubles a year. She also received a benefit and 15 roubles per performance. In August of the same year, she signed a three-year contract which guaranteed that the per performance fee would be increased by 5 roubles each year. In 1878, she requested that her contract be renewed for 1,143 roubles in salary, the usual benefit, 35 roubles for each performance, and an additional 500 roubles for wardrobe costs. In 1881, she kept the same salary, but her wardrobe subsidy was increased to 3,000 roubles, the per performance fee was increased to 50 roubles, and she contracted to perform four times a week, excluding benefits.[17] It was in 1883 that her salary took a tremendous leap from 1,143 to 12,000 roubles a year. She was also given an additional 10,857 roubles for "maintenance." In addition to the unprecedented salary increase, she negotiated a contract for sixty performances each season; if the directorate wanted her to play more than sixty times, they had to pay her 200 roubles for each performance. She also asked for and received a four-month vacation each year. After 1884, Savina's base salary remained constant for many years, but she continued to receive special subsidies for wardrobe (up to 5,000 roubles) as well as large gifts and loans.

Because actors of both sexes relied heavily on benefit performances to supplement their incomes, salaries and fees per performance tell only part of the story. Savina herself understood the importance of these occasions when she wrote: "Benefits! For actors, they're like birthday celebrations; they mean tremendous revenue and in most cases, they are an actor's security for the whole winter."[18] Savina would surely know, inasmuch as her own benefits were among the most lucrative. In 1876, she received a mere 2,118 roubles and 55 kopeks for her benefit. By 1880, she was taking in an average of 4,700 roubles per benefit; in the late 1880s and 1890s, 5,500 was average and in 1900, she received almost 7,000 roubles for a single benefit performance marking the anniversary of her twenty-fifth year of service to the Imperial theatres. A rough estimate, then, of the total income during a good season for an actress of Savina's stature would fall between 35,000 and 40,000 roubles, a figure that does not include income earned during summer tours. In light of this rather substantial figure, it is surely not cynical to suggest that at least some women had mercenary rather than altruistic motives for pursuing careers on the stage. Although actresses often justified their professional activities on the basis of self-effacing service to art and country, the possibility of acquiring tremendous wealth and its attendant luxuries must have enticed more than one woman into the theatre.

In general, however, women and girls who fantasized about making their fortunes in the theatre were either ill-informed about the realities of actresses' lives or chose to ignore them. The average actress did not enjoy a permanent position in one of the Imperial theatres, but was constantly on the move from one provincial enterprise or "*tovarishchestvo*" to another, and she would have been lucky to have earned 40,000 roubles over the course of ten years, much less in a single season.[19]

When The First All-Russian Congress of Representatives of the Stage was convened in 1897, its charge was to consider the crisis in private provincial theatres.[20] For that reason, when Tarlovskaia-Rastorgueva spoke to the Congress about the appalling situation of Russian actresses, her point of reference was the provincial theatres; the Imperial theatres, which had their own problems, were only implied in her remarks. Although actors of both sexes suffered from the theatre crisis in the provinces, certain issues were peculiar to women. Tarlovskaia and other respresentatives at the Congress identified them as prostitution, sexual patronage, excessive wardrobe costs, and unwanted pregnancy.[21]

Charges of sexual patronage and prostitution are, of course, endemic to theatre. And because theatre has been associated historically with sexual promiscuity, it is difficult to determine whether patronage and prostitution increased among Russian actresses during the period or whether there was simply a heightened awareness of the problem within the theatre community as pressure for reform of the profession increased. Available evidence suggests that the problem was genuine. Between approximately 1880 and 1917, journal and newspaper articles, as well as reports to various Congresses, indicate a conspicuous increase in commercial sexual activity among Russian actresses.

According to Tarlovskaia, sexual exploitation of women was new to Russian theatre; twenty or thirty years ago, she claimed, actresses were still true disciples of art, respected by all for their talent, knowledge, and divine spark. Now, they must be "accessible" in order to succeed.[22] Prostitution and patronage did not, however, arise spontaneously at the end of the nineteenth century. For that reason, Tarlovskaia's suggestion that actresses enjoyed universal respect and that sexual extortion was virtually unknown in Russian theatre before the 1870s was either naive or disingenuous: actresses' status was low throughout the eighteenth and nineteenth centuries and serf actresses were clearly subjected to sexual exploitation.[23] Nonetheless, as conditions in the theatre changed at the end of the nineteenth century, sexual patronage and prostitution were more prevalent, public condemnation of the theatrical marketplace was more insistent, and pressure on the theatre community to take a more rigorous position with respect to questions of personal morality increased.

"Accessibility" was defined and manifested variously, and many critics took pains to distinguish between patronage and prostitution. Some insisted that the infiltration of professional prostitutes into the theatre had reached epidemic proportions. Writing in 1904 about the "actor's marketplace," S. Svetlov used the term "courtesan" to describe women who were hired by provincial entrepreneurs primarily on the basis of particularly desirable physical qualities that would attract large numbers of male spectators and who were not fastidious in their choice of admirers.[24] In 1905, a critic complained on the pages of *Theatrical Russia* (*Teatral'naia rossia*) that the presence of so many "women of easy virtue" in the theatre ruined opportunities for serious actresses who found themselves forced out of the job market by untalented strumpets with pretty faces and large wardrobes.[25] In 1909, another critic charged that for years professional prostitutes had been masquerading as actresses and that even after finding respectable positions in legitimate theatres, they refused to renounce their "other," more lucrative profession.[26] But in spite of the fear among morally indignant critics, directors, and actors that prostitution was widespread in the theatre community, evidence suggests that professional prostitutes were still exceptional. The real problem was not professional prostitution, but sexual patronage, which manifested itself in several more or less noxious forms and affected most actresses.

It was the exceptional provincial actress who did not have personal experience with sexual extortion. The bartering of actresses by provincial entrepreneurs was so common that Tarlovskaia called it "white slave trade." By her account, no actress could advance in her career without a patron: regardless of how pretty or talented she might be, an actress without protection (*pokrovistel'stvo*) lost "nine-tenths of her value as an actress."[27] According to one critic, the root of the problem lay in the fact that actresses, like women generally, had few rights.[28] For that reason, they were at the mercy not only of unscrupulous entrepreneurs and directors, but also of their "admirers." These local Lotharios, most of whom did not distinguish between actresses and prostitutes, often enjoyed considerable authority with the directors and entrepreneurs who hired actresses.

Speaking before the Theatre Congress in 1897, N.F. Arbenin related a conversation between a provincial entrepreneur, his regular patrons, and the city fathers. The men had only one question for the entrepreneur, who had just hired a new company in Moscow: "Are there any women?" The entrepreneur replied that "A. is a real beauty, B. is simply candy, and C. is an enchanting blonde. I had to take D. because although she is completely inept, she has a string of admirers." Arbenin also protested the increasingly popular practice among provincial entrepreneurs of requiring actresses to stay after a production and "entertain" the local "lovers of art." Actresses who refused were fired immediately.[29] In 1910, an anonymous critic described the conditions which prompted one actress to commit suicide, another to attempt it, and a third to attempt murder. The first had nothing left to sell but her body; the second was beaten and raped by a local merchant; the third was not given any roles until she yielded to the sexual demands of the local representative of the theatrical commission.[30] The consequences of according excessive privilege to male patrons are reflected in Kremlev's address to the Women's Congress, in which he told of a provincial theatre habitué who shot an actress because the entrepreneur did not consult him before hiring the female personnel.[31]

Because married women had little appeal for male spectators, many entrepreneurs refused to hire married couples.[32] For actresses, however, the presence a husband or lover helped protect them against unwanted advances by male patrons. Single actresses could not afford to reject or even ignore the men who importuned them. Aleksandra Shubert, who performed in both Imperial and provincial theatres, told in her memoir of the consequences of turning down an invitation to a party thrown by one of the city's wealthiest men because he tried to dictate what she would wear. Friends in the company cautioned her not to risk her benefit by offending him. Standing firmly on her principles, Shubert did not attend the party and, sure enough, on the day of her benefit, the theatre was mostly empty.[33] Since actresses could receive half their yearly earnings from a single benefit performance, this kind of revenge constituted a genuine financial crisis.

Zinaida Kholmskaia, a prominent actress who worked in private theatres in both the provinces and capital cities, related an unpleasant incident that occurred during her first professional engagement at the theatre in Briansk.[34] According to Kholmskaia, because the governor of the province was an "eccentric, abnormal man" who hated women (zhenonenavistnik) and preferred to let local bureaucrats administer their own districts, the police chief of the city of Briansk had acquired an unhealthy amount of power not only over the city, but over the actresses working in the local theatre. Although Kholmskaia was a novice, her experience with him might have unnerved even an experienced actress.

Following the first act of her debut performance in Briansk, the police chief's footman was waiting at her dressing room with a large glass of cognac and several oranges. After the second act, he appeared with more cognac, candy, and apples. Although embarrassed by his unsought and unwanted attention, following the curtain call Kholmskaia thanked the police chief for his gifts, had a good laugh with the other actors about his foolishness, and thought no more about it until he and the footman appeared late one night at her apartment demanding "entertainment." Although Kholmskaia's brother-in-law heard the commotion and drove the intruders away, the theatre's entrepreneur was less sympathetic. "What were you thinking of," he cried the next morning, "you would have drunk a little wine with him and that would have been all. Now he'll show you!" And he did.

For her first benefit, Kholmskaia chose Daughter of the Age (Dochveka), a role she had already played successfully. Rehearsals began, but on the eve of the performance, the police chief suddenly forbade the production. The entrepreneur advised Kholmskaia to petition him personally. She went to his office where she was kept waiting until 9 o'clock in the evening only to be told that he had no intention of changing his mind. Instead, he demanded that she produce The Maid of Orleans, a role she had not prepared and for which there was no time to rehearse. She ran back to the entrepreneur, who had already spoken to the police chief and agreed that she must play the Maid. Backed into a corner, she went home to study the role, but complained in her memoir that never had she performed so badly or been so humiliated. The final insult came when the police chief attempted to prevent her from leaving Briansk at the end of the season. Like most actors, she was desperate to get to the Theatre Bureau in Moscow to find a new position. Had he succeeded in detaining her, she would have been without work for the next season.

If male entrepreneurs, directors, and actors had offered actresses consistent support, their relationships with male patrons would surely have been less arduous. Unfortunately, rather than challenging the exploitation of actresses,

28

their male colleagues often initiated and participated in it. Some critics accused entrepreneurs and directors of deliberately debauching their actresses. Arbenin, for example, charged that entrepreneurs viewed actresses as "living goods" (*zhivoi tovar*).[35] An article on actresses and prostitution, which appeared in 1909, relates the story of a director who complained that after he took the trouble to introduce a particular actress ("insolent woman," as he called her) to a wealthy merchant, she later had the nerve to come crawling to him for a salary![36] In an anonymous appeal to entrepreneurs, one actress complained that when she protested at the minuscule salary of 30 roubles a month offered to her by one of their provincial brethren, she was told to "arrange something" with one of the many wealthy men loitering about the theatre.[37]

Augustina Izborskaia described the Moscow Theatre Bureau at Lent as a "genuine hell" for actresses. The unscrupulous manager of the Bureau willingly arranged jobs for actresses in exchange for money or sexual favors, and the entrepreneurs who came there seeking new talent for their companies were no better. At the beginning of Lent, they maintained a respectful attitude toward the actors and actresses with whom they negotiated contracts. But after five or six weeks, as desperation to sign with someone, no matter how disreputable, increased, the entrepreneurs grew correspondingly rapacious. Izborskaia wrote that when she returned to her hotel room after a full day at the Theatre Bureau, she felt as if people had been spitting in her face and beating her with sticks. Her brief memoir concludes with a plaintive wail: "I have said enough. I do not want to remember all the abominations a provincial actress without a substantial reputation had to swallow."[38]

Although actors and actresses might seem to be natural allies, relationships between them were complex, precarious, and often unsatisfactory. The peripatetic life of the average provincial actor and actress did not encourage monogamy or permit many to establish settled family lives. Writing for *Theatre and Art* in 1904, S. Svetlov argued that before serfdom was abolished, provincial troupes were constituted on a family model: married couples traveled and performed together and, when they were old enough, the children usually took up their parents' profession. The abolition of serfdom permanently altered the face of provincial theatre: it ruined many existing companies, created a new class of spectators, and forced entrepreneurs constantly to seek novelty in order to satisfy the tastes of this new public. One strategy for luring them into the theatre was to hire a new stable of actors and actresses each year, which had the adverse effect of discouraging domestic stability and "family values" in the theatre community.[39]

The problem of pregnancy among unwed actresses is clear from the popularity of cautionary tales about innocent young women led to perdition by actors who promised wedlock, got them pregnant, and then disappeared.[40] Domestic instability exacerbated the problem of unexpected and unwanted pregnancy. Relationships between actors and actresses typically lasted for a season or two until one member of the couple moved on. In general, these temporary arrangements did not benefit actresses, many of whom found themselves pregnant and abandoned at the end of the season. Because the contractual regulations governing pregnancy were so disadvantageous to actresses, careers – to say nothing of lives – could be temporarily interrupted or permanently destroyed by it.[41]

Although actresses were often victimized by male colleagues and patrons, the more pragmatic among them understood and accepted the necessity for patronage and protection. Frequently, they were not only complicit in their own exploitation, but engineered the oppression of other women. In a series of humorous stories published in *Footlights and Life* (*Rampa i zhizn*), Evgeniia Garting criticized unscrupulous actresses who cynically manipulated the existing situation to their own advantage. "The Director's Wife" (*Zhena rezhissera*), concerns a young actress who lands her first job after drama school in a small provincial theatre.[42] Drama school pedagogy prepared her to advance her career by marrying an influential man – preferably a troupe's entrepreneur, his son, or the director. For that reason, her first task upon arrival is to search out a suitable victim. She snares a director, but is astonished when he forbids her to continue acting after their marriage. Because she married a director not in order to stay at home and have babies but to get leading roles, she quickly divorces him and moves on.

In another of Garting's stories, "His Excellency's Wife" (*Zhena ego prevoskhoditel'stva*), a starring actor insists on a sizeable contract for his wife before agreeing to sign his own contract.[43] The wife, who is simultaneously attractive and embarrassingly inept on stage, requires her husband's influence because she could not make 50 roubles a month on her own.

In a third story, Garting recounts the machinations of a professional walk-on (*vykhodnaia*) actress.[44] After long years of wandering from one theatre to another, this woman, described as "uncombed, unkempt, slovenly, and generally repulsive," has conceived a strategy for advancing her fortunes in each new theatre. Her scheme consists of swooning repeatedly in front of the leading actor so that he will take pity on her and offer financial assistance or help obtaining roles.

A provincial director told of serving in a small theatre where the leading lady – a very attractive woman and a very bad actress – enjoyed complete authority over the repertoire and distribution of roles. Her power was derived from the intimate relationship she enjoyed with the entrepreneur.[45] This lustful fellow, also one of the town's most respected citizens, was so enamored of the talentless harlot that he tailored the entire repertoire to suit her. Unfortunately, the audience, who would have preferred a real actress and some attempt on the part of the entrepreneur to maintain satisfactory artistic standards, abandoned the theatre. As a result, the entrepreneur lost thousands of roubles and, when he could no longer promote her career, his leading lady unceremoniously replaced him with a new patron.

Apparently, directors were painfully aware of the proliferation of self-serving actresses. In "The Actor's Marketplace," Svetlov also complained about the type of primadonna who was without talent, had the intellectual qualifications of a "pretty hen," and received a huge salary because she was surrounded by admirers and owned a stunning wardrobe.[46]

THE COSTUME CRISIS

If a small number of actresses profited from prevailing conditions, most commentators agreed that they degraded not only women but the concept of theatre as a "temple of art" as well. Because the abolition of serfdom fundamentally altered the composition of the audience, this otherwise progressive measure could conceivably have damaged the status of women in provincial theatres. This rather revisionist critique of the emancipation has the advantage of historical distance. During the period only a handful of particularly perspicacious observers recognized the profound effect of post-reform audience diversification on attitudes toward actresses. Most members of the theatre community were persuaded that the twin plagues of prostitution and patronage issued from a single source: excessive wardrobe demands. Mariia Velizarii, a moderately successful character actress who traveled the provincial circuit for several decades, understood the significance for actresses of a suitable wardrobe. When the theatre in which she worked went bankrupt, Velizarii was forced to pawn her entire personal stock of costumes. "This was," she wrote in her memoir, "an absolute disaster for an actress because how could you have a career without a wardrobe. What is an actress without costumes? She is a beggar; her route to the stage is cut off."[47]

Although the "wardrobe crisis" affected both actresses and actors, the burden on women was far greater. Actors were contractually obligated to supply their own costumes for plays requiring contemporary dress, but the theatre paid for historical costumes. Actresses, on the other hand, were required to supply both contemporary and historical costumes, including headdresses."[48] According to Arbenin, until recently this arrangement was not especially onerous because an actress's entire wardrobe consisted of three dresses: one for historical dramas and two for contemporary plays.[49] This convention apparently satisfied consumers of theatrical art until the Meiningen tours in 1885 and 1890 stimulated an antiquarian craze and Western touring stars like Bernhardt, Duse, and Rejane created a vogue for extravagant costuming in the capital cities.[50] Having learned from their Western competitors that audiences would pay good money to see a fashion extravaganza, Russian actresses working in the Imperial theatres began imitating them. The vicious circle was complete when the native stars, many of whom toured the provinces during the summers with their magnificent wardrobes, stimulated an appetite for extravagant costuming among provincial spectators and entrepreneurs.[51]

At the Women's Congress in 1908, Grinevskaia claimed that although salaries for actors and actresses were roughly equivalent, actresses spent up to two thirds of their salary on costumes.[52] This expenditure was not caprice but a condition of employment. Claiming that they were simply responding to public pressure, playwrights and entrepreneurs refused to hire actresses who did not own a substantial stock of costumes. Arbenin charged that entrepreneurs valued wardrobe over talent, preferring fashionably attired actresses to actresses with authentic ability and experience.[53] This trend, which became alarming during the final decades of the nineteenth century, provoked one witty fellow to observe that if he dressed up a mannequin in fine clothing and sent it to the Theatre Bureau during Lent, it would leave with a contract for 600 roubles a month.[54]

Grinevskaia complained that the tendency of avaricious entrepreneurs and directors to pander to the low and often capricious taste of provincial spectators for vapid amusement was a principal cause of the costume crisis. The public wanted spectacle, but entrepreneurs, who were too mean to pay for the necessary scenery and costumes out of their own pockets, refused to produce the historical dramas and spectacle melodramas that would satisfy the audience's appetite for elaborate sets and costumes. Instead, they transformed contemporary domestic plays into extravaganzas by requiring actresses to make multiple costume changes for even the simplest salon dramas.[55] One critic of excessive costuming told of his experience with a play, the action of which required a very modest environment. Unfortunately, the playwright included a "ball" scene. Given the milieu established by the text, this "ball" should have been little more than a small party thrown by a civil servant for friends and family. Not satisfied with such modest surroundings, however, the director and entrepreneur decided to enhance the spectacle by requiring the leading actress to purchase a completely new wardrobe for the scene. Protesting that she already had a perfectly acceptable ball gown, the actress resisted their demands. But because she had already worn the existing gown more than once, they forced her to buy a new one.[56]

The author also noted with a touch of irony that if spectators demanded new sets for each production, entrepreneurs and directors would refuse to pander to public taste because the money would come from their own pockets. Instead, the producers of provincial theatre preferred to "decorate their own often wretched productions at the expense of women's honor, soul, and body."[57] He added that actresses bore the entire burden of costuming. Actors, who could get by with the same frock coat for every production, often looked as wretched as the scenery and were largely exempt from excessive expenditures for costumes. According to Grinevskaia, entrepreneurs and directors who preferred actresses with wardrobes to actresses with talent not only encouraged moral depravity among theatre workers, but also fostered the current level of mediocrity on the Russian stage.[58]

Demands on actresses for sexual favors were certainly not new at the end of the nineteenth century. The only novelty was the connection established by contemporary commentators between excessive demands for elaborate costumes and the growing problem of prostitution. For most provincial actresses, the economic equation was simple: entrepreneurs demanded elegant wardrobes; actresses needed money in order to buy them, but their salaries were not sufficient.[59] In "Actresses and Wardrobe" (*Aktrisy i tualety*), N.I. Aberdukh observed that the obligation to obtain their own costumes and the necessity to own a fine wardrobe discouraged virtuous behavior among actresses.[60] In the same article, A. Murski told of a young actress who, in spite of her best intentions, could not avoid the necessity to "sell her body" when she was forced by an unscrupulous entrepreneur to buy a boyar's costume, a ball dress, and a fashionable hat on a salary of 25 roubles a month.[61]

Provincial actresses' average monthly salaries ranged from 30 to 50 roubles for walk-ons to 300–400 for particular types (*na amplua*).[62] Although these salaries may seem attractive when compared to the renumeration for typical low-level government jobs, teaching positions, and skilled crafts, critics of existing conditions argued that the hidden costs of life in the theatre left actresses with little discretionary income. Arbenin pointed out that a discrepancy often existed between an actress's reported and actual salary.[63] In addition, because the regular theatre season lasted only six months, the average monthly salary must be reduced by half in order to obtain an accurate picture of economic reality.[64] The peripatetic existence of a typical provincial actress also required more substantial expenditures than the settled lives of teachers and government employees. Actresses had to move at least twice a year, travel to Moscow at Lent, eat in restaurants, and live in hotels.

A leading actress receiving an average salary of 400 roubles a month during the regular season, could, if she lived modestly, spare between 200 and 300 roubles for costumes. Actresses who received smaller salaries could hardly afford to sew one or two new dresses each season and remake the old ones in accordance with current fashion. After paying for travel and living expenses, walk-on and second-level actresses had not a kopek left to spare for costumes. Considering that in 1897 an average historical costume cost between 70 and 100 roubles, few actresses could afford substantial, and at the same time elegant, wardrobes.[65] And because entrepreneurs and directors demanded such wardrobes, actresses from all categories were compelled to engage on some level in commercial sex. As one observer noted, if women had no thought of prostitution before going on stage, necessity compelled them to become acquainted with "the life" once they joined a theatre.[66] Although many Imperial actresses received wardrobe subsidies, even they were not exempt from financial pressures related to costuming. During one season, Mariia Savina spent 7,000 roubles on her onstage wardrobe and, according to Grinevskaia, the amount of money Vera Michurina-Samoilova spent in one year on costumes was sufficient to support ten middle class families in relative comfort.[67]

Although most observers agreed that rapacious entrepreneurs and predatory directors created, profited from, and perpetuated this abusive system, several saw the problem differently. In 1897, one anonymous critic argued that, because they insisted upon dressing in the most elegant contemporary fashions regardless of the requirements of the play itself, actresses themselves were to blame for the existing state of affairs. By his account, actors had resigned themselves long ago to wearing costumes appropriate for the role even if their personal appeal was diminished. But if a director suggested to an actress that she should wear a historically authentic costume for the sake of the play, her reply would invariably be: "Is it pretty?" Unlike their male colleagues, actresses, driven by personal vanity alone, were exclusively concerned with pleasing and impressing the "various princes and Petr Ivanychs" sitting in the first row. Even the most secure actress would, he claimed, play Marguerite sitting in her prison cell dressed in a white cashmere peignoir.[68]

In 1909, N.I. Aberdukh tried to convince the readers of *Footlights and the Actor* (*Rampa i akter*) that drama schools were to blame. Arguing that they encouraged "cruel competition" among young women and reinforced unhealthy "marketing" practices (*reklama*), Aberdukh called upon these institutions to reconsider their pedagogical methods. He also suggested that, attracted by romantic fantasies of luxury and comfort, too many young women fled to the stage not because they loved art, but in order to escape violent, unhappy, poverty-stricken family situations. The theatre would not solve the problem of prostitution, Aberdukh insisted, until financially secure, well-educated, morally irreproachable women from the upper classes began pursuing careers in the theatre.[69] When such supposedly exemplary women did begin to appear on stage, however, they were also deemed unsatisfactory. In 1911, two years after Aberdukh called for greater refinement among actresses, N.S. Vasil'eva complained of the appalling mediocrity of the current crop of actresses, a group which consisted primarily of neurasthenics in search of "experience, emotion, and transformation." These "ladies" (*damy*), most of whom had little talent and were concerned exclusively with outward appearances (*vneshnost*), came to the stage because they simply had nothing else with which to occupy their time.[70]

At the end of the period, during the war years, a new perspective emerged as critics such as N. Smirnova simultaneously excused and censured actresses. Arguing that vanity and excessive stylishness were necessary and inevitable in the theatre, she nonetheless encouraged actresses to set an example for others: when soldiers were dying and people starving, actresses had, according to Smirnova, a moral responsibility to discourage public preoccupation with high fashion.[71]

That wardrobe was the most pressing issue for provincial actresses is clear from the protocol of the First All-Russian Congress of Representatives of the Stage. Although many challenged the accuracy of Tarlovskaia's general assessment of actresses' degraded status, even her critics agreed that the burden of increasingly elaborate production values fell primarily on actresses and that excessive elegance on stage had to be curbed.[72] But what could be done?

In an ineffectual attempt to address the problem, members of the Congress proposed to change rule seventy-three of the standard contract so that it read: "Actresses receiving between 50 and 75 roubles a month must have at least four dresses, including a ball gown and a visiting dress, even if they are inexpensive. Those receiving less than 50 roubles are not obliged to purchase a ball dress, but may obtain one from the theatre's wardrobe."[73] This well-intentioned, entirely inadequate proposal, which did little to change existing conditions, suggests that Russian actresses had little authority within the very organization charged with protecting their interests. Because issues peculiar to actresses were largely ignored by the Congress and the Russian Theatre Society, their situation continued to deteriorate: after 1900 the chorus of complaints about excessive demands for elegant costumes grew louder and instances of professional prostitution and sexual extortion were documented more frequently.

FAMILY LIFE AND WORKING CONDITIONS

Although prostitution, sexual patronage, and excessive wardrobe costs caused tremendous anxiety among actresses in both the Imperial and private theatres, other issues also affected the quality of their lives. Many women who chose to devote themselves to the theatre were motivated at least in part by a desire to escape the oppressive, state-sanctioned conditions of marriage and family; but because actresses were not a homogeneous group, some also yearned for the stability and respectability provided by traditional domestic arrangements. The bourgeois nuclear family model was, however, difficult to replicate within the theatrical context.

Russian marriage laws did not encourage monogamy or family stability among members of the theatre community. One observer argued that statute 103 of the civil code, which obliged married couples to live together, and Senate resolution 1790, which established a husband's absolute authority to circumscribe his wife's activities, discouraged actresses from marrying.[74] Although these statutes were burdensome to all Russian women, because their profession demanded mobility and flexibility actresses were particularly disadvantaged. For that reason, in spite of social disapprobation, many actresses avoided legal marriage in favor of temporary or permanent cohabitation.

Writing in 1900 about the challenge of establishing and maintaining family stability while simultaneously pursuing a career in the theatre, V. Linski observed that three types of marriage were possible for actresses and actors: 1) between an actor and a woman outside the theatre; 2) between an actress and actor; 3) between an actress and a man outside the theatre.[75] The first arrangement was possible, although many such unions did not last; the second was ideal because both parties understood and accepted the conditions imposed by their profession. The third arrangement was inevitably disastrous for two reasons: no man could tolerate being an appendage to his more visible – and perhaps highly paid – wife; and actresses, who were too highly strung and inclined to madness, did not possess the proper "soft femininity" (*miagkaia zhenstvennost*) to be suitable wives. Linski's views were not exceptional. Like many critics he loathed emancipated women and decried the pernicious effect of feminism on actresses, which in his opinion encouraged them to renounce traditional values in pursuit of self-gratification.

Although some actresses persisted in the effort to satisfy both personal and professional imperatives, many others were overwhelmed and eventually had to renounce one or the other. Shortly after Polina Strepetova began her career in the 1860s, she asked a prominent playwright, Count Vladimir Sollogub, to evaluate her chances for success. His first question was whether she intended to marry. She answered: "No. I not only don't want to get married, the word marriage itself is revolting." Pleased by her response, he advised: "Forget about marriage for as long as possible.... A family woman (*zhenshchina – semianinka*) and an actress are incompatible."[76]

Mariia Velizarii, whose experience confirms Sollogub's admonition, wrote: "The stage is a jealous lover. If you betray it, it will betray you."[77] Before marrying Ivan Shuvalov in the late 1890s, Velizarii had already established a solid reputation on the provincial circuit. Once she was obliged to accompany her husband, however, Velizarii found herself at a considerable professional disadvantage. On those rare occasions when husband and wife found employment in the same theatre, Velizarii received slightly more than half of Shuvalov's salary.[78] Then, in 1898, the birth of their first child forced her to reevaluate her priorities. Although professing satisfaction with the altered circumstances of her professional life, Velizarii complained bitterly when she was forced to follow Shuvalov to St. Petersburg for the sake of family unity. He was offered a substantial contract with the Imperial Aleksandrinskii Theatre, but in order to accompany him and remain professionally active, she had to accept a greatly reduced salary at Lidia Iavorskaia's Novyi Theatre. Grumbling that "the actress had paid for the woman's happiness," Velizarii charged Iavorskaia with taking advantage of her desperate family situation by cutting her salary to 400, rather than her usual 600, roubles a month.[79]

If marriage hindered an actress's career, children presented an even greater obstacle to professional achievement. Perhaps for that reason, only a small number of successful actresses had children. Indeed, Velizarii's most grievous professional misfortune was not her marriage to Shuvalov, but his sudden death, which forced her into the extraordinarily disadvantageous position of a single parent. When he died, Velizarii had no job and 12 roubles in her pocket. Without a husband and burdened by the full responsibility for a young child, she became easy prey for unscrupulous entrepreneurs and directors as she wandered from one provincial theatre to another in search of steady employment. Zinaida Kholmskaia echoed Velizarii's complaint when she was forced to abandon a lucrative tour with M.E. Darskii because of the inconvenience of traveling in the middle of the night from one town to another with children in tow.[80] Augustina Izborskaia observed that the forced separation of families for five or six months at a time often led to the permanent fracture of the family unit. To be the child of an actor, she argued, was to have a cheerless, distorted childhood. Materially deprived and barred by circumstance from receiving an adequate education, actors' children were severely handicapped in the existing social situation.[81] Most actresses who wanted a traditional family arrangement understood that it required stability, a luxury few of them could afford.

The views of Aleksandr Kugel on the pathology of women artists were not exceptional in Russia. For Kugel, a woman who succeeded as an artist was one who had failed to realize her true creative impulse through love and motherhood.[82] But women who exchanged traditional domestic relations for an autonomous existence in the theatre were usually motivated by a complex combination of economic, aesthetic, and personal factors. As we have seen, for many actresses, a strong dose of economic reality cured any illusions they may have entertained about acquiring substantial wealth. But because so many women justified their extra-domestic activities on the basis of service to art and humanity, questions of aesthetic satisfaction and personal development were important to them. Actresses exchanged sex not only for money, but also for advantageous roles. But were the roles worth the bargain and did the conditions under which plays were produced promote artistic sensitivity and excellence?

Because Russian theatre was so diverse, it is difficult to generalize broadly about aesthetic objectives and working conditions at the end of the nineteenth century. Throughout the nineteenth century, theatres in the capital cities and provinces served the disparate needs of audiences widely separated by class, ethnicity, economics, and even geography. To complicate matters further, at the end of the century many theatres attempted to redefine their objectives and reform working conditions in response to fundamental shifts in cultural values.

Traditionally, the Imperial theatres in Moscow and St. Petersburg were considered to be exemplary models of artistic excellence in which authentic talent could be nurtured and exhibited, while private provincial theatres were anti-aesthetic and "profaned sacred art."[83] Exceptions to conventional wisdom existed throughout the period, however. Good theatre could, for example, be found in several provincial cities, including Kiev, Kharkhov, Odessa, and Saratov. Ironically, beginning in the 1870s, the formerly exemplary Imperial theatres began to deteriorate; the Aleksandrinskii was especially vulnerable to harsh criticism for its obsolete scenic conventions, absence of ensemble, and less than ideal repertoire. With the rise of private art theatres in the late 1890s and increased emphasis on universal actor training, distinctions between Imperial and private theatre in both the capitals and provinces broke down further. Nonetheless, some divisions remained operative throughout the period. For example, although Imperial theatres were often managed by incompetent, ignorant bureaucrats, they had enormous resources at their disposal, which allowed them to provide substantial salaries and perquisites. In contrast, the private commercial theatres, which employed the largest percentage of actresses, often had few material resources and were managed by unprincipled, exploitative entrepreneurs who cared only for profit, squeezed the actors unmercifully, and often absconded at the end of the season, having lined their pockets with the box office receipts.

Although Imperial actresses often complained of having to perform popular rubbish, of mistreatment by disrespectful administrators and directors, and of absurdly long working hours, conditions in the private theatres, especially those in the provinces, were much worse.

According to Nikolai Urvantsov, the repertoire could not be planned in advance because the typical provincial entrepreneur was in bondage to the whims of the public. The tastes of this coarse collection of merchants, peasants, and assorted civil servants determined the types of plays – usually crude farces, melodramas, and "pornography" – that could be produced.[84] The theatres had little money or time to spend on proper staging: productions were slapped together with great speed, their quality was poor, and repetition was, by necessity, rare. Nikolai Karabanov wrote that to compare typical provincial actors and actresses to those fortunate creatures who worked for Imperial and private art theatres was like comparing housepainters and artists. Provincial performers, who learned between fifty and sixty new roles during a four or five month season, could not afford to be concerned with art. What could these pathetic toilers achieve as artists, Karabanov asked, when they produced three new plays a week and were in rehearsal and performance at least ten hours each day?[85] Under such conditions, it is hardly surprising that even at the end of the nineteenth century, most actors and actresses placed greater value on the prompter than on the director, who was often viewed simply as a nuisance. Urvantsov concluded that on those rare occasions when good theatre was produced in the provinces it was thanks to the "heroic efforts" of actors and directors; only their "inexhaustibly fanatical love for the theatre" made it possible for them to surmount such lousy working conditions.[86] Given the existing situation, is it any wonder, then, that actresses' fantasies of artistic satisfaction and personal self-realization often culminated in bitter disillusion?

The art theatres and formal training programs that appeared at the end of the nineteenth century eventually had a salutary effect on Russian theatre, but for many years their presence did little to improve life for the vast majority of actresses.[87] Although many evinced a heartfelt desire to devote themselves to "pure art," there were too few art theatres to accommodate all who wished to join; most such enterprises were extraordinarily unstable; and at least some actresses resisted the authority of the autocratic actor-managers who controlled them. With respect to theatre schools and training programs, shortly after the Imperial monopoly was abolished in 1882, demands for better trained and educated actors became more insistent.[88] Although a significant number of programs were established in the 1890s and first decade of the twentieth century, many actresses and actors firmly rejected the idea that acting was a learned skill. In addition, even the most rigorous theatre schools ill prepared their graduates for the commercial, anti-aesthetic realities of both the Imperial and private theatres. In 1896, one critic advised beginning actors and actresses to conceal their theatre school credentials. In order to maintain a position in a provincial troupe, he admonished them to forget everything they learned in school and begin to perform like "experienced actors" – that is, they must accept any role, regardless of suitability to type, and "perform without knowing the contents of the play or even reading their own roles."[89]

In "The Pure Actress" (*Chistenkaia aktrisa*), a critic mocked the new type of actress being created by well-intentioned drama schools. The "pure actress" had a "pure appearance," which included "big, bewildered eyes and a completely flat chest, upon which she wore a medallion with a picture of her teacher and an inscription from Lope de Vega."[90] Upon receiving her first genuine engagement, this naive waif wrote to her beloved teacher:

> Ah, what a horror! I expected so much, but not what I encountered. We perform with one rehearsal, no one sticks to quarter tones or even half tones, the entrepreneur calls me his little sweetheart, no one ever heard of Brandes, and our leading actress swigs cognac like a boatswain. This is what they call service to art! When I began rehearsing Sashen'ka from *Ivanov* in accordance with your theory of the half-pause, the director called me a "duffer." My God, what kind of atmosphere am I stuck in – and all this after you and I translated Calderon together![91]

Having received no useful advice from her former mentor, after a month the "pure actress" married the company's *raisonneur*, started drinking heavily, pawned her medallion, put on a little weight, and occasionally was heard to whisper the name of Calderon.

The question posed at the beginning of the chapter – was life in the theatre as congenial as its optimistic devotees imagined? – is not easily answered. N.S. Vasileva observed in 1911 that women had always been attracted to the stage by the phantom of independence, but asked whether their thinking was dangerously delusional.[92] Clearly, a small minority of actresses boasted yearly earnings far beyond those of women in any other profession, but many barely scraped by. In addition, during much of the period the social stigma of professional acting was so great that even Imperial actresses did not emerge unscathed. Nevertheless by the 1890s, a few prominent actresses in both the capitals and provinces were beginning to enjoy the more elevated status of genuine artists. For the majority of Russian actresses, however, life in the theatre consisted of a daily struggle to overcome seemingly insurmountable physical, financial, emotional, and moral obstacles. Complaints about existing conditions were largely ignored and proposals to unionize and address actresses' problems collectively fell on deaf ears.[93]

As irrational as it may seem, and in spite of the odds and obstacles confronting them, ever larger numbers of Russian women flocked to the newly established actor-training programs, gathered at the Theatre Bureau during Lent, and begged recalcitrant entrepreneurs and directors to give them a chance. Perhaps Polina Strepetova expressed the appeal of the theatre for women when, upon stepping into the train that would carry her to her first independent job as an actress, she cried: "Freedom, freedom! Oh what a marvelous feeling."[94]

3

MARIIA SAVINA
Privilege and power in the Imperial theatres

In 1915, an obituary notice in the *Woman's Herald* (*Zhenskii vestnik*) proclaimed: "Mariia Gavrilovna Savina demonstrated what a Russian woman can be and what she can accomplish when her path is freely chosen."[1] Mariia Savina, the most powerful actress of the Silver Age, may also have been the most powerful individual, male or female, in Russian theatre between the late 1870s and 1900, the point when private theatres began to pose a genuine threat to the Imperials. Savina, whose reign on the Imperial Aleksandrinskii stage in St. Petersburg lasted for more than four decades, is, unfortunately, little known in the West. Her relative obscurity is not difficult to explain. In certain respects, Savina was the most audacious actress of the era. But because she remained within the Imperial system and preferred to exploit popular trends rather than encourage aesthetic innovation, she was often identified with the forces of reaction. Western histories of Silver Age theatre tend to focus almost exclusively on the progressive avant-garde. For that reason, actresses associated with the stolid, often reactionary traditions of the Imperial theatres are neglected in favor of those few, like Vera Kommissarzhevskaia, who abandoned the Imperial system in order to explore theatrical modernism independently.

Savina's significance in Silver Age theatre, in terms of concrete achievements and as a marker of shifting gender ideology, is considerable. She was not only a wildly successful actress, but also founded the Russian Theatre Society (RTO) and was the first woman to be granted the title "Actress Emerita" (*zasluzhennaia artistka*).[2] Perhaps more than any actress of the era, Savina successfully exploited both Western trends and Slavophile traditions. A product of the provincial theatres, she was a nakedly ambitious, yet astonishingly unpretentious pragmatist who enjoyed unprecedented authority both onstage and off. More than any of her contemporaries, Savina's career marked the limits of what an actress could achieve within existing institutional hierarchies. In an essay published not long after Savina's death, one admirer observed that "if Savina had been born male, she would probably have reached the pinnacle of authority and power, and who knows, she might have secured a place in the pages of world history."[3] She was simultaneously admired, envied, and hated; in an age when many actresses were dismissed as morally depraved, vacuous imitators of Parisian fashion, her carefully cultivated feminine charm and reputation for intellectual acuity attracted the attention and admiration of some of the most prominent men of the period, including Ivan Turgenev, Aleksei Suvorin, and Aleksandr Koni;[4] at the same time, her restrained elegance, a tasteful blend of Paris and St. Petersburg, was widely admired by those Russian women who could afford to imitate it. Indeed, with Savina we begin to see a disintegration of the social boundaries that existed between actresses and respectable women and a new receptivity to Western-influenced "*zhenstvennost.*" Savina fully exploited the appetite for women's themes on stage and she was the first Russian actress to understand the value of marketing. Like Sarah Bernhardt, with whom she was sometimes compared, fashion and personality were significant factors in her success, so much so that she was also the first Russian dramatic actress to cultivate a personality cult. Although Savina was enormously popular, neither during her long career nor after her death was she saddled with the symbolic baggage that so burdened Mariia Ermolova and Vera Kommissarzhevskaia. And although Russian theatre is deeply indebted to Savina for her activism on its behalf, no heroic mythology exaggerates her accomplishments or clouds her deficiencies. She was never effective or comfortable in romantic heroic roles; her heroines were for "everyday" use (*povsednevnost*).[5] Perhaps for that reason, Russian critics and theatre historians have never agreed on the nature of Savina's significance: some insist she was nothing more than a mediocre actress whose success was the product of a Machiavellian instinct for power, while others called her one of the creative geniuses of Silver Age theatre.[6]

The transitory nature of the stage actor's art, the subjectivity of critical response, and the fact that Savina was a pre-Moscow Art Theatre actress caught in a transition of styles and techniques, make speculation about the quality of her artistry difficult. After her death, even Aleksandr Koni, one of Savina's closest friends, was frustrated by the impossibility of communicating her magic to readers who had not seen the deceased actress on stage.[7] In addition, like most powerful women, she had rabid detractors and fanatical admirers, few of whom deserve to be called objective observers; indeed, no prominent actress of this period was free from the critics' ideological agendas and crusades. If the quality of Savina's artistry is now shrouded with ambiguity, one thing about her career is certain: from the perspective of gender, it embodied both the best and worst of Silver Age culture as it affected women.

Savina was born on March 30, 1854. After a brief career as an actress, her mother left both the theatre and her husband. Savina's father, a former teacher who preferred the life of an intinerant provincial actor, dragged his daughter with him as he chased jobs from town to town on the circuit. For that reason, it is no surprise that Savina's theatrical career began before age ten and, like many prepubescent actresses, she debuted in a boy's role. Although as a child,

Mariia Gavrilovna was not particularly attracted to the stage, because few other professions were accessible to a girl of her class, she was inevitably drawn to it as a means of survival.[8] Her formal education consisted of a brief sojourn in a private pension in Odessa, but from her earliest years, theatre was Savina's milieu and she seems to have had few interests or ambitions beyond it.

Savina married three times, but like most successful actresses remained childless. She escaped her birth family by means of her first marriage to a young provincial actor named Savin, from whom she took her stage name.[9] Shortly after the wedding, they set off on the provincial circuit where, at least initially, theatres were interested in the husband and agreed to hire the wife for minor roles at a minimal salary primarily in order to obtain a serviceable, though far from brilliant, leading man.[10] In his memoirs, a retired actor who met Savina in this period suggested that her genius was not readily apparent to her provincial colleagues; no one who knew her during these years expected her to become such an accomplished actress or have such phenomenal success on the Imperial stage.[11] Shortly after she and Savin arrived for their first engagement at the Kazan theatre in 1871, Savina's luck began to change when the leading actress deserted the theatre in mid-season and her entire repertoire was assigned to the seventeen-year-old utility player.[12] This was, perhaps, the first example in Savina's professional life of her extraordinary ability to seize an opportunity and pursue her advantage with aggressive tenacity. She played the entire spectrum of genres, from serious dramatic to vaudeville; one night she danced, tambourine in hand, in light operetta, and the next night played Maria Antonovna in *The Government Inspector*. Apparently the young actress charmed the locals because from that moment she established a reputation as a desirable commodity. Her star rose rapidly – so much so that by the time Savina went to Saratov in 1873 at a salary of 400 roubles, she, not her husband, was the main attraction.[13] Generally speaking, Savina's experiences in the provinces were not atypical, but three aspects of her early work help to clarify both her general position in Silver Age theatre and also her specific role in the shifting sexual ideology as it affected theatre: the intensely competitive, frequently hostile relationships she began to establish with other actresses; her pragmatic, but frequently criticized propensity for wasting her considerable talents on popular rubbish; and the fact that even in the very early stages of her career Savina's individuality tended to overshadow the playwright's text.

Legend has it that Savina found herself on the Imperial Aleksandrinskii stage largely by accident. Because Savina rarely did anything "by accident," this seems unlikely; but because the story appears repeatedly in both contemporaneous sources and more recent biographical materials, it is central to the actress's mythology and merits attention. Already estranged from her first husband, by 1874 Savina was enjoying substantial popularity on the provincial circuit. During Lent (*velikii post*), when theatrical entrepreneurs swarmed to the capital cities on a quest for new talent for the coming season, she just happened to travel to St. Petersburg, ostensibly for a medical consultation. While in the city, Savina was invited to perform in a benefit being staged by one of the club theatres. Still virtually anonymous in the capital, Mariia Gavrilovna was particularly anxious to appear in this production because key members of the Imperial Aleksandrinskii company were likely to be present. The experience nearly culminated in disaster, however. Not being familiar with the peculiarities of her rehearsal technique, the entrepreneur was stunned and dismayed when, during rehearsals, Savina muttered and fumbled about the stage like a novice.[14] Everyone, even the familiar theatrical parasites loitering about the rehearsal hall, offered her advice until she became so discouraged that she nearly bought a ticket for the first train back to Saratov. The story had a cheery ending, however, when the "experienced actors [from the Aleksandrinskii] noticed her extraordinary gifts" and recommended to the director of the Imperial theatres that she be given a debut.[15] Two weeks later, Savina had her Aleksandrinskii debut; she received overwhelmingly positive responses from St. Petersburg critics, but the Imperial directorate, which was not especially receptive to provincial talent, required two additional debut performances before they agreed to offer her a contract.

Mariia Gavrilovna was an anomaly among Imperial actresses because, unlike most of them, she was not "trained by the pedants of the theatre seminary"[16] and had, according to Aleksandr Kugel, no stage education except the school of experience.[17] For that reason, she breathed life and energy into the stagnant atmosphere of Aleksandrinskii Theatre. Although it was undoubtedly true that, in 1874, the Aleksandrinskii was desperate for female talent, it seems unlikely, as one Moscow critic later charged, that Savina's success was largely the result of fortuitous circumstances rather than individual merit, and that if any of several other competent actresses had beat her to a debut, they would have become the darling of St. Petersburg.[18] Until Vera Kommissarzhevskaia was hired in 1896, Polina Strepetova, another ambitious, talented provincial actress, was Savina's only serious competition. As we shall see, Strepetova was a thoroughly populist (*narodnik*) actress whose major triumphs were in Ostrovski's plays. Although she enjoyed a brief vogue in St. Petersburg, she had little flexibility and was an abject failure in the Western-influenced society comedies and dramas that became the mainstay of the Aleksandrinskii repertoire during Savina's reign. Strepetova, who was apparently unaffected by the example of the Western touring stars, also lacked Savina's physical attractiveness and her uncanny ability to exploit Western trends while simultaneously remaining identified with Russian traditions. What distinguished Savina from lesser talents produced by the Imperial training program was that, perhaps as a result of her experiences in the provinces, she had acquired a deeper understanding of women from various social strata. According to Kugel, it was Savina who brought the

Russian "new woman," with her "new content" and "assertive will," to the stage;[19] thus the images of women she popularized were quite unlike those of other young Aleksandrinskii actresses, most of whom knew little of life beyond the privileged environs of the theatre.

During her forty-year career, Mariia Gavrilovna redefined theatrical "*zhenstvennost*" several times; her first innovation was the ingenue. Savina's most recent biographer called her the first proper Russian ingenue, but Kugel, who knew the actress well, asserted as much in 1923: "What," he asked, "was the Russian ingenue before Savina? Did she exist? I doubt it. There were the internationally familiar vaudeville fidgets, the oppressed innocents of melodrama, but outside of several excellent folk (*narodnyi*) characters, our stage did not know Russian girls and women."[20] Because the ingenue was not a native Russian flower, her appearance on the Russian stage initiated a controversy that dragged on for years. This sensuous, coquettish, largely alien character type, who affected the latest trends in Western fashion, simultaneously fascinated fashionable audiences in St. Petersburg and Moscow – who tended to worship anything Western – and disturbed conservative, Slavophile critics who saw her as a corrupting influence.[21] Savina seems to have understood perfectly the attraction for Russian audiences of this exotic Western blossom, but she also understood Russian nationalism and, perhaps for that reason, rarely performed in the Western repertoire. Like many of her competitors, Mariia Gavrilovna played Ostrovski's young women; in these roles she was competent, but not exceptional. She occasionally played the classical repertoire, but was not particularly comfortable in costume dramas. Instead, Savina's early successes were based primarily on frequent collaborations with popular hacks such as Victor Krylov and Aleksei Potekhin, playwrights who adapted – often to the point of plagiarism – Western society comedies and dramas (primarily French) especially suited to her particular talents. She was also closely associated with Turgenev's heroines, particularly Vera and later Natalia Petrovna from *A Month in the Country*.[22] Turgenev, who, like Ostrovski, is associated with early Russian realism, was an expatriate whose style, stories, and characters were clearly influenced by years of Parisian living. Vera, for example, is not a standard Western ingenue, but she also bears little resemblance to more typically Russian characters like Ostrovski's Katerina (*The Storm*). The ingenue introduced by Savina, then, was a hybrid derived from both native and foreign models. Her success with this controversial character type indicates the degree to which she was able to play both sides of the escalating controversy over sex/gender ideology to her own advantage.[23] She could wag her finger at, and gently admonish Turgenev for his Western tastes and trumpet her own patriotism – and at the same time exploit certain Bernhardtesque qualities and marketing strategies, which eventually became a principal source of her enormous popularity.

Figure 1 Mariia Savina as Marguerite Gautier
in *Lady of the Camellias*. Courtesy
of the St. Petersburg Theatre Museum

The fact that Savina was able to make the ingenue acceptable to Russian critics and spectators reflects one effect of shifting sex/gender ideology on audience taste. But Mariia Gavrilovna did not emerge unscathed from the controversy; her ingenue was implicated in the charge that, assisted by Krylov, she ruined the exemplary Russian stage during the 1870s and 1880s.[24] The attitude of Ostrovski and Aleskei Suvorin toward Savina was typical. Though both were Mariia Gavrilovna's ardent supporters when her presence in the cast guaranteed the success of *their* productions, Suvorin otherwise directed a barrage of criticism at the actress for her taste in dramatic literature and Ostrovski held her responsible for lowering the quality of the Aleksandrinskii's repertoire.[25] This is not altogether untrue, but the situation was not quite as simple as Savina's detractors would have had it and Savina herself was saddled with much more of the blame than she merited.

It was a question of power. Because she was the first Imperial actress to use the power of her popularity effectively, Savina became a lightning rod for disgruntled critics.[26] It is tempting to speculate that the attacks on her may have been motivated by the predominance of women's themes during the period, a trend instrumental to the rise of starring actresses. The fact that she, not Krylov, Potekhin, or the directorate of the Imperial theatres, was held responsible by contemporaneous critics for the decline of the Aleksandrinskii repertoire suggests the degree to which she was perceived as a powerful, intelligent, often threatening force. Complaining that she was entirely self-interested, Savina's detractors accused her of sacrificing the integrity of the Aleksandrinskii stage – and of Russian theatre as a whole – to her zealous pursuit of cheap celebrity in fatuous plays. In the declining years of Savina's career and after her death, critics and eulogists began to reevaluate opinions expressed earlier, suggesting that the popularity during the 1870s and 1880s of French adaptations and ingenues was largely a factor of the times. Rather than pinning the blame on Savina for the decline of Russian theatre, they excused her, explaining that her popularity was simply a response to changing audience tastes and expectations.[27] Though Savina exploited the appetite for Western society comedy, she did not create it.

Neither point of view reflects the reality of Savina's situation. To suggest that Savina was not implicated in the decline of the repertoire is to deny the reality of her power, which increased considerably over time.[28] If Savina did not single-handedly alter the Aleksandrinskii's repertoire, her talent was undisputed, her authority unprecedented, and her influence on the nature of the repertoire was clear. Her personal popularity guaranteed the success of almost any play and, like Bernhardt, she often chose popular rubbish if it had a showcase role for her. But as her apologists justly pointed out, Savina was occasionally innovative: she was the first Russian actress to play Nora in *A Doll's House*, thereby introducing spectators in St. Petersburg to Ibsen; she helped to popularize Turgenev's plays; after many years of arguing with the censor, she succeeded in mounting Tolstoi's *Power of Darkness* (*Vlasttmy*) at the Aleksandrinskii; and she was a sensitive interpreter of Chekhov.[29] Statements by Savina's partisans regarding her progressive tendencies should, however, be understood in context. In the first place, Savina was already a monument when they were made. In the second, her record as an advocate for progressive playwrights and thoughtful drama was desultory at best. For example, her support for Turgenev was probably motivated as much by calculation as by a genuine desire to raise the artistic level of the repertoire; *A Doll's House* was produced on Savina's initiative as her benefit in 1884, but after the play was ravaged by critics, she did not attempt another Ibsen for years; and although she was a sensitive interpreter of Sarah in *Ivanov*, she was generally hostile to modernist tendencies and rarely performed in Chekhov's plays.

Savina's heritage is the triumph of professional pragmatism over her own artistic, intellectual, and perhaps even political sensibilities. As she matured, friends and foes alike acknowledged Mariia Gavrilovna's great talent and extraordinary intelligence; she was certainly able to distinguish the social, political, artistic, and literary merits of a play, but because both she and the Aleksandrinskii directorate apparently cared more about financial than artistic success, they ignored these considerations in favor of immediate gain. Savina's instinct for marketing her own talents was remarkable; if she was occasionally mistaken, the mistake was not repeated. The example of *A Doll's House* is instructive. Ibsen's play was not forced on an unwilling starring actress by a progressive director; she chose it freely because, it may safely be assumed, like many Western actresses, she recognized a good role in an interesting, progressive play. Had critics responded positively to the production, it seems likely that Savina would have done Ibsen more frequently – but they were hostile and she refused to risk her career on a controversial playwright. Her relationship to the Russian women's movement was similarly ambivalent. She frequently did benefit performances in support of women's higher education; among other books on women, her personal library included all of the documents (*trudy*) from the first Russian women's convention; and a letter to Savina from Aleksandr Koni suggests that she was quite interested in women's rights and advocacy for women.[30] Nonetheless, *A Doll's House* was her first and only attempt to use the stage as a pulpit for women's rights. Although the women's movement enjoyed a certain amount of influence, it had little general support in Russia, especially from theatre critics. To be publicly associated with feminism was a risky business for any actress who valued her popularity, and Savina, whose popularity penetrated more deeply into the ranks of Russian society than that of most Imperial actresses, seems to have valued it above any private political convictions.

In addition, her correspondence with Suvorin reveals two important factors in Savina's success: she understood the dynamics of an effective production better than many directors and playwrights and she was supremely confident of her own stage instincts. During rehearsals for *Tatiana Repina*, Suvorin wrote lengthy letters to the actress which included revisions to the text, explications of new material, and instructions for playing the role. At first, listening patiently, trying to comfort the playwright and reassure him of her skill, she replied: "Every mother trembles for her child, but I am a good, experienced nanny and I won't put your daughter's eyes out: she is too dear to me." Nine days later, her patience worn thin by his badgering, she demands that he stop fiddling with the play, accusing him of a complete lack of stage sense and claiming that he has caused her to have three gall bladder attacks. Finally, she threatens to leave for a cure in Carlsbad if he continues to natter at her.[31] The incident with Suvorin was typical of her relationships with playwrights; Savina did not simply act in their plays, she was the playwright's principal collaborator. Indeed, so many critics remarked on Mariia Gavrilovna's skillful transformation of bad plays into good productions that there is no doubt who was responsible for their success.[32] But if critics appreciated Savina's extraordinary gifts and authority with spectators, they simply could not understand, and would not accept, her resistance to plays with literary and artistic merit. The insistent carping by critics had little effect on her repertoire, however. When she changed, it was by force of necessity, not because she was convinced of the merits of their argument.

For actresses, the phrase "force of necessity" is a polite allusion to age. Although Savina metamorphized successfully several times during her career, like most actresses, she resisted the final transition to older character types. Arguing that women were subject to a "different law" and that older actresses were disadvantaged by a repertoire that privileged young women, Kugel compared Savina's situation to Konstantin Varmalov's, who continued to get good roles no matter how old and fat he was.[33] Actresses and female playwrights were also painfully aware of the situation. In 1892, one of the most successful playwrights, K.V. Nazareva, published a short story, *Stage Illusions (Stsenicheskaia illiuziia)*, which recounts the declining years of an aging ingenue. Terrified of being mocked by critics for playing roles inappropriate to her age, this still youthful actress switches voluntarily to older character types before she is mentally, emotionally, or even chronologically prepared. Other ingenues, one indistinguishable from the other, wait hungrily, like birds of prey, to replace her, not realizing that in a few short years they will be in the same humiliating position. After changing types, the older actress quickly recedes into the background, eventually disappearing into the purgatory of provincial theatre where she becomes so despondent that suicide is the only viable alternative. If there is an irony to this parable, it is that the actress was probably not even thirty when she was forced out.[34]

Despite her fear of growing old, Savina aged well professionally precisely because, at least through middle age, she anticipated each stage of the process and turned it to her advantage. Like Nazareva's fictional prima donna, Savina knew when the ingenue was out of her range. When Chekhov gave *The Seagull* to the Aleksandrinskii in 1896, he asked that the now forty-two-year-old actress be given the role of Nina Zarechnaia. When Savina discovered the role had been assigned to her, she wrote to Suvorin, who was still close to Chekhov, asking him to extricate her from an impossible situation. Explaining that the success of Nina depends entirely on the actress's "exterior" (*vneshnost*), Savina acknowledges that she simply cannot disguise her age with wigs and makeup. Instead, she asks that Chekhov consider Vera Kommissarzhevskaia for the role and expresses her own desire to play Masha, who interests her much more than Nina.[35] Ironically, the role best suited to Savina was, of course, Arkadina, but throughout the latter part of her career, the actress studiously avoided maternal roles, even those as "unmatronly" as Kolia's self-absorbed mother.[36] In the end, however, Savina extricated herself entirely from the *The Seagull* and did not participate in the disastrous premiere.

Like Nazareva's unfortunate creature, many actresses who remained in the theatre past their youth moved from ingenue roles to comic older women (*komicheskaia starukha*) or grand dames, a transition that affected their employment opportunities, salary, and stature in the company, to say nothing of their personal vanity. Refusing to allow the passage of time to destroy her career, Savina not only survived the transition to middle age but prospered. Although she popularized the ingenue in Russia, Mariia Gavrilovna's reputation rests primarily on another type that became a staple of her repertoire near the end of the nineteenth century: the unsympathetic "fashionable lady" (*svetskaia dama*). As she matured during the late 1880s and 1890s, Savina was crowned queen of both high fashion and fashionable high comedy; her ingenue, described by critics as "fresh," "charmingly naive," and "sympathetic," was gradually replaced by an independent, worldly, sharp-tongued society woman. Critical response to this character was surprisingly positive. Kugel credited Savina with freeing Russian actresses from the necessity to be eternally sympathetic: her characters had "a will to action," they were "egotistic and passionate."[37] In 1891, a critic for the Moscow-based journal *Artist* praised Savina above Glikeriia Fedotova and Mariia Ermolova, the reigning prima donnas of the Imperial Malyi theatre, because they insisted upon idealizing every role. In contrast, Savina was interesting precisely because she dared to be unsympathetic, something few actresses of her stature would risk.[38] Given the hostility of Russian critics to Bernhardt, who also dared to be unsympathetic, it is ironic that Savina, the most unequivocally ambitious actress ever to assault the Imperial theatre fortress, a woman who dared to be unsympathetic both on stage and off, was crowned by critics as a model of "eternal femininity" (*vechnaia zhenstvennost*).[39]

Savina's transition to sophisticated, caustic society women reflects both the actress's personal transformation from provincial "*devochka*" (girl) to fashionable "*dama*," as well as more universal changes in Russian society and, by association, in Russian theatre. As democratic sentiments became stronger in Russia, traditional class stratification gradually began to break down.

Although women often had greater mobility than men in transgressing class boundaries, Russian actresses were more constrained than most by their association in the minds of the public with prostitution. During Savina's reign at the Aleksandrinskii, however, formerly insurmountable barriers between actresses and women of the upper classes began to disintegrate as larger numbers of women sought higher education and independent employment outside the home, as the composition of the audience became increasingly bourgeois, and as the profession of acting became more respectable for both men and women. Although Savina did not consciously construct a stage image informed by feminist ideology, she was the most visible emblem of what an ambitious provincial girl could achieve. Not only was she financially independent, she was also known and respected throughout Russia for her stage artistry. Even Tolstoi, who considered that, as a general rule, women should confine themselves to caring for a husband and children, was impressed by Savina's intelligence and wit.[40] Her second marriage (to Nikita Vsevolozhski, a *bona fide* aristocrat) was, at least in the eyes of other ambitious young women, a fairy tale come true. Although this unfortunate liaison was the cause of much personal grief (her husband's family refused to accept her; he was forced to retire from his military post; and he lost all of his money and most of hers through gambling and high living), it was also a profitable marketing ploy which fed the public's inexhaustible appetite for scandal among the *beau monde*, kept Mariia Gavrilovna in the public eye, and brought her universal sympathy.[41] Indeed, the marriage to Vsevolozhski elevated her in the eyes of everyone except the most conservative advocates of class privilege.

In his memoirs of Savina, a fellow actor remarked that when plays are mediocre, the actor's personality tends to dominate;[42] although Savina acquired considerable skill as an actress, it was her ability to market personal style and fashion without resorting to mindless imitation of Western trends that made her the idol of St. Petersburg. Women admired her, men fell in love with her, playwrights, critics, and fellow actors courted her favors – and the eternally pragmatic Savina created her image, managed her ascendancy, and maintained her position with more energy and tenacity than any actress before or after. Apparently Savina's authority with the public was so great that tradesmen, craftspeople, and commercial enterpreneurs asked her for product endorsements.[43] Like Bernhardt, Savina was a canny businesswoman who understood the importance of publicity and effective marketing, but as we have already seen, Bernhardt's eccentricities and excessive flamboyance were problematic for many Russian critics and spectators whose appetite for Parisian decadence was not without limits. Having made the transition to "fashionable ladies," Savina, who had already sounded the depth of her audience's taste for Western-influenced drama, continued to perform primarily in adaptations; but now, borrowing yet another page from Bernhardt's book, she began to exploit fashion for its own sake.

Because she did not perform in exotic spectacles, her expenditures rarely matched Bernhardt's excesses. By Silver Age standards, however, she spent enormous sums on elegant, contemporary fashions suited to the genres in which she specialized.[44] Her purchases were apparently motivated less by personal vanity than by an almost perfect understanding of her audience. "What kind of public is this?" she asked. "On Sundays it is no worse than a fairground mob, but usually it is a lazy, bloated crowd that attends the theatre in order to digest dinner while watching Madame Vsevolozhski and her wardrobe. These people are not in the least bit interested in extending their minds or stimulating their brains. What does this bunch care about Ibsen?"[45] Unlike Ermolova and later Kommissarzhevskaia, Savina did not seek to challenge or elevate public taste, but to exploit it. A full wardrobe was essential and no actress could hope to land a job without an adequate stock of suitable costumes. Like Bernhardt, however, Savina understood that an "adequate" wardrobe was not sufficient; high fashion and multiple costume changes drew the St. Petersburg *beau monde* into the theatre. For that reason, her performances were often pretexts for elegant displays of new gowns. Changes in fashion were, however, implicated in changes in sex/gender ideology and Savina seems instinctively to have understood the danger of imitating Bernhardt too closely. If Russians were fascinated by the French, they were also repelled by what seemed to them to be the French tendency toward decadence and immorality – both of which were incarnated for many critics in Bernhardt. Although many Russians admired foreign fashions, carried to an extreme, outrageous costumes alienated critics and spectators. Savina was the first Russian actress to indulge the audience's taste for high fashion, but she carefully maintained an image of restrained elegance.[46]

It is not difficult to understand Savina's special appeal for the middle- and upper-class women who could afford to attend the Aleksandrinskii Theatre: their lives, aspirations, and fantasies were reflected in her characters. Unlike Mariia Ermolova, who specialized in idealized, romantic-heroic caricatures from the classical repertoire, or Strepetova, whose skills were limited to Ostrovski's coarse realism, Savina excelled in society comedies and dramas adapted to the Russian context; these were known generically as "*bytovaia dramaturgiia*," or "drama of everyday life." This is not meant to suggest that Savina was a realist in the tradition of the later Moscow Art Theatre actresses. Although her career may be understood as a stage in the development of realistic acting, she never pretended to subordinate herself to the role and was, as many critics observed, a virtuoso performer for whom ensemble acting was an undesirably alien concept.[47] Savina can, however, be seen as a prototype for the genuinely realistic actresses that followed; the barriers between Mariia Gavrilovna and her female audience broke down precisely because women in the audience began to see characters and situations with which they could identify. In regard to costume and manners, "*bytovaia dramaturgiia*" required that Savina imitate current fashion; thus she reflected an image back to women in the audience that the higher ranks had already achieved and the lower ranks aspired to imitate.[48] These were the women they wanted, or imagined themselves, to be: witty, attractive to men, and always beautifully dressed. If Savina's favorite type during the late 1880s and 1890s was a "new woman," the term should not be confused with the more familiar Western New Woman. Savina's "new woman" had a quick wit and a sharp tongue, but she rarely trangressed the bounds of bourgeois propriety, preserved many conventional, non-threatening qualities of traditional "*zhenstvennost*," and was, therefore, acceptable to conservative spectators and critics.

If Savina rejected the New Woman as a desirable stage image, more so than any starring actress of the period, she lived the role off-stage. After her second marriage failed, she devoted much of her energy to forwarding her own career and expanding her power base both within the Aleksandrinskii and in the larger theatre community. Her device, which neither she nor her admirers ever tired of repeating, was "theatre is my life" (*teatr – moia zhizn*). And on the occasion of her twenty-fifth jubilee, she is rumored to have proclaimed: "I am the Aleksandrinskii Theatre."[49] Her authority at the Aleksandrinskii was still based on her broad popularity; as long as she remained the theatre's most marketable commodity, management and directors did not challenge her.[50] Like many of Savina's colleagues, Vera Michurina-Samoilova, who joined the Aleksandrinskii in 1866, disliked Mariia Gavrilovna and resented her power, but respected her talent and discipline. According to Samoilova, rehearsals were scheduled at Savina's convenience. During rehearsals, absolute silence reigned and everyone, right up to the director "danced attendance on her."[51] Evtikhi Karpov, an aspiring playwright who enjoyed Savina's support, observed that Mariia Gavrilovna's interests went well beyond her own role. She consistently "interfered" in all aspects of the rehearsal and production process; for that reason her career was a record of constant skirmishes with the front office, the author, and the director.[52] Michurina-Samoilova complained that Savina was often cold, capricious, and hostile off stage, but added that she was a delight to perform with. Karpov suggested that Mariia Gavrilovna's seriousness of purpose and intolerance for slackers won her many enemies. Khodotov observed that, although playwrights were often astonished at her individuality, artistic sensitivity, and "masculine logic," many members of Aleksandrinskii directorate hated, feared, and intrigued against her.[53] Her will to power was such that conflicts with directors were inevitable. Taking into account her talent, managerial skills, and readiness to assert her will, it is difficult to avoid speculation that, had Savina been male, she would have been appointed managing director of the Aleksandrinskii. Indeed, when V.V. Chekhov observed in 1904 that Savina had no need to found her own theatre because she already owned the Aleksandrinskii, he was not far from the truth.[54] It is hardly surprising, then, that she was eventually eclipsed not by another actress, but by the string of neo-Wagnerian "master artists" hired by the Aleksandrinskii after 1900. As she aged, these men, who saw Savina as an impediment to their own ambitions, were increasingly able to outmaneuver her because her power, which was based on her value as a marketable commodity, decreased as she reached the point in her career when "fashionable ladies" went out of fashion and advancing age prevented her from finding an equally attractive substitute.[55]

Savina's power was not, however, limited to the Aleksandrinskii Theatre. Although she was often criticized for her indifference to national and international affairs, politics in the theatre community began to consume much of her energy after 1884. Her reputation for private philanthropy and public advocacy on behalf of provincial actors was so great that M.G. Svetaeva called her "the first authentic actress-social activist (aktrisa-obshchest-vennitsa) in Russia."[56] Without devaluing the reality of Savina's contribution to the Russian theatre community, the term "social activist" as it applies to actresses requires both explanation and qualification.

During the second half of the nineteenth century, Russian women became increasingly involved in the public life of the nation and, according to Barbara Engel, they "brought moral fervor to everything they did.... Hundreds of them devoted their lives to educating or providing medical care for the Russian masses" and "hundreds more participated in movements for social and political change."[57] Russian women were involved in the entire spectrum of social activism, from benign charitable associations to plotting and executing assassinations as members of the People's Will, but even as they moved away from an exclusive preoccupation with domestic affairs, there was tremendous pressure to maintain traditional gender roles. Because most *legal* forms of social activism required women to apply conventional feminine skills to extra-domestic activities, they did not threaten the already strained social fabric. Thus, most social activists could escape the domestic sphere without being censured as self-serving, ambitious harridans. Actresses were not exempt from the necessity to frame their activities in the rhetoric of social activism. Indeed, perhaps because the profession of acting had the reputation of being a refuge for prostitutes, alcoholics, and slackers of all sorts, actresses were under even greater pressure to justify their activity in terms of social service. Thus, when Savina celebrated her twenty-fifth jubilee at the Aleksandrinskii, one critic rhapsodized about her "quarter century of irreproachable, selfless devotion to national art."[58]

Because the attitude toward artists and artistic endeavor in the West, especially in the United States, is comparatively cynical, it is tempting to dismiss sentiments like these as sanctimonious bombast. But, steeped in their own cultural bias, which tends to see all art in commercial terms, Western historians are ill-equipped to judge objectively whether Russian actresses were genuinely motivated by moral fervor and selfless devotion to serving their country through art, or whether the purple prose of social service simply masked personal ambition. Savina's case is even more difficult because, although her brand of acerbic *"zhenstvennost"* had broad appeal, she had few of the maternal, nurturant qualities so valued by social critics. Even close friends and ardent admirers acknowledged that Savina's philanthropy and activism on behalf of her profession were not motivated by sentiment or any repressed maternal feelings, but by rational calculation. Although the reasons for her decision to become actively involved in theatrical reform remain obscure, she was one of the few prominent actresses to do so, and ultimately, she did more to advance acting as a respectable profession than any other actress of the period.[59]

Mariia Gavrilovna, who toured Russia each summer, never forgot her roots in provincial theatre; for that reason, she devoted tremendous energy to improving conditions for provincial actors. With respect to her private philanthropic activities, one eulogist emphasized that people from all walks of life came to Savina for help, most of them complete strangers, and that she responded generously to their requests for assistance whether or not she was sympathetic to their various causes or liked them personally. She was, he claimed, motivated not by "unctious Christian piety," but by a strong, though completely unsentimental, social conscience.[60] Not everyone viewed Savina so uncritically. Pavla Vulf, an actress who worked with Mariia Gavrilovna during one of her provincial tours, acknowledged her colleague's largesse, but added that Savina had much to atone for, suggesting that her philanthropy was a sort of backhanded compensation to the many victims of her capricious anger and pride.[61]

Her organizational efforts on behalf of Russian actors are, however, far more significant than her personal magnanimity. In 1877, the Society for Reciprocal Relief for Russian Artists (*Obshchestvo vzaimnogo vspomozheniia russkikh artistov*) was established; in 1883 it was transformed into the Society for Assistance to Stage Artists (*Obshchestvo dlia posobiia stsenicheskim deiateliam*) and Savina, an active member of the Society, was appointed secretary. She devoted considerable energy to strengthening the organization by broadening its scope and attracting the support of influential people.[62] Thanks largely to her extraordinary gift for organization, it was re-formed a third time in 1894 and renamed the Russian Theatrical Society (*Russkoe teatralnoe obshchestvo*, hereafter, RTO).[63] Shortly thereafter, Savina became chair, a post she held for many years. If the objectives of the first two organizations were purely philanthropic, the objectives of the third were much broader and included a commitment to the general development and improvement of theatre as a profession, especially in the provinces. In a letter to Suvorin, she argues that an association to protect the interests of theatre artists is absolutely necessary because: "We are like birds in the sky, we live in the present – in all of Russia there might be ten people who will enjoy security in old age; the rest need a Society."[64] Under Savina's leadership, the RTO organized the First All-Russian Congress of Representatives of the Stage in 1897, which is usually mentioned in passing by Western historians as the impetus for Stanislavski's and Nemirovich's theatrical reforms. The published record, which includes all of the reports and papers (*doklady*) given during the conference, suggests, however, that aesthetics were peripheral to the real purpose of the conference, which was to address concerns dear to Savina's eternally pragmatic heart: the generally pathetic state of provincial theatre, the exploitation of performers by unscrupulous entrepreneurs, the need to standardize contracts, pregnancy as an obstacle to employment, inadequate salaries, and other equally practical issues that affected the daily lives of performers of both sexes.[65] An odd feature of the Congress is, however, that, although she was one of the principal organizers and, during the proceedings, sat on one side of Prince Sergei Mikhailovich, the titular president of the RTO, Savina's name is virtually absent from the published record. Svetaeva claims that she gave a brief closing speech, but it is not included in the "*trudy*."[66] In addition, on the occasion of Savina's death, V. Nikulin, a provincial actor, reminded readers of *Theatre and Art* that she was a powerful mediating influence at the Congress, but none of this activity was recorded in the minutes.[67] Whether the absence of documentation is evidence of her fundamental modesty or simply historical erasure, the result has been to obscure Savina's genuine contributions to professionalizing acting in Russia and to organizing what was essentially the first theatrical union in the country.[68] In 1913, several angry younger members of the Society complained that Savina and other representatives of the RTO "old guard" were impediments to progress and should be unceremoniously eliminated.[69] But when she died in 1915, the RTO panicked because the one person who had held the entire organization together, who had reconciled the various factions and interest groups, was now gone.[70]

In addition to their work at the RTO, Savina and her third husband, A.E. Molchanov, conceived of, created, and subsidized both the Shelter for Retired Actors (*Ubezhishche dlia prestarelykh stsenicheskikh deiatelei*) and the Orphanage for Actors' Children (*Priiut dlia akterskikh detei-sirot*). These were standard philanthropic activities of the sort Russian society expected from women. More unusual is an event that was framed by Savina and her admirers in the rhetoric of selfless service to the international interests of Russian theatre: the event was Savina's tour in 1899 to Berlin, the first by a Russian actor to Western Europe.[71] This tour assumed tremendous significance for Russians, especially for actresses, many of whom felt, thanks to ruthless comparisons in the Russian press between native and foreign stars, that they could not compete with the likes of Bernhardt, Duse, and Rejane. Well before the Berlin adventure, however, Savina had toyed with the idea of touring abroad. She was invited to Paris in 1892, but although flattered, turned the invitation down.[72] Between 1892 and 1899, her nationalist convictions and desire to demonstrate to the world that Russian actors could compete internationally apparently motivated her to risk her reputation with a foreign tour. In addition, on the eve of her twenty-fifth anniversary on the

Aleksandrinskii stage, locked in "mortal combat" with Vera Kommissarzhevskaia, she was desparate for a gimmick that would swing the focus of St. Petersburg critics and spectators back to herself.

Ten years after the tour, Savina published excerpts from her Berlin diary, prefaced by her reasons for venturing beyond the secure boundaries of the Aleksandrinskii. In a moment of frankness, she acknowledged that lust for international recognition and an intense desire to compete with Bernhardt and other Western touring stars may have played a role in the decision, but argued: "In general, I think that an actor's desire for fame is more natural and legitimate than anyone else's. And besides, who wouldn't want to rise over the common crowd!? People can moralize all they want, but fame and notoriety are like oxygen for an actor."[73] This momentary candour is followed by a defensive tirade in which she protests that Russians do not imitate the West, the West imitates Russia and that if foreign actors can succeed in Russia without knowing the language, Russian actors should not be ashamed to tour abroad in their native tongue.[74] The remaining seven installments of the diary are a record of unremitting self-praise, obsession with being "as good as Duse," and repeated declarations of Russian superiority.

Savina's defensiveness reflects an important reality of Silver Age theatre: the members of its community were extremely conscious of, and sensitive to, their reputation in the West. Characterized on the Russian side by alternate feelings of inferiority and superiority, the relationship with the West was ambivalent and intensely competitive. Savina's tour gave Kugel occasion to publish several feuilletons that offer clues to Russian anxiety about foreign touring. From the combined perspective of nationalism and gender, the most interesting is one he wrote about the special obstacles for actors of translating their art into an alien cultural context. But the problem was not simply competition between native and foreign actors. Savina's admirers demanded that she bear the standard for Russian culture and art; in his essay, Kugel cites several "open letters" appealing to her to proclaim Russia's fame abroad by including Russian plays in her repertoire. He argues, however, that certain Russian plays, especially anything by Ostrovski, should not be shown abroad. Given Ostrovski's stature as the leading Russian realist, this advice seems odd. But Kugel rationalizes that Westerners will not understand Ostrovski's women "with their passivity, which borders on stupidity, their mystical fear of sin ... their irresponsibility, cowed condition, submissive behavior, and inability to understand even the simplest of life's questions," adding that Savina would be doing a "bad service" to both Russia and Ostrovski if she took these plays abroad.[75] Inside Russia, Ostrovski was praised for his unsparing portraits of "real" Russian life, but what Kugel's advice reflects is a well-founded fear that Westerners would be dismayed by the reality of Russian women's lives. Although for Kugel, their condition was an embarrassment, he did not suggest that steps be taken to improve their situation. Rather, he simply wanted Savina to represent the pride of Russian theatre, without airing national dirty linen with respect to the status of women.[76]

According to Savina, the tour was an unprecedented success, and perhaps in her own terms, it was.[77] In her diary, she carefully calculated the number of curtain calls Duse received for her German debut in relation to the number she received. By her count, Duse received two after the last curtain call; in contrast, she received three after acts one and two, five after act three, and seven after act five.[78] She also noted that following a performance of *Camille*, a tearful German spectator rushed to tell her that she was "better than Duse," and several critics declared that the farewell scene with Armand was superior to either Duse or their best native stars.[79] Competition with foreign stars was a part of life for Russian actresses; if Savina's need to be "as good as" Duse (and to a lesser degree, Bernhardt) was more intense than most, it was not particularly unusual. Savina's competitive impulse was, however, symptomatic of a more serious illness that afflicted Russian theatre throughout the Silver Age: the bitter, fractious rivalries among native actresses for pre-eminence in the hearts and minds of Russian critics and spectators. Created largely by critics, this pathologically competitive situation was exacerbated by the actresses themselves – and Savina, who enjoyed the reputation of a merciless competitor, was particularly guilty of suppressing other women.

Puzzled by the state of affairs at the Aleksandrinskii, Kugel asked why this unhealthy competition existed only among actresses. Actors, he claimed, are appreciated as individuals; each has his own gifts and all coexist peacefully. Actresses, however, rule singly and each theatre has a prima donna around whom everything revolves.[80] Assuming that Kugel's assertion is legitimate, several responses to his question are possible. The Imperial system, which had a long tradition of privileging exclusive cliques of starring actors and actresses, shamelessly elevated and rewarded favorites, often at the expense of the rest of the company.[81] Though this affected performers of both sexes, the smaller number of roles available to women meant that fewer of them had access to high-status positions, a situation which made vicious competition inevitable. The fact that women were treated differently by critics and spectators, many of whom apparently enjoyed the spectacle of actresses savaging each other as they maneuvered for advantage, was equally destructive. Some critics encouraged competition by playing the women off each other; others used military rhetoric to describe stratagems used by rival actresses to secure advantage. Thus, when Savina and Strepetova shared first the Kazan and later the Aleksandrinskii stages, critics and spectators formed camps around their favorites.[82] When Savina toured to Moscow, a group of Ermolova zealots booed her during the performances for no other reason than her very presence in Moscow was perceived as a threat to their idol's supremacy.[83] In 1884, a critic compared Savina's struggle for power at the Aleksandrinskii to the battle at Sevastopol, and ten years later, the *St.*

Petersburg Gazette used military rhetoric to describe Mariia Gavrilovna's triumphant Moscow tour.[84] Factions arose around actresses because their admirers did not see them simply as artists or even skilled craftswomen; rather, they were the concrete manifestations of sexual fantasy and gender ideology. It is hardly surprising, then, that this extreme partisanship had a pernicious effect not only on individual women, but on the theatre community as a whole. If actors were largely exempt, it was because they were not subjected to the same kinds of pressures: their careers were not perceived as a series of tactical maneuvers and they were not encumbered by similar kinds of symbolic and ideological signification.

Savina's reputation for suppressing other women was established during conflicts with Strepetova in the provinces and reaffirmed over several decades by a series of minor skirimishes with lesser rivals. But it was the battle between Savina and Vera Kommissarzhevskaia that ruptured the theatre community and foretold of more serious divisions to come. Kommissar-zhevskaia's engagement at the Aleksandrinskii in 1896 posed the first serious threat to Savina's power since Strepetova in the early 1880s. Savina's apologists claimed that the conflicts with both Strepetova and Kommissar-zhevskaia were impersonal: Mariia Gavrilovna was not motivated by personal animosity, but by genuine concern for the artistic direction of the Alek-sandrinskii theatre.[85] This is a partial truth. Savina, Strepetova, and Kommissarzhevskaia did represent antagonistic aesthetic tendencies and, by implication, contrasting constructions of "*zhenstvennost*," but it is inaccurate to suggest that Savina did not suppress other actresses or that her conflicts with them were purely impersonal. Khodotov, who knew both Savina and Kommissarzhevskaia intimately, argued that the two actresses were so completely disparate that there *should not* have been competition between them; it was, he charged, the unhealthy atmosphere at the Aleksandranskii that made personal emnity inevitable.[86] V.V. Chekhov suggests that Savina was actually quite taken with Kommissarzhevskaia when the younger actress debuted on the Imperial stage.[87] Nonetheless, hostilities arose, camps formed around each, Kommissarzhevskaia was outmaneuvered and eventually re-signed, the modernist revolution which might have taken place at the Aleksandrinskii was postponed indefinitely – and Savina was deeply implic-ated in the whole fiasco. If her concern about the art of Russian theatre was genuine, what motivated her ruthlessness?

Among the panegyrics that appeared immediately after her death in 1915 was an anonymous article entitled "Tsarina of the Russian Theatre" (*tsaritsa russkoi stseny*). Although, like most authors of posthumous tributes, this one was given to hyberbole, he expressed a fundamental truth about Savina's position when he wrote: "Powerful, energetic, charming, she did not recog-nize or tolerate competition. She was born with rights to the throne and preserved it from any encroachments with the persistence and intelligence of a true sovereign."[88] As Kugel observed, an implicit quota governed the policies of the Imperial theatres: one queen per theatre. A product of her environment, Mariia Gavrilovna understood the unspoken rules of the Imperial theatre game and played it more skillfully than any actress of her generation. Once she ascended the throne, she had no intention of relinquishing it to some bubble-headed bimbo who had nothing to offer the exemplary Russian stage but a pretty face.[89] Nonetheless, critics frequently reminded Savina that her time was limited and Mariia Gavrilovna herself made sporadic efforts to mentor younger actresses. The most ironic aspect of the situation with Kommissarzhevskaia was that, according to Pavla Vulf, Savina had once hoped Vera Fedorovna would be her successor.[90]

Although there are no records of what transpired to poison the relationship between the actresses, two possibilities are likely. Kommissarzhevskaia, who entertained lofty ideas about the role of art and artists in society, had her own reputation for intolerance. The more commercially minded Savina, whose success was based on Krylov's shallow adaptations, would hardly have tolerated any gestures of disrespect from the younger woman. In addition, Kommissarzhevskaia's appearance created a surge of energy among St. Petersburg critics, many of whom still blamed Savina for the decline of the Aleksandrinskii repertoire. Although their response to Kommissarzhevskaia was not universally enthusiastic, most acknowledged that she represented a breath of fresh air and several wanted to present her with Savina's crown before the queen was prepared to abdicate. An article by A. Volynski was fairly typical of critical response to the two reigning Aleksandrinskii stars. Although his essay on the current state of St. Petersburg theatre included several pleasant remarks about Savina, much of it was devoted to Kommissarzhevskaia, often at Savina's expense. Volynski wrote: "With respect to depth and sincerity, Kommissarzhevskaia is much more significant than Savina; she has no competition among the other women in the company."[91] Given Savina's ambition, ego, and elevated status at the Aleksandrinskii, this kind of rhetoric, which seemed designed to exacerbate an already difficult situation, would surely have discouraged further impulses to mentor Kommissarzhevskaia.

The hostility between Savina and Kommissarzhevskaia was, however, symptomatic of a much deeper rupture in the theatre community. In the late 1890s Russian theatre was on the eve of an extended period of innovation and reaction which, by 1905 critics had christened the "theatre crisis" (*krizis teatra*). Predicated largely on the rise of modernism, the "crisis" increased the pressure on bastions of tradition like the Aleksandrinskii to accommodate modernist tendencies in drama and production style. As part of that trend, the ineffectual stage managers and regisseurs of the nineteenth century were rapidly being replaced by directors in the tradition of the Wagnerian "master artist." In contrast to Kommissarzhevskaia, who quickly became the idol of progressives in both art and politics, Savina did not understand the need for either modernism or directors and energetically resisted both. Perhaps because her earlier attempts at innovation were either castigated by critics or obstructed by the state censor, or perhaps because she had grown too accustomed to the privileges of the Imperial system to challenge it, Mariia Gavrilovna was now in no hurry to associate herself with revolutionaries in art or society.[92] In St. Petersburg, the two actresses marked polar points on the theatrical continuum: Kommissarzhevskaia stood at the head of the modernist movement, which for Savina marked the decline and fall of the Russian theatre.

Even today, the Russian theatre's reputation, especially in the West, rests on innovations associated with modernism. Unfortunately, Savina's reputation rests largely on her resistance to it. If, during the early years, progressives reproached her for supporting Krylov and Potekhin, after 1900, a new wave of advanced critics and practitioners censured her for plotting to keep modernist influences at bay. Although she was occasionally forced to play the modern Western European and Russian repertoire, Savina rarely ventured into the new drama willingly. In an interview in 1905 with *Theatrical Russia* (*Teatral'naia rossia*), she articulated several reasons for her opposition to modernist drama and production practice. Queried about the current practice of using theatre as a weapon of social justice, Savina responded that the stage was no place for "topical revues" (*zlobodnevnye obozreniia*). Asked why she refused the role of Ranevskaia in *The Cherry Orchard*, she replied that she could not understand what was meant by Chekhovian "mood" or distinguish it from the "mood" required to play *A Month in the Country*, and that she could not play a style that she simply did not understand. She defended the Aleksandrinskii's policy of protecting the repertoire from the encroachment of Western European modernism on the basis that its mandate was to produce Russian authors. Finally, having expressed the opinion that Ibsen was the only tolerable symbolist playwright, she rejected most symbolist drama on the basis that it was too obscure. "It is not enough," she asserted, "that an author's idea is comprehensible to other artists: what is important is that the public understands it."[93] Because suitable roles became increasingly scarce after the turn of the century, Savina grudgingly experimented with the modernist repertoire, but was rarely successful in it. Her ill-concealed scorn was reflected in the correspondence with Aleksandr Koni. During rehearsals for Tolstoi's *The Living Corpse* (*Zhivoi trup*), which was produced under Meierhold's direction in 1911, she wrote to Koni: "We're rehearsing 'Corpse'. But the staging [of this play] is the real corpse; and Tolstoi knew it because he would not allow it to be produced. It's not even a synopsis of a play, it's just a sketch."[94] When asked to consider a play by Leonid Andreev, she asked Koni to read it. The accompanying note observed caustically: "Either I am a fool, or he is a charlatan, not a playwright."[95] It is surely true that modernism did not suit Savina's aesthetic and literary preferences. Kugel, who once called Mariia Gavrilovna "the healthy sense of the Russian theatre," emphasized that she was firmly anchored in the tangible world.[96] Preferring human beings to Andreev's abstractions and Chekhov's neurasthenics, she had little taste for mysticism or heavy-handed symbolism. Under pressure from modernism, "*zhenstvennost*" sustained another conceptual metamorphosis, but age kept Savina on the periphery of new developments in the theatre. The modernist repertoire contained few showcase roles for an actress of Savina's stature, temperament, age, and type. Despondent over the lack of suitable new material, she turned with increasing frequency to inappropriately youthful roles and, long before the movement in the 1920s, she went "back to Ostrovski."

Her objections to modernism were not confined to the literature. With respect to modernist acting style, she reproached the new generation of actresses who relied on personal style rather than craft, while simultaneously inveighing against innovations introduced by the Moscow Art Theatre. As a result of MAT's experiments, she claimed, talent can no longer be distinguished from technique because at the MAT, technique gives the illusion of talent.[97] The demand for ensemble performance was at the root of Savina's hostility toward modernism as it was practiced at the Moscow Art Theatre. Well before modernism appeared in St. Petersburg, critics identified Mariia Gavrilovna's fatal flaw: she could not see beyond her own role. In Savina's defense it must be emphasized that she was not alone in this: the Imperial practice of privileging an exclusive gaggle of popular actors did not promote the kind of cooperation necessary for an effective ensemble. As long as the star system prevailed, her unwillingness to consider the *whole* play was not challenged, but as the modernist movement gained momentum, the public's taste for virtuoso acting and powerful personalities diminished.

This trend, which was accompanied by the rise of the omnipotent, Wagnerian director, hastened the demise of starring actresses, most of whom could not adjust to ensemble playing or subordinate themselves to the authority of a director. Convinced of her own superior aesthetic sensibilities and commercial instincts, Mariia Gavrilovna had a proud history of resisting attempts by directors to mould her performances. One might even speculate that her notorious habit of mumbling her way through rehearsals was a defensive posture designed to protect her private creative process against intrusions by directors. In her memoirs, she observed that at the Aleksandrinskii the director's duties consisted of nothing more than appointing roles and scheduling rehearsals; the author rehearsed the play and the actors worked out their own blocking.[98] Since authors generally knew little about staging, this arrangement suited Savina perfectly. Although, in the absence of an author, Mariia Gavrilovna had to deal with directors, her unprecedented authority at the Aleksandrinskii cowed most of them: when a director's work did not suit her, she simply asked him to sit down while she restaged the scene to her satisfaction.[99]

Not surprisingly, her combined hostility toward modernism and directors was most fully expressed in her attitude toward Vsevolod Meierhold. For

Savina, even more than Kommissarzhevskaia, Meierhold stood at the head of forces bent on the destruction of Russian theatre. In one of her late memoirs, she wrote of the controversial director and his disciples: "Ignorant, alien people with an agenda completely foreign to ours came [to the Aleksandrinskii Theatre]; knowing that their invasion of our church was unlawful and hating us with all their hearts, these 'caliphs of the hour' rushed to destroy our monuments."[100] Her final vow to counter and overcome Meierhold's "blasphemy" sounds like the death rattle of a mortally wounded heroine of melodrama. In retrospect, perhaps it was. Savina's final creative gesture was to collaborate with Meierhold in 1915 on Zinaida Gippius's *The Green Ring* (*Zelenoe koltso*).[101] She died shortly thereafter.

Evaluating Savina's significance as a woman in Silver Age theatre is fraught with contradictions. She was a remarkable individual who, in spite of her modest roots, achieved tremendous authority within hegemonic institutions that normally deny women access to power. Unfortunately, having secured her own position, she did little to advance the cause of women as a class and might even be accused of sabotaging opportunities for other women to advance. As her authority increased, critics, many of whom saw Savina as an exception to commonly held beliefs about women, used the term "*chelovek*" (person/human being) rather than "*zhenshchina*" (woman) to refer to her. Rarely applied to actresses (or to women generally), the term "*chelovek*" was intended as a great compliment. Male critics, who appreciated her intelligence, pragmatism, and capacity for rational discourse with men, also praised the absence in Savina of particularly negative qualities universally associated with both actresses and women as generic groups. She was not, for example, impulsive, irrational, emotionally capricious, or sexually manipulative. And although there is evidence of an embryonic feminist consciousness in Savina, she avoided political controversy and rarely presented any serious challenges to existing hierarchies. Thus, although she broke down certain barriers that existed between actresses and other women, Savina was not perceived as a threat by men who saw her as a benign exception to the general rules set down by nature to govern her sex. Understood in terms of individual achievement, Savina was certainly a New Woman in the most Western sense of the term. But her position and authority, both of which were granted on the basis of exceptionality, had little immediate effect on the status of Russian actresses collectively.

4

AN UNEASY ALLIANCE
Glikeriia Fedotova and Mariia Ermolova at the Malyi Theatre

Each capital city had its own Imperial dramatic theatre: St. Petersburg supported the Aleksandrinskii and Moscow, the Malyi. Both were state subsidized and enjoyed Imperial patronage; both were also subject to rigid censorship and suffered from bureaucratic mismanagement. Between 1870 and 1917, however, the two theatres had little in common besides the mixed blessing of being subject to the Imperial bureaucracy. Differences between the Aleksandrinskii and the Malyi theatres reflect differences between the cities that harbored them. Geographical location accounts for at least some of the cultural discontinuity between Peter the Great's "window on the West" and Russia's historic capital. The presence of the tsar and his court in St. Petersburg influenced the tastes, expectations, and mores of fashionable society, a segment of the population that included the Aleksandrinskii's regular audience. St. Petersburg was a decidedly Westernized city. For that reason, its residents' aesthetic preferences were clearly distinguished from those of the more traditionally Russian Muscovites. Not surprisingly, their tastes in actresses were equally dissimilar.

During the period, the simmering rivalry between Imperial dramatic theatres in Moscow and St. Petersburg intensified. Their competitive relationship is apparent in the response of critics and spectators to their respective starring actresses. Although Savina ruled the Aleksandrinskii Theatre in St. Petersburg for almost 40 years and enjoyed considerable authority as the founder of the Russian Theatrical Society, she was not particularly admired in Moscow. St. Petersburg audiences were correspondingly ambivalent about Moscow actresses. Without question, Savina was the dominatrix of the Imperial stage. Her Moscow competition was, however, impressive and, for that reason, Savina must be understood as one member of a triumverate of starring actresses that included Glikeriia Fedotova and Mariia Ermolova. These three women dominated the Imperial theatres between the late 1870s and approximately 1900. Fedotova, who debuted on the Moscow Malyi stage in 1862, was the darling of Moscow audiences until Ermolova mounted a successful challenge to her supremacy in the mid-1870s. Following her victory, Ermolova remained the "idol of Moscow" until the vogue for her heroic-romantic style abated in the mid-1890s.

Rivalries were commonplace among actresses: if Savina was excessively competitive, her attitude toward other actresses was not extraordinary. Savina's relationships with her female colleagues at the Aleksandrinskii can be characterized as a series of strategic, largely hostile maneuvers. The relationship between Ermolova and Fedotova was, however, unique among starring actresses of the period precisely because it was a relationship of shared power. Although Ermolova largely displaced Fedotova during the late 1870s and 1880s, her conquest did not drive the older actress from the Malyi to wander the provincial circuit, nor did it force her to retire from the Imperial stage and open her own private theatre in order to continue playing desirable roles. Until 1905, when a crippling illness obliged Fedotova to retire, an uneasy relationship of equality existed between the two leading actresses; although Malyi spectators engaged in fierce, partisan warfare, any personal animosity between Fedotova and Ermolova was kept within the walls of the theatre and largely concealed from the press and the public.[1]

Neither Ermolova nor Fedotova was a product of the provincial circuit: both graduated from the Malyi's "theatre school" and, like most Imperial actresses, played a repertoire consisting primarily of Russian and Western classics, contemporary "*bytovaia*" drama, and popular rubbish. In marked contrast to Savina, Fedotova and Ermolova were considered "serious" actresses. The seriousness attributed to them by critics and colleagues refers not only to the types of roles in which they specialized, but also to their attitude toward the art of theatre and its role in Russian culture and society. Because they were persuaded that Russia's exemplary theatre, the Malyi, should be an instrument of public enlightenment and that actresses had a serious responsibility to the public to advance theatre as an art, Fedotova and Ermolova were credited with enhancing, rather than corrupting, the Malyi's repertoire. They were further distinguished from many starring actresses of the period by their scorn for the kind of notoriety produced by marketing schemes and publicity gimmicks.

Nonetheless, they were quite different in terms of type, temperament, and the image of "*zhenstvennost*" each projected. Fedotova was the principal link between the Shchepkin school and contemporary realism as exemplified by the Moscow Art Theatre. A highly disciplined, astonishingly versatile actress who took great pride in her mastery of technique, Fedotova conquered even the most unsuitable roles by means of systematic analysis and dogged study. Although rarely brilliant, she was consistently capable and occasionally extraordinary. Fedotova's tremendous popularity during the 1860s and 1870s surely reflected the tastes and tenor of the times; it was not, however, based on personality, but on conscious artistry and attention to craft. Because she cultivated versatility and flexibility, the relationship of her created images to cultural shifts in gender ideology is more difficult to assess. In contrast to

Fedotova, Ermolova was an actress of tremendous temperament and little range. She was, perhaps, the last representative of the heroic-romantic ideal, and her most effective roles, Laurencia in *Fuente Ovejuna* and Joan in *The Maid of Orleans*, marked her as a herald of revolutionary protest during the 1880s. If Fedotova was content to be an actress, Ermolova transformed herself – perhaps unwittingly – into a symbol of rebellious, almost masculine "*zhenstvennost*" that had tremendous appeal for progressives during the late 1870s and 1880s.

TRAINING AN IMPERIAL ACTRESS: FEDOTOVA AND ERMOLOVA AT THE MOSCOW THEATRE SCHOOL

For the most part, Imperial theatres trained their own actresses and actors. If Savina's provincial background and lack of formal training made her exceptional among starring Imperial actresses, Fedotova's and Ermolova's experiences were more typical. Like most of their colleagues at the Malyi Theatre, Fedotova and Ermolova were educated at the Moscow Theatre School, which supplied the Malyi's actresses.[2] This exclusive, sex-segregated institution put considerable pressure on students to conform to the social and aesthetic standards of Russia's "exemplary stage," and by so doing, became a principal purveyor of gender ideology. For that reason, its organization, curriculum, and objectives are of interest.

Before the late 1880s, well-trained, highly skilled actresses were rare in Russia. Because entrepreneurs so often hired actresses on the basis of physical appeal rather than theatrical expertise, training in craft was largely unnecessary for professional advancement. Furthermore, because actor-training programs were virtually unknown outside the Imperial theatre schools, even actresses who evinced a sincere commitment to art had little access to formal training. It is ironic, however, that although the Imperial schools had substantial human and financial resources, and offered courses of study in both general education and craft, they were woefully inadequate and did little to prepare actresses for the dramatic stage – or for life. The alleged purpose of the Imperial schools was to provide all of the Imperial theatres, including the ballet theatre, with a steady supply of talented, well-trained, exemplary young dancers, singers, and actresses. In fact, both dramatic art and general education played second fiddle to ballet, which formed the nucleus of the Moscow Theatre School's program.

One obvious reason for the neglect of actor training is located in the attitude of actors themselves to formal training. Nadezhda Vasileva, who taught at the Aleksandrinskii's school during the 1880s and 1890s, observed that few dramatic actors felt compelled to study their own craft. Arguing that "systematic training, school exercises, and pedantism," diminished rather than enhanced authentic talent, they studiously avoided formal training.

According to this school of thought, real actors required nothing more than "instinct" (*nutro*) and a good voice.[3] Perhaps for that reason, Fedotova's and Ermolova's first years at the Moscow Theatre School included little, if any, formal study of dramatic literature, theatre history, dramatic theory, or acting technique. In the late 1850s and early 1860s, Fedotova and her contemporaries were exposed to a "rather primitive" program consisting of "Russian grammar, geography, French, and the laws of God."[4] Besides these subjects, they studied ballet for three hours each morning and, when the Malyi needed walk-on or secondary actresses, they performed in the evenings.[5] By the time Ermolova and her classmates entered the school in 1862, the curriculum had deteriorated and opportunities to study for the dramatic stage were even more limited.

All new students were required to study ballet; after several years of general education and dance, a small number were permitted to study drama. Most of these students either displayed remarkable aptitude for the dramatic stage or remarkable ineptitude for ballet. Because ballet was considered a more serious and sublime calling than theatre, students who chose drama were relegated to the school's periphery; given the nature of the training available to them, it is not clear whether student actresses felt privileged or mortified.[6] Fedotova's and Ermolova's experiences in the drama program suggest the reasons for their ambivalence.

Because she was not the offspring of a theatrical family, Glikeriia Fedotova was an oddity in the Moscow Theatre school.[7] At age ten, she transferred to the theatre school from a German pension and followed the standard program of instruction. Although Fedotova proved to be a competent dancer, her real talent was for acting.[8] At the point when she received permission to study drama, the school's lone instructor was so occupied with his own career at the Malyi that he had little time for the young women at the theatre school. His pedagogical methodology consisted of telling his students to read "sincerely and truthfully."[9] Fedotova was fortunate that Ivan Samarin, who took his pedagogical responsibilities seriously, soon replaced him. A former student and disciple of Mikhail Shchepkin, Samarin was favorably impressed by Fedotova's natural gifts and took great interest in developing them. Samarin introduced Fedotova to Shchepkin, who also evinced sincere interest in her technique and encouraged her to cultivate a serious attitude toward the art and craft of theatre. The two men assumed responsibility for mentoring the young actress.

Samarin introduced significant philosophical and structural changes into the Malyi's drama program. Convinced that exemplary actresses should be well educated, he insisted that students be assigned fewer roles at the Malyi so that they could devote more time to their lessons. He also introduced them to great literature, which helped to develop their literary tastes and aesthetic sensibilities. Although all of the students surely benefitted from Samarin's reforms, his interest in Fedotova was more intense and personal. He not only worked with her privately, but also gave his young protégée the leading female role in his benefit in 1862. Thanks to Samarin and Shchepkin, Fedotova's debut performance in *The Child* (*Rebenok*) was the talk of Moscow. Spectators and critics were struck by the truthfulness and sincerity of her acting; her performance was distinguished by "unprecedented simplicity, naivete, and restraint."[10]

Shchepkin's role in her training and education was less formal, but equally significant. He invited Fedotova into his home where she spent considerable time with him and his family. He coached her during rehearsals and performances, which helped to shape her attitude toward her work. During the first production of *The Child*, he stood behind the curtains so that he could encourage her each time she came backstage. During the performance and at the final curtain ecstatic spectators called the novice actress out repeatedly, rewarding her with deafening ovations. When the celebratory mood finally abated, Shchepkin took Fedotova aside and asked her to consider the nature of her success. Explaining bluntly that it was the product of her youth and "pretty little mug," he asked rhetorically: "How do you think they would have responded if I had played like you? They would have dragged me off the stage. Remember that."[11] Apparently Fedotova did remember, for even as a young woman, she never allowed youth, beauty, or natural charm to take precedence over systematic analysis and disciplined study of each role she undertook.

Because two prominent, well-established actors took a personal interest in her professional development, Fedotova was one of a handful of actresses whose development was actually enhanced by her experience at the Moscow Theatre School. But even she acknowledged that, if not for her early education at the German pension, she would have been functionally illiterate.[12] Mariia Ermolova was less fortunate, but perhaps more typical.

The daughter of the Malyi Theatre's second prompter, Mariia Nikolaevna Ermolova was the most successful member of a theatrical family that included several generations of Malyi employees.[13] Unlike Fedotova, Ermolova was a theatre brat who spent most of her childhood playing backstage or observing performances from the prompter's box. She entered the Moscow theatre school at age nine, partly because she wanted to be an actress and partly because the family expected it.[14] The same year Ermolova started the program, Fedotova finished it – and if Glikeriia Nikolaevna was the faculty's prize pupil, Mariia Nikolaevna was their scapegoat.

Like Fedotova before her, Ermolova was immediately assigned to a ballet class. Unlike Fedotova, who was at least competent, the tall, awkward, serious, and painfully shy Ermolova hated ballet and could not master even the simplest exercises and choreography. Nicknamed the "ugly duckling," Ermolova did not fit the reigning feminine ideal; perhaps for that reason, the ballet instructors disliked and ignored her, and her peers teased her mercilessly.[15] Like other students who could not handle the dance curriculum, she was sent to the theatre "department" for evaluation.[16] Once accepted, she should have studied declamation and engaged in practical exercises, but in fact, by the time Ermolova entered the drama program it was in utter disarray. Samarin had abandoned teaching and in his place another actor appeared once or twice a month to recruit student actresses for adolescent roles at the Malyi. Because the general education curriculum had also deteriorated, Ermolova's tenure at the Moscow theatre school had few practical results: it failed, as one observer remarked, to "develop either the person or the actress in her."[17]

Seeing that she required special attention and instruction, Ermolova's father asked Samarin, who had done so much to advance Fedotova's career, to tutor her privately. Samarin conducted several lessons with Ermolova, then sent her back to her father with a message that any further effort would be wasted: Mariia Nikolaevna would never be an actress.[18] Not discouraged, in 1866 her father arranged for her to have a prominent role in his own benefit – which may have harmed rather than advanced her career.

Because no mentors attended to her education and training, Ermolova was forced to rely on her own resources. She and a group of friends organized private, improvised theatricals. These entertainments, which were her "sole preparation, the only school through which she passed," brought her to the attention of one of the Malyi's leading actresses, Nadezhda Medvedeva.[19] In 1870, intending to produce Lessing's *Emilia Galotti* for her benefit, Medvedeva asked Fedotova to accept the title role. Fedotova, who was by that time the Malyi's leading box office attraction, agreed to play Emilia, but shortly before the performance, she fell ill and was forced to withdraw. Because the Malyi Theatre maintained only a small complement of salaried actresses, Fedotova was virtually impossible to replace. Perhaps because a substantial portion of her annual earnings depended on this benefit, Medvedeva refused to postpone or cancel the performance; instead the panicked actress searched frantically for a surrogate. She finally appealed to the Moscow theatre school. Because Samarin's opinion of Ermolova was well known at the Malyi, Medvedeva had no intention of asking Mariia Nikolaevna to play Emilia Galotti until Lisa Semenova, a participant in Ermolova's amateur theatricals, persuaded Medvedeva of her friend's extraordinary gifts.[20] After hearing Ermolova read the role, Medvedeva decided to take a chance on the young actress whose stage experience consisted primarily of extracurricular improvisations.

Ironically, Samarin agreed to coach Ermolova for the role. In general, however, Medvedeva's colleagues felt that by inviting an inexperienced, completely unknown student actress to play the great Fedotova's role, she had simultaneously subverted a long-established, carefully preserved hierarchy and transgressed the boundaries of professional courtesy. Perhaps for these reasons, although Ermolova gained a mentor in Medvedeva, she encountered extreme hostility from other members of the cast during rehearsals.[21] And although spectators responded enthusiastically to Ermolova's performance and she was largely responsible for the production's stunning success, it had little immediate effect on her career.

Following successful completion of the Moscow Theatre School's program, Fedotova and Ermolova encountered similar obstacles on their separate journeys to professional advancement. The Malyi hired both actresses immediately, but in spite of their obvious gifts, neither advanced as rapidly as might be expected. An unduly rigid, hierarchical system of assigning roles and types (*razovaia sistema*) severely impeded professional development among Malyi actresses, especially the younger ones. In any given period, the theatre kept one prominent comic actress and one prominent serious actress for all leading roles. At the same time, two promising younger actresses were groomed to replace them in the repertoire when the older actresses made the inevitable transition to mature roles.[22] Because actresses received so little authentic training at the Moscow Theatre School, many were desperate to either refine their craft or simply develop basic performance skills – but this unfortunate system severely limited their access to appropriate roles. According to Baron Drizen, who was for many years an adminstrator at the Imperial theatres, the deliberate suppression of young talent was not unusual and probably discouraged significant numbers of gifted actresses. A minority of the most tenacious "extricated themselves from the vice" and negotiated successful careers; the majority, however, were sucked into the maelstrom of backstage life and never rose beyond utility positions.[23]

Before their eighteenth birthdays, both Fedotova and Ermolova had already enjoyed phenomenally successful debut performances, but thanks to this system, neither was able to turn it to her immediate advantage. Fedotova, however, advanced more rapidly than Ermolova for several reasons: Shchepkin and Samarin trained her well; they helped her negotiate the Malyi system; and, when she debuted in 1862, the theatre's pathetic cadre of salaried actresses offered little competition.[24] In contrast, Ermolova had to surmount three seemingly impossible obstacles: her training was inadequate; she had no powerful patrons; and, when she debuted in 1870, Fedotova's unprecedented popularity effectively suppressed any competition. The Malyi directorate refused to offer Ermolova advantageous roles as long as Fedotova's box office attraction remained strong. Fortunately for Ermolova, when Fedotova became seriously ill in 1874 and was forced to take an extended leave of absence, the directorate offered her Fedotova's repertoire. Ermolova's ascendancy might otherwise have been delayed indefinitely.[25]

If training in craft at the Moscow Theatre School was inadequate, indoctrination in the traditions, values, and ideology of Russia's exemplary stage was not. In contrast to ambitious, self-educated actresses like Savina, who came to the Aleksandrinskii Theatre by way of the provincial circuit, Fedotova and Ermolova understood, and apparently accepted, the expectations and restrictions imposed upon them by the Moscow Theatre School and the Malyi Theatre during the late and post-Shchepkin eras.

Mikhail Shchepkin and his disciples not only encouraged their students and colleagues to adopt a serious attitude toward the art of theatre and craft of acting, but also set themselves up as exemplary models of this "new" attitude. Although some critics reproached representatives of the Shchepkin school for placing excessive emphasis on technique and education at the expense of instinct and inspiration, most held the Malyi – nicknamed the house of Shchepkin (*dom Shchepkina*) – and its company in high esteem.[26] Comparisons between the Malyi Theatre and the Aleksandrinskii, which, according to its critics, pandered shamelessly to the debased tastes of its fashionably shallow audience, consistently favored the Malyi. The Malyi's administrators, directors, and acting company were apparently committed to maintaining their status as Russia's exemplary theatre. Not only did the Malyi attempt to sustain an exemplary repertoire, but Malyi performers were regarded as exemplary artists. In contrast to typical Aleksandrinskii actresses who, like Savina, cared only for their own careers, Malyi actresses were praised for their commitment to the ensemble, their elevated aesthetic sensibilities, and their personal discretion.[27] If the pragmatic, commercially minded Savina was guilty of corrupting the Aleksandrinskii's repertoire and diminishing the theatre's status, Fedotova and Ermolova were determined to exert a salutary influence on the Malyi. For the most part they succeeded: from the point of view of the critics, their presence in the company enhanced, rather than detracted from, the theatre's reputation.

VESTAL VIRGIN AND MADONNA: GENDER IDEOLOGY AND *"ZHENSTVENNOST"* AT THE MALYI THEATRE

Perhaps because they were less personally ambitious and wielded less power than Savina, Fedotova and Ermolova were not as threatening or controversial from the standpoint of gender. Although the two Moscow actresses were distinctive with respect to gender ideology, both favored idealized representations of *"zhenstvennost"* that inspired lofty panegyrics from Moscow critics and spectators about the relationship between eternal *"zhenstvennost"* and the sublime in art.

Glikeriia Fedotova is the more difficult of the two to locate on an ideological continuum. Because Fedotova's reputation was based largely on craft rather than personality, her connections with particular ideological trends are more difficult to establish. Although she clearly preferred certain types, unlike most of her contemporaries, Fedotova was a meticulous craftsperson who took great pride in her ability to analyze, rehearse, and perform any role competently. She was not, therefore, closely identified with one role or type, nor did a cult of personality develop around her. Accounts of her tenure at the Moscow Theatre School suggest that she had tremendous natural talent, but by the late 1870s, critics had already begun to complain that her performances, although technically irreproachable, lacked warmth, spontaneity – and the most precious commodity in a Russian actress, temperament.[28] Fedotova viewed her role in the theatre as an elevated mission and, perhaps for that reason, in 1912 V. Ermilov called her the "vestal virgin of the temple of art" (*vestalka stseny-khrama*).[29]

The sobriquet "vestal virgin" suggests not only Fedotova's stage image, but her self-discipline and what critics, colleagues, and spectators perceived as her selfless devotion to perfecting her own skills and maintaining the Malyi's reputation as Russia's exemplary theatre. Fedotova first came to the attention of the Moscow public in 1862 in *The Child*, by P.D. Boborykin. Although she did not choose the play or the role and cannot, therefore, be given credit for advancing the cause of enlightened contemporary drama on the Malyi stage, *The Child* was, according to A.I. Urusov, an early example of the "woman's theme" genre.[30] Questions of family relations and women's rights within the family are central, and the playwright critiques patriarchal relations in the family, especially the continued power of the "*domostroi*," or rules governing domestic order, to circumscribe women's lives.[31] In his review of the performance, Urusov observed that relations between fathers and children in Russia were among the worst in the world: nowhere, he complained, was there such inequality.[32] Perhaps for these reasons, *The Child* struck a nerve among progressives in the Malyi's audience.

The phenomenal success of *The Child* was due not only to Fedotova's inspired performance, but also to the progressive spirit that prevailed in the Malyi auditorium during the period. The Malyi Theatre's audience consisted largely of the Moscow aristocracy and intelligentsia, and, as Linda Edmondson observed: "A society ... whose intelligentsia was passionate for change, was one in which ideas of women's liberation found a ready audience."[33] Questions of women's emancipation were being discussed in educated society by the late 1850s; for that reason the story of *The Child*, which traces the consequences of a young girl's awakening to her own "*zhenstvennost*" and to the reality of women's oppression, resonated with Moscow spectators in 1862. Fedotova's performance so impressed Ostrovski that in 1863 he asked her to play the role that still epitomizes women's oppression in provincial Russia, Katerina in *The Storm*.

Although Fedotova played provincial domestic realism (*bytovaia dramaturgiia*) more skillfuly than most of her colleagues at the Malyi Theatre and kept Katerina and other Ostrovski protagonists in her repertoire for more than thirty years, she was not particularly attracted to the domestic "*bytovaia*" genre. In the theatre, the populist vogue for Russian realism did not mature until the 1870s, and in general, the provincial characters and environments depicted by the realists were alien to Imperial actresses.[34] Unlike Polina Strepetova, whose populist zealotry included a commitment to Russian realism, Fedotova had no apparent ideological inclinations and did not identify strongly with Ostrovski's characters or with the issues raised by his plays. For that reason, whatever Fedotova's social attitudes and political predilections may have been, they must be distinguished from those of the Russian realists. If Fedotova was the principal conduit for Ostrovski's ideas and ideology in Moscow, there is little evidence that she played his heroines because she harbored embryonic populist or feminist sympathies, or even that she played them by choice.[35]

Because actresses selected their own plays for benefit performances, their preferences can be inferred from their benefits. In Fedotova's case, her preference for Western classics, especially Shakespeare, was established in 1864 when Vasili Samoilov, a prominent touring star who performed at the Malyi, asked her to play Cordelia and Ophelia to his Lear and Hamlet. Delighted by this experience, she proposed to produce *Romeo and Juliet* for her first benefit, and although it was a disaster, for many years Fedotova continued to choose primarily Western classics for her benefit perform-ances.[36] Beatrice in *Much Ado About Nothing* and Kate in *The Taming of the Shrew*, two of her most effective roles, established her reputation as a skillful comedienne, and her success with the public encouraged other Malyi actors to attempt Western classics. One critic wrote in 1892 that "no actress did as much as Fedotova to establish Shakespeare on the Russian stage."[37]

In fact, although Fedotova clearly preferred the exemplary Western repertoire, she was enormously flexible and could play a broad spectrum of genres competently, including comedy, native domestic realism, Western and Russian classical and romantic genres, as well as French salon comedies. Although she did not perform in Ibsen's realistic plays, she was one of the few to attempt his romantic-historical drama.[38] Many contemporary obser-vers suggest that her real talent was for comedy, but like Mariia Savina, Fedotova resisted attempts by critics to relegate her to the debased status of professional comedienne.[39] The only genre that eluded Fedotova was tragedy: one contemporary commentator observed that, although she was a competent dramatic actress, nature simply did not give her the force for tragedy.[40] Tragedy was reserved for actresses with temperament, and at the Malyi, Ermolova dominated the genre.

Fedotova's public image was appropriate for a Russian woman of the 1860s: a serious, professional artist and craftsperson who sacrificed her personal interests and happiness to a sublime mission. Her fame was not based on personality; she did not respond to the capricious tastes of her audience by constructing and marketing an attractive stage image; she did not employ self-promotion gimmicks; and the events of her private life were not grist for public consumption. Although she preferred the Western repertoire, Fedotova did not cultivate the fashions or affectations of Western touring stars who passed through Moscow. There is little disagreement among contemporary commentators and theatre historians about the distinguishing characteristic of Fedotova's work: it was an almost perfect union of talent, intelligence, and technique.[41]

Figure 2 Gilkeriia Fedotova in Ibsen's *The Vikings at Helgeland.* Courtesy of the St. Petersburg Theatre Museum

Ironically, Fedotova and Savina, who received such disparate treatment by critics, shared certain fundamental characteristics: both were perceived as formidable women whose personal discipline and seriousness of purpose intimidated directors and colleagues alike; both had considerable natural talent, but acquired the less elevated status of skilled technicians; both were admired for their intelligence and analytical skills (in another era, they might have been directors); and in both, the instinct for theatre as a professional enterprise was primary.[42] Nonetheless, Fedotova won the admiration of critics and spectators as a serious artist and craftsperson, while Savina constantly fought the reputation of an aggressive, self-absorbed, Machiavellian prima donna who cared for nothing but self-aggrandisement. Several factors account for many of the real and perceived differences between the two actresses.

The first is an issue of class. Savina arrived at the Aleksandrinskii Theatre by way of the provincial circuit. Relying entirely upon her own resources to overcome the tremendous bias against provincial actresses, she enjoyed none of Fedotova's advantages. Glikeriia Fedotova did not carry the stigma of the provinces with her into the Imperial Malyi Theatre.[43] A product of relative privilege, who spent all but the first years of her life in Moscow and who received an education beyond the expectations of most women in the 1850s and 1860s, Fedotova was accepted without question or opposition into the Malyi fold. Her taste in drama, sense of artistic mission, and understanding of appropriate personal and professional decorum were inculcated by the schools she attended and the mentors who saw to her development. Had Fedotova encouraged the growing taste for contemporary, popular Western drama and Russian adaptations of French salon dramas and comedies à la Victor Krylov, the wrath of critics would surely have descended upon her as well.

Throughout her life, Fedotova faithfully practiced and promoted Shchepkin's principle that "science is the foundation of all art."[44] When she was struck by a serious illness in the 1870s, she used her convalescence to begin a steady program of self-education. She read widely, especially critical literature, and studied foreign languages so that she could read primary texts of plays, criticism, and theory. When she returned to the stage, her performances were increasingly distinguished by thoughtful working out of the central idea and by intelligent choices based on knowledge acquired specially for each role. Unlike so many gifted actresses of the period who played instinctually – "as God moved their spirits" – Fedotova investigated each character thoroughly. Rather than leaving her roles to the inspiration of the moment, she "designed" each according to a carefully laid out plan.[45] According to one critic, spectators always understood the precise nature of Fedotova's objective in each role and the direction she would move with it. Her characters were unified by a guiding concept and appeared to be the result of careful consideration.[46]

Although Savina was also a careful craftsperson, critics frequently reproached her for the uniformity and monotony of her characterizations, for her apparent unwillingness to appear in unflattering roles, for playing only roles that came easily, and for sacrificing art to commercial expediency. In contrast, from her earliest years, Fedotova was distinguished by flexibility, eclecticism, dogged diligence, and respect for theatre as an art. Critical reviews did not stop her from attempting difficult roles or roles that did not suit the limited range of types critics and directors assigned to her during her first years at the Malyi.

Fedotova's initial forays into Shakespeare were, for example, largely unsuccessful: although critics praised her courageous choice of material and thanked her for bringing exemplary Western drama to Moscow, they pointed out that neither she nor the ensemble were adequately prepared to handle the verse or the characterizations.[47] In contrast to Savina, who responded to similar criticism by abandoning individual roles and even entire genres, Fedotova did not abandon the Western classical repertoire, but applied herself to mastering it. Critics advised her to avoid tragedy, but rather than eliminating tragic and strong dramatic roles from her repertoire, she insisted upon playing them. By approaching the characters analytically and rehearsing them thoroughly, she played these roles competently, if not always brilliantly. She even agreed to perform in plays that did not meet her aesthetic standards because, by her reasoning, "no matter how bad a play is, no matter how poor the quality, once we begin rehearsals, we must say to ourselves that the role is splendid and we must do what we can with it."[48]

If Fedotova's claim to membership in the new generation of actresses is legitimate, it is not because she inspired a cult of personality, identified with a particular ideology, or specialized in a particular stage image. In fact, although Fedotova's eclecticism, discipline, and studied approach to her profession endeared her to Moscow Art Theatre and post-Moscow Art Theatre generations, she did not enjoy universal appeal, especially among critics and spectators who preferred inspirational, ecstatic actresses with clearly defined ideologically associations. Fedotova was an actress of the new generation not on the basis of personality politics, but because she established a model of exemplary professional behavior for Russian actresses. Fedotova demonstrated that intellect and emotion are compatible, and that a serious, disciplined approach to the art and craft of theatre was not only possible for actresses, but desirable.[49] According to critics like Boris Alpers, however, her very versatility, professionalism, and failure to grasp the fundamental relationship between art and ideology were liabilities that kept her from attaining the summit of artistic achievement.[50] Critics who shared his views preferred Mariia Ermolova.

During the late 1870s and 1880s, enthusiasm for Mariia Ermolova surpassed the bounds of rational discourse and moved into the realm of ecstatic idolatry. Vlas Doroshevich wrote that the inhabitants of Moscow could question the existence of God, but not the skill, beauty, and perfection of Mariia Ermolova.[51] Another of Ermolova's ardent admirers, A. Amfiteatrov, imagined a dialogue between a young man and woman about the relative merits of acting as an occupation for women. "Do intelligent girls," the young man asks his companion, "really believe that performing in plays by Victor Krylov is useful lifework?" Wishing to defend actresses, the young woman mentions Ermolova. Deeply offended, her companion retorts that Ermolova is not an actress: "She's the great soul of Russian women . . . the embodiment of a social ideal . . . the tragic muse, but certainly not an actress."[52]

In spite of the young man's poetic hyberbole, Ermolova clearly *was* a gifted actress, but her mimetic skills alone do not account for the hysteria engendered by her performances or for the legends and cult of personality that developed around her. Doroshevich understood the secret of her unprecedented popularity when he proclaimed with a touch of irony: "Happy is the artist who reflects the spirit of her times. . . . [for she] will become the object of national worship."[53] In contrast to Fedotova's reputation as a meticulous craftsperson and Savina's as a commercial wizard, only Ermolova achieved the lofty status of national icon. For all of their many contributions to the art and practice of theatre, Fedotova and Savina remained actresses, while Mariia Ermolova was transformed by a generation of rebellious, idealistic youth from an actress into a compelling national symbol of heroic self-sacrifice.

An enigma to critics, spectators, colleagues, and even her closest friends, Ermolova earned a reputation for modesty, virtue, dignity, tolerance, and extreme reticence. This self-effacing actress and reluctant star, who became the idol of disaffected youth of the 1880s, was appropriately nicknamed by critics "the great silent one" (*velikaia molchalnitsa*), and by admiring throngs of students, "the Madonna."[54] Although Ermolova could not eliminate entirely all of the emotional and physical quirks that so vexed her instructors at the Moscow Theatre School, she did manage to exorcise or conceal many of the most damaging. The road from "ugly duckling" of the Moscow Theatre School to darling of the progressive intelligentsia, university students, and assorted revolutionaries required six years and tremendous transformative effort on Ermolova's part. She was assisted, however, by the assassination of Aleksandr II, an event that altered the prevailing temper of the Malyi auditorium, thus creating an environment in which Ermolova could flourish.

Ermolova's professional life is best understood in terms of three phases. The first was marked by her remarkably successful debut in 1870 in *Emilia Galotti*; the second began in 1876 when she played Laurencia in Lope de Vega's *Fuente Ovejuna*; the third began in 1884 with Joan of Arc in Schiller's *The Maid of Orleans*.[55] These three roles not only mark the major stages in her professional development, but also, according to Baron Drizen, the boundaries of her "creative imagination;" in all her other roles, she copied herself.[56]

The *Emilia Galotti* period was simultaneously the most discouraging and, from a developmental point of view, the most significant. Following her tremendous success with Emilia, Ermolova went back to school, the Malyi directorate largely ignored her, and for almost six years she received walk-on and secondary roles. Entries in Ermolova's journal from this period reveal an impatient young woman whose mental and emotional health was determined by the caprices of the Malyi directorate. Because she so desperately wanted recognition and affirmation, each rumor of a new role became a cause for despair or ecstasy.[57] Frustrated by her enforced idleness and bored by the roles assigned to her, Ermolova began a process of self-education and physical transformation. Between 1870 and 1876, she began consciously to "break herself" of those personal idiosyncracies that hindered her professional advancement.[58] Her metamorphosis was assisted by a group of liberal students who encouraged her intellectual development.

Ermolova's process of "breaking herself" is of particular interest from the standpoint of gender ideology. As an adolescent, Ermolova, who had little of the natural grace and plasticity so necessary for success on the stage, did not conform to the reigning model of "*zhenstvennost.*" Certain rather masculine qualities – excessive height, awkward bearing, occasional vulgarity, and a tendency toward introspection – distinguished her from her more popular and successful colleagues. One observer suggested that qualitative gender differences between Fedotova and Ermolova accounted for Samarin's negative response to Mariia Nikolaevna. Fedotova appealed to him because she was "playful, coquettish, soft, tender, cunning, elegant, expressive, and graceful;" but he was indifferent to the "withdrawn, constrained, and awkward Ermolova."[59] Ermolova accepted the necessity to eliminate her gender deficiences and cultivate qualities associated with the reigning stage model of "*zhenstvennost.*" Besides physical grace, these included "softness, nobility of tone, and variety of intonation."[60] By spending hours alone in front of a mirror practicing poses, developing plasticity, and refining her mimicry, Ermolova successfully erased many of her imperfections. This process of solitary self-instruction left her with the external qualities of a standard ingenue, but she still lacked the requisite "naivete, sugariness, and tearful sentimentality." Instead, the fundamental feature of her early performances was "deep sadness and grief."[61] For that reason, during the late 1870s, Ermolova began to resist ingenue roles and specialize in the genre upon which her reputation was established: romantic-heroic tragedy with political implications.

Like Fedotova, Ermolova enjoyed the reputation of a serious actress in an exemplary repertoire; unlike her rival, Ermolova's ideological inclinations were unequivocally manifested in her work at the Malyi Theatre. *Fuente Ovejuna*, the play she selected for her first benefit in 1876, marked a turning point in her career. This pivotal event was, however, prepared for by the friendships she formed with radical students after 1870.

When Ermolova arrived at the Malyi Theatre, her intellectual development and range of interests were severely limited. She was not ignorant by choice; rather, Ermolova was the inevitable product of an intellectually and economically impoverished environment. Ermolova's childhood was marked by extreme poverty; her father, who ruled the family with an iron hand, allowed his children little physical or intellectual freedom; faculty at the Moscow Theatre School evinced little concern for students' intellectual development; and except for cheap, popular plays, books were virtually absent from both her home and school environments. Several months after her debut in *Emilia Galotti*, Ermolova fell in with a group of radical students imbued with the liberal ideals of the 1860s. During this period, she not only acquired an intellectual life, but also began to develop the ideals and principles that informed much of her later work at the Malyi.[62]

Although the intensity of Ermolova's involvement with radical politics abated after several years, university students remained her most ardent admirers and her early activism left an imprint on her later life and work.[63] Unlike so many starring actresses, Ermolova was excited by ideas and took a thoughtful attitude toward life and literature. She did not live ostentatiously or behave "like a star"; she read serious newspapers and journals; and she took cabs to work rather than riding in her own carriage.[64] Instead of chasing after dissipated aristocrats or even members of her own profession, she married N.P. Shubinski, a distinguished lawyer and activist. Although her letters to Shubinski suggest how deeply inadequate she felt in the presence of this prominent representative of the Moscow intelligentsia, the relationship inspired her to read widely and study diligently.[65]

The effects of her involvement with progressive people and politics were apparent not only in the roles she selected, but also in the response of Malyi audiences to her performances during the late 1870s and 1880s. On a friend's advice, Ermolova chose the role of Laurencia in *Fuente Ovejuna* for her first benefit; in addition to suiting the temper of the times, this role set the tone for much of the rest of her career. Baron Drizen reported that when Ermolova spoke the monologue in which Laurencia challenges the people of Fuente Ovejuna to rise up against tyranny: "An electric shock ran through the auditorium. Trembling as if from fever, spectators were prepared to burst from their seats and follow this heroic girl. . . . The little dramatic ingenue was suddenly a great tragic actress."[66] Although Ermolova's tendency was always to idealize her roles, with *Fuente Ovejuna* the sorrowful, aggrieved quality of her previous work was replaced by furious protest and sublime ecstasy. Her idealism, love of the people (*narodoliubie*), and rejection of autocratic authority resonated in the Malyi auditorium. She was transformed into a spokesperson for the oppressed; no longer simply an actress, Ermolova became "an artist-warrior," prepared to fight and perish for a "beautiful idea."[67] Although *Fuente Ovejuna* quickly disappeared from the Malyi's repertoire, the Malyi directorate could no longer ignore Ermolova.[68]

Following the success of *Fuente Ovejuna*, playwrights deserted Fedotova to write for the public's new idol, Mariia Ermolova. By adapting their principal female characters to her best qualities, they encouraged the emergence of a new type of heroine in Russian plays of the 1880s: a woman of strong spirit trapped in an oppressive environment. The typical Ermolova heroine must confront social prejudice and arbitrary abuse of power by parental, conjugal, or state authorities. Conscious of her own superior virtue, she does not submit, but challenges the forces of oppression and ultimately triumphs.[69] At least one critic claimed that because she was so effective in romantic-heroic roles, Ermolova singlehandedly created a vogue for romantic-heroic women on the Russian stage.[70] Given the social and political tensions of the period, his interpretation seems naive. Whether by intention or by accident, Ermolova tapped into the growing dissatisfaction of progressives and students with current social conditions. The opposition saw in this powerful actresses a standard bearer for the cause of social justice. It is not surprising that, after *Fuente Ovejuna*, Ermolova was transformed by her admirers into a chaste symbol of rebellion against the arbitrary authority of the autocracy.

Ermolova's fame peaked in 1884 when she produced *The Maid of Orleans* for her benefit. Although Schiller's Joan has much in common with Lope's Laurencia, because the tragic sensibility is predominant in Schiller's play, many Russian critics mark the beginning of Ermolova's third phase with her production of *The Maid*.

Joan of Arc was not only Ermolova's favorite role, she also considered it to be her sole authentic contribution to the Russian theatre.[71] Although a translation of the text was published in Russia in 1822, its production was prohibited. Ermolova tried several times to obtain permission to stage the play, but did not succeed until 1883 when she persuaded the censor to allow selected scenes from *The Maid* to be produced on the occasion of the one-hundreth anniversary of the translator's birth. The following year, she finally received permission to produce the entire play.[72] Even so, the Imperial theatre's directorate attempted to discourage Ermolova by refusing to build new sets or costumes for the production. Instead, she was given sets and costumes from Tchaikovski's opera, which had been produced several years before.[73] If the directorate's objective was to sabotage the production, they failed. According to colleagues and critics, Ermolova's performance was so inspired that no one in the audience noticed the wretched scenery and costumes or the weakness of the ensemble.[74]

Although Emilia Galotti and Laurencia marked stages in Ermolova's development, Joan of Arc was her signature role. Even more than *Fuente Ovejuna*, *The Maid of Orleans* resonated with students and members of the progressive intelligentsia, many of whom felt that, in Ermolova, the Malyi

М.Н. ЕРМОЛОВА ~ ИОАННА Д'АРК.
„ Орлеанская дева " Ф. Шиллера.
1884 г. (фото 1893 г.)

Figure 3 Mariia Ermolova in Schiller's *The Maid of Orleans*. Courtesy of the St. Petersburg Theatre Museum

Theatre had satisfied the national yearning for a Russian Joan of Arc.[75] It is significant that Ermolova produced the play during the period of reaction that followed the assassination of Aleksandr II. Perhaps spectators responded so enthusiastically to her because they were hungry for a voice that could, as one commentator noted, "summon them to battle and affirm the strength of the human spirit."[76] In Ermolova's Joan, Malyi audiences were treated to the spectacle of a *woman* triumphing physically, morally, and spiritually over the forces of repression. If a woman could behave so courageously, surely the people of Russia could overcome their legendary passivity and challenge the legitimacy of the tsarist autocracy. Nemirovich-Danchenko confirmed that, from both aesthetic and social points of view, Ermolova raised the art of theatre to new ideological heights – and by so doing, she became the "genuine idol of liberals and revolutionary youth."[77]

Ermolova's uniquely heroic, sexually detached brand of *"zhenstvennost"* was finally established by her performance in *The Maid of Orleans*. Although a few critics still pressured her to search out and develop the more conventionally feminine aspects of her characters, in fact Ermolova's somewhat masculine appearance and demeanor served her well in romantic-heroic drama, and the very ambiguity of her gender identity contributed to her effectiveness in heroic roles.[78] In 1906, A. Amfiteatrov observed that although Ermolova did not provoke his generation to "hysterical idolatry," she enjoyed unprecedented admiration and respect from the "cultured mass of spectators," and her devotees worshipped her with a fervor bordering on fanaticism.[79] The feelings expressed by two ardent disciples of Ermolova's divinity suggest the degree to which she was transformed into a cultural icon and deified by students during the 1880s and 1890s.

A. Rostislavov wrote that Ermolova did not have the "proper tender womanly beauty:" she lacked "physical grace" and her voice was not "softly melodious." She had little interest in high fashion, but "the inner elegance of her appearance was so great and so illuminated her outer appearance" that it was not necessary to resort to "special costume contrivances." Her image was not marred by "cold female intelligence." Rather, she was a "surprisingly unified combination of simplicity, vitality, and strength; an intuitive revelation of the most profound principles of female and male spirituality." Ermolova was, Rostislavov continued, the "students' Madonna" and before her divinity, only the "purest thoughts and feelings" were possible. In the attitude of students toward Ermolova, there was not a trace of the usual "coarse, debased worship of actresses."[80]

Echoing Rostislavov, N. Rossov wrote that Ermolova "renewed" her spectators "physically and morally." In roles from the classical repertoire, she had a "magical, curative effect on the soul." She "opened heaven for us," he wrote, "she made the very air of the theatre pure and fresh like a child's kiss." Ermolova "elevated women" so that "all of the coarse feelings of envy and maliciousness momentarily vanished from our souls in the presence of the sweet aspect of the Maid of Orleans' unearthly beauty."[81]

Pointing out that the deification of Ermolova had reached absurd proportions, Vlas Doroshevich complained that she was not only beyond criticism, but that a general, albeit unspoken, agreement existed among critics not to write honestly about her. "How," he asked rhetorically, "do you dare to criticize a gift from God, a national symbol?" Several pages later he continued: "What kind of idolatry is this that blinds people to her deficiencies and keeps them from speaking their minds?"[82] Doroshevich and many of his colleagues were simultaneously puzzled and enthralled by the enigmatic actress, and although most critics admired Ermolova, some had misgivings about the uncritical adulation surrounding her. Perhaps it was Ermolova's mystery that prompted critics to produce a significant body of book and journal literature devoted to examining the secret of her power over spectators. In this body of literature, several features of her art and practice stand out: temperament, idealization, optimism, and personal modesty.

Until the Moscow Art Theatre effected the triumph of technique, "temperament" was an essential component in the art of acting in Russia. "Existence without temperament," Aleksandr Kugel observed, "is unthinkable, for without temperament there is neither suffering nor joy." "Temperament," he explained, "is a will to, or passion for, life." Many critics and spectators shared his opinion that the most effective actresses were those, like Eleonora Duse, who relied on temperament rather than calculation. Temperament was instinctual – a gift of God – and for that reason, it did not yield to technique, nor could it be learned. The only skill necessary was the ability to "extract or peel away buried layers of emotion."[83] Perhaps it is not surprising that Ermolova, whose reputation rested on temperament, was the first Russian actress to be compared favorably with Duse. Temperament not only distinguished Ermolova from both Fedotova and Savina, but also made her the only genuinely tragic actress among them.

According to Nemirovich-Danchenko, Ermolova, who was instrumental in promoting the trend toward authentic emotion, or "truth on stage," in Russia, represented a tendency that ran counter to Fedotova's. Fedotova was a virtuoso, a solid artist whose strength lay in her flexibility and firm grasp of technique. In contrast, Ermolova's talent consisted in her "stunning temperament," in the extraordinary ease with which she "lit her emotional flame and set the spectators on fire." Nemirovich claimed that Ermolova's talent was not subject to rational analysis; it simply possessed the crowd. Ermolova's temperament was even more effective because it was combined with elevated ideology, romantic pathos, and demands for heroic action.[84] Although her stage technique was often flawed, during the 1880s the apparent authenticity, spontaneity, and depth of her emotive powers made her the idol of liberal and revolutionary youth.[85]

Writing about stage ideals associated with particular actresses during the

1880s, G.A. Zhernovaia suggests that Ermolova embodied an idealized type of "new woman."[86] From Zhernovaia's perspective, the wild enthusiasm generated by Ermolova was situational: after the assassination of the relatively liberal Aleksandr II, the paranoid and reactionary Aleksandr III reversed many of his predecessor's reforms and further curtailed the already limited freedoms enjoyed by Russians during the 1860s and 1870s. Although students, members of the liberal intelligentsia, and other radical groups were outraged, they had little power to resist state-imposed repression. In Moscow, their anger found an outlet in Ermolova and the Malyi Theatre. Although Ermolova's reputation rested upon classical Western heroines like Laurencia and Joan, she "Russianized" them.[87] Using Lope de Vega's and Schiller's texts, Ermolova summoned the people to oppose tyranny, and by so doing, became a relatively benign vehicle for protest against the Russian autocracy. Zhernovaia even suggests that Ermolova's romantic-heroic "new women" were prototypes for the professional female revolutionaries and assassins who enjoyed a significant presence in the People's Will (*Narodnaia volia*).[88]

Ermolova actively resisted unsympathetic or villainous characters.[89] Throughout her life, she specialized in heroic types who suffered tremendously, but ultimately triumphed – morally, if not physically – over their persecutors. On those rare occasions when she played unsympathetic characters, Ermolova inevitably found ways to make them sympathetic. For example, Ermolova so ennobled Lady Macbeth when she played the role in 1896, that she evoked sympathy rather than horror.[90] In the same season, she idealized the role of a "mercenary adultress" to the point that one reviewer feared her performance would damage the moral fiber of impressionable female spectators. In Ermolova's interpretation, he complained, the character was so "heart-rendingly sympathetic," that young women might be tempted to imitate her immoral behavior.[91]

Because Ermolova and Savina were contemporaries who represented not only competing theatres, but competing cities, ideologies, and lifestyles, comparisons between them were inevitable. Spectators and critics who appreciated multi-dimensional female characters with sharp edges favored the unsentimental Savina, whose personal pragmatism and keen sense of irony kept her roles firmly grounded in "real life." Those who preferred romantic, highly idealized, heroic figures leaned toward Ermolova.[92] In her biography of Ermolova, Tatiana Shchepkina-Kupernik included a long-cherished, frequently repeated assumption about the fundamental difference between two actresses who played many of the same roles: "Ermolova always defended her heroines, while Savina prosecuted them."[93] With a touch of irony, Vlas Doroshevich joked that both Ermolova and her husband, Shubinski, were defense lawyers, but that Ermolova's court proceedings were far more significant and difficult.[94]

Regardless of an author's intention, Ermolova played every role sympathetically. Whether the play called for it or not, she consistently emphasized intense suffering as a permanent quality of women's lives. Some critics observed that her suffering began before the curtain rose: "In the first act," they complained, "she always seems to have already read the fifth."[95] Others located Ermolova's appeal in the capacity of her characters to endure extreme suffering, while maintaining an aura of nobility and elevated spirituality. Although intense, her suffering was never coarse or hysterical. For Aleksandr Kugel, Ermolova was "one of the most beautiful creations of our 'old' culture." She was like a "guest from classical antiquity – a sort of Diana-Artemis with the wisdom of Athena and the warm sincerity of Penelope." Ermolova was, he concluded, the "stage affirmation of the Platonic ideal."[96]

Most Moscow critics agreed that Ermolova reached for and touched the sublime. Two of the most prominent, Vladimir Nemirovich-Danchenko and Nikolai Efros, tried to articulate the implications for women of Ermolova's interpretive framework. In 1910, Efros wrote that Ermolova's career was a history of "service to a single, fixed, elevated ideal.... Taken as a whole, all of her performances were apologies for women, artistic refutations of all the slander against the female heart and soul." Ermolova did not, he continued, "violate the author's image or lie to please feminist tendentious-ness.... In her performances, she always emphasized women's merits." By concentrating on the nobility of women, she raised her female spectators. Ermolova showed them that "women were capable of elevated impulses, hero-ism, self-sacrifice, and deeds of faith and love."[97] Nemirovich-Danchenko took a similar point of view when he wrote of Ermolova: "For fifty years you sang of women's deeds, first in sorrowful images of exquisite suffering, then in fiery images imbued with love for freedom and hatred of oppression.... A theatrical miracle was realized through you when whole generations were inspired by the images you created."[98] When Ermolova died in 1928, Metropolitan Trifon eulogized her for leading the people to eternal ideals of God's truth, good, and beauty.[99]

STRATEGIES OF "*ZHENSTVENNOST*" IN THE IMPERIAL THEATRES: FEDOTOVA, ERMOLOVA, AND SAVINA

Although many Russians understood the deification of actresses like Ermolova as a universal affirmation of women, the trend was not necessarily progressive. In point of fact, glorification of an ideal, abstract "Woman" was not new in Russia.[100] Sobriquets like "vestal virgin of the temple of art" and "Madonna" suggest that, much more than Savina, Ermolova and Fedotova operated within the framework of traditional gender ideology. Although none of the Imperial triumvirate was progressive in the sense of supporting Western European modernism, Savina understood better than her Moscow competitors how to exploit Western popular culture. Assisted by Victor Krylov, she not only tailored French salon plays to the tastes of fashionable

St. Petersburg audiences, but also willingly subscribed to prevailing Western fashion imperatives. Because the Malyi was not free from box office pressures, Fedotova and Ermolova were also compelled to play the Savina–Krylov repertoire. But their preference for plays by Shakespeare, Schiller, Lope de Vega, Calderon, Lessing, and other Western European classics was clear. It is, perhaps, ironic that the two Moscow actresses were simultaneously more identified than Savina with Western dramaturgy and more acceptable to conservative critics and spectators. The reasons are not difficult to locate.

Although they preferred a Western repertoire, neither Fedotova nor Ermolova subscribed publicly to values, fashions, ideas, and ideologies associated with popular trends in Western Europe and America. They not only understood, but also enthusiastically endorsed the more austere, traditional values of the Malyi Theatre and its regular audience. From a semiotic point of view, Fedotova and Ermolova retained distinctively Russian systems of signifiers and signifieds: relative to many other actresses, both dressed modestly on stage and off, conducted their private lives discreetly, and refused to enhance their careers with Bernhardtesque marketing gimmicks.[101] Unlike Savina, Fedotova and Ermolova were successful with Russian realist genres, and even when they played classical Western tragedy and comedy, both tended to "Russianize" their heroines. In addition, neither aspired to tour foreign countries or compete with Western stars. Although Fedotova toured Russia extensively, Ermolova, who contrived to avoid any extra-theatrical public appearances, could hardly be persuaded to leave Moscow even for command performances in St. Petersburg.

The rhetorical devices used by critics and historians to position Ermolova and Fedotova within the culture reveal the degree to which both projected images of "*zhenstvennost*" that did not threaten dominant gender ideology. The same critics who accused Savina of debasing the Aleksandrinskii repertoire and promoting Parisian excess praised Fedotova and Ermolova for maintaining the high standards of Russia's exemplary theatre. While Savina served her own ambition, the Moscow actresses served the people through self-sacrifice and uncompromising devotion to the highest aesthetic and ideological ideals. For Savina, theatre was a lucrative profession; for Fedotova it was an elevated artistic calling; for Ermolova, it was a sublime moral mission. Thanks in large part to the salutary influence of Ermolova and Fedotova, until approximately 1905, the Malyi Theatre enjoyed the reputation of an institution of cultural enlightenment rather than a house of debased popular entertainment.[102] Many critics remarked that they left performances by Ermolova spiritually uplifted and with a renewed appreciation for "the beautiful" in life. Amfiteatrov, one of Ermolova's most ardent admirers, called her influence a "great moral disinfectant."[103] In this sense, the Moscow actresses cannot be distinguished in any significant way from female radicals, revolutionaries, and other social activists who "drew on feminine ideals of altruism and self-sacrifice that were rooted deep in the Russian past" to justify their non-traditional, extra-domestic activities.[104]

Although critics identified Fedotova and Ermolova with Russian traditions, in fact the Moscow actresses were popular precisely because, like Savina, they successfully negotiated Western and neo-Slavophile gender ideologies. The principal difference between them with respect to gender ideology is located in class. Savina, a pragmatic child of the provincial circuit, constructed an image of *"zhenstvennost"* based in popular Western and Russian culture. As products of the Moscow Theatre School, Fedotova and Ermolova constructed images based on academic and "high art" models from Russia and the West. Not surprisingly, the Moscow actresses were more acceptable to critics, most of whom claimed membership in the intelligentsia.

Although Fedotova and Ermolova served the highest aesthetic, moral, and ideological ideals, and enjoyed the respect and love of critics and colleagues, they did not age as well as Savina, nor did they achieve the kind of power she enjoyed within the Aleksandrinskii Theatre and the Russian Theatre Society. Fedotova's career was interrupted abruptly in 1905 by a progressive, physically debilitating illness, but distress over the direction of Russian theatre and of her own career hastened her retirement. The transition to "mature" roles was particularly difficult for her. In 1895, Fedotova formally announced her intention to move into middle-aged roles and petitioned the Director of the Imperial Theatres for a two-year leave of absence.[105] During this period, she intended to develop a new repertoire, perfect it through a series of provincial tours, and finally unveil it in Moscow. She accepted no salary, but asked that upon her return, she be given her old salary of 12,000 roubles a year plus benefits. The Director agreed to her conditions. When she returned, however, he "unofficially" offered her a salary of 9,000 roubles. His rationale? The change to middle-aged types reduced her value to the theatre. Thirty-five years of selfless service to the Malyi Theatre meant little to the Malyi's administrative hierarchy. The outraged Fedotova wrote to the Director: "I cannot tell you how offensive this is to me as a woman and as an artist."[106]

Ermolova's situation was different, but equally painful. Mariia Nikolaevna was closely identified with a particular genre and a particular style of inspirational acting. As modernism displaced romantic-heroic drama and temperament yielded to technique, she found herself without a repertoire and without the skills – or desire – to adapt to the new drama of Ibsen, Chekhov, Maeterlinck, and other modernists. "Eagles are not in fashion today," Stanislavski observed. "The time of temperament is past," Kugel echoed.[107] In 1907, Baron Drizen acknowledged that Ermolova had little to look forward to. "Genius is a product of its time," he wrote. "Our century cannot boast of optimism. Conditions like these are not propitious for an actress of heroic temperament, one who believes in a brighter future. Society does understand or value her."[108]

It is, perhaps, ironic that Savina, who was entirely pragmatic, who professed no ideological or aesthetic ideals, and who suffered extremely at the hands of critics, not only survived but even prospered at a time when Fedotova's and Ermolova's authority was greatly diminished. Debilitated by ill health, the Moscow actresses struggled to adapt simultaneously to middle age and to a rapidly changing social environment. Eventually both withdrew from public life. In a letter to Savina, Ermolova expressed admiration for her colleague's "energetic nature," and acknowledged that the imperative to learn new roles and a new repertoire distressed and exhausted her: "You're right, there are other roles," she wrote, "but I have to compose myself before I can switch to them."[109] All three of the Imperial stars resisted new tendencies, clung to familiar roles, faced down challenges from younger actresses, and fought to retain their privilege in the face of increasingly frequent assaults by powerful directors who saw the aging actresses as impediments to progress. Perhaps Savina negotiated the situation more successfully because she was not burdened by self-imposed obligations to art or ideology.

It was Savina's good fortune to die in 1915 when Imperial actresses still enjoyed considerable privilege and status. Conditions in the post-revolutionary period did not favor the Imperial theatres and many members of the community, including starring actresses, were left in great need. Although Fedotova and Ermolova survived into the 1920s, their final years were marked by deprivation and chronic illness.[110] From an ideological perspective, however, starring actresses who achieved fame during the 1870s and 1880s were, for the most part, already obsolete by 1900.

5

NARODNICHESTVO, NATIONALISM, AND NEURASTHENIA

Polina Strepetova as populist icon

When Polina Antipevna Strepetova lay dying of stomach cancer in 1903, sympathetic friends and admirers sought to console the embittered actress by reminding her of the remarkable service she had performed for Russian theatre. Not in the least comforted by their well-intentioned banalities, the perpetually pugnacious Strepetova responded with self-righteous indignation: "Savina served the theatre, I served the people."[1]

Strepetova, a strident supporter of both populist (*narodnichestvo*) and Slavophile (*slavianofilstvo*) ideals, provoked considerable controversy during the period. An oddity among starring actresses, her ideological and aesthetic convictions distinguished her from even moderate advocates of Westernization like Mariia Savina and Mariia Ermolova. Riding on a rising tide of populist fervour, Strepetova became, for a brief period in the 1870s and early 1880s, the most popular actress in Russia.[2] In contrast to her most successful competitors in the provincial and capital theatres, Strepetova refused to capitulate to Western trends in ideology, art, theatre, or fashion. Given her resistance to the growing Westernization of Russian theatre, it is curious that many critics, both contemporaneous and current, credit Strepetova with assisting in the "process of women's emancipation" in Russia.[3]

Her distaste for Western fashion, drama, and culture set her apart from most other starring actresses of the period, especially Savina, whom many, including Strepetova herself, saw as her principal rival. Strepetova, who rarely performed in either the popular or progressive Western repertoire, did not evince palpable interest in the Woman Question or the Ibsenian "New Woman"; rather, she established a liberal reputation in the late 1860s with emotionally wrenching renditions of Aleksandr Ostrovski's and Aleksei Pisemski's "purely Russian" heroines. In the 1870s and early 1880s, contemporaneous commentators associated Strepetova's work with progressive populism and with the women's emancipation movement. As she aged, Strepetova's conservative instincts prevailed over earlier liberal tendencies, making the discrepancy between her public persona and private convictions more apparent. Indeed, her later alliances with reactionary movements, including neo-Slavophilism, Russification, antisemitism, and Russian nationalism, made her one of the most ideologically contradictory, yet emotionally compelling actresses of the age. Because Strepetova expressed her political convictions openly, they eventually impeded her career. For that reason, more than any other actress of the period, Strepetova's example persuaded Russian actresses of the necessity to subordinate private convictions to professional pragmatism.

With respect to dominant trends in gender ideology, aesthetics, and representation, Strepetova was surely an anomaly among starring actresses of the period. Plain-featured, stoop-shouldered, ill-tempered, and deliberately unfashionable, she had little in common with the elegant, Western-influenced stars of the Imperial theatres with whom she was so often compared – usually to her disadvantage. Nonetheless, during the 1870s and early 1880s, Strepetova's performances provoked enthusiastic, even frenzied reactions from impassioned admirers in the capitals and provinces. Her repertoire, which consisted primarily of physically exhausted, emotionally impoverished, spiritually depleted mothers, wives, and daughters of peasants (*krestianstvo*) and petty bourgeois merchants (*kupechestvo*), was considered by many to be the most progressive in the country. Strepetova's position in Russia's war of gender ideology with the West was determined by the strength and intimacy of her relationship with the Russian "people" (*narod*). In the world of late nineteenth-century theatre, she represented a decidedly Russified, neo-romantic conception of "*zhenstvennost*," which appealed to an ideologically diverse coalition of spectators ranging from conservative nationalists to revolutionary populists.

THE ORIGINS AND EDUCATION OF
AN UNLIKELY STAR

On October 4, 1850, in the provincial city of Nizhnii Novgorod, a sack containing a newborn infant was deposited, probably by her mother, on the doorstep of Antip Grigorevich Strepetov and his wife, Elizaveta Ivanovna.[4] Although no conclusive evidence of her biological parents' identity exists, Nizhnii gossips whispered that the tiny girl was the unfortunate issue of a brief romance between a young actress, Glazunova, who spent one season at the Nizhnii theatre, and an officer of the Guards. Like so many unseasoned provincial actresses Glazunova was apparently ill-prepared for the crisis of an unwanted pregnancy or the prolonged burden of motherhood. Relying on the couple's kindly reputation, she must have hoped that Antip Grigorevich, the Nizhnii theatre's hairdresser, and Elizaveta Ivanovna, an established provincial actress, would be able to provide for the child better than she could. Glazunova calculated accurately: loath to turn an orphaned infant over to the local constabulary, the Strepetovs adopted the child, christened her Pelageia, and raised her as their own.[5]

The atmosphere of Strepetova's adoptive family was remarkable for its effect on her personal and professional development. Although fundamentally well-intentioned and benevolent, the Strepetovs were a conservative, deeply religious couple who maintained strict control over their children's activities and education. Because Antip Grigorevich and Elizaveta Ivanovna viewed with suspicion any "depraved pedagogical innovations" that might corrupt Russian youth, they refused to allow their own children to attend the local *gimnaziia*, which was, from the parental point of view, a breeding ground for liberals and freethinkers.[6] Strepetova's general education was, therefore, haphazard: for a brief period, her parents hired an ancient seminarian to instruct the children privately in geography, calligraphy, and, most important, the laws of God. Later, Polina studied French with a local gentry girl who, after discovering her pupil's intention to go on the stage, tried desperately to dissuade her from pursuing the road to perdition.[7]

Her parents' and tutors' influence was, however, benign beside that of a fanatically religious aunt to whom Strepetova was particularly attached. Beniash, who takes a dim, typically Soviet point of view on the subject of religion, argues in his biography that the baneful influence on Strepetova of this pious relative irreparably damaged the actress's emotional and intellectual development.[8] By all accounts, this aunt was sincerely devoted to Polina, but the mystical, highly superstitious character of her faith apparently encouraged the child to have religious hallucinations. As an adult, Strepetova continued to have what Beniash calls "sickly visions," and her acting, which was often trance-like in its intensity, simultaneously inspired, disturbed, and sometimes even frightened her partners.[9] Perhaps as a result of the heavy-handedness of her early religious indoctrination, she developed the humorless, intolerant, unaccommodating nature for which colleagues and critics so often reproached her.

Strepetova's ambivalence about developments in the theatre at the end of the nineteenth century may have been fostered, at least in part, by her parents' attitude toward their profession. As the offspring of serfs, Antip Grigorevich and Elizaveta Ivanovna were pragmatic rather than idealistic about the theatre. Harboring few illusions about "art as an elevated calling, about talent, or about service to the theatre," they regarded their profession as necessary, but difficult work: for the Strepetovs, theatre was simply a way of life, a way to earn a living wage.[10] Although there were certain advantages to being raised in a theatrical family, acquisition of systematic training was not one of them. Indeed, Strepetova's theatre education was even more haphazard than her general schooling. Like most provincial performers, her formal instruction in acting was minimal, and although her appreciation for literary drama increased over time, conditions in the Strepetov household did not encourage Polina to refine her literary and aesthetic sensibilities.

Strepetova's amateur debut took place on the Nizhnii stage when she was seven. Subsequently, she spent hours at the theatre observing rehearsals and performances, and, like many provincial girls living on the edge of poverty, was dazzled by the artificial opulence of the sets and costumes, particularly the gowns worn by the elegant Moscow and St. Petersburg touring stars who occasionally passed through Nizhnii Novgorod. Her fascination with actresses bordered on obsession. She desperately wanted a mentor to initiate her into the secrets of acting, but complained that for lack of a "professor," she had to rely on self-instruction. As a child, her method consisted of practicing poses and rehearsing monologues of her own composition in front of a large mirror. Exercises in mimicry were the most pleasurable part of her self-imposed lesson plan, and in view of her later success with neurasthenic personalities, it is not surprising that she derived particular satisfaction from feigning insanity. For the rest, her "training" amounted to experiential learning: she began with walk-on roles and, having demonstrated considerable natural ability, quickly moved through the ranks.

In early adolescence, Strepetova began begging her mother's permission to act professionally, not because she was particularly idealistic or felt called to aesthetic self-expression, but because, as an unwed young woman, she had already become a burden to her increasingly impoverished family.[11] By her own admission, she turned to theatre because she wanted to be useful and knew no other calling.[12] When Polina turned fifteen, therefore, Elizaveta Ivanovna, who was skeptical about her daughter's chances for success, but felt that theatre was her only "honorable" option, wrote to an entrepreneur in Iaroslav asking him to hire her for older women's roles (*starukhi*) and Polina for "whatever was available at whatever salary he could afford." The entrepreneur, Smirnov, was sufficiently impressed by Polina's debut as a maid in a vaudeville to offer her a salary of eighteen roubles a month.[13]

Strepetova's engagement at the theatre in Iaroslav, where she enjoyed considerable success with local spectators, but began a lifelong pattern of alienating entrepreneurs, directors, and colleagues, marked the beginning of her life as an itinerant, albeit enormously successful, provincial player. Her career advanced rapidly: in 1867, she went to Simbirsk at a salary of 25 roubles; in 1868, she moved to Vladimir where she received 100 roubles; by the 1871/72 season, she had already built a considerable reputation as a dramatic actress on the provincial circuit when Petr Medvedev, a prominent provincial entrepreneur, hired her to work at the Kazan theatre for the unprecedented salary of 50 roubles per performance.[14] Although historians usually categorized Strepetova as a provincial actress, during her career she moved repeatedly between theatres in the provinces and capital cities. After stunning successes in Kazan, she accompanied Medvedev to Moscow. In 1873 she debuted at the Moscow Popular Theatre (*Obshchedostupnyi teatr*), an early club theatre that took pride in its accessibility to the "simple people" (*prostoi narod*).[15]

Well before she arrived in Moscow, however, Strepetova had already established the line of business for which she became famous. Like most provincial players, she was compelled to perform in the jejune, popular entertainments favored by provincial entrepreneurs and spectators, but her aptitude was for thoughtful "drama of everyday life" (*bytovaia dramaturgiia*), rather than fashionable comedies and dramas, operettas, and melodramas.[16] Her seemingly natural facility for "*bytovaia*" roles was established during her first season at Iaroslav when she inspired considerable enthusiasm among spectators for her performance in *The Child* (*Rebenok*). The pivotal point in Strepetova's career, however, was the 1869/70 season at Samara. There she met Modest Pisarev, who exerted considerable influence on the future course of her career by persuading her to consider more seriously her aesthetic, literary, and social objectives. The entrepreneur's decision to cast her as Lizaveta in Aleksandr Pisemski's *Bitter Fate* (*Gorkaia sudbina*) was equally important. With Lizaveta, Strepetova emancipated herself from the standard provincial repertoire and demonstrated her formidable talent for serious Russian realism.[17]

A HEROINE FOR PROGRESSIVES AND REACTIONARIES: STREPETOVA AND POPULISM

Two factors determined Strepetova's stunning success first in *Bitter Fate* and later in Ostrovski's dramas of merchant life: the growing interest (especially among the intelligentsia) in the "people" (*narod*) and the actress's own astonishing ability to "live inside" her characters, experience their emotions, and communicate them effectively to an audience.

Claiming that it was unique in the Russian dramatic oeuvre, A.I. Urusov called *Bitter Fate* Russia's first authentic "peasant tragedy" (*muzhitskaia tragediia*).[18] Like Aleksandr Ostrovski, with whom he was closely allied, Aleksei Pisemski through his association with the realistic trend in Russian art and literature that flourished in the mid-nineteenth century, gained the reputation of a "chronicler of the life of the common people."[19] The plot of *Bitter Fate*, which was written in 1859 and first produced after the reforms in 1863, is simple: a peasant woman, Lizaveta, willingly enters into intimate relations with the owner of the estate on which she and her husband, Anani, serve, and eventually bears his child. Anani, who is depicted as a sympathetic, loving husband, eventually discovers his wife's infidelity, deduces the identity of the child's father, and murders the child with an axe. Anani is sentenced by the jury to hard labor and, accompanied by the now subdued and repentent Lizaveta, he is sent to Siberia. Pisemski's neo-romantic, populist ideology is clear: the play idealized the peasantry by pitting a noble peasant (*muzhik*) against a decadent aristocrat in a struggle for possession of the body and affections of the peasant's wife.

Although *Bitter Fate* was fresh and modern in 1863, it provoked surprisingly little reaction from audiences at the Imperial theatres in Moscow and St. Petersburg. Box office receipts were poor and critical reception was tepid: most critics sympathized with Anani, but dismissed Lizaveta as an un-

Figure 4 Polina Strepetova in Pisemski's *Bitter Fate*. Courtesy of the St. Petersburg Theatre Museum

pleasantly coarse, decidedly tedious secondary character – which was apparently the author's intention.[20] If Pisemski romanticized the peasant commune and peasant men, he was less sympathetic toward the women: calling Lizaveta a "rascally woman" (*shelma-baba*), he actively discouraged actresses from idealizing her.[21] Although Strepetova was not the first to play the role, she was the first to ignore Pisemski's admonitions and make something of Lizaveta by approaching her sympathetically.[22] With Strepetova in the role, for the first time *Bitter Fate* drew large, enthusiastic audiences. A new generation of critics congratulated the actress for vitalizing Lizaveta and positioning her as a central figure in the story. Calling Strepetova Piscmski's "co-author," Urusov attributed much of the play's new success to Strepetova's performance rather than the playwright's text.[23]

Following her triumph in *Bitter Fate*, Strepetova could begin to reject offers that required her to play the popular repertoire and specialize in plays that reproduced the daily lives of common people. Her association with, and eventual marriage to, Modest Pisarev, a gentle, soft-spoken university-educated actor, had a salutory effect on her aesthetic and literary tastes and, at least temporarily, helped to smooth her rough edges.[24] Although Strepetova established her reputation as a "*bytovaia*" actress under Pisarev's tutelage, he also encouraged her to broaden her range by playing Western classics, including Shakespeare. But her sporadic – and consistently unsuccessful – forays into the Western repertoire only confirmed the limits of her natural talent: Strepetova could not convincingly depict characters who fell beyond the boundaries of her own personal and cultural experience. One prominent critic, Vlas Doroshevich, wrote that Strepetova was a great "*artistka-narodnitsa*," the literal translation of which is "actress-populist." According to Doroshevich, when she tried to play Shakespeare's Beatrice, Schiller's Maria Stuart, or Scribe's Adrienne Lecouvreur her performances resembled "aristocratic life as depicted in 20-kopek novels."[25] Her strength, he said, was with simple Russian women: "She promoted the cult of the Russian woman, decorated with . . . the martyrs' wreaths of Lizaveta and Katerina (*The Storm*). She showed us the martyrdom of Russian women. And we saw not only its horror, but also its imperishable beauty."[26] Even though many actresses played the "*bytovaia*" repertoire, none were as closely associated with the "cult of the Russian woman" as Strepetova. Through this cult, Strepetova promoted a distinctively Russian image of "*zhenstvennost.*"

In the early 1870s, the speed and intensity of Strepetova's success accelerated. Even her harshest critics acknowledged the strength of her extraordinary emotive powers, but her dizzyingly rapid rise and equally swift decline in the mid-1880s, as well as the fanatical devotion she inspired among admirers, suggest that the dynamics of her popularity were motivated by forces beyond the purely aesthetic. It is surely not coincidental that Strepetova's shifting fortunes parallel the rise and fall of Russian populism (*narodnichestvo*).

Populism in Russia is neither a single nor a simple phenomenon. Polish historian Andrzej Walicki suggests that the term has at least two meanings. In the broadest sense, populism was "the name given to all Russian democratic ideologies – revolutionary as well as reformist – that expressed the interests of the peasants and small producers and advocated the view that Russia could skip the capitalist stage of development."[27] Viewed in its more narrow, historical sense "the term 'Populism' is applied to a single trend within Russian radicalism, a trend that made its appearance in the mid-1870s after the experiences of the first 'go to the people' movement, and that differed from other revolutionary trends by its advocacy of 'the hegemony of the masses over the educated elite.'"[28] Both definitions are useful and help to position Strepetova in late nineteenth-century culture.

Russian populism, as it evolved in the 1870s, borrowed several ideological assumptions from two pre-reform political camps: the reactionary "Slavophiles" and the enlightened democrats. Like Slavophilism, populism was fundamentally romantic and backward looking. Both movements idealized the "people" (narod); celebrated a purely Russian spirit, with its concomitant rejection of Westernization; and glorified the primitive, self-sufficient peasant commune (conservative utopianism). But in the nineteenth century, Slavophilism, which in its broadest application means simply "love of Slavs," came to refer specifically to a "group of ideologists belonging to the conservative nobility."[29] Their ideals, which included autocracy, Orthodoxy, and "nationality" (narodnost), were formulated in reaction to the influx of Western ideas and values (from socialism to constitutional monarchy to deism and atheism). Populists, on the other hand, like the pre-emancipation enlightened democrats, were drawn primarily from the intelligentsia and claimed to represent "the broad masses, which in nineteenth-century Russia meant the peasantry above all."[30] The populists, whose chief enemy was capitalism, were devoted – at least in the abstract – to the Russian peasantry. During the populist crusade of 1873–1874 thousands of young men and women went out to the countryside to discover "the people:" "Clad in peasant clothes . . . they went to the villages in order to taste the authentic, healthy, simple life."[31]

Given her preference for "dramas of everday life" and moving representations of "ordinary" people, it is not surprising that the period of Strepetova's greatest popularity during the 1870s coincides with the rise of revolutionary populism. Peasant agitation was commonplace, a self-conscious proletariat was beginning to form, and populist ideology began to influence art and sharpen interest in the lives of common people.[32] The underclasses needed heroes and martyrs. Even Aleksandr Kugel, whose distaste for actresses like Strepetova was palpable, acknowledged a certain symbiosis between Strepetova and the "people." In his obituary, he called her an authentic representative of "populism" (narodnichestvo). "No one," he argued, "was more 'narodnaia' than Strepetova: her spirit was turned toward the people and, better than anyone else, she expressed the social feelings and ideas of her period."[33]

Strepetova's association with populism evolved during her nomadic years on the provincial circuit. When she joined Medvedev's company in 1871, Strepetova was still married to the scurrilous, self-absorbed Mikhail Strelski. Pregnant with her first child and oppressed by her husband, she found herself temporarily relegated to the background. When her domestic situation became unbearable, without a word, Strepetova abandoned Strelski and the company. When she returned during the following season, it was with renewed energy fuelled by a mutually supportive relationship with Pisarev. Working together, they established a solid reputation throughout the provinces for moving renditions of Ostrovski's and Pisemski's plays, especially *The Storm*, *The Forest*, and *Bitter Fate*. V.N. Davydov, a member of Medvedev's company at the time, was profoundly annoyed by Strepetova's growing notoriety. According to Davydov, Pisarev and Strepetova were sufficiently popular to make unprecedented demands on the entrepreneur with respect to salary and repertoire, and to push several accomplished actors and actresses into the background – among them, Mariia Savina.[34]

The response of spectators to Strepetova and Savina and the relationship that developed between them, both in the provinces and later in St. Petersburg, provides a gauge of populist sentiment during the period. Although the actresses were so dissimilar that competition between them should have been minimal, like most entrepreneurs Medvedev was apparently unable to satisfy or accommodate more than one "leading lady" (*premersha*) at a time. Savina, who had attracted considerable attention during several seasons with Medvedev, was the public's favorite. Hostilities quickly escalated as the "naive, spontaneous, democratic" public's enthusiastic preference for Strepetova gave her the authority to challenge Savina's privileged position in Medvedev's troupe.[35] Disciples of the plain-featured, straight-talking, unfashionable "woman of the people" (*narodnitsa*) and the attractive, diplomatic, unfailingly stylish ingenue arranged themselves in camps around their favorites.

Gender ideology was central to the controversy. Strepetova and Savina represented antagonistic concepts of "*zhenstvennost.*" Even in the provinces, Savina's appeal was primarily to spectators who affected catholic tastes, preferred lighthearted entertainments, and tended toward Westernization. Because she was fashionable, gregarious, and loved to dance and flirt, Savina was a favorite with men in the audience, who inundated her with candy and flowers.[36] Strepetova was of another type altogether, and her anomalous position among Russian actresses is clear from the amount of energy expended by critics and colleagues on describing her physical appearance and analyzing why she succeeded in spite of it. From Michurina-Samoilova's disparaging "short, stooped, poorly shaped, and very unattractive" to Urusov's ardent defense of her "unusually expressive face and splendid eyes," everyone had something to say about Strepetova's outward appearance.[37]

In fact, she was neither a standard beauty, nor a monster, but simply a "plain Jane" (*durnushkaia*).[38] What distinguished Strepetova from other actresses, many of whom were also cheated by nature, was her refusal to accept the growing influence of the fashion industry on theatrical style. Many of her colleagues were absurdly preoccupied with Parisian fashion and advanced their careers by spending thousands of roubles each season on the latest styles in clothing and makeup. But Strepetova firmly resisted commercial pressure.[39] In a rather unlikely comparison between Sarah Bernhardt and Strepetova, Zinaida Kholmskaia identified an important difference between Paris and the Russian provinces: "All of the French actresses I've seen," she wrote, "have an overwhelming need to pursue beauty at the expense of sincerity." Although many Russian actresses modeled themselves on the French, Strepetova's purely Russian modesty provided a refreshing break from Western decadence. "When she was alive," Kholmskaia continued, "I don't remember her wearing anything but a black dress without the slightest trace of decoration, not even a ribbon or a piece of lace."[40] Aleksandr Kugel' concurred with Kholmskaia: "When you imagine Strepetova's figure without a corset, in a simple blouse, and her smooth coiffure without a trace of curl, you begin to understand the 'evolution' of the Russian theatre and especially of the Russian actress."[41]

When they wearied of disparaging her physical appearance, Strepetova's critics turned to her "difficult" personality. In contrast to Savina's reputation for charm, wit, lively conversation, and political savvy, Strepetova was morose, reserved, straightforward, quarrelsome, and openly bigoted. Although some admired her candid honesty and "wicked intellect" (*zlostuma*), others were repelled by her vulgarity and obvious lack of breeding.[42] Strepetova, who regarded these qualities as a mark of Russian authenticity, took great pride in them. Her modest appearance, irascible temperament, provincial coarseness, and inability to dissemble effectively marked her as a "woman of the people." Unfortunately, they also marked her as an outsider in certain circles. Although her popularity was impressive, she was also an object of disdain. The response of one pretentious provincial spectator to Strepetova suggests that class identity was an important issue for some members of the audience. The man, a member of the local gentry who had lived in Paris, remarked after seeing her: "This is village bread and even worse, it's badly baked. My stomach can't digest it."[43]

Nonetheless, in the 1870s many spectators not only ate this coarse village bread, but preferred it to the Imperial theatres' refined French baguettes. The image of "*zhenstvennost*" popularized by Strepetova had broad appeal for two categories of Russian spectators: neo-Slavophile and populist sympathizers anxious about the effects of Westernization on traditional culture; and progressives, including advocates of women's emancipation, concerned about the continuing abuse and suppression of lower-class women within the rigidly patriarchal framework of the peasant commune.

Noting that Strepetova's characters were not "young ladies (*baryshni*) disguised in national costumes, but real women (*baby*), authentic Russian merchants' daughters," Strepetova's conservative supporters were delighted by the "purely Russian element" in her acting.[44] Her portrayals of Lizaveta and Katerina, not only "confirmed the beauty and powerful spirit of women from the people," but also made her a "prophet of populism."[45] Sergei Iablonovskii, who first saw the actress in *The Storm* 1895), argued that her class origins and continued commitment to the "people" enabled Strepetova to relate to "real" people better than most starring actresses. Although both Fedotova and Ermolova played "*bytovaia*" roles, neither could claim to share any life experience with the women they depicted. Savina, whose own class origins were only slightly more elevated than Strepetova's, tried to erase any trace of them. Although she persuaded the Aleksandrinskii directorate to produce Tolstoi's *The Power of Darkness* and, like most actresses of her generation, played Ostrovski's female heroes, Savina's enduring popularity with the sophisticated, cosmopolitan St. Petersburg audience was based at least in part on her discretion with respect to class identity. In contrast, Strepetova wore her class identification like a badge of honor. For that reason, unlike others who "pretended" to be "from the people" (*narodnyi*) or condescended to lower-class characters when forced to play them, Strepetova respected and believed in the peasant and merchant women she depicted.[46]

Because she was so closely identified with purely Russian traditions, conservative polemicists not only defended Strepetova, but used her as a standard bearer for their nationalist agenda. When, for example, the Imperial theatres resisted public pressure to hire her in the late 1870s, the ultra-conservative, antisemitic publicist, Aleksei Suvorin, defended her passionately in his newspaper, *The New Times* (*Novoe vremia*). In the short term, support from Suvorin and other conservatives was important to Strepetova's career, but she paid dearly for it. By attributing her effect on spectators to national pride and framing his thesis in right-wing rhetoric, Suvorin placed her squarely in the center of a raging controversy between liberals and conservatives.[47] According to Altshuller, she was unwittingly transformed by conservative supporters into "the representative of our 'original' (*samobytnyi*) Russian national genius and art."[48] Calling her the "leading actress of *The New Times*," Beniash claimed that, unbeknownst to Strepetova herself, by 1890, Suvorin had transformed her into a weapon of chauvinist ideology.[49]

Strepetova was not, however, an entirely passive observer of the process of politicizing her image. Following her divorce from Pisarev, who had encouraged her liberal tendencies, she looked for support elsewhere – and found it among conservative nationalists. Strepetova's reactionary posturing alienated many in the theatre community; the wrath of the liberal majority descended upon her during a session of the second theatre congress in 1901, when she spoke in favor of limiting the rights of Jewish actors.[50] Although later apologists tried to minimize her right-wing tendencies, Kugel argued that her convictions were those of a genuine "dissenter" (*raskolnitsa*) and that her antisemitism was a mark of "*narodnyi*" authenticity.[51]

Given her ideological ties to conservative neo-Slavophiles, populists, and nationalists, the fact that Strepetova also found support among progressives seems oddly contradictory – but perhaps the contradiction lies within populism itself. The "back to the people" impulse included not only simple-minded, uncritical panegyrics to a uniquely Russian spirit embodied in the "people," but also a liberal critique of the oppressive, patriarchal primitivism characteristic of the peasant commune and, by implication, of Russian society as a whole.[52] Between approximately 1850 and 1880, Ostrovski and Pisemski produced detailed depictions of Russian peasant and merchant life, many of which, whether by intention or by accident, touched on "women's themes." For that reason, until their plays became unfashionable in the late 1880s, critics tended to dismiss Ibsen as redundant. One even argued that *Bitter Fate* was the Russian equivalent of *A Doll's House* and Strepetova's Lizaveta, the prototype not only for Nora, but even for the Western European suffragists.[53]

Perhaps critics overstated the feminist implications of Strepetova's performances, but if she was not consciously progressive with respect to issues affecting women, Doroshevich's retrospective remarks on her significance suggest an aspect of her work that might be considered unintentionally feminist. "From under the oppressive influence of the '*Domostroi*,' the tatar mentality, and serfdom," he wrote of Strepetova, "the simple Russian woman, who preserves within her the best of the human spirit, appeared before us."[54]

The salient term is "*Domostroi*," or "rules of household order." Originally written and disseminated in the Middle Ages, the "*Domostroi*" is a manual for the governance of household relations.[55] Although significant portions of the manual are devoted to benign instructions for food preparation, clothing construction, and general organization of a model Orthodox home, it also authoritatively establishes the relative status of men and women in the social hierarchy. Thus, the instructions for "educating" a wife begin from the premise that her duty consists of "pleasing God and her husband and arranging his house and submitting to him in everything."[56] The rules for conducting a harmonious Christian home include guidelines for beating a wife or female servant without permanently crippling her or causing a miscarriage.[57] Although the authority of the "*Domostroi*" was diminished by the nineteenth century, many of its premises and principles were still enforced, especially among the lower classes. And if the document itself was weakened, popular beliefs about women's inferiority and the necessity for male domination were constantly reinforced by the Orthodox clergy and the state, both of which had a "vested interest in supporting the patriarchal system as a means of social control."[58]

The domestic principles articulated in the "*Domostroi*" were still operative in the social system depicted by Ostrovski and Pisemski. And although they might, like Ibsen, have argued that no conscious feminist agenda informed the composition of their plays, in Strepetova's hands spectators began to respond to the themes, and especially to the central female characters, as if they were composed with consciously feminist intent. Interestingly, although Ostrovski did write one play specifically for her, Strepetova was not the first to play any of the roles upon which her reputation rests. Apparently, social and political instability in Russia during the 1870s and early 1880s, including a growing sensitivity to women's oppression, produced an altered audience sensibility. These factors, combined with Strepetova's impassioned performances, compelled critics and spectators to respond differently to her than they had to earlier interpreters. If Ostrovski's and Pisemski's texts depicted a universally oppressive milieu, Strepetova's performances drew particular attention to the oppression of women within it. Doroshevich suggested that Russian women owed her a debt of gratitude for revealing the depth of their oppression.[59] Iablonovski wrote that Strepetova was effective precisely because she so convincingly portrayed "simple Russian women who had toiled and suffered for centuries."[60] Urusov quotes a "smart, sensitive woman," who remarked after seeing her in Ostrovski's *The Poor Bride*: "It seemed to me that the auditorium was half full of suffering, forgotten, unhappy people, who saw in Strepetova the embodiment of their own suffering and the offenses they had endured."[61] Selivanov argued that "she came to us not just as an actress, but as a freedom fighter."[62]

In the battle of the actresses, Strepetova's fortunes were determined largely by the vitality of populism. Her popularity was by no means limited to the provinces where, by virtue of her ideological associations, she might logically have been expected to prosper. During the early 1870s, when she and Savina worked together in Medvedev's troupe, Strepetova overshadowed her rival. In 1873, when Strepetova followed Medvedev to Moscow, audiences at the Moscow Popular Theatre received her enthusiastically, progressive critics compared her favorably to the Malyi Theatre's Glikeriia Fedotova, another successful interpreter of "*bytovaia*" roles, and she was perceived as a genuine threat to the hegemony of the Imperial actresses.[63] One sure index of her popularity was the invitation she received in 1876 from Elizaveta Levkeeva to participate in her benefit performance at the Imperial Aleksandrinskii Theatre. During this extraordinary event, a provincial actress stepped onto the hallowed boards of an Imperial stage without having first received an official invitation from the directorate for a formal debut.

Following the benefit performance, Strepetova worked in a series of progressive club and private theatres, but in spite of a wildly enthusiastic response from the public, the Imperial theatres continued deliberately to slight her. Even pressure from powerful critics and playwrights like Suvorin, Urusov, and Ostrovski, who eulogized her in the press and championed her behind the scenes, did not persuade the Imperial directorate to invite Strepetova into an Imperial company until 1881, when the enthusiasm for both populism and its most celebrated representative in the theatre was already beginning to abate.

Strepetova was ambivalent about the Imperial theatres: like most provincial celebrities, she was tempted by the status, respectability, and benefits that accrued to Imperial actresses – but could she subordinate her unruly temperament to the discreet, circumscribed life of an Imperial employee? Apparently not. Her calamitous experience at the Aleksandrinskii neither satisfied her aesthetic and political sensibilities nor reinforced her faith in, or respect for, her colleagues. Most ironic was the fact that a contract with an Imperial theatre, which should have advanced her professionally, was instead a fatal blow to her career. After two successful seasons in St. Petersburg, public enthusiasm for Strepetova's repertoire – and, by association, for Strepetova – began to pale. The Aleksandrinskii directorate responded to her diminished box office appeal by severely curtailing the amount of "*bytovaia*" drama in their repertoire. Because her repertoire consisted of one genre, their decision was deadly for Strepetova. The directorate assigned her to play in the fashionable salon comedies and dramas that formed the core of the Aleksandrinskii's repertoire, but she was so awkward and unconvincing that directors could do nothing with her. By the mid-1880s she was receiving fewer and fewer choice assignments, her career began to stagnate, and she became increasingly invisible, desperate, and angry.

Reflecting Strepetova's own paranoia, many of her supporters accused Savina of sabotaging their favorite during her ill-starred, nine-year tenure at the Aleksandrinskii.[64] Certainly Savina was not a neutral observer of Strepetova's declining fortunes. She did, after all, have unprecedented influence with the Imperial directorate, there was little love lost between the two, Savina did not tolerate competition, and she undoubtedly intrigued against her old enemy. But Strepetova, who preferred conspiracy theories, refused to acknowledge that other factors beyond the control of either actress damaged her career far more than individual enmity or backstage intrigue could. Political events exerted considerable influence on the theatre, and in this instance, changes in the social and political climate occasioned by Aleksandr II's assassination accelerated Strepetova's downward spiral.

The period of thaw during Aleksandr II's reign was followed after his assassination in 1881 by a period of repression and intolerance, which forced most progressive movements temporarily underground. The Imperial theatres, which were part of the state bureaucracy, conducted their operations, selected their repertoires, and hired their actors under careful surveillance by the government. If the Imperial directorate resisted innovation and controversy under the relatively liberal Aleksandr II, it had even less reason to innovate under his successor, Aleksandr III. The Aleksandrinskii Theatre, which had already added several prominent provincial actors to its company, did not invite Strepetova because the ideological, aesthetic, and class issues separating them were too great, and neither side evinced much willingness to compromise.[65]

When the directorate finally signed a contract with Strepetova, her impact was minimal because she insisted upon maintaining her class identity and "*bytovaia*" repertoire. It is not surprising, then, that she could not penetrate, or feel comfortable in, the Aleksandrinskii's exclusive, often arrogant, ensemble. In addition, even though "back-to-the-people" themes were fashionable during the 1870s and early 1880s, the intelligentsia, urban gentry, and aristocracy were generally scornful of "plebian art."[66] Once the vogue for "*bytovaia*" drama passed, therefore, spectators distanced themselves from Strepetova. Ostrovski observed that Strepetova was always somehow superfluous at the Aleksandrinskii. Despite nine years in the company, she was "like a guest artist who comes for five or six shows and leaves."[67] Attempts to assimilate her into the repertoire failed largely because, according to Ostrovski, her talent was "too extraordinary." After 1884, she was relegated to the periphery, often collecting her rather substantial salary without having been onstage for weeks.

ACTRESSES, ACTING, AND ACTOR TRAINING: STREPETOVA AS "*SAMORODOK*"

Although Ostrovski may have overstated the breadth of Strepetova's talent, he did not exaggerate its emotional depth. Her stage presence was extraordinary and her appeal, which went well beyond the purely ideological, was partially grounded in her approach to the craft of acting. Applied to Strepetova, however, the phrase "craft of acting," which implies a certain self-conscious artistry, may be misleading: her training was minimal and her approach to characterization, largely instinctual. For this reason, she was caught not only in the ideological maelstrom engulfing Russia, but also, like several other actresses in this study, in the growing controversy within the theatre community over the relative merits of talent and technique.

Complaining about the scarcity of authentic tragic actresses, Urusov noted that those few who succeeded in spite of the hegemony of comic actresses were of two types: the first was the actress who "played analytically, observed and imitated nature, seized upon certain aspects of reality, and delved deeply into [character] detail"; the second played "'by nerves' (*nervami*), did not observe or imitate nature, but was subordinate to it, and lived and suffered passionately in the role."[68] If critics were divided about virtually every other aspect of Strepetova's career, most agreed that she represented the second category: according to Iablonovski, she played entirely "by the force of intuition (*nutrom*), without subjecting the role to strict, cold analysis."[69] She was, he continued, a great "*samorodok*," by which he meant that she was an actress without education, but whose tremendous natural talent made training not only unnecessary, but perhaps even undesirable.[70]

Because both Strepetova and Savina specialized in plays from the "*bytovaia*" repertoire, critics rather indiscriminately employed the term "naturalistic" to describe their acting styles. Strepetova, however, emphasized authenticity of emotion and sincerity of feeling. "In comparison with her," I. Petrovskaia wrote, "even a brilliant realist like Savina was perceived as the representative of an alien style. However real or close to the truth Savina's acting was, the spectator was always aware that she was acting – even if it was good acting, it was acting all the same."[71] Strepetova's gift was for transporting spectators out of the auditorium into the world of the play and its characters by strength of inspiration alone. Because she appeared to "live and suffer inside the character," the audience felt what she felt and suffered what she suffered.[72] In 1884, an admirer wrote that, "like a ray of light in the dark realm of Russian art," her performances literally stunned the public. "There are many actresses," he continued, "who can perform certain roles effectively, but few who can create an indelible impression with their playing."[73]

Pisemski characterized Strepetova as "Mochalov in a skirt."[74] Pavel Mochalov, who represented the spirit of revolutionary romanticism in Russian theatre, was famous during the first half of the nineteenth century for his emotionally riveting performances. Strepetova's emotional intensity and the energy and absolute commitment with which she threw herself into a role inspired frequent comparisons with Mochalov. Like her predecessor, she was also unpredictable – brilliant at one moment, uninspired and pedestrian at the next. After seeing her in *The Storm*, Iablonovski, who appreciated the complete absence of restraint in Strepetova's performance, complained that the "yawning abysses, steep slopes, and terrible upgrades" in her acting compromised its consistency and quality. For that reason, he continued, "even the most mediocre actresses could triumph over Strepetova, who could not play as accurately, moderately, or correctly as they. But then they were not able to raise their pretty little heads to where Strepetova soared, like an eagle in the sky, during moments of inspiration."[75]

If Strepetova's critics picked up on the "soaring," neo-romantic elements of her style, her interpretive approach also presaged another, more ominous trend: the neurasthenic in the theatre. Although actors rather than actresses tended to specialize in neurasthenic characters, Strepetova, whose depictions of hysterics and madwomen were frighteningly real, was one of the first neurasthenics on the Russian stage.[76] During a performance of *The Storm*, for example, she was so transported, so completely possessed by the role, that she fainted before the curtain call and could not be revived without a doctor's assistance.[77] Most actresses who played Katerina tried to maintain a modicum of rational restraint, but Strepetova created the impression of a woman whose "brain worked abnormally."[78]

This pathological quality was a prominent feature of Strepetova's acting from her earliest years in the provinces. It became so extreme after she left the Aleksandrinskii that one critic wrote about a performance of *Family Reckonings* (*Semeinye raschety*) in 1895: "If I was a professor of nervous illnesses, I would certainly invite Madame Strepetova to my clinic and ask her to recreate the last scene for my students, which she played in a complete stupor."[79] As her popularity waned, Strepetova, who relied almost entirely upon temperament, tried to recapture spectator interest by turning up the emotional heat. But the sincerity, naturalness, and genuine emotional intensity that characterized her early work and attracted such ardent admiration now seemed unpleasantly forced, artificial, and frenzied, which in turn further alienated spectators. As one critic remarked: "This is not dramatic art; it only appeals to people who want strong emotional experiences and who enjoy watching torture, attending executions, and visiting hospital wards."[80]

Strepetova was incandescent onstage – but finally, like the proverbial moth and the flame, she burned herself out. Although critics and spectators professed to appreciate the unrestrained, unpredictable intensity of her performances, and Strepetova herself rejected suggestions that formal training might improve them, her inability to formulate a reliable, systematic method for creating a role eventually became an obstacle to sustained success. She did not, for example, have much physical strength, did not learn to pace herself on stage, and often could not sustain the impossibly high level of emotional intensity she established at the beginning of a performance. Davydov observed that she expended so much strength and physical tension on stage that, already exhausted by the second or third act, she was completely drained by the curtain.[81] Her natural talent was impressive, but she had little technique to support her emotional intensity or intuitive character choices.

More damaging was the effect of inadequate technique on her ability to play a wide variety of interesting characters. Notorious for inflexibility onstage and off, Strepetova, who specialized in victimized women, portrayed intense suffering more convincingly than any of her competitors. Regardless of the playwright's intent, in Strepetova's hands, all of her most effective characters suffered extremely from the twin plagues of class and gender oppression. Strepetova's astonishing talent for reproducing the outward signs of severe emotional distress may explain why a formerly disagreeable character like Pisemski's Lizaveta suddenly became sympathetic in her interpretation, especially during a period of heightened gender and class sensitivity. Unfortunately, however, Strepetova's natural talent was limited to variations on one theme. Although some critics, Vladimir Nemirovich-Danchenko among them, were not bothered by the absence of specifity in her historical and non-Russian characters, others complained that she was not only unconvincing, but even absurd in roles other than the "simple Russian women," which she played to such great effect.[82] Although Strepetova's inability to cross genres had already attracted negative comment in the early 1870s, it was not a professional obstacle until populism and populist drama became unfashionable after 1881. By the mid-1880s, her inability to adapt to rapidly changing social and theatrical conditions or respond to new audience expectations, had effectively halted the forward motion of her career.

Because she relied so heavily on inspiration, affected spectators deeply, but could not adapt to new roles or sustain a career, partisans on both sides of the growing controversy over training and natural talent used her example to support their own often contradictory positions. Her critics argued that training might have broadened her spectrum, thus extending the life of her career.[83] Crying that her art, which was the product of divine inspiration rather than pedestrian pedagogy, could neither be taught nor learned, Strepetova's most ardent disciples rejected the idea that formal training could improve her acting. Elated by her performance in *Bitter Fate*, Turgenev's enthusiastic response epitomized the "anti-schooling" mentality. "This was not acting, but reality," he exlaimed. "Everyone talks about schools, but what kind of school could produce the performance we saw today? You cannot learn to act like this. You can only experience the spark God put in your heart."[84] Urusov's defense of Strepetova's "art" rested upon three points: temperament is genetic; no recipe for producing an effective actor has yet been devised; and formal training, which is for mediocrities, often ruins real talent.[85]

Debate over the relative merits of actor training dragged on for decades in prerevolutionary Russia and was never resolved to the satisfaction of either party. Long before tempers cooled, however, Strepetova had receded into the background. Ultimately, it mattered little which side was "right;" her lack of formal education and training left Strepetova vulnerable to accusations of vulgarity and ignorance. Hostile critics and colleagues often used these accusations to discredit her with Aleksandrinskii administrators and audiences.

The absence of both formal actor training and a liberal education should not, however, be taken to mean that Strepetova was insufficiently serious about theatre. Her artistic integrity and sense of social responsibility were beyond question. For that reason, nothing angered the actress more than what she perceived as her colleagues' blithe indifference to their God-given calling. And, in point of fact, much of the enmity directed against her by colleagues and critics was engendered by her self-righteous intolerance of their negligence. A harshly vocal critic of theatre administrators, directors, and fellow actors, she saw no necessity to cultivate the political skills necessary to survival in any theatre, Imperial or private. The notoriously undiplomatic actress earned a reputation for saying aloud what others only dared to think. Upon being introduced to an influential director who could have promoted her career, her first words were: "Hello, I hear you're a real son of a bitch."[86] She explained to her fellow actors and actresses that they were "vulgar, disgusting, inveterate liars."[87] During a rehearsal of *The Storm*, her dissatisfaction with the actress playing Varvara rose to such a pitch that she asked another member of the company to try the role. When that unfortunate young woman confessed her ignorance of the play, Strepetova "stepped back, measured her from head to toe, and with a murderous look said: 'My dear, why are you on the stage – you might as well be a laundress or a cook.'"[88]

Strepetova's bitter disillusionment with her colleagues, with acting, and with the whole business of theatre was the subject of a posthumous article published in 1904 in *The Historical Herald (Istoricheskii vestnik)*.[89] The author, who identified herself simply as "A.G.", met Strepetova during the actress's honeymoon with her third husband, a strikingly handsome and very devoted young man whose excessive jealousy was the cause of Strepetova's third domestic tragedy.[90] On the long journey by train to Moscow, the author and the actress struck up an acquaintance. "A.G.," who claimed she wanted to see only the best in her traveling companion, was overwhelmed by Strepetova's bitterness and alienated by her vitriolic attacks on her colleagues in the theatre, all of whom were "talentless, empty-headed intriguers with no respect for their own art."[91] Because she had endured so much baseness and intrigue during her own career, Strepetova refused to allow her daughter, who had both the talent and desire to be an actress, to pursue a career in the theatre. "Today," she declared emphatically, "the more talented an actress is, the worse her life will be; talent simply engenders envy and enemies."[92]

RECONCILIATION

For all practical purposes, Strepetova's career as an Imperial actress ended when the directorate dismissed her in 1890.[93] It is odd that, in spite of her fierce anger at, and obvious dissatisfaction with, every aspect of the Aleksandrinskii Theatre, she fought to stay, first by recruiting Ostrovski, who championed her until his death in 1886, and later by futile attempts to renegotiate her contract. Before his death, Ostrovski not only interceded for her with the Imperial administration, but, hoping that the combined force of his name and her inspired acting would revive her flagging fortunes and strengthen her influence in the theatre, he wrote a play for her benefit in 1884.[94] The play, *Guilty Without Guilt (Bez viny vinovatye)*, was not one of his best, and although critics responded positively to Strepetova's performance, her position in the theatre remained tenuous.[95] Ostrovski claimed the Aleksandrinskii did its best to make her failure inevitable.[96] When he died, she lost her strongest pillar of support within the theatre – but his popularity had already diminished to such a degree that, alive or dead, he could have done little to help her. By the mid-1880s, as interest in "*bytovaia*" plays – and, by association, Strepetova's heroines – rapidly decreased, she lost her repertoire and neither she nor the Aleksandrinskii directorate could find suitable roles. Strepetova tried to counter the directorate's visible anxiety over maintaining an idle actress on a star's salary by offering to play any role they assigned her and agreeing to waive her per-performance fee – but to no avail. Arguing that Strepetova's inability to adapt to changing times and tastes forced them to take decisive action, the Aleksandrinskii directorate dismissed her in 1890.

Convinced that Machiavellian machinations and personal vendettas were behind her professional misfortunes, Strepetova left the Aleksandrinskii full of hope that a warm welcome awaited her in the provinces. She was disappointed. Her populist themes no longer resonated in Russia and the "simple Russian woman" was obsolete. Strepetova's old roles did not arouse sympathy even among her most ardent supporters, including Aleksei Suvorin.

Suvorin, whose enthusiasm for the theatre prompted him to establish his own in 1895, invited her to play Matriona in the first production in St. Petersburg of Tolstoi's *The Power of Darkness*. Although Tolstoi himself preferred the Moscow production with Olga Sadovskaia, Strepetova, who earned the sobriquet "Lady Macbeth of the provinces" for her performance, enjoyed tremendous success in St. Petersburg.[97] It was to be her last significant role. During the run of *The Power of Darkness*, Strepetova informed Suvorin's artistic director, Evtikhi Karpov, that she had been promised several additional productions if she agreed to play Matriona.[98] Karpov reported this to Suvorin, who said she was crazy, but agreed to produce them for her when she threatened to desert the cast of *The Power of Darkness*. Two of the three productions were disastrous. The production of *An Equal Fighter* (*Ravenskii borets*) was sabotaged, probably by one of Strepetova's many enemies. Hoping to disrupt the performance, someone threw a dog into the chandelier. Its howling distracted the audience and sent Strepetova into hysterics. But it was her performance as Katerina in Suvorin's revival of *The Storm* that reduced even her old ally to stunned silence. It was clear to all who witnessed it that the qualities that made Strepetova's earlier work so powerful had vanished.

Strepetova's box office was so poor after 1900 that, except for occasional philanthropic performances and dramatic readings, she performed little during the final years of her life. She remained popular with university students, many of whom supported her even through the worst years at the Aleksandrinskii.[99] Perhaps nostalgia prompted the new generation of radical youth to turn to Strepetova, who once enjoyed a reputation as a progressive artist; or perhaps they simply had so few heroes that they could overlook her increasingly reactionary, antisemitic inclinations. Not long before her death, Lidia Iavorskaia initiated negotiations with her, but they could not agree on the terms of the contract, so Strepetova, who would probably have been deeply offended by conditions at the Novyi Theatre, never worked for Iavorskaia.[100]

Although many critics decried Strepetova's shabby treatment by members of the theatre community, most also agreed that her own "difficult personality" and stubborn resistance to change were significant factors in the series of personal and professional catastrophies that befell her with frightening regularity.[101] Zinaida Kholmskaia understood perfectly the gender implications of Strepetova's fall from grace when she suggested that this "true daughter of the people" had been "betrayed by her beloved stage." Indigenous images of "*zhenstvennost*" now seemed embarrassingly primitive. For that reason, Russian theatre as an institution, as well as the majority of spectators who supported it, increasingly rejected native forms of *"zhenst-vennost"* in favor of elegant French imports.[102]

There is a final irony in Strepetova's story. When she died in 1903, her funeral service was a testament to public indifference: few spectators, journalists, critics, or playwrights paid their last respects to the actress who, just a few short years before, had been hailed as the pride of pure Russian *"zhenstvennost."* Not everyone ignored the proceedings, however, and one mourner in particular stood out among the small group gathered to pay tribute to Strepetova: Mariia Savina.[103] Always a complex and contradictory figure, Savina was distraught by the news in 1903 that Strepetova was suffering from terminal stomach cancer. According to Davydov, Savina was literally tormented by the need to reconcile with her old rival. She went to the hospital twice, but could not bring herself to cross the threshold of the woman who had considered Savina her "mortal enemy." Finally, when Strepetova's death was imminent, Savina gathered enough courage to go to her. No one was in the room with them, so what passed between the two women who represented such disparate trends in Russian theatre is unknown – but apparently Savina was satisfied that Strepetova would not carry her hostility into the grave. "When I left the hospital," Savina reported, "Strepetova blessed me with her emaciated hand and said weakly: 'God be with you.'"[104]

Whether Davydov's touching tale of deathbed reconciliation is sentimental fiction or hard fact is largely irrelevant: the story not only provides necessary closure, but also contains a grain of symbolic truth. Although Strepetova and Savina were personally hostile and represented antagonistic constructions of *"zhenstvennost,"* from a generational point of view, they shared certain cultural values and assumptions that were under siege by 1900. The new offensive was mounted not by the advocates of "elegant French imports," but by the modernists, whose aesthetics and ideology were alien to both Savina and Strepetova. Although Strepetova's populist "women of the people" went out of fashion well before Savina's chic bourgeois ladies, from the perspective of gender ideology, when Strepetova died in 1903, both she and Savina were obsolete. The Silver Age of decadence and symbolism required new constructions of *"zhenstvennost,"* most of which were inaccessible to actresses of Savina's and Strepetova's generation. The source of Savina's desire for reconciliation with her old enemy may have been her own sense of vulnerability; perhaps she preferred reconciliation with Strepetova to capitulation to a new generation of actresses headed by Vera Kommissar-zhevskaia.

6

ENTER THE
ACTRESS-ENTREPRENEUR
Anna Brenko and her successors

For the most part, Mariia Savina, Glikeriia Fedotova, Mariia Ermolova, and even Polina Strepetova functioned successfully within the constraints imposed by existing theatrical institutions, legal regulations, and social decorum. The Imperial triumvirate, consisting of Savina, Fedotova, and Ermolova, flourished within the rarefied atmosphere of the Imperial theatres. Strepetova, whose uncompromising pride in class and stubborn support for populist ideals estranged her from the three actresses with whom she might otherwise have enjoyed collegial relations, did not suit the class, ideological, or aesthetic disposition of the Imperial theatres and their audiences. Nonetheless, until the vogue for populist issues and drama diminished, she was wildly popular as a touring star on the provincial and club theatre circuit.

Because existing conditions privileged this tiny, fiercely competitive, hierarchical clique of starring actresses, few of its members were moved to challenge the dominant order. How would it profit Fedotova, Ermolova, or Savina to become actively engaged in the battle for general theatrical reform, for the rights of actresses, or even for their own artistic autonomy? Among non-aristocratic Russian women, most of whom could not aspire to social equality or professional equity, starring actresses were exceptional because they had contrived to acquire substantial wealth, autonomy, authority, and even a degree of respectability. Perhaps from the point of view of the Imperial stars, there was much to lose and little to gain from challenging the very system that guaranteed their elevated status. For that reason, despite frequent squabbles with administrators, playwrights, and directors, Fedotova and Ermolova were content to remain within the protective patriarchal embrace of the Malyi Theatre; Savina's activities were philanthropic rather than revolutionary; and even Strepetova, who had so many good reasons to protest the existing conditions of actresses' employment and seek alternatives to established institutions and conventions, was passive. Her response to her own considerable experience of discrimination consisted primarily of strident – and largely ineffectual – complaints about witless colleagues, shallow plays, and obtrusive administrators. But like the other female stars, she said little publicly about the collective exploitation and oppression of actresses.

That Russian actresses endured their situation for so long is a tribute to their patience, but because few realistic alternatives were available to them until the 1880s, especially in the capital cities, patience was less a virtue than a necessity. The monopoly of the Malyi Theatre in Moscow and the Aleksandrinskii Theatre in St. Petersburg severely limited theatrical expansion in the capital cities until after the monopoly was rescinded in 1882.[1] As long as the monopoly remained in force, actresses who were not invited to debut at one of the Imperial theatres, who failed to debut successfully, or who could not adjust to the Imperial milieu, had either to abandon acting altogether or resign themselves to the even more oppressive conditions of the provincial circuit. Following the abolition of the monopoly, however, another attractive alternative presented itself: independent entrepreneurship in the formerly interdicted capital cities.

Independent Russian actress-entrepreneurs were not unknown before 1880, but their activities were confined primarily to the provinces. The only exceptions were starring actresses who hired temporary companies for summer tours. Between 1880 and approximately 1910, however, as increasingly vociferous protests against autocratic authority began to undermine traditional hierarchies and destabilize the conditions of social life in Russia, theatrical enterprises owned and managed by women proliferated: at least fourteen women, most of them actress-managers of one sort or another, opened theatres or initiated sharing companies (*tovarishchestvo*) in Moscow, St. Petersburg, and various prominent provincial cities. This flowering of entrepreneurial spirit among women was one consequence of the ideological and aesthetic tumult that altered the course of Russian theatre during the final decades of the prerevolutionary period. The abolition of the monopoly removed a major obstacle for aspiring theatrical entrepreneurs of both sexes; several other factors, however, encouraged women, most of whom still had few legal rights and were, for that reason, at a tremendous disadvantage in the world of commerce, to set off on the risky path of independent entrepreneurship. Among the many social and theatrical factors that stimulated interest among actresses in greater professional autonomy were the women's movement and the tours by Bernhardt and Duse.

The outspoken critique by representatives of the Russian women's movement of women's dependent status was discussed in mass circulation newspapers, popular magazines, feminist publications, and theatre journals. Although few actresses identified publicly with bourgeois feminism, they were certainly familiar with the issues raised by the women's rights movement and, as working women, found some of them quite sympathetic. If actresses were rarely in the vanguard of the women's movement, many were aware of, and distressed by, economic discrimination and sexual extortion within their own profession. On a macrocosmic level, the movement increased the number of actresses by encouraging Russian women to challenge their subordinate, dependent status in society and seek paid employment; on a microcosmic level, it encouraged actresses to challenge their subordinate, dependent status within the theatre community by becoming actress-managers.[2] For that reason, after the principal legal barrier to establishing private theatrical enterprises in Moscow and St. Petersburg was eliminated, independent entrepreneurship became an increasingly attractive alternative to the hegemony of actor-managers in the private theatres and (mostly male) bureaucrats and regisseurs in the Imperials.

Shifts in gender ideology encouraged independent theatrical entrepreneurship. Although actresses in the capitals and provinces were familiar with "New Woman" rhetoric by 1880, most still preferred to play the New Woman onstage rather than behave like her offstage. If the women's movement provided Russian actresses with a theory of financial and artistic autonomy, Sarah Bernhardt and Eleonora Duse provided them with the first exemplary models of independent entrepreneurial practice. Whatever their relative merits as actresses, both Bernhardt and Duse enjoyed financial and creative autonomy unknown to even the most successful Russian actresses. The example set by Bernhardt, who traveled with her own company, owned her own theatre in Paris, and flaunted her freedom in the most outrageous fashion, must have been particularly attractive to Russian actresses, who had so few opportunities for professional self-determination. If Russian actresses hesitated to countenance publicly the more indecorous aspects of Bernhardt's escapades, they surely must have admired her entrepreneurial skill. And since critics were encouraging native actresses to imitate their Western rivals in everything else, why not as actress-managers too?

Although few were openly feminist, actress-entrepreneurs put the rhetoric of financial and artistic autonomy into practice; in that sense, they were the "New Women" of the Russian theatre. As a group, they were not homogeneous. Memoirs and other records suggest, however, that female entrepreneurs who established theatres in Moscow and St. Petersburg between 1880 and 1910 had remarkably similar experiences with respect to the commercial aspects of theatre management. Most were actress-managers who conceived of their theatres as vehicles for personal and professional advancement. Ironically, many were so overwhelmed by their new management responsibilities that acting became only an occasional pleasure once their theatres opened. Even among those who continued to perform regularly, few were motivated primarily by commercial considerations. Although a small minority of actress-managers were uncontrite profiteers, the majority were motivated by a complex combination of aesthetic dissatisfaction and desire for financial independence. Ultimately, if the criteria for success are longevity and substantial returns on their investments, none of the female entrepreneurs succeeded. It is also unfortunately true that most were not on the cutting edge of the avant-garde, nor as a group were they particularly politically progressive. Although many proclaimed publicly their devotion to elevated aesthetic and literary ideals, in reality, most produced traditional fare, the production quality of which varied with the taste and financial resources of the individual entrepreneur.

The phenomenon of the female theatrical entrepreneur is not unique to the period or to Russia. Indeed, women who owned and managed their own theatres, either independently or with a male partner, can be found in many Western European countries at least since the Renaissance, and after women began more aggressively to pursue their rights at the end of the nineteenth century, actress-managers became more common. Russia's uniqueness with respect to the proliferation of female theatrical entrepreneurs lies in its social, political, and cultural situation. Throughout the nineteenth century, pressure for social, political, and economic reform intensified in Russia, but although some progress occurred under Aleksandr II, when measured against more advanced Western nations – France, Great Britain, and even the United States, the countries with which Russians most often compared themselves – it remained remarkably repressive, autocratic, patriarchal, and generally backward. If by the end of the century, conditions in Russia were more propitious than ever before for female theatrical entrepreneurs, they were certainly not as hospitable as those in the United States or the more progressive nations of Western Europe.[3]

Although conditions in Russia were not particularly conducive to female entrepreneurship, an astonishing number of actresses, both starring and non-starring, managed their own theatrical enterprises. This chapter considers the activities of four actress-entrepreneurs who established theatrical enterprises in Moscow and St. Petersburg between 1880 and 1900. The most significant, Anna Brenko, founded and managed the first legal private professional art theatre in Moscow in 1880. Following Brenko's example, Mariia Abramova, Elizaveta Goreva, and Elizaveta Shabelskaia attempted to establish theatres in the capital cities in the 1890s. Their memoirs, articles about their theatres, and reviews of their productions provide a valuable source of information about the experiences and status of actress-entrepreneurs in the prerevolutionary period.

ANNA BRENKO AND THE PUSHKIN THEATRE

Bernard Shaw once said of Edy Craig, the manager of the Pioneer Players in Britain, that her brother, Gordon, had "made himself the most famous producer in Europe by dint of never producing anything, while Edith Craig remains the most obscure by dint of producing everything."[4] If Shaw had known Anna Brenko, Russia's first prominent actress-manager, he might have said the same of her. Although no famous brother overshadows her, Brenko remains one of the most undeservedly obscure figures in the history of Russian theatre. Undervalued, underutilized, and undistinguished during her tenure as an actress at the Imperial Malyi Theatre, Brenko was one of the earliest to respond to calls for theatrical reform when she established

Moscow's first continuously producing, professional private theatrical enterprise, the Pushkin Theatre. Much of the credit for advancing the concept of a private "art" theatre, for emphasizing the ensemble over starring actors, and for using the theatre as a vehicle for serious ideas must go to Brenko, a progressive actress-entrepreneur whose ideas and achievements can best be understood against the general background of theatrical conditions and conventions in the capital cities.

Despite the brilliance of a few part-time playwrights and inspired actors, generally speaking, Russian theatre and drama were, according to many critics, pitifully debased during the last decades of the nineteenth century. In St. Petersburg and Moscow, vaudevilles, melodramas, and salon comedies predominated in the repertoires of the Imperial theatres; neo-Slavophile factions and advocates of Westernization squabbled over the relative merits of Western European influence; the Imperial monopoly and rigid censorship severely inhibited both the writing and production of thoughtful native drama; production practices were obsolete and careless and most plays were woefully under-rehearsed; even in the last decades of the century, the Wagnerian concepts of the unified artwork and omnipotent master artist were little understood or appreciated; the Imperial theatres continued to use a benefit system that rewarded actors arbitrarily and gave them too much authority over the repertoire; and, finally, theatres in the capitals were usually managed by incompetent state-appointed bureaucrats. It is no wonder that, in 1871, an anonymous critic observed in *The European Herald* (*Vestnik evropy*): "The theatre is disintegrating. People who love art and take it seriously have completely stopped attending Russian theatre because they cannot find anything in it except zealous cultivation of 'amusements' that are not appropriate for a respectable theatre."[5] The author offered three simple solutions: abolish the Imperial monopoly, increase the authority of the *regisseur*, and emphasize the ensemble.

Arguing that the future health of Russian theatre would be determined by the outcome of an ongoing struggle by private theatres for legal recognition, A.I. Urusov called the Imperial monopoly a "comedy." Russian theatre, which was stagnating in a sort of "pre-reform" (*doreformennyi*) purgatory, was, he complained, a bureaucratic rather than an artistic activity. For Urusov, the two most frequently offered justifications for maintaining the monopoly – social control and profit – were specious: it was, he argued, the business of the police, the court, and the censor to preserve social order, and state supported theatres should be dedicated to art, not profit.[6]

Urusov began publishing his polemics on the theatre in the 1870s, but even in the 1860s, murmurs of discontent were audible among progressive actors, playwrights, and critics. Calls for theatrical reform, which became increasingly insistent during the late 1870s and 1880s, did not go unheeded. Although Anna Brenko mounted the most successful challenge to the hegemony of the Imperial theatres before 1882, she was hardly the first to try; her Pushkin

Theatre, which was founded in 1880, had several important antecedents. During the 1860s and 1870s, spectators in Moscow and St. Petersburg who wanted alternatives to the fare offered by the Imperial theatres could attend a variety of amateur performances (*liubitelskie spektakli*). So-called "club stages" (*klubnye stseny*) produced "readings" (*chtenie*), "family evenings" (*semeinye vechera*) with music and dancing, as well as scenes from plays, usually without makeup, costumes, or scenery. In addition, many prominent actors and actresses participated regularly in philanthropic performances.[7] In the early 1880s, Urusov proposed an "evolutionary" model for the rise of private theatres in Russia: private theatres "were born in amateur productions, crawled on all fours in philanthropic performances, strengthened in the club theatres, and now they've finally achieved semi-legal status."[8]

Although a few semi-legal club theatres dotted the landscape in St. Petersburg and Moscow during the 1870s, their stability was precarious. The ministers and bureaucrats who determined government policies on the arts generally represented the interests of the state rather than the interests of artists. Because they could not agree on the desirability or feasibility of private theatres, the regulations governing them changed with alarming frequency. Today's laws might be obsolete tomorrow, and entrepreneurs, directors, and performers could not predict what new tax, fee, or regulation might be imposed next. Managers of the club and semi-legal private stages were required to pay an arbitrary per-performance fee to the Imperial theatres and all of their posters had to be designed and manufactured by the state's printer at exorbitant costs. Urusov remarked that, under existing conditions, only the strongest, most persistent individuals could establish and sustain theatrical enterprises.[9]

The club stages and semi-private theatres were amateur undertakings: they did not enjoy fully legal status; they could not produced plays in their entirety; their entertainments were strictly regulated; and their actors were either moonlighting from the Imperial theatres, on tour from the provinces, or strictly amateur. Brenko's was the first fully professional private theatre: called variously the "Theatre near the Pushkin Monument" (*Teatr bliz pamiatnika Pushkina*), The Pushkin Theatre, or simply Brenko's theatre, it occupied an important rung on Urusov's evolutionary ladder.[10] Although two prominent provincial actors, Modest Pisarev and Vasili Andreev-Burlak, later shared management responsibilities with her, Brenko was solely responsible for initiating and organizing the new enterprise.

In his memoirs, Iuri Iurev, a friend of several Pushkin actors who was familiar with the theatre's operations, observed that Brenko was a woman "fanatically devoted to art."[11] That her fanaticism was accompanied by amazing energy and devotion to the theatre is confirmed by her astonishing resiliency: in spite of a series of demoralizing experiences with unscrupulous actors, directors, bureaucrats, and lawyers, which contributed to the ruin of her theatre, left her with considerable financial debt, and wrecked her

Figure 5 Actress-manager Anna Brenko of the Pushkin Theatre.
Courtesy of the Central State Archive of Literature
and Art (TsGALI)

personal life, she maintained an abiding faith in the theatre. First she acted, then she tried her luck at management and playwriting, and finally, she turned to directing and teaching. Her directorial activities confirm Brenko as an anomaly among actresses of the period: if female entrepreneurs were oddities in the late nineteenth and early twentieth centuries, female directors were even more unusual. In the case of Brenko, not only did she open the first private professional art theatre two years before the abolition of the Imperial monopoly, but she also established the first worker's theatre three years before the revolution and directed its productions.[12] Given her achievements, Brenko's obscurity seems even more remarkable.

Brenko staged her first independent productions with an amateur troupe:

in the summer of 1879, she produced several outdoor performances in support of students arrested by the police.[13] Although this action may have had a political subtext, in her memoirs, Brenko suggests more benign motives: she wanted to open her own theatre, but had no experience producing plays. Staging philanthropic performances on behalf of the students presented a perfect opportunity to acquire the requisite knowledge and skills.[14] According to Brenko's biographer, R. Vitenzon, dissatisfaction with working conditions at the Malyi Theatre and with its aesthetic principles galvanized Brenko to challenge the monopoly by opening her own theatre.[15] In her memoirs, Brenko states her preference for "Shakespeare and all the classics," and complains about the Malyi Theatre's inadequate, obsolete production practices. In her opinion, the absence of strong directors at the Malyi damaged both the company and the quality of their productions.[16]

Brenko's frequent observations in interviews and in her memoirs about the treatment of performers offer further clues to her objectives. Like many secondary players, Brenko chafed under the restrictions imposed upon her by the Malyi directorate. Calling her employment at the Malyi "bondage," she proclaimed the necessity for "free art." The time had come to rise up against the "evils" of state institutions like the Malyi and create theatres based on new principles: her theatre would be one in which "principles of brotherhood and fellowship reigned."[17] Her motives were not, however, entirely altruistic; like many actresses, she also dreamed of creating a theatre in which she could not only perform on a regular basis, but also play her favorite roles. She wrote: "When I read Shakespeare, Schiller, and Calderon, my mind roamed freely, but [in the Malyi] with its trivial repertoire, everyone felt dispirited and oppressed. Because my own aesthetic sensibilities and desires diverged from more widely held views on art, I pulled myself together and began planning my escape. The imperative to break away was even stronger because I hated operetta and vaudeville and was dissatisfied with the roles I had to play in them."[18] Her emancipation fantasies extended to her colleagues: "When I joined the Imperial stage," she wrote, "I was struck by the fact that these great actors lived like slaves instead of free artists."[19] Did she succeed in freeing them? At least one Soviet critic thought so when he proclaimed in 1924 that the fall of "serfdom in the theatre" was finally accomplished by Brenko.[20]

Soviet revisionism and Brenko's own elevated rhetoric complicate the task of establishing the Pushkin Theatre's original objectives. Soviet theatre historians often impute revolutionary and philanthropic motives to Brenko. Undoubtedly, she was an unusual actress: she enjoyed a higher level of education than most of her peers and she leaned toward liberal politics.[21] There is, however, little more than circumstantial evidence that the Pushkin Theatre intentionally provoked social unrest or that it was a "people's theatre" in the sense of an organization with an ideological agenda whose objective was to make popular or educational drama accessible to lower-class audiences.[22] Her later associations with workers' theatre were unambiguously political, but during the Pushkin period, Brenko's motivations were primarily literary and aesthetic. The Pushkin Theatre, which appealed predominantly to the intelligentsia, was designed not as an antidote to the Malyi, but as its rival.[23]

Perhaps the only certain conclusion that can be drawn about Brenko's entrepreneurial objectives is that they were multiple and complex. She was dissatisfied with her position at the Malyi for personal and professional reasons; she was interested in innovation and reform; she wanted artistic and financial independence – and, like most ambitious performers, she was self-interested. Brenko's experiences staging summer performances in the park spurred her ambition and she began to explore new ways to circumvent the Imperial monopoly. The Pushkin Theatre officially opened on September 9, 1880, but Brenko began hustling her scheme for a fully legal professional private theatre well before this. In the winter of 1880, she traveled to St. Petersburg to petition the Society for Christian Assistance for their support in producing a series of philanthropic performances. The Society agreed to sponsor her, but the money to support the performances came from Brenko's own pocket. She rented the Solodovnikov Theatre for the presentation of several musical-literary evenings which included readings of scenes from plays. Although these were "evenings with songs and declamation without scenery, makeup, and costume," several prominent provincial actors and friends from the Malyi Theatre (including Mariia Ermolova) agreed to participate.[24] Elated by the success of her enterprise, she wrote enthusiastically about the relationship with her new colleagues: "because everything was done by general consensus and no oppressive forces constrained us, the work was easy: we were free people working on our own initiative."[25] The ambitious, indefatigable Brenko pushed the boundaries of the state monopoly. Even in the early stages of her career as an independent entrepreneur she disregarded many of the government's restrictions and each day she grew bolder.

Although Brenko lost 6,000 roubles on her philanthropic entertainments, she was not discouraged. The experience taught her a great deal about lobbying the government for permission to stage theatrical entertainments and she used the Solodovnikov performances to arrange debuts for provincial performers. Once she was familiar with the best the provinces had to offer, she could choose among them for her future theatrical enterprise.[26] Ultimately, however, the relationship with the Society for Christian Assistance was not satisfactory. Brenko returned to St. Petersburg to petition for a private theatrical enterprise that could produce fully mounted plays in their entirety. With the help of her husband, Osip Levenson, a distinguished lawyer and music critic, she cultivated useful relationships with several prominent state officials who helped her to obtain permission from the Ministry of the

Imperial Court to open a private theatre, but with the proviso that she produce only "scenes from plays."[27]

Advertisements in *The Russian Gazette* (*Russkie vedomosti*) suggest that, at least publicly, Brenko complied with the Ministry's restrictions, but in point of fact, she was offering audiences fully mounted productions with all the trimmings.[28] Brenko argued that had the restrictions been reasonable, she would have complied, but because "no one paid attention to amateur performances" she had to risk the Ministry's displeasure and produce plays in their entirety in order to attract paying spectators.[29] As one critic noted, however, the theatre was in a perilous position: "If one civil servant had decided to inform his superiors that Brenko was producing entire plays – the business would have been finished."[30] In the spring of 1880, Brenko contracted for renovations on the building that would open in September as the Pushkin Theatre. The Pushkin's first production, Nikolai Gogol's *The Government Inspector*, featured a cast of distinguished professional actors who were lured from the provinces by promises of high salaries, a voice in management, and increased artistic satisfaction.

Brenko accomplished the transition from staging readings, family evenings, and scenes from plays to administering a full-scale private theatrical enterprise with astonishing rapidity. Because she and her husband were relatively wealthy, she had both the leisure and the financial resources to manage and pay for her initial forays into independent entrepreneurship. As the enterprise expanded, however, she was quick to understand the need for additional financial, administrative, and artistic support. Because commercial theatres were suppressed in the capital cities, few of the idealistic theatre artists who aspired to independent entrepreneurship in Moscow and St. Petersburg had enough experience with the exigencies of private enterprise to understand that creating and sustaining a private theatre required firm personal commitment, iron-willed tenacity, and significant financial resources. Early entrepreneurs like Brenko had to find creative ways to finance their ventures and persuade professional actors to accept the legitimacy of theatres operating on the periphery of the familiar system. With respect to financing her enterprise, Brenko hit upon a method that many subsequent independent theatrical entrepreneurs found indispensable: she persuaded a philanthropic millionaire with a prediliction for theatre to subsidize her.

S.M. Malkiel, who made his fortune supplying footwear to the Russian military during the Russo–Turkish War, became Brenko's silent partner.[31] Malkiel had purchased two mansions on Tverskaia Street, one of which was supposedly haunted. Having concluded that his private needs could be satisfied by one mansion, he allowed Brenko to use the other – the haunted one – and agreed to subsidize the extensive interior renovations necessary to transform it into a luxurious private theatre.[32]

By all accounts, the Pushkin Theatre exuded elegance. The exterior resembled the Renaissance Theatre in Paris. The interior included brass bannisters, oriental carpets, foyer walls covered with portraits of famous actors, and a hall lined with busts of classic playwrights.[33] The stage and auditorium, designed by Chichagov, a distinguished Moscow architect, were the "pearls" of the theatre. The trimming and curtain were light blue, the decorations were simple and tasteful, and the dressing rooms were so ample that one actress remarked: "the director of this theatre certainly cares about actors."[34] The resources both Malkiel and Brenko put into the theatre suggest that they did not conceive of it as a peripheral, amateur enterprise, but rather as a genuine alternative to the Malyi.

In the process of hiring her first company of actors, Brenko skimmed the cream off the top of the provincial circuit. Her luxurious new theatre, which housed a troupe of the most accomplished, professional provincial actors in Russia during the period, included several stars, among them Pisarev, Andreev-Burlak, and Polina Strepetova. Giliarovski claimed that Brenko paid the actors "sky-high sums of money" for their services.[35] Indeed, many Pushkin actors were highly paid even by Imperial theatre standards. Strep-etova, who was especially well paid for her services, received 300 roubles per performance.[36]

Although Brenko herself had no experience of life on the provincial circuit, while staging the performances for the Society for Christian Assistance with Pisarev and Andreev-Burlak, she became painfully aware of the abuses and inequities heaped on provincial actors. Perhaps conversations with the two provincial actors, along with her own experiences at the Malyi, raised her consciousness about acting as an honorable, professional activity. In turn, the company's initial enthusiasm for the new enterprise was fueled by more than the profit motive. Glama-Meshcherskaia, whose memoirs provide an excellent picture of the Pushkin experiment's positive features, argued that Brenko had created something unique in Russia. "My first acquaintance with the Pushkin Theatre and its personnel," she wrote, "left me with the impression that I was in a new world."[37]

Elegant, fully equipped dressing rooms and high salaries certainly contributed to the new company's general enthusiasm, but perhaps equally important was the emphasis placed by Brenko, Pisarev, and Andreev-Burlak on ensemble performance.[38] If, like so many actress-managers, Brenko originally intended to create a vehicle for her own stardom, that part of her scheme failed to materialize. Brenko rarely performed except in emergencies, and although the company included a star of Strepetova's magnitude and Pisarev and Andreev-Burlak tended to monopolize the leading male roles, in general the Pushkin was not a theatre of starring performers.[39] A.I. Urusov, an ardent supporter of the private theatre concept, said of the Pushkin company that it was an "excellent, highly disciplined ensemble of provincial actors." From his point of view, Brenko had demonstrated that in the right context and with adequate support, "good things could come from provincial actors."[40] Glama-Meshcherskaia wrote that the company lived like one big family; another actor observed that he had never before experienced such friendly working relations among actors. The Pushkin was, in Glama's words, "an authentic actors' artel" rather than an autocratic theatrical enterprise.[41]

The sense that the Pushkin was a democratic association of actresses and actors was reinforced by its formal organization. Although D.I. Zolotniski complained about the retrospective hyperbole surrounding Pushkin Theatre, even he acknowledged that its democratic form of management was genuinely innovative.[42] Together, Brenko, Pisarev, and Andreev-Burlak formed an "Artistic Council." Brenko and Andreev-Burlak assumed most of the administrative responsibilities and Pisarev was the titular "artistic director."[43] Because it was organized democratically, the Pushkin was not subject to the whims of a single starring actress or actor. Rather, artistic and administrative decisions were made and implemented collectively by the Artistic Council.

Brenko also reformed the rehearsal system. For the first production, the company gathered to rehearse a full two weeks before the opening – an unfamiliar luxury for provincial actors who were in the habit of throwing productions together with one rehearsal. Later, the usual rehearsal period was between three and four weeks. The Pushkin also gave their productions longer consecutive runs than was customary in either the provincial or the Imperial theatres, which continued to change bills almost nightly.[44] The Pushkin's innovations lend credence to the idea that the reform of Russian theatre was underway long before 1898 when the Moscow Art Theatre opened its doors, and that Nikolai Sinelnikov, and later the MAT's directors, were not the first to recognize the desirability of ensemble playing and the need for extended rehearsals.[45]

If Brenko was not prepared to initiate radical departures from traditional staging, she was certainly progressive. Perhaps she is best understood as a transitional figure, a sort of Russian Marie Wilton.[46] Brenko sought a certain degree of historical accuracy in production, but even though she complained of the absence of strong directors at the Malyi, like most actress-managers of the period, she had little appreciation for the Wagnerian concept of the omnipotent master artist.[47] "The stage," she argued, "is not an orchestra; for that reason, the leadership of that type of director is not only unnecessary, but patently absurd because it would inhibit the development of talented actors."[48] Nonetheless, Brenko fulfilled many of the functions of a *regisseur* as it was then defined in Russia, and her position at the Pushkin required her to be involved in every aspect of production.[49]

There is no question that Brenko directed later in her career and may even have been the first legitimate female *regisseur* in Russia. It is doubtful, however, whether she "directed" at the Pushkin in the Saxe-Meiningen sense of the word; the definition of a *regisseur* as a glorified stage manager better describes Brenko's role in the Pushkin's production process. Among the-atrical enterprises managed by women, however, this arrangement was not unusual: actress-entrepreneurs employed male regisseurs and, by Glama-Meshcherskaia's account, Modest Pisarev was the Pushkin's "artistic director." Brenko had only a modest performance résumé when she initiated the Pushkin experiment and never distinguished herself as an actress, but the fact that she did not govern her theatre autocratically does not necessarily mean she considered herself less of an artist or that she simply handed the artistic reigns over to Pisarev. Indeed, her concern for, and influence on, aesthetic quality was confirmed when she hired Aleksandr Fedotov to direct at the Pushkin after critics reproached the company for the poor quality of several productions.[50]

Brenko's own artistic and literary predilictions were clearly visible in the policies governing the Pushkin's repertoire. That she conceived of the Pushkin as an "art theatre" is clear from her insistence upon maintaining a repertoire that would appeal primarily to the intelligentsia. Both Giliarovski and Glama-Meshcherskaia reported that while Brenko managed the company, commercial considerations never superseded artistic. Iuri Iurev claimed that the Pushkin's directors tried to protect their theatre from "the mediocre tastes of the shallow, bourgeois public."[51]

Although Brenko, Pisarev, and Andreev-Burlak applied democratic principles to managing the theatre, Brenko's authority over the repertoire was absolute. When she hired Fedotov, it was with the understanding that he would not take it upon himself to alter the theatre's fundamental nature, that the repertoire would remain strictly literary, and that she would continue to choose the plays.[52] Brenko, who cared deeply about the quality of the repertoire, wanted to introduce audiences to plays by the best foreign and native dramatists. In keeping with its founder's objectives, in the first month alone the Pushkin produced five plays by Ostrovski, two by Gogol, one by Turgenev, Shakespeare's *Hamlet*, Lessing's *Emilia Galotti*, Moliere's *The Forced Marriage*, as well as comedies and serious dramas by several respectable, native *"bytovaia"* playwrights. In subsequent months, Brenko and her collaborators staged plays by Schiller, Griboedov, Saltykov-Shchedrin, Lermontov, Hugo, Dumas *fils*, Aleksei Tolstoi, and Zola, among others.[53] The occasional Scribean melodrama also crept into the repertoire, but for the most part, Brenko maintained the standards of a genuine art theatre even in the face of growing opposition from her actors. Her choice of plays was not, perhaps, revolutionary, and she did not have the good fortune to discover a Chekhov among the native playwrights, but she fought to preserve literary and artistic standards throughout the theatre's two-year history.

Extant reviews of Pushkin productions are bewilderingly contradictory. Although Brenko insisted upon a thoughtful repertoire, spent considerable sums on production, introduced popularly priced matinees for students, and emphasized ensemble playing, reviews suggest that the aesthetic quality of Pushkin productions was uneven and did not always match its founder's elevated ideals.[54] Still a student when he began reviewing productions at the

Pushkin, Nemirovich-Danchenko praised Brenko's repertoire. The Pushkin, he wrote, "offered food for the mind," while the Malyi's repertoire was an idle "plaything." Nemirovich was often critical, however, of the "absence of a stable standard of acting." Although he did not care for romantic dramas like Lermontov's *Masquerade*, Nemirovich acknowledged that the production values were impressive.[55] Urusov, who consistently supported private theatres in principle and in fact, wrote that the Pushkin Theatre's success established private theatres as a reality in Russia, and singled out Pisarev, Andreev-Burlak, and Strepetova for special praise.[56] In a brief review of one of Fedotov's productions, Urusov expressed his delight with the careful staging, new sets and costumes, and effective lighting, and added that the actors, who had enjoyed sixteen rehearsals, formed an impressive ensemble. Although Urusov occasionally criticized the Pushkin's repertoire, he commended the Artistic Council for their willingness to produce plays that had been censored by the Malyi's literary-theatrical committee: "This private enterprise," he wrote, "does honor to the production of plays that are contrary to the reigning repertoire, plays that cannot rely on great commercial success."[57] Ostrovski, whose relationship to Brenko's enterprise oscillated between harsh criticism and active support, complained that management problems and a noticeable lack of discipline among some of the actors undermined the rehearsal process and spoiled several productions. Nonetheless, he acknowledged that the Pushkin competed successfully with the Malyi and praised its support for playwrights.[58]

Despite its promising beginnings and generally enthusiastic reception, Brenko's experiment lasted only two years, failing just before the monopoly was officially repealed in 1882. At the time, the Pushkin seemed to be enjoying substantial success. Glama-Meshcherskaia claimed that box office receipts were good, perhaps the best in Moscow, and the Pushkin attracted the same spectators that attended the Malyi Theatre.[59] During the second season, Brenko won Ostrovski's support and enjoyed congenial relations with many theatrical luminaries, including Mariia Ermolova and Ivan Turgenev. She and her husband were wealthy, well-connected, and enjoyed the financial support of their silent partner, Malkiel. If the Pushkin's success seemed so certain, why did it collapse?

Contemporaneous sources offer divergent, often contradictory accounts of the Pushkin's demise, but most agree that when Malkiel was forced to withdraw his support, collapse was inevitable. Although Brenko made many enemies during her tenure at the Pushkin, there is no evidence of personal enmity with Malkiel. His reasons for withdrawing were apparently purely economic. Giliarovski's explanation of the breakdown of their relationship is particularly novel. By his account, the financial arrangement between the actress and her millionaire was jeopardized by an architectural accident. A balcony attached to Malkiel's personal residence collapsed, injuring several pedestrians on the street below. Newspapers sensationalized the incident, lawsuits followed, and the resulting financial pressure on Malkiel forced him to withdraw support from the theatre. Although box office receipts were good, they did not cover the theatre's expenses and, bereft of her patron, Brenko was left without a kopek.[60]

A.V. Anisimov offers a more plausible explanation. Malkiel was spending outrageous sums of money on the Pushkin Theatre until his wife suddenly returned to Moscow from Paris and put a stop to it. In addition, Malkiel was under criminal investigation for selling poor-quality shoes and boots to the military. Pressure from his wife, along with the enormous expenditures required to mount a legal defense, forced him to curtail his support for the theatre. When Brenko's creditors discovered Malkiel's financial instability, they refused to compromise on her debts; because box office alone could not cover expenses, she was forced to close the theatre.[61]

V. Maslikh fails to mention the balcony, the wife, or the lawsuit, but does agree that box office receipts were not sufficient to cover expenditures. He blames the limited dimensions of the Pushkin's auditorium. Even if the company had played to packed houses every night, they could not, Maslikh argued, have taken in enough money to cover the theatre's expenses.[62]

Glama-Meshcherskaia suggested that Brenko herself unwittingly undermined the closely knit artistic ensemble by staging productions outside the Pushkin Theatre itself (*vyezdnye spektakli*) while the building was undergoing further renovations. "These productions," she wrote, "had a pernicious effect on the company's unity; our routines were altered, and the ensemble that had developed during a year of working together was undermined."[63]

All of these factors were implicated in the theatre's ruin: Malkiel did withdraw his support, the Pushkin auditorium was too small to generate substantial box office receipts, and Brenko was a victim of her own ambition. Anna Brenko was an energetic entrepreneur with expansionist inclinations; renovations to the Pushkin may simply have been a convenient rationalization for the external productions. In her own memoirs, she acknowledged that by 1882, she was supporting three theatres and a troupe of fifty actors: her company performed at the Pushkin Theatre, the Solodovnikov Theatre, and the German Club. On Sundays, they mounted as many as five productions within the three venues.[64]

The most frequent charge laid by her critics was that Brenko lacked the common sense to run a business. Complaining in 1886 that the promise of a post-monopoly theatre had not been fulfilled, P.A. Kanshin called Brenko's theatre the first major disappointment of the post-reform era. The problem, he argued, was Brenko herself. She was an "extremely impractical" woman, who "could not deal effectively with provincial actors, and who behaved in an inappropriately careless and unconstrained manner."[65] Her company of fifty actresses and actors included far too many inessential people, and even worse, she lured provincial stars by offering them excessively high salaries.

The theatre was conceived too expansively from the beginning, Kanshin concluded, which made bankruptcy inevitable.

Echoing Kanshin, B.A. Shchetinin also blamed the Pushkin's collapse on Brenko's managerial inexperience.[66] An anonymous critic suggested in *Theatre and Art* that the Pushkin's deficit resulted from the enormous sums Brenko spent on productions; another wrote in *The Theatrical Gazette* (*Teatralnaia gazeta*) that, although the theatre was eventually torn apart by internal dissension, the root of the problem lay in the Pushkin Theatre's novelty – it was neither an Imperial, nor a provincial theatre, and no one was prepared to manage it properly.[67] Many unkind things were written about Brenko and about her alleged mismanagement of the theatre. Perhaps for that reason, she felt compelled to defend herself by telling her version of the events leading to the theatre's collapse. Her unpublished memoirs and *Sovremennyi liud*, a play she wrote in 1882, paint a picture of a woman who put all of her resources – financial, emotional, and physical – into her enterprise, only to lose control of her company through plotting and betrayal by the people she most trusted.[68]

In the memoirs, Brenko assumed responsibility for some managerial misjudgments. She wanted her theatre to be "perfect and brilliant," and was so encouraged by the Pushkin's initial successes that she made hasty, immoderate expenditures, which left her deeply in debt when good fortune ceased to smile upon the enterprise. She had good reason to feel confident, however: during the winter season, the Pushkin's auditorium was full while the Malyi's was half empty. Brenko saw no reason to be anxious about going into debt, so she spent thousands of roubles on costumes, scenery, and salary increases, confident that all would be repaid by Lent. But when the People's Will assassinated Aleksandr II and the state ordered her to close the theatre for six months of mourning, financial disaster struck.[69]

For three days Brenko sat in her room contemplating the situation: "I suddenly emerged from an enchanted world of hope and rapture," she wrote, "into a very nasty reality."[70] The theatre was sold out two weeks in advance and she had already spent the income – but if there were no productions, spectators had to be reimbursed. Brenko pawned her most valuable possessions and gave the money to the box office manager to return to the public. Her financial situation was made more desperate by the fact that she had already rented an Imperial summer theatre in Petrovskii Park and spent considerable sums on renovations, scenery, costumes, and properties. When friends advised her to save herself by relinquishing the summer theatre, Brenko balked. Instead, she announced to the company that if they would agree to work temporarily at half salary, she would not cancel the summer season. Desperate for jobs, the actors and actresses rejoiced and thanked her repeatedly. The unfortunate Brenko, who relied on their "word of honor" (*chestnoe slovo*) and did not negotiate written contracts, lived to regret her ill-considered benevolence.

During the summer season, Brenko divided her time between producing plays in Moscow and petitioning bureaucrats and ministers in St. Petersburg for full legal status. While negotiating with the government in St. Petersburg, she began to lose control of the company: the actors behaved irresponsibly, skipping rehearsals and altering the repertoire without her permission. The quality of the productions deteriorated and business was uneven. The actors, who quickly learned to play Brenko and her partners against each other, wanted more money and increased control over the repertoire. When she returned from St. Petersburg, they had already forgotten their "word of honor" and demanded full salaries; Brenko paid them at a personal loss of 18,000 roubles. Pisarev and Andreev-Burlak, who responded sympathetically to the actors' complaints, pressured Brenko to give up her rights as entre-preneur, reorganize the enterprise into a *tovarishchestvo*, and release it into the hands of the actors. Brenko refused to yield. From her point of view, a sharing company was simply not feasible; if these provincial bumpkins, who wanted to produce "melodramas and other worthless genres," acquired any power over the repertoire, everything she had worked to create would be destroyed. At one point, emotions reached such a pitch that the actors began screaming: "Down with the enterprise, down with the exploiter, Brenko is an exploiter!"[71]

Brenko was persuaded that Fedotov, Pisarev, and Fedor Korsh were deliberately stirring up the company as part of a plot to take the theatre from her. Perhaps because he was not an artist, but a wealthy lawyer and a sharp, callous businessman, her anger was directed primarily at Korsh. As a sort of investment, Korsh rented the Pushkin's cloakroom from Brenko for 23,000 roubles a year, pocketing the profit from the 20 kopeks spectators paid to hang their coats. According to Brenko, Korsh insinuated himself with her husband, Osip Levenson, then persuaded Levenson to hire one of his toadies and give him an office. This informant reported to his boss that the theatre earned as much as 600,000 roubles a year. Impressed by the theatre's value, Korsh resolved to create dissension among the partners and turn the company against Brenko so that he could acquire it.

According to Brenko, Korsh ruined her financially by undermining the faith of her creditors in her financial stability. He achieved this by bribing an already hostile critic to plant stories in the *Moscow Leaflet* (*Moskovskii listok*) about the Pushkin Theatre's imminent financial collapse.[72] The moment her panicked creditors read the articles, Brenko was ruined: they demanded immediate satisfaction of debts that she had counted on paying over time. Simultaneously, Korsh instigated rebellion among her distraught actors by hinting that Brenko intended to abandon the theatre, leaving them without wages or future employment. He and Fedotov calmed the actors' fears by persuading most of them to sign contracts with *their* new company. Eventu-ally, they succeeded in wresting the Pushkin Theatre from her, and Brenko and Levenson, who had invested all of their resources in the theatre, were left without a kopek.[73]

ANNA BRENKO'S HERITAGE

Ironically, during the summer of 1881, while Korsh, Fedotov, and Pisarev were intriguing against her in Moscow, Brenko was winning the battle over the Imperial monopoly in St. Petersburg. Having secured letters of support from influential representatives of the Moscow aristocracy, Brenko set off for St. Petersburg. There she found sympathy for her cause among various ministers and government officials, several of whom enjoyed the tsar's confidence. Upon arriving in the city, she went straight to Count Vorontsov to complain about the suppression of private theatres and the unreasonable conditions imposed upon her by Baron Kister, an enormously powerful court inspector who formulated and enforced the policies governing theatre in the capital cities. Kister, a formidable figure in the history of late nineteenth-century Russian theatre, wielded considerable power over both Imperial and private theatres in Moscow and St. Petersburg. For that reason, a brief digression on the Baron and his policies helps to explain the urgency of Brenko's mission.

According to F.A. Budrin, who worked for the Imperial theatres between 1843 and 1883, during the ministry of Count Adlerberg, the independence of the director of the Imperial theatres was almost completely undermined.[74] Contracts with actors and salary increases were granted by the minister himself; expenditures on productions were determined not by the director, but by a ministry inspector. During this period, S.A. Gedeonov was appointed director of theatre and Baron Kister rose to a powerful position in Adlerberg's circle. Although the spirits of many theatre artists were buoyed by the appointment of the youthful, liberal Gedeonov, the hostility between him and Kister, who enjoyed Adlerberg's sympathy, rendered him powerless. Thwarted in his attempts to introduce reform, Gedeonov eventually withdrew and simply refused to participate in governance of the Imperial theatres.

Following Gedeonov's resignation, the director's position remained vacant, leaving Baron Kister, then an inspector for the Imperial court, free to assume management of the Imperial theatres. Kister, an ex-officer and insignificant civil servant (supervisor of the Botanical Gardens), was an energetic, cunning *parvenu* who achieved a brilliant career by making himself indispensable to Adlerberg. A man with little interest in or love for art, his request to manage the Imperial theatres was entirely self-interested. Kister's theory and practice of theatre management were dictated by the profit motive; he quickly gained a reputation for economy by cutting expenditures to the bone in the Imperial theatres and imposing substantial fees and taxes – both legal and illegal – on anyone connected with theatre in Moscow and St. Petersburg.

According to Budrin, Kister's machinations were assisted by a certain "L," who surpassed his mentor's example. "L" eliminated subsistence salaries for graduates of the theatre schools; he promised salary increases that were never bestowed; and the fees he assessed on private theatres were so excessive that few entrepreneurs could afford to pay them. He closed club theatres capriciously and in Moscow literally robbed entrepreneurs with demands for money and favors. As a result, the Imperial theatres became increasingly filthy and unpleasant, and settings and costumes turned to rubbish. Private theatres simply could not flourish under the terms imposed on them. Under these conditions, it is no wonder that people who cared about the future of theatre in Russia finally challenged the monopoly.

Having listened sympathetically to Brenko's complaints, Vorontsov carried her petition for legalization of the Pushkin Theatre personally to the tsar, who signed it.[75] Assuring Brenko that official notification would arrive shortly, the Count sent her home – where she waited for three weeks before receiving a letter informing her that the tsar had refused the petition. Brenko's first reaction was to rush back to her most influential champion in Moscow, Prince Dolgorukov, who composed a new letter of support.[76] Then, letter in hand, she hastened to St. Petersburg where, upon arrival, her enemy's identity was revealed: acting against the tsar's instructions, Baron Kister had refused to recognize the legitimacy of her petition. Vorontsov and her other intercessors went back to the tsar who, reacting furiously to Kister's insubordination, dismissed him and appointed a commission to investigate conditions in the theatres. Brenko returned to Moscow to await the results of their investigation. Eventually, the commission repealed the monopoly, granted legal status to the Pushkin Theatre, and devised new regulations for governing theatre in the capital cities.

Unfortunately, the good news arrived too late to save the Pushkin Theatre as it had been conceived and managed by Brenko: in the spring of 1882, only a few short months before the monopoly was officially abolished, the theatre went bankrupt. The company, most of whom had already signed contracts with Fedotov and Korsh, left Brenko and her husband with nothing but the Pushkin's debts.

A combination of adverse internal and external circumstances determined the fate of the Pushkin Theatre. Brenko's naivete and entrepreneurial inexperience surely contributed to the theatre's failure, but she was also operating under impossible conditions. She challenged the entrenched system of Imperial privilege; although the government was already under considerable pressure to make concessions to private entrepreneurs, the battle still raged and Brenko's enterprise existed in a state of semi-legal limbo. Her attention and energies were divided between managing a theatre and badgering state ministers and bureaucrats to support her petitions for fully legal status. Her financial problems were exacerbated by Kister's policies and by her own commitment to paying the members of her company a respectable living wage, to supplying them with a decent theatre in which to perform, and to subsidizing fully mounted, aesthetically satisfying productions.

Long after the wounds between Brenko and Fedotov healed and their friendship was rekindled, Fedotov introduced her to an acquaintance saying: "This is Anna Alekseevna. She's a good person, and that's why she doesn't have anything."[77] Indeed, Bertolt Brecht might have recognized Shen-Te and Shui-Ta in Anna Brenko and Fedor Korsh or Aleksandr Fedotov. Brenko tried to treat her company decently, but provincial performers were by necessity cunning survivalists; perhaps for that reason, the more agreeable and accommodating she tried to be, the more they challenged her managerial authority and exploited her financially. In spite of his expertise as a director, when she hired the iron-fisted Fedotov, many actors were angry because they knew he would not be as malleable as Brenko. Ironically, when Fedotov abused the actors, their anger was directed not at him, but at Brenko, who had foisted the tyrannical director on them.

Having assumed management of the company, Fedor Korsh quickly earned a reputation for ruthlessness; for that reason, actors like Pisarev, Andreev-Burlak, and Glama-Meshcherskaia were soon alienated by his "commercial politics." After one disastrous season with Korsh, Pisarev tried to persuade Malkiel to rent the theatre to what was left of the company. Failing that, they returned to the provinces. Glama-Meshcherskaia observed that Korsh was an "honorable merchant-entrepreneur," but, in contrast to Brenko, he was always a merchant first. A careful businessman whose perpetual haggling exhausted and angered the actors, Korsh was courteous and pleasant to people who could do things for him and a demon with everyone else.[78] But which qualities best serve an aspiring theatrical entrepreneur? Perhaps the answer lies in longevity and profitability: in spite of its founder's elevated aspirations, the Pushkin theatre lasted for two years and, following its demise, Brenko spent the remainder of her life in poverty. The Korsh Theatre lasted until the Revolution, and the sharp, commercially savvy lawyer-entrepreneur not only maintained, but enhanced his personal fortune.

Perhaps Anna Brenko was satisfied with her moral victory. In 1905 and 1915, when the theatre community celebrated Brenko's twenty-fifth and thirty-fifth "jubilees," three commemorative articles eulogized her contributions to the Russian theatre.[79] In 1905, one of the anonymous authors wrote: "Today Brenko lives in poverty in Moscow, giving drama lessons to students. But at least she has the satisfaction of thinking each time she looks at Moscow's free private theatres, 'I did this!' "[80] In 1915, another proclaimed the Pushkin Theatre the phoenix out of whose ashes all other private theatres in Russia arose.[81] Brenko's thirty-fifth jubilee also coincided with the first production of her newly established worker's theatre. Stanislavski, who attended the opening celebration, stood up before the crowd to eulogize Brenko as a "pioneer of democratic theatre." "You are," he proclaimed, "the mascot of the Russian stage."[82]

Although they expressed their appreciation retrospectively, most of Brenko's contemporaries appreciated the Pushkin Theatre's significance within the general scheme of pre- and post-monopoly reform; few, however, grasped the gender implications of her accomplishments. By demonstrating that a woman could create and manage her own theatrical enterprise, Brenko, the first important native female theatrical entrepreneur in Russia, set an example for Russian actresses. Russian actresses admired and envied Bernhardt and Duse, but they remained distant, alien idols. In the eyes of (mostly male) critics, few Russian actresses could measure up to them and those who tried were reproached either for the palidness of the imitation or for aping Western decadence. Differences in context were also important. Although Bernhardt and Duse surely confronted considerable oppression and gender bias in their own countries, the situation for women in Western Europe was clearly distinguished from the situation facing Russian women. Brenko demonstrated that a Russian actress-manager could succeed in the Russian context. If the Pushkin Theatre was the paradigm for the private art theatre in Russia, Anna Brenko was the native prototype for the actress-entrepreneur.

BRENKO'S SUCCESSORS

The experiences of most subsequent actress-managers mirrored Brenko's. Three less celebrated actress-managers – Mariia Abramova, Elizaveta Goreva, and Elizaveta Shabelskaia – also left records of the theatres they founded and managed in Moscow and St. Petersburg between 1889 and 1901. Existing memoirs, articles about these women, and reviews of their productions suggest both significant differences among individual actress-entrepreneurs as well as a certain homogeneity of experience. For that reason, a brief account of their activities helps to fill out the picture of the first Russian actress-managers.

Brenko's most immediate successors, Mariia Abramova and Elizaveta Goreva, were provincial actresses who established theatrical enterprises in Moscow in 1889. Abramova's objectives were slightly less elevated, but similar to Goreva's: her stated intention was to produce Russian classics, especially Ostrovski; Goreva's was to produce international classics.[83]

According to an anonymous "friend," Abramova was an unusually intelligent, well-educated, and sensitive woman who had little in common with other actresses.[84] The daughter of an expatriate Hungarian count and his Russian wife, Abramova attended a women's *gimnaziia* for ten years before enrolling in the medical courses in Kazan. Her distaste for blood prompted Abramova to exchange medicine for the peripatetic life of a provincial actress.[85] Like many provincial girls, she saw in the theatre a glittering alternative to life in the provinces: "Every provincial girl dreamed about the theatre," her anonymous friend wrote, "because, after all, only the stage could give women everything they wanted in life."[86] Abramova set off on the provincial circuit, where she eventually earned a salary of 200 roubles a month. According to her niece, she less interested in money, than in being "a useful member of society who brought good to the people." Imagine her astonishment when she discovered this was not possible in the provincial "cesspit" where actresses were viewed as sexual commodities.[87]

In 1889, Abramova received a substantial inheritance, used it to rent the Shelaputin Theatre in Moscow, and organized her own company under the name Theatre of Abramova (*teatr Abramovoi*). Despite her financial resources, elevated objectives, and public-spirited intentions, Abramova's theatre lasted less than a year. The *Theatrical Encyclopedia* suggests that "financial mismanagement" was the occasion of its untimely demise, but contemporaneous reviews indicate a rather more complex situation.[88]

Like Brenko and many other post-monopoly actress-entrepreneurs, Abramova claimed to be motivated by literary and aesthetic rather than commercial considerations. Her promise to produce a serious program in which Ostrovski's plays would occupy a prominent place won the sympathy of critics and the educated public. But as one reviewer observed, just because Abramova put Ostrovski's name and likeness on her front curtain didn't necessarily mean good theatre would emerge from behind it. Carried away by the "exaggerated success of its [first] productions," the new theatre had, he complained, already forgotten about "inner content." The Theatre of Abramova, which showed such early promise, was already suffering from two potentially deadly disorders: a less than exemplary repertoire and an inattentive, immodest, easily satisfied company of actors.[89]

Subsequent reviews of Abramova's productions do not fully support one critic's complaint that competition from other private theatres forced her to resort to popular trash.[90] Indeed, Chekhov got his first production at the Theatre of Abramova; Evtikhi Karpov, a progressive if not particularly skillful playwright, was produced there; Abramova did stage the classics; and the production values – sets and costumes – were often stunning.[91] Clearly, Abramova's repertoire was less pristine than her early pronouncements promised, but Fedor Korsh prospered for decades on a similar repertoire. Reviews in *Artist* indicate that a major source of Abramova's instability was the acting company: from the perspective of Moscow critics, provincial performers simply did not have the skills or proper attitude toward their craft to handle either the exemplary Russian or Western European repertoires. Abramova's managerial "incompetence" complicated an already difficult situation: such an "inexperienced novice entrepreneur," could not, one critic argued, control her company or realize her objectives.[92] Embittered by the failure of her enterprise, Abramova attributed its demise to her own charitable, open-hearted nature: "Running a theatre required crueler hands than mine," she later observed.[93]

When the Theatre of Abramova collapsed in the middle of its first season,

Elizaveta Goreva invited many of Abramova's now unemployed actors to work in her newly established theatre. Like Abramova, Goreva was a provincial actress with grand ambitions, but unlike her relatively obscure competitor, Goreva was a minor star: she enjoyed a substantial (albeit brief) reputation as a tragic actress, had a following in both the provinces and capital cities, and was the first Russian actress to tour abroad.[94] According to Aleksandr Kugel, much of her appeal was physical. A great beauty of the "purely Russian type," Goreva had a "softly rounded figure, bluish-gray eyes, and a reserved manner. Her voice resembled Bernhardt's, but with a pleasantly Russian sing-song quality."[95] After 1884, Goreva's star rose quickly, but in spite of two debuts at the Aleksandrinskii Theatre and considerable pressure from supporters, the Imperial directorate refused to offer her a contract.[96] Her experience with the Imperial theatres resembled Strepetova's, but unlike her ill-starred colleague, Goreva confounded her detractors by opening her own theatre. Although the enthusiasm for Goreva's particular brand of romantic-heroic performance had already abated by 1889, when the Theatre of Goreva (*teatr Gorevoi*) opened, it stimulated considerable interest in Moscow and enjoyed substantial support from critics.

Goreva, an ambitious, eccentric, self-assured actress with considerable natural talent and little formal training, tried to avoid the provincial label by specializing in the classical Western repertoire and uninterrupted touring. She always stayed at the best hotels, rode in carriages, and spent money freely. Wherever she went, her capricious escapades and personal extravagence engendered excitement, gossip, admiration – and enemies. Glama-Meshcherskaia met Goreva in Odessa in the mid-1880s when rumors were already flying about Goreva's grand scheme to organize a theatre "the likes of which had never been seen before in Russia."[97] Before her departure, Goreva asked Glama-Meshcherskaia to join the theatre. Persuaded that Goreva's fantasy would not materialize, Glama signed a contract with Fedor Korsh and forgot the actress's offer.

Several years elapsed before Goreva and her "inseparable companion" (*nerazluchnaia sputnitsa*), T.F. Karpenko, actually took steps to realize a new private theatre in Moscow.[98] Goreva, who hoped her reputation and marketing instincts would draw spectators, provided the impetus and energy for the project; Karpenko, the widow of a millionaire, provided the financial backing. Like Brenko and Abramova, Goreva claimed a serious literary and aesthetic mission for her enterprise. To demonstrate her seriousness of purpose, she engaged noted playwright and critic P.D. Boborykin to serve as literary manager/artistic director, spent 35,000 roubles on renovating the theatre, and acquired "a whole constellation of eminent actors" by offering them excessive salaries.[99]

A sort of poor man's Ermolova, Goreva preferred strong, romantic-dramatic roles in plays like Schiller's *Maria Stuart*; for that reason, her repertoire initially promoted Western classics. Reviews suggest that, in contrast to many other actress-managers, she also produced several plays by Russian women.[100] Although critics noted certain faults in the productions, most were generally supportive and Goreva enjoyed considerable artistic, if not financial, success during her first season. Critics responded favorably to the repertoire and, because Goreva and Karpenko spent enormous sums of money on them, the sets and costumes were stunning. One critic applauded Goreva for bringing plays like *The Misanthrope* and *Don Carlos* to the attention of Moscow audiences; another praised *Maria Stuart*'s elegant scenery and generally high production standards.[101]

In spite of its initial promise, the Theatre of Goreva experienced serious setbacks before the end of the first season: Boborykin resigned, leaving the theatre without a strong literary and artistic conscience, and it was losing substantial amounts of money. Sounding the doleful refrain of "financial mismanagement," The *Theatrical Encyclopedia* cites Goreva's alleged impracticality as the source of the theatre's problems.[102] Goreva's situation resembled both Brenko's and Abramova's, but the failure of all three to sustain their theatres cannot be so easily reduced to charges of individual incompetence. If Brenko's, Abramova's, and Goreva's managerial inexperience was one factor in the failure of their theatres, three others surely contributed: audience taste, the necessity to hire provincial actors, and gender bias.

After productions of Ostrovski's *The Storm* and Chekhov's *The Marriage Proposal* at the Theatre of Goreva in 1890, one critic wrote that the new theatre's management was clearly committed to satisfying the public's taste for "serious art."[103] Unfortunately, critics did not accurately represent the reality of "public taste." The educated public's desire for a serious repertoire was undoubtedly sincere, but since the educated public constituted a small minority of the population, it could not provide sufficient support to sustain theatrical enterprises with elevated literary and artistic ambitions. Like Abramova, Goreva quickly discovered that the classical Russian and Western European repertoires spelled financial disaster. In contrast to Brenko, who tried to maintain the quality of the repertoire over the objections of her company, Abramova and Goreva tried to rescue their floundering enterprises by producing melodrama and other popular genres – but to no avail. When Goreva altered the philosophy and design of her theatre, formerly supportive critics attacked her furiously for betraying her solemn promise to produce exemplary plays.[104] Caught in a web of competing demands, Goreva tried to negotiate the interests and needs of a fragmented audience – and by so doing, satisfied no one.

Like Brenko, Goreva also suffered from the necessity to hire provincial actors. Initially, many critics overlooked or forgave the quality of the acting, preferring instead to focus on the repertoire and *mise en scene*. Interestingly, Goreva repeated Brenko's pattern in the sense that she hired a company of genuinely prominent provincial actors, several of whom displayed sufficient talent and skill to win contracts with the Imperial theatres. From the beginning, however, critics gently observed that only a few members of Goreva's company had the skills to handle classical Western or Russian texts, but they also praised individual actors and actresses for the strength of their performances and acknowledged the company's competence in contemporary popular genres.[105] As impatience with Goreva and her ailing enterprise grew, critics began to attack every aspect of production, especially the acting. Astonished by the "unusual carelessness and slovenliness" of Goreva's actors, one critic argued in 1890 that the company should not even attempt classical drama.[106] Another charged that Goreva foisted inferior actors on the public because her ticket prices were low: cheap prices apparently justifed poor quality.[107] *Artist*'s most ferocious attack, which was mounted at the end of the 1890 season and continued into 1891, faulted Goreva for bringing the most primitive, unaesthetic, openly chaotic form of provincial theatre into Moscow. If she had conducted her affairs properly, an *Artist* critic argued, she could have acquainted Muscovite audiences with the best provincial talent. But through egregious mismanagement of her theatre, Goreva had simply reinforced existing prejudices against provincial actors and provincial theatre.[108]

By repeating many of Brenko's mistakes, Goreva did create some of her own problems. In her rush to create a megatheatrical empire, she expanded her operation at the very moment when wisdom dictated caution. In 1890, when she should have been reassessing the first Theatre of Goreva, she opened a second, popularly priced theatre. Disabused of their illusions about Goreva's practice, critics lost no time in attacking the new theatre for its shoddy production standards and trite repertoire. Arguing that the responsibility to enlighten their public required managers of popular theatres to be more, rather than less, selective and attentive to production values, critics accused Goreva of pandering to the lowest tastes of the audience. Goreva could not solve her theatres' problems, and as her frustration mounted, her passion for entrepreneurship cooled. Karpenko, who had already lost thousands of roubles, finally stepped in, measured the business with her "merchant's eye," and persuaded Goreva to give it up.[109]

Gender bias was a third factor in the failures of Brenko, Abramova, and Goreva to sustain their enterprises, but because instances of gender discrimination are less concrete and more open to subjective interpretation, its effect is more difficult to assess. Russian women were collectively disenfranchised; logically, then, actresses were legally, socially, and economically disadvantaged when they undertook the organization and management of their own theatres. Only one actress-manager, however, addressed issues of gender bias and sex discrimination directly: the eclectic novelist, playwright, theatre critic, and actress-entrepreneur Elizaveta Shabelskaia, who began her career in Brenko's Pushkin Theatre.[110] In 1900, having already established a reputation as a playwright and critic, Shabelskaia opened the Petersburg Theatre, which operated for two seasons. When the theatre went bankrupt in 1902, Shabelskaia was accused – and later fully exonerated – of forging promissory notes in the name of her principal backer, V.I. Kovalevski, the Minister of Finance. Even after the trial, she felt compelled to defend herself in the court of public opinion; to that purpose, Shabelskaia published *The Woman Entrepreneur's Promissory Notes* (*Vekselia antreprenershi*), a bitter, thinly disguised "fictional" account of her experiences managing the Petersburg Theatre.[111]

Although marred by her disturbingly self-serving, pretentious portrait of herself as the naively trusting, scrupulously honest victim of a gang of rapacious scoundrels, Shabelskaia's memoir is exceptional for its expression of gender outrage. Her experiences as an actress-manager mirror those of Brenko, Abramova, and Goreva; in seeking to explain her theatre's failure, however, she did not point a self-accusatory finger, but rather looked for the cause in sex/gender bias within the existing social, theatrical, and economic context. Shabelskaia's critique begins early in the memoir: "Other entrepreneurs," she wrote, "shook their heads when they saw a stupid woman, who understood nothing about theatre management," running a theatre. "People said of her," Shabelskaia continued, "she's a good, but impractical woman who lets everyone rob her." Shabelskaia claimed that only the word "good" wounded her because in Russian "good" is synonymous with "stupid."[112]

Shabelskaia also identified a problem that affected actress-managers exclusively: most were excluded from the tight circle of theatre "habitués" – men who attended the theatre regularly, were its principal patrons, and expected favors from the entrepreneur. The denizens of the Petersburg Theatre were hostile to her because the atmosphere she promoted was too "dull and prim." They were disturbed by the absence of an "experienced leader" who would drink with them after performances and be prepared to acquaint them with "girls."[113]

Finally, the most striking feature of Shabelskaia's and Brenko's memoirs is that both are permeated by the incessant refrain of financial anxiety. The two actress-managers apparently expended considerable time and energy juggling promissory notes, calculating production costs, wheedling current and potential backers, and putting off creditors. Of course, all but the most wealthy entrepreneurs of both sexes would have faced similar demands, but women-managed enterprises were particularly vulnerable to economic collapse because women's access to the world of commerce and trade was severely limited.[114] If there is any validity to Shabelskaia's charge that actress-managers were considered incompetent by male (and some female) colleagues, then women became easy prey not only for unscrupulous lawyers like Korsh, but also for actor-managers like Pisarev and Fedotov, and critics-turned-managers like Boborykin, who clearly imagined that they could manage theatrical enterprises better than the "stupid" women who initiated them.[115] If women had a collective reputation for incompetence, how could potential backers justify the risk of investing in enterprises managed by actress-entrepreneurs?

In 1909, Isabella Grinevskaia suggested that actress-managers, many of whom saw their theatres as an escape route to freedom, were dangerously self-deluded.[116] Although several female entrepreneurs enjoyed a measure of economic, artistic, and personal autonomy, even the most ambitious and powerful among them were not free agents, forever liberated from male hegemony in the theatre. Although Grinevskaia's skepticism is understandable, her equivocal attitude toward the achievements of actress-entrepreneurs belies the progress of women in Russian theatre.

The visibility of women like Brenko, Abramova, Goreva, and Shabelskaia in the St. Petersburg and Moscow theatre communities suggests not only a sea change in the status of actresses, but also indicates the broad spectrum of women pursuing independent theatre management as a viable alternative to existing institutions. Although several starring actresses, including Lidia Iavorskaia and Vera Kommissarzhevskaia, managed their own theatres between 1900 and 1910, star status was not a prerequisite for independent enterpreneurship: Goreva was a minor provincial celebrity, but neither Brenko, Abramova, nor Shabelskaia were starring actresses. In addition, collectively actress-entrepreneurs were better educated and tended to be from higher social classes, which indicates not only the broader effects on women of Aleksandr II's educational reforms, but also a change in the demographics of the theatre community. Pre-reform actresses were largely reconciled to their subordinate status; after 1880, however, the more emancipated and ambitious among them began probing the boundaries of existing institutions and hierarchies. Perhaps by necessity, the most audacious were actress-entrepreneurs.

7

LIDIA IAVORSKAIA
The Silver Age actress as
unruly woman

In order to establish and sustain independent theatrical enterprises, actress-entrepreneurs needed either great wealth, access to a patron with great wealth, or enough personal charisma and celebrity to draw large numbers of paying spectators into their theatres. In view of the conditions for successful entrepreneurship, perhaps the theatres founded by Brenko, Abramova, Goreva, and Shabelskaia were doomed from the first. Although Goreva enjoyed a brief vogue, the first female entrepreneurs were minor celebrities who lacked sufficient private resources to sustain their theatres during times of economic crisis. In contrast to their predecessors, the two most prominent actress-managers of the late Imperial period, Lidia Borisovna Iavorskaia and Vera Fedorovna Kommissarzhevskaia, did enjoy the combined advantages of tremendous celebrity and considerable private resources.

Although most of the actresses considered in this study worked past the turn of the century, in the sense that their careers coincide chronologically with the rise of decadence and symbolism in Russia, Iavorskaia and Kommissarzhevskaia are the first authentic Silver Age actresses. There is not, however, a clean break between actresses of Savina's and Ermolova's generation and actresses who came of age during the late 1890s. Iavorskaia and Kommissarzhevskaia clearly represent new tendencies in Russian theatre, culture, and gender ideology, but both were also influenced by the aesthetics and ideologies of the previous generation. By the late 1890s, Western European influences were so strong that actresses like Iavorskaia and Kommissarzhevskaia could identify openly with the Western European New Woman and pursue progressive social agendas in their theatres. Nonetheless, the fact that critics dubbed Iavorskaia "Little Bernhardt" and Kommissarzhevskaia the "Russian Duse" suggests that gender categories established in the 1880s were operative at least through the first decade of the twentieth century.

Although both Kommissarzhevskaia and Iavorskaia were enormously popular and controversial during the Silver Age, Vera Fedorovna was clearly the preeminent actress of the era. In the sense that both favored Western ideas and values, they were alike. But Kommissarzhevskaia and Iavorskaia represented contrasting trends: Kommissarzhevskaia was identified primarily with academic and art theatres, while Iavorskaia was caught somewhere between art and commercial theatre in a sort of aesthetic and ideological limbo. Because she occupied much the same place in late nineteenth-century Russian culture as Madonna does in twentieth-century American, the term "high camp diva" as it has been applied to Madonna offers a point of entry into Lidia Borisovna's career and significance.

Since the 1980s, Madonna, the high priestess of American pop culture, has constructed a multi-million dollar performance empire, the success of which rests primarily on her extraordinary ability to behave outrageously and market it. In spite of – or perhaps because of – her immense popular following, press pundits loathe Madonna. Mainstream critics deplore her debauched lifestyle, sexual athletics, and public exhibitionism, while avant-garde critics regard her performances as trendy schlock rather than legitimate art. All of this negative attention has little effect on Madonna except to increase sales of her recordings, books, and videos to average citizens who might otherwise be indifferent to the Madonna phenomenon. Although some cultural critics are intrigued by the psycho-social implications of her performances, others complain that, in spite of being singularly mediocre, Madonna has acquired tremendous fame, wealth, and cultural authority by cunning marketing and ruthless exploitation of the public's seemingly insatiable appetite for scandalous behavior.

Viewed within her own context, several aspects of Lidia Iavorskaia's image and career resemble Madonna's – foremost among them, she dressed outrageously and was deliberately provocative. Part-time political activist, brazen self-promoter with aspirations to art, enormously popular with audiences, but scorned by legitimate theatres and mainstream critics, like Madonna, Iavorskaia provoked extreme responses from all sides.[1]

Tatiana Shchepkina-Kupernik, who was for several years Iavorskaia's closest friend and collaborator, wrote after the actress's death in 1921 that the media's attitude toward Lidia Borisovna was unprecedented and bewildering. No other actress, she claimed, was "subjected to such persecution."[2] One of the most vicious attacks appeared in 1902 in *Theatre and Art* (*Teatr i iskusstvo*). Prefacing his critique of Iavorskaia's Parisian tour with several malevolent personal remarks, N. Negorev declared that her entire career was "marked by her desire for notoriety at any cost." According to Negorev, Iavorskaia had none of the qualities of a real theatrical artist: she was lazy and undisciplined, her voice was harsh and unpleasant, she had no range, and her creativity consisted of "roaring and throwing herself around the stage."[3] He also argued that she stimulated an artificial appetite for her performances by publishing anonymous eulogies to herself in various St. Petersburg newspapers. Complaining that Iavorskaia had neither talent nor craft, Negorev maintained that publicity alone created the vogue for her peculiarly unpleasant brand of performance. He was stunned that her following, which included people of refinement and taste, could be so duped by an actress whose sole talent was for self-promotion and exhibitionism.

The tone and rhetoric of Negorev's complaint were not exceptional; many contemporaneous reviews, especially those authored by St. Petersburg critics, dismissed Iavorskaia as a brazen egotist of mediocre talent. For several reasons, however, she merits renewed attention. Along with Brenko and Kommissarzhevskaia, Iavorskaia was one of a handful of controversial, genuinely innovative actress-entrepreurs who were prominent in Silver Age theatre. She was, as Nikolai Efros wrote, a genuine "seeker" who often chose intriguing, intellectually audacious material. Although she did stage her share of schlock, Iavorskaia also produced plays by Ibsen, Maeterlinck, and other representatives of the avant-garde. Furthermore, the scope of her interests went beyond Russia and Western Europe to encompass even Indian drama.[4] Charging that she had no genuine ideological or aesthetic convictions, her detractors accused her of "showboating" each time a new liberal cause appeared on the horizon. Nonetheless, her political and aesthetic views were astonishingly consistent: in 1900, she almost singlehandedly instigated the most serious theatre riot in the history of Russian theatre; in the same year, she opened her own theatre, which earned a reputation for producing progressive plays and supporting liberal causes; she was the first to demonstrate support for the workers' strike of 1905 by closing her theatre temporarily; and she was one of the few prominent Russian actresses to identify openly with feminism.

Iavorskaia's support for the British suffrage movement was widely publicized, but perhaps more importantly, she was part of a circle of "new women" that included writers, actresses, professors, journalists, newspaper editors, and critics. According to Shchepkina-Kupernik, before this new professional class appeared, Russian women fell into two categories: respectable society women (mothers, sisters, wives) and prostitutes. In contrast to these tedious traditional stereotypes, Shchepkina argued, the "new women" were not only respectable, but also good comrades and the intellectual equals of men.[5] It is too simple, then, to dismiss Iavorskaia as a cunning publicist with a penchant for exhibitionism. Her experience raises intriguing questions about women who publicly flaunt the boundaries of the bourgeois and about female transgression in general. Most importantly, her career, public persona, and the responses to it reflect changes in Russian theatre and society that had tremendous resonance for women.

THE MAKING OF A DIVA

Born in Kiev in 1871 to a family with aristocratic pretensions, Iavorskaia was a child of privilege. Her German mother's family was wealthy; her father, a retired general, served for many years as Kiev's chief of police; and her uncle was a government minister. By Iavorskaia's own account, her stage career began at the age of nine when she participated in an amateur theatrical staged in her parents' home. The response by representatives of "good society" was, she explained to interviewer Iuri Beliaev, unanimously positive: "Hearing how I spoke the line '*Je veux un negre, je veux la lune*,' everyone predicted that I had a great future as an actress."[6] Hoping the experience would dispel any fantasies about a career in the theatre, her parents sent her to a *gimnaziia*. It did not, and after a brief marriage at age seventeen to an alcoholic libertine, Iavorskaia moved to St. Petersburg where she spent three years studying with V.N. Davydov in the Aleksandrinskii Theatre's training program.

Although Iavorskaia apparently passed her examination performance in 1893, she was not invited to continue in the program or join the Aleksandrinskii company. In their memoirs, Iuri Iurev and Shchepkina-Kupernik suggest that the directorate snubbed Lidia Borisovna because she and Davydov, one of the Aleksandrinskii's veteran luminaries, disliked each other intensely.[7] Iavorskaia does not mention Davydov or discuss her experiences at the school in any interviews, which suggests that the experience was unpleasant and better forgotten. The Aleksandrinskii's rejection did not, however, discourage her and she set off immediately for Paris where she studied with Edmund Got, a retired actor from the Comédie Française and one of Sarah Bernhardt's mentors.[8]

While in Paris she developed a taste for the French style of acting and Western European drama, especially the repertoire popularized by Bernhardt and Rejane. Although Iavorskaia borrowed freely from Duse and other Western European actresses, her sympathies were clearly with the French: she acquired a taste for flamboyant French fashions, absorbed the French romantic style of acting, and, based on Bernhardt's example, further refined her talent for self-promotion. When she returned to Russia in the summer of 1893 and joined a provincial summer theatre in Revel, it was as a grand coquette in the French style. Although Iavorskaia described her debut in Chekhov's *The Bear* as "modest," she quickly became a favorite with local spectators. Her notoriety attracted the attention of the Korsh Theatre, which invited her to join the company in Moscow for the regular season. She debuted at the Korsh in August 1893 in a one-act comedy entitled *Tête à tête*, which was followed a week later by *The Flirt* (*Igra v liubov*).

During her first two years at the Korsh, Iavorskaia enjoyed considerable attention from the press and public. Her first spectacular success with audiences, if not with critics, came in Victorien Sardou's *Madame Sans-Gêne* and she went on to win acclaim in plays by Rostand, Dumas, and D'Annuncio. Shchepkina-Kupernik noted that when Lidia Borisovna burst onto the Korsh stage, threw off her "eccentric dark red cloak and with her passionate, raspy, nervous voice uttered the first line: 'Ah, how my head aches,'" people sat up in their chairs for the first time in many years.[9] Although spectators were charmed by Iavorskaia's novelty, her colleagues were less enthusiastic. Actors at the Korsh theatre, one of the most prominent – and stagnant – in Moscow, were openly hostile to this presumptuous girl "who came out of nowhere and commandeered the entire theatre."[10] Critical response to her early performances in Moscow was overwhelmingly positive and, perhaps provoked by critics who suggested that Iavorskaia was the best thing to happen to the Korsh Theatre in years, animosity toward her within the theatre intensified. In addition, in an era of increased nationalism and "bourgeoisification" of the theatre, her patina of Europeanism provided yet another pretext for malicious backstage slander. For all of these reasons, by the end of the first season she was Korsh's most popular and controversial actress. But the reputation she established at the Korsh as a "little Bernhardt," whose instinct for the public relations coup rivalled her model's own, seriously hampered Iavorskaia's professional development over the years.

Her tenure at the Korsh Theatre was characterized by feverish activity: she not only spent long hours at the theatre, but also established a Parisian style literary salon which attracted a circle of artists, actors, and writers, including Anton Chekhov, with whom she had a brief romantic interlude.[11] During this period, Chekhov was still friendly with the notoriously conservative St. Petersburg essayist, Aleksei Suvorin, whose activities included publishing *The New Times* (*Novoe vremia*) and managing the St. Petersburg Malyi Theatre (Society for Art and Literature). Chekhov, who often shared his impressions of Moscow theatre with Suvorin, recommended to his friend that he take note of this young actress who "might make something of herself if she's not spoiled by her schooling."[12] After seeing her on tour, Suvorin was not particularly impressed, but decided to extend an invitation to her to join the newly formed Society for Art and Literature. Longing for more autonomy and frustrated with conditions at the Korsh, Iavorskaia accepted in a move which seemed advantageous at the time.[13]

The Society for Art and Literature was founded by Suvorin in 1895 for the purpose of "acquainting the public with new theatrical and artistic movements."[14] The repertoire was to be "completely literary" and the directorate proclaimed its intention to avoid "tendentiousness and politics."[15] The new theatre opened in 1895 with Ostrovski's *The Storm*, followed by *A Doll's House* with Iavorskaia in leading role. The production was repeated five times and enjoyed moderate success, but Iavorskaia was not satisfied. For all of her internationalism, Lidia Borisovna did not intend to build an image or promote her career on the basis of progressive Western European drama. Her objectives were apparently quite different from Suvorin's and her marketing instincts were much sharper. For those reasons, before agreeing to join the Society, she obtained his promise that the theatre would produce Rostand's *Princess of Reverie* for her first benefit. Although Suvorin considered the play nonsense, he agreed; to his chagrin, the production was not only popular, but extremely profitable.[16] Influenced by Iavorskaia's success in Rostand's play, the Society began featuring Iavorskaia in plays from the French repertoire – especially plays written for and popularized by Sarah Bernhardt. Not everyone was pleased with the theatre's new direction. By 1898, Kugel was complaining that the Society's original purpose had been entirely subverted; it had been transformed from an art theatre into a commercial enterprise.[17]

Kugel did not name Iavorskaia as the source of the Society's unwelcome metamorphosis, but given her ambition and Suvorin's relative inexperience as a theatre manager, she may well have driven the changes. It is difficult to establish precisely the extent of Iavorskaia's authority at the Society. Because her presence in a production guaranteed its success, she clearly enjoyed a certain measure of power. Perhaps that is why some critics were persuaded that her power was excessive. According to Nikolai Efros, Iavorskaia immediately established herself as the company's "lawmaker" and Negorev maintained that the theatre's repertoire and general management were largely under her control.[18] Whatever the reality of her influence, most critics agreed that it was pernicious.

Iavorskaia's status in the St. Petersburg theatre community was further complicated by her "scandalous" personal life. Shortly after her arrival in St. Petersburg, Iavorskaia rocketed into public view and shocked the city's elite by marrying a genuine scion of the aristocracy, Prince Bariatinski. Far from an impoverished member of the minor aristocracy, Bariatinski, the grandson of a famous field marshal on his father's side and of a wealthy count on his mother's, was a genuine prince whose family was on intimate terms with the tsar. According to Kugel, Bariatinski "did a bit of reading and writing," and was skeptical of the fashionable society in which he moved.[19] Perhaps for that reason, he found Iavorskaia's "bohemian" circle of artists, actors, and writers alluring, and easily succumbed to Lidia Borisovna's charms. The prince, who willingly entered into this arrangement, lost his inheritance and prominent place in society, but Iavorskaia bore most of the social disapprobation. Although the furor over their marriage temporarily enhanced Iavorskaia's celebrity, the gossip engendered by it further damaged her aspirations to be taken seriously as an artist.[20]

Whatever power Iavorskaia enjoyed at the Society for Art and Literature, she could not sustain it without Suvorin's support. Simultaneously fascinated and repulsed by actresses, Suvorin was vulnerable not only to Iavorskaia's considerable charm, but to the aura of the *beau monde* surrounding her.[21] Although Iavorskaia's reign at the Society lasted only five years, during much of that period, Suvorin tolerated and even encouraged her. His attitude began to change when she and Bariatinski established a progressive newspaper, *The Northern Courier* (*Severnyi kurer*), that aspired to compete with *The New Times*. According to Kugel, Suvorin feared only two things: death and competition from another journal, thus the moment of *The Northern Courier*'s conception was marked by rapidly escalating tensions between actress and entrepreneur. They culminated with Suvorin's production of a second-rate antisemitic melodrama entitled *The Smugglers* (*Kontra-bandisty*).[22] The production of this play sparked the worst theatre riot in the history of Russian theatre, and Iavorskaia, who placed herself at the center of the controversy by refusing to perform in it and by publicly denouncing the production in the pages of *The Northern Courier*, was blamed.

The history of Suvorin's production of *The Smugglers* is both ideologically complex and frustratingly vague. The ideological complexity arises from the fact that *The Smugglers* reflected a rising tide of antisemitic reaction in this period; the information vacuum surrounding the event itself is the result of state censorship: within hours of the crisis, critics and commentators were forbidden to write about the production, the riot that ensued, or any of the events leading up to it.[23] Nonetheless, it is possible to reconstruct at least some of the most significant parts of the story.

The production in 1900 was not Suvorin's first attempt to mount *The Smugglers*. In 1898 Litvin-Efron and Krylov offered the play under its original title, *Sons of Israel* (*Syny izrailia*), to the Imperial Theatre directorate which, fearing controversy, decided not to produce it. The authors then turned to the notoriously antisemitic Suvorin, who accepted the play, distributed the roles among the actors, and started rehearsals.[24] He did not, however, anticipate the reaction of several members of the company who, once they read the script, refused to participate in such unabashedly anti-semitic propaganda. For that reason the production had to be canceled.[25] The ill-starred script disappeared for approximately a year only to resurface when Suvorin published it in 1899 in his journal, *The Historical Herald* (*Istoricheskii vestnik*). In November 1900, rehearsals began at the Society for Art and Literature for a new production of the play, this time under the title *The Smugglers*.[26]

Petr Gnedich, a regisseur at the Society, suggests in his memoirs that simple pigheadedness motivated Suvorin to move ahead with the production of *The Smugglers*. As a social commentator and essayist, Suvorin often took reactionary positions, but generally he had the good sense not to mix art and personal politics; indeed, he admired the skill – if not the politics – of playwrights such as Ibsen, Chekhov, and others associated with liberalism and the realist school. According to Gnedich, Suvorin knew that *The Smugglers* was aesthetically inferior and politically incendiary, but insisted on the production largely because Iavorskaia and Bariatinski mounted a public protest against it.[27] Lidia Borisovna, who was assigned a leading role in the production, sent the script back to the director, Evtikhi Karpov, with her apologies for being unable to accept a role in such a disgustingly reactionary play. The accompanying note read: "Dear Evtikhi Pavlovich! Having carefully reread *Sons of Israel*, I've concluded that my principles will not permit me to perform in it. It seems to me that this play will excite nationalist hatred and awaken the worst instincts of the mob. I am sincerely sorry, but I must refuse this role. Although you sent it, I suspect that, in the depth of your soul, you sympathize with me."[28]

Whatever tangled maze of personal animosity and political convictions motivated Suvorin and Iavorskaia to lock horns over *The Smugglers*, when the production opened on November 23, 1900, it quickly escalated into a scandal of major proportions. Open warfare between liberal and conservative newspaper and magazine columnists prepared spectators for an evening of controversy, but apparently few anticipated violence. On opening night the upper gallery was packed with St. Petersburg students, and upon peeking through a chink in the curtain, a member of the local police department stationed behind it exclaimed, "The whole staff of the revolution is here."[29] In spite of (or perhaps because of) their earlier protests against the production, Iavorskaia and Bariatinski attended, concealing themselves from public view in their private box near the stage. Indeed, only Suvorin was conspicuous by his absence.[30]

The atmosphere in the auditorium was tense, and when the curtain rose, the actors, who were greeted by whistling and cries of "Down [with the play]! Curtain!" could not speak their first lines above the noise. Suddenly a navy siren sounded from somewhere in the auditorium, and a rumor spread rapidly that it emanated from Iavorskaia's box. Privileged spectators seated in the parterre were furious; they turned on Iavorskaia shouting: "Adventuress, blockhead, throw her out of the theatre."[31] The police were perplexed; they wanted to evict the students seated in the galleries, but because much of the disturbance was actually being initiated by the parterre, they ran back and forth not knowing whom to accuse. The actors could not continue and the curtain fell. In a futile attempt to calm the auditorium, Karpov ventured out in front of the curtain only to be met with a hail of boots, cucumbers, potatoes, and onions.[32]

The actors and A.P. Kolomnin, who was left in charge by Suvorin, wanted to cancel the performance, but an official representative of the police department insisted that they continue to play under police protection. The moment the actors appeared on stage, however, the vegetable bombardment began again with renewed force, this time directed not at the actors, but at the policemen who were visible in the wings. Finally, troops positioned in the galleries began dragging students out of the auditorium, and when sympathetic spectators flew to their rescue, chaos reigned in the theatre. The actors cowered against the back wall of the stage and the performance was finally canceled. In the aftermath of the riot, more than a hundred people were arrested, newspaper and journal editors were forbidden to report the event, and the search for a scapegoat began.[33] In the theatre community, one question overshadowed all others: what was Iavorskaia's role in *The Smuggler*'s scandal?

Lidia Borisovna was probably neither as innocent in this affair as she claimed, nor as guilty as others believed her to be, but her open protest against the production and her reputation as a brazen publicity seeker made her a natural target for the investigation that ensued. She proclaimed her innocence in a note to Suvorin: "I sincerely hoped the play would fail and be hissed off the stage," she wrote, "but that is all. All of the other the stories about me are pure slander."[34] Although no civil action was initiated against her, in response to pressure from the Society's actors, the board of directors convened to consider the case. Their evidence consisted of a petition signed by thirty-seven actors and a statement from Karpov describing events leading up to the disturbance.

Although they offered little concrete evidence of her guilt, the actors charged Iavorskaia with instigating the riot and humiliating them publicly. Concluding that further association with her was impossible, they unanimously called for her dismissal. Karpov argued that even during rehearsals, the cast was furious with Iavorskaia for airing backstage politics in a public forum. He further charged that Iavorskaia's newspaper, *The Northern Courier*, provoked the disturbance by publishing incendiary attacks on the play before it opened.[35] Having concluded that the legal aspects of the case should be argued in civil court, the board of directors confined its deliberations to questions of professional conduct. The board determined that Iavorskaia's refusal to perform in *The Smugglers* was an attempt to discredit the theatre and that she betrayed both the organization and her colleagues by publicizing an internal conflict. Iavorskaia was charged with breach of contract, the Society fired her, and the government shut down *The Northern Courier*.[36] Because they doubted Iavorskaia's motives and sincerity, St. Petersburg critics were not sympathetic. As Negorev observed caustically several years later: "It makes little difference whether we denounce Iavorskaia or eulogize her, she turns it to her advantage."[37]

THE NOVYI THEATRE: IAVORSKAIA AS ACTRESS-MANAGER

Shchepkina suggests that the *The Smugglers* debacle was a pivotal moment in Iavorskaia's career, that it broke something in her spirit.[38] Nonetheless, it did not stop her feverish activity and, within a year, she opened her own theatre, the Novyi, in St. Petersburg. The theatre provided new grist for the critics' mill. Crying that Iavorskaia's new enterprise was simply further evidence of her boundless egotism, many dismissed the Novyi from its inception as yet another example of exhibitionism and self-aggrandizement. There is, however, evidence that Iavorskaia had few choices after the *The Smuggler's* debacle. In 1897, after debuting unsuccessfully at the Imperial Mikhailovskii Theatre, she was not invited to join the company. Although progressive art theatres proliferated after 1898, they were not likely to hire her. The trend in Russian theatre at the beginning of the century was toward ensemble production, but Iavorskaia's reputation, which was based on personality rather than craft, would not appeal to men like Stanislavski or Nemirovich-Danchenko. Finally, if *The Smugglers* increased her popularity with the

145

theatre-going public, it further damaged her reputation amongst her colleagues. Many actors simply refused to work with her, and, as she remarked to Shchepkina after being fired from the Society, she was a woman with nowhere to go.[39]

Although critics gave Lidia Borisovna little credit for seriousness of purpose and the theatre's repertoire always consisted of an eclectic blend of light French comedy, serious Western European "new drama," and native domestic realism with pretensions to social relevance, the Novyi established the reputation of a progressive, moderately left-wing theatre. In addition to Iavorskaia's usual popular fare, the Novyi produced Ibsen, Strindberg, Maeterlinck, Tolstoi, and they even staged Nikolai Evreinov's first play, *The Foundation of Happiness* (*Fundament schastia*). Production practice was not radically innovative, but Iavorskaia had the good sense to hire competent, "advanced" directors and designers, and critics acknowledged that the quality of the *mise en scene* was generally high.[40] The Novyi was also the first theatre in St. Petersburg to affirm its sympathy with the workers by joining the strike of 1905.[41]

Nonetheless, critics ravaged Novyi productions mercilessly, primarily for the quality of the acting. Not surprisingly, the problem was traced to Iavorskaia herself, but because Lidia Borisovna provoked such extreme responses, it is difficult to gauge the objectivity of existing memoirs and reviews. Nadezhda Skarskaia, for example, remarked in her memoirs that Lidia Borisovna's "sensual temperament" was such that people either worshipped or despised her; there was no middle ground.[42] Shchepkina affirmed that, for better or worse, no one was indifferent to Iavorskaia, and further observed that the malicious personal attacks directed at her by critics, colleagues, and even casual acquaintances often had little foundation in fact. In his obituary, Efros acknowledged that Iavorskaia's behavior was enormously problematic in a society that demanded "modest constraint," particularly from women.[43]

The principal problem for Iavorskaia was that the paradigm for her image of "*zhenstvennost*" was exclusively Western. She exhibited herself on stage in excessively expensive Parisian fashions; she specialized in Parisian grand coquettes; she spoke several languages and toured more widely in Western Europe than any actress of the period; and she was an aggressive, combative personality whose freewheeling lifestyle – so inappropriate for a modest Russian woman – offended many critics and colleagues. The task of evaluating Iavorskaia as an artist is further complicated by the fact that existing criticism was authored almost exclusively by male critics, many of whom reacted in horror to the lack of traditional feminine modesty displayed by French actresses and their Russian imitators. Although most popular actresses borrowed from the West, Iavorskaia's example illustrates the danger for actresses of constructing an excessively Westernized image of "*zhenstvennost*."

Because Iavorskaia did not leave memoirs and the celebrity interview was still largely unknown in Russia, it is difficult to reconstruct precisely her own views on acting or her technical approach to creating a role. It is clear, however, that her style and technique changed over time; and as Iavorskaia changed, so did the attitude of critics toward her. Throughout her career, Iavorskaia's performances were marred by poor vocal quality, a physical deficiency that she was apparently unable to correct. In her early years, however, Moscow critics overlooked minor technical defects, preferring to emphasize the novelty, sincerity, and spontaneity of her performances.[44] When she debuted at the Korsh in 1893, a critic for *Artist* observed that, although one should not rush to judgment on the basis of one performance, Iavorskaia was a "very valuable acquisition for the stage."[45] In Shakespeare's *Twelfth Night*, she was praised for her "naturalness and simplicity," and in *The Mother-in-law* (*Teshcha*), the same critic noted with approval that, in contrast to many well-meaning but misguided Moscow actresses, Iavorskaia did not idealize her characters. Rather, she created "living people" with both negative and positive qualities.[46] When Iavorskaia undertook the role of Dumas's notorious courtesan in *The Lady of the Camellias*, a role already made famous in Russia by Bernhardt and Duse, another *Artist* critic suggested that, given Iavorskaia's relative youth and inexperience, spectators should not expect the depth of characterization and emotional sublimity offered by the more mature foreign stars; nonetheless Iavorskaia acquitted herself admirably in the role and even had moments of brilliance. She hit the emotional high notes convincingly and persuaded critics and spectators alike of her versatility: she had proven that both serious and comic drama were well within her range.[47] In a review of Sardou's *Madame Sans-Gêne* in 1894, a production that was wildly popular with spectators, Iavorskaia was reproached for planning and executing the externals of the role so carefully that her technique became an obstacle to spontaneity.[48] In general, even when Moscow critics were not entirely satisfied with Iavorskaia, they reproached her gently, making certain to balance negative and positive criticism. This was in marked contrast to the harsh criticism she received in St. Petersburg from critics who carped unceasingly about her carelessness, obsession with externals, and tendency to improvise wildly during performances. The St. Petersburg pundits forgave her nothing.

Iavorskaia actually had more formal education and legitimate theatrical training than most actresses, but the training was firmly grounded in two increasingly retrograde traditions: the antiquated methods of the Imperial stage and the more controversial techniques of the French romantic style as exemplified by Bernhardt. In the early 1890s, trends that would later be associated with the Moscow Art Theatre were gaining currency among Russian actors: ensemble playing, emotional authenticity, and "naturalness" had begun to supplant both the more formal, declamatory methods of the Imperial stage and the contrived emotionalism of romantic acting. Iavorskaia's style was a sort of hybrid derived from these earlier schools of acting, and for that reason Negorev's claim that her technique amounted to screaming and rushing wildly around the stage must be regarded with a certain degree of skepticism. She had more "technique" than most actresses, but by the late 1890s, it was not the technique *Theatre and Art* critics wanted to see.

It is clear, however, that Iavorskaia was most comfortable with the Bernhardt repertoire and that following her initial successes at the Korsh Theatre, her approach became increasingly artificial and emulative; her emphasis on style at the expense of soul was a source of constant irritation to critics. The lesson of Sarah Bernhardt's Russian tours was that excessive emotion, melodramatic action, exoticism, sensuality, and extravagant costumes both onstage and off sold tickets. Always a quick student, Iavorskaia absorbed the lesson well and marketed herself very effectively in plays that had all or most of these qualities. Indeed, in this respect, her instincts were much sharper than either Korsh's or Suvorin's. Nonetheless, for two reasons, Iavorskaia failed to achieve the international "superstardom" she craved or even the elevated status of native stars like Savina and Ermolova: the Russian appetite for commercial Western theatre and fashion – especially Parisian – was limited, and Iavorskaia failed to establish an image free from associations with Bernhardt.

Still, it is too simple to dismiss Lidia Borisovna as a Bernhardt clone. Several critics saw in her the potential for serious artistic achievement, and when she performed scenes from Schiller's *Maria Stuart* as part of her examination at the Imperial school, an *Artist* critic wrote: "It will be difficult for Madame Iavorskaia to maintain a place in the modern repertoire. She has a naturally elevated, rather melodramatic tone – and if she can play tragedy, she will be a valuable actress."[49] Although Iavorskaia nested comfortably in the French sentimental and neo-romantic repertoire, she was a strong advocate of more thoughtful plays and performed in a variety of styles and periods ranging from Ibsen's *When We Dead Awaken* to Shakespeare's *Antony and Cleopatra*. She was apparently unremarkable in these roles, but it is doubtful whether her training prepared her to play them, or whether her reputation encouraged spectators and critics to take her seriously when she did.[50]

In spite of her early training and sporadic forays into more intellectually challenging material, it is true that over time Iavorskaia began to rely more on personal magnetism and sensuality than she did on solid technique.[51] As early as 1895, defects that became more pronounced in later years were already apparent in her performance of Iudif in *Uriel Akost*. According to one *Artist* critic, Iavorskaia's approach to the role was completely misguided; rather than the poetic image envisioned by the playwright, her Iudif was a "shrill, fussy, nervous, unhinged woman, affected and completely lacking in that femininity, spiritual grace, simplicity, and strength" that is the essence of the character. Even more damning is his suggestion that, driven by her pathological need to be the center of attention, Iavorskaia deliberately upstaged the other actors by mugging at inappropriate moments. Finally, he reproached her for being too ambitious in her choice of roles. Two years earlier this adventurousness was evidence of her versatility; now it was seen as an indication of her inability to recognize her type (light comic ingenue) and stick to it. The critic advised Iavorskaia to avoid roles that were beyond her talent, training, and discipline and further suggested that she was an *"aktris na khoroshie roli."* This, he explained, is an actress who loves her own success more than she loves the art of theatre, an actress who is interested only in effective roles. In a delightfully caustic moment, he observed that Iavorskaia's gifts were not so great that she could unite in one person Bernhardt, Duse, Rejane, Savina, and Ermolova.[52]

With respect to Iavorskaia's work at the Novyi Theatre, there is a certain unanimity of opinion among critics and colleagues that it had degenerated: the discipline characteristic of the Korsh and Suvorin years was dissipated by a whirlwind of social activities and her personal charisma had been replaced by arrogance and insensitivity. Persuaded that her mesmerizing persona and stylish wardrobe were the principal attractions, she surrounded herself with a weak ensemble of actors and her technique became increasingly slipshod. Based on memoirs and contemporaneous reviews and articles, one must conclude that actors and directors feared and disliked Iavorskaia because she treated them like indentured servants, encouraged careless, undisciplined rehearsals, improvised freely onstage during performances, and ignored the current trend toward ensemble production. Actors' anecdotes paint an unpleasant picture of the Novyi Theatre as an abyss of anarchy and caprice. Because she wanted to join her husband in St. Petersburg, Mariia Velizarii accepted a position at the Novyi Theatre, but was furious with Lidia Borisovna for hiring her at a reduced salary and for monopolizing the most desirable female roles. Velizarii also complained about the haphazard rehearsals: most theatres started at 11 o'clock in the morning, but rehearsals at the Novyi started whenever Iavorskaia deigned to appear. Lidia Borisovna's casual attitude toward memorizing and performing the author's text was another source of discontent. According to Velizarii, actors lived in fear of performing with Iavorskaia because they could not predict what she might say or do next.[53] Vera Kommissarzhevskaia, whose Dramaticheskii Theatre competed with the Novyi, suggested that Iavorskaia's management policies consisted of caprice and large quantities of champagne.[54] One of Iavorskaia's actors offered the most damning assessment: complaining that the Novyi theatre included too many "titled individuals of the female sex who give collective consultations on a wide range of questions," he dismissed it as a "ladies enterprise" (*damskaia zateia*).[55]

In spite of its detractors, the Novyi enjoyed five relatively prosperous years before attendance began to decline in 1906. Iavorskaia finally closed the theatre in 1907, and subsequently her notoriety rapidly diminished. Between 1907 and 1918, she toured extensively in Russia and abroad, took part in the struggle for women's suffrage in England, divorced Bariatinski, married an

Englishman, and after the Revolution, settled permanently in London where she died in 1921.[56]

In light of her "checkered" past and inflammatory public persona, it might well be argued that Lidia Borisovna would have been controversial in any age, but in the prerevolutionary context, she was even more so. It is, perhaps, ironic that a woman who so disrupted traditional values and conventions was an inevitable product of the very culture that so often scorned her. The complexities of Iavorskaia's position and the ways in which it reflects collective cultural anxiety about the changing role of women suggest a curious cause–effect relationship between several related phenomena: theatre reform, the growing influence of bourgeois ideology, and the consequences for theatre of the Woman Question.

Between 1890 and 1917, Russian theatre was in a constant state of crisis and flux. Obsolete theatrical conventions, social and political unrest, and rigid censorship were among the factors that inspired concerned actors, directors, playwrights, and designers to convene the First All-Russian Congress of Representatives of the Stage in 1897. The convention in turn inspired Stanislavski's and Nemirovich-Danchenko's famous eighteen-hour meeting at the Slavianski Bazaar, which culminated in the founding of the MAT and ushered in the renaissance of Russian theatre and drama. Much has already been written about this "golden age" of Russian theatre and drama, but little attention has been given in existing histories to an issue that may arguably have had broader social significance: the effects of social, political, and aesthetic reform on actresses as a class.[57] Iavorskaia, the inevitable product of a transitional, reformist age, faced a dilemma common to all Russian actresses: how to reconcile the new moral, intellectual, and aesthetic imperatives being articulated by theatre critics with an intense craving for artistic autonomy, financial independence, and popular success at any cost.[58]

Many of the critics and practitioners active in drama and production reform were also engaged in a relentless struggle to persuade both the viewing public and the theatre community itself that theatre was a legitimate craft, a responsible adult activity managed by serious, disciplined professionals. Between approximately 1897 and 1905, prominent mainstream theatre journals, especially *Theatre and Art* and *Theatrical Russia* published a veritable deluge of articles on the proper education of actors, on theatre as a tool of public enlightenment, and on the need to establish elevated moral/ ethical behavioral codes in the theatre community. The first two issues affected actresses indirectly; the third singled them out as a group for censure. All were detrimental to starring actresses.

The proper relationship between talent and craft was the focus of vigorous debate at the end of the century.[59] Advocates of systematic actor training, who gradually gained the upper hand, declared that the ability to act convincingly on stage was not a gift of nature, but a craft accessible to anyone with a modicum of talent, strong discipline, and dogged determination.

Successful performers, as they appeared in these essays, resembled efficient civil servants more than the inspirational artists of romantic and neo-romantic fiction. The emphasis on acting as a learned craft requiring self-sacrifice, discipline, and seriousness of aesthetic purpose had a negative effect on starring actresses, few of whom had formal training or believed that such training was necessary. Rather than craft, they relied on the physical and intellectual gifts with which nature had endowed them, suitability for established character types, the goodwill of munificent male patrons and actor-managers, a stylish personal wardrobe, and their own marketing instincts. Ironically, Iavorskaia was one of a handful of starring actresses who had actually attended actor training programs both at home and abroad, but that did not save her from repeated – and often justifiable – attacks by critics who reproached her for her apparent inability to play any role if she hadn't seen Bernhardt in it first, for her limited range of roles, for her onstage improvisations, and for her emphasis on the external trappings of spectacle, especially extravagant costumes.[60]

Discussions of theatre education were often accompanied by sermonizing about theatre *as* education.[61] The theme of theatre's proper role in society – its potential to inspire its devotees to lives of vice or virtue – is as old as Plato's *Republic*, but it took on new life in Russia at the end of the century when everyone wanted to hitch a ride on the cultural enlightenment bandwagon. Unfortunately, the low status of the profession hindered efforts by critics, playwrights, and actors to set the theatre up as an institution of moral instruction and to establish themselves as society's educators. For that reason, critics such as Aleksandr Kugel instructed actors that, if they aspired to teach their audiences how to live, their own lives must be beyond reproach.[62] Thus, the idea that theatre should be a tool of moral instruction was accompanied by a moral imperative for the theatre community itself. But behind Kugel's idealization of the actor as one who must stand above the crowd lies the reality of actors' and actresses' lives – and critics were quick to trace the profession's low status to the virtual absence of proto-Victorian bourgeois family values.

In 1900, *Theatre and Art* and *Theatrical Russia* launched a public discussion of backstage morality with a series of articles that appeared over a five-year period, all of which focused primarily on the moral responsibility of actresses to provide proper feminine role models, to forsake elaborate dress and foreign influences, and to cease the widespread practice of exchanging sexual favors for roles. Perhaps most significantly, they exhorted women to accept nature's gender imperative which assigned them to hearth and home. If family values were absent from the theatre community, gender roles were warped, and actors disregarded middle-class moral codes, it was, critics cried, because actresses had renounced their femininity and duty toward the family.[63]

Like the systematization of actor training, the introduction of middle-class morality into the theatre community was part of a calculated move to professionalize and "bourgeoisify" Russian theatre, trends that were simultaneously problematic and propitious for an actress of Iavorskaia's type and temperament.[64] Lidia Borisovna seemed to derive special glee from flaunting all restrictions, both implicit and explicit, that smacked of middle-class values and morality. Taken together, her independence, left-wing politics, patina of Western Europeanism, personal vanity, intellectual and aristocratic pretensions, taste for the exotic, and love of publicity created a public persona that simultaneously attracted large, enthusiastic audiences and repulsed critics and practitioners, many of whom were heavily invested in the process of bourgeoisification.

In addition, Shchepkina revealed a peculiarity of Iavorskaia's personality that would have particularly disturbed theatre critics busy dashing off essentialist diatribes on the "natural" inclinations and duties of women. Lidia Borisovna, she claimed, had nothing of the feminine, as it was then defined, in her personality. She could not hold a needle; she had no taste for the things that usually occupied women's attention (flowers, music, and domestic activities); and she had no special fondness for children.[65] Although few successful actress had the leisure to pursue traditional feminine activities, what apparently damned Iavorskaia was that she did not even pretend to be interested.

Her relationships with male colleagues, critics, and admirers were often strained. Lidia Borisovna was a stunningly attractive woman by the standards of the period, but, according to Shchepkina, she was cold as an alpine sky: "her eyes were very strange ... sometimes one felt a certain emptiness in them, as if they didn't reflect or perceive the outside world, sometimes they were vague, sometimes they watched cruelly, not blinking; these could be the eyes of a *rusalka*, which have no human feeling and no depth."[66] Men were often charmed by, and attracted to Iavorskaia, but when she failed to respond to their advances, passionate admiration was quickly transformed into violent dislike.[67] She was, in short, the antithesis of the self-sacrificing, ideal actress/ woman for whom love and feminine duty were paramount. Self-centered, vain, arrogant, and enormously confident, Iavorskaia worshipped brazenly at the altar of self-gratification, and by so doing, came to epitomize those features of contemporary theatre that most antagonized moralists and reformers.[68]

Finally, Iavorskaia was often reproached for her preference for Western European ideas and values, and especially for her tendency to imitate Bernhardt both onstage and off. Before 1900, critics assailed Iavorskaia for promoting shallow, Western commercial drama and theatre. After the turn of the century, the addition to her repertoire of progressive plays by Ibsen, Strindberg, Maeterlinck, and other Western modernists proved equally controversial. After she opened her own theatre, like Kommissarzhevskaia, Iavorskaia gravitated toward roles clearly influenced by the Western model of the New Woman.

During the Silver Age, the New Woman, the Woman Question, and the Women's Movement provoked renewed hostility from Russian theatre critics. In 1897, Kugel responded to the effects of the Women's Movement on theatre by claiming that it had produced a whiney, disordered, dissatisfied type of emancipated woman. He further suggests that because the movement inspired women to question traditional roles, the theatre was being inundated with hordes of talentless, aggressive aspiring actresses for whom there were no jobs.[69] Another *Theatre and Art* critic, V. Linski, wrote in 1900 that it was as dangerous to marry an ambitious, career-minded actress as it was to marry a female scholar (*zhenshchina nauka*): they represent two extremes, tropical heat and polar cold, but neither makes a satisfactory wife.[70] In 1903, distressed by the implications of Ibsen's female characters, Linski wrote another series of articles entitled "The New Woman" (*Novaia zhenshchina*); in them he argued that the New Woman strives above all else "to destroy the foundation of the contemporary family;" she will even "destroy another's happiness to satisfy her own needs."[71] Given the distaste expressed by many critics for Western European realism, especially with respect to its representation of women, it is hardly surprising that Iavorskaia, who came to symbolize everything critics found most repellent in the New Woman, would become the well into which they poured their venom.

Were critics and colleagues just? Was Iavorskaia simply a mediocre actress with an instinct for self-promotion that rivaled Bernhardt's in her own time and Madonna's in ours, and does she now rest in well-deserved anonymity? In his obituary, Efros observed that Lidia Borisovna wanted more fame than she got and got less than she deserved.[72] After Iavorskaia's death, Kugel expressed regret for the gratuitously cruel feuilletons he wrote about her at the turn of the century. Recalling her role in the *The Smugglers* scandal, he remarked with a touch of nostalgia that, in certain respects, Iavorskaia was quite a pleasant woman.[73] Although both Efros and Kugel acknowledged that Iavorskaia received disproportionately negative criticism from the theatrical press, neither suggests that her role in the development of Silver Age theatre merits further serious scrutiny. Even her most sincere apologist, Shchepkina-Kupernik, who, in a brief flash of divine inspiration, actually suggests that certain gender expectations may have handicapped Iavorskaia, avoids the temptation of painting her as one of the great figures of the period. Soviet historians, apparently not amused by her publicity stunts and unreconstructed elitism, not only failed to resuscitate her reputation, but even erased her as a key figure in the *The Smugglers* debacle and the 1905 theatre strike.[74]

Traditional theatre historiography does not permit reconsideration of Iavorskaia as a major force in Silver Age theatre, but feminist historiography instructs us to view with suspicion the erasure of controversial women. Within a feminist framework, Iavorskaia can profitably be understood as a sort of bellwether whose exploits (and the reactions to them) reveal how precarious the position of women in Russian theatre was during a supposedly reformist age, and how easily the patina of liberalism rubbed off when patriarchal privilege was threatened by a genuinely unruly woman. Iavorskaia wanted to be taken seriously as an artist, but was hampered by an unfortunate confluence of circumstances: endowed by nature with considerable physical beauty and personal magnetism, she was bereft of those conventional feminine sensibilitites that would have allowed her to exploit them effectively. Ambitious and impatient for fame, she was hostile to suggestions that she reconcile herself to the status of appendage – a competent actress forever doomed to play second fiddle to more prominent actors. Dazzled by Bernhardt's "superstardom," inspired by her autonomy, assertiveness, and flair for the bizzare, Iavorskaia chose a route to fame at odds with both Russian theatrical tradition and the quickening trend toward bourgeoisification. For this reason, more graphically than any actress of the period, Iavorskaia symbolized the ambivalence and liminal status of Russian women as they stood on the threshold of cultural revolution.

8

LITTLE GIRL LOST
The deification of Vera Kommissarzhevskaia

Vera Fedorovna Kommissarzhevskaia, the actress whose seemingly un-pronounceable last name still twists the tongues of Western critics and historians, is little known outside Russia except as the creator of Nina Zarechnaia in the *The Seagull*, and as the actress who dared to fire Vsevolod Meierhold. In contrast to Brenko, Goreva, Iavorskaia, and other less promin-ent actress-entrepreneurs, most of whom are unknown in the West and largely forgotten in Russia, Kommissarzhevskaia's name is still spoken with great reverence in her native land. Wildly popular during the last decade of the nineteenth century and first decade of the twentieth, she inspired her admirers with the passionate enthusiasm of religious zealots. Engimatic, ambitious, frequently tormented by personal, political, and aesthetic contra-dictions, Kommissarzhevskaia stands as a complex symbol of the Silver Age itself. Although Iavorskaia and Kommissarzhevskaia promoted many of the same playwrights, supported many of the same causes, and followed Western trends in art and literature, critics and progressive spectators responded very differently to them. Despite her efforts to project the image of an enlightened, progressive artist, Iavorskaia was associated in the collective public consciousness with debased Western commercialism. In contrast, Kommissarzhevskaia embodied elevated modernity tempered by just the right touch of national identity.

According to Aleksandr Kugel, her unprecedented popularity was based not upon conscious artistry, but upon the carefully cultivated image of "a fragile, suffering child of our times."[1] Although Kommissarzhevskaia has been compared by critics and historians to both Ermolova and Strepetova, she was neither a classical heroine nor a true neurasthenic. For several reasons, however, the comparison is legitimate: like her predecessors, Vera Fedorovna tended to approach acting as an extension of self rather than a process of creating discrete characters; she was the focus of a personality cult; and she relied primarily on inspiration rather than craft. Although critics leveled charges of inflexibility and monotony against Ermolova, Strepetova, and Kommissarzhevskaia, their capacity for suffering and astonishing ability to depict profound emotional anguish on stage counterpoised their apparent inability to creat a broad spectrum of distinctive characters.

Ermolova, Strepetova, and Kommissarzhevskaia also resembled each other in the sense that their extraordinary popularity was based, for the most part, on the needs of particular social and political environments rather than on purely artistic accomplishments. Strepetova was a product of populism; Ermolova appealed to a spirit of social protest current during the 1870s and 1880s; Kommissarzhevskaia's popularity was a response to the growing confusion surrounding the collapse of Imperial Russia. Her celebrity coincides chronologically with the *fin de siècle* and the Silver Age of art and literature. This transitional period was marked by political agitation, social unrest, and escalating conflict within the artistic, literary, and theatrical communities. The fragile peace between the autocracy and its restive constituents was rapidly crumbling. Dissatisfaction with the existing social order eventually culminated in the failed uprising of 1905 and the successful revolution of 1917. The desire among university students and representatives of the progressive intelligentsia for fundamental structural change in the social, political, and cultural life of the country was reflected in the world of art. The "theatre crisis" (*krizis teatra*) that began in the late 1890s and was resolved, at least temporarily, by the revolution, was part of a broader trend in Russian art that paralleled current social and political tensions.

Kommissarzhevskaia, whose image sustained several transformations both during her life and posthumously, was surely the most controversial actress of the era. Her appeal was primarily to the alienated, to the oppressed, and to the soulful seekers of perfect beauty, truth, and spirituality in art. She was also the first starring actress to enjoy enthusiastic support from women, especially women of the intelligentsia and female university students (*kursistki*). Not surprisingly, Kommissarzhevskaia's signature role was for many years Chekhov's Nina Zarechnaia. The concomitant ascendancy of Chekhov's dramaturgy and the hypersensitive actress most closely identified with his fragmented heroines marks the last significant shift in Russian gender ideology before the Revolution.

LIFE WITH FATHER: THE VICISSITUDES OF AN ARTISTIC CHILDHOOD

Born in 1864, Vera Kommissarzhevskaia was the eldest child of opera star Fedor Petrovich Kommissarzhevski and Mariia Shulgina, the only daughter of the commander of the Preobrazhenskii regiment. From a class perspective, their marriage caused much comment in that segment of St. Petersburg society that cared about such things. Although Kommissarzhevski was the reigning star of the Imperial Mariinskii Theatre and the union was apparently one of mutual affection, he was a performer and therefore considered beneath the daughter of an Imperial officer.[2] According to popular legend,

Kommissarzhevski "abducted" Mariia Shulgina – much to her family's dismay. The marriage, which lasted until the late 1870s, produced four children: Vera, Nadezhda, Olga, and Grisha.[3]

Firmly positioned at the center of the family universe, Fedor Petrovich was the sun around which the lesser planets – his wife and children – circulated. According to Vera Kommissarzhevskaia's friends, colleagues, and relatives, Kommissarzhevski was an impulsive, romantic figure whose ideas, caprices, and desires dominated his daughter's life and imagination. A well-educated man who graduated from the St. Petersburg University, he entered the civil service, but could not adjust to the restrictive routines and regulations governing civil servants. Persuaded that he was endowed by nature with a superlative vocal instrument, Kommissarzhevski left government service and set off to study opera in Italy. When he arrived, civil war was raging. Kommissarzhevski postponed his opera career, fought with Garibaldi, and finally, following the war, arrived in Milan to take up his studies. He enjoyed success on concert stages in Europe and South America before returning to Russia to join the Imperial Mariinskii opera, where he cultivated an enthusiastic following.

While her parents' marriage lasted, Vera Fedorovna and her siblings enjoyed a privileged existence. The family was comfortable financially, had homes in St. Petersburg and the country, and counted many distinguished artists, including Stravinski, Mussorgski, and Shaliapin among their friends. Bourgeois values were largely absent from their home and the children were raised in an atmosphere of "artistic chaos."[4] Liubov Gurevich, a friend of Vera Fedorovna's and editor of the progressive journal *The Northern Herald* (*Severnyi vestnik*), suggested that Mariia Shulgina enjoyed considerably more influence in the family than Kommissarzhevskaia's admirers wished to acknowledge.[5] By most accounts, however, Vera was her father's child.

Kommissarzhevski's authority in the home and influence over his daughter had both positive and negative consequences. For example, he encouraged her to distinguish between low and high art and to cultivate a taste for the high. In addition, although he did not encourage any of his daughters to act professionally, he provided them with ample opportunities to attend his own rehearsals and performances, and supported their domestic amateur theatricals. Finally, as a member of the progressive intelligentsia, he set an example for the family of liberal politics. On the other hand, because he moved her from one school to another in rapid succession, Vera Fedorovna's formal education was inadequate. When she did attend school, she wasted her time playing practical jokes on teachers and classmates, failed her final exams, and did not prepare for anything. Indeed, until her late twenties, Kommissarzhevskaia was a dilettante who knew neither system nor discipline. Either genetically or by example, she acquired many of her father's most questionable characteristics: a tendency to flit from one ephemeral passion to the next, chronic impulsiveness and inconsistency, and intolerance for anything or anyone that did not meet her exalted aesthetic and spiritual standards.[6]

Vera Fedorovna maintained a childlike devotion to her father even after he deserted the family and sold their property – purchased with Mariia Shulgina's inheritance – in order to support his new wife.[7] Shulgina and the children were reduced to a standard of living like the one depicted by Dostoevski in *Poor People*. Following the divorce, Vera Fedorovna lived alternately with her mother and father. Perhaps the insecurity and uncertainty of her domestic situation slowed her maturation: in 1880/81, a friend of the family observed that although she was almost sixteen years old, Kommissarzhevskaia "seemed much younger and behaved like a child. She was not interested in clothing, courting, or parties with dancing."[8] Her apparent indifference to adolescent sexual rites of passage vanished when Count Muravev, an impoverished artist-aristocrat, entered her life. In an improvident move, the infatuated Kommissarzhevskaia married the count in 1883. The marriage was a disaster, and after numerous infidelities on his part and incidents of domestic violence, she left him in 1885.[9]

Following six years of emotional distress and boredom, Kommissarzhevskaia began searching for direction. Not surprisingly, she turned to the theatre. In 1891, she persuaded Vladimir Davydov, an old friend of her father's and one of the Aleksandrinskii's most prominent senior actors, to give her lessons. Perhaps because Davydov did not predict a brilliant future for her, she gave up the lessons in 1892 and, hoping for a career in opera, moved to Moscow to live with her father. Kommissarzhevski, now a professor at the Moscow Conservatory, was deeply involved in pedagogical activities. Together with Aleksandr Fedotov and Konstantin Stanislavski, he had recently founded the Society for Art and Literature, which included musical-dramatic courses.[10] Kommissarzhevskaia took singing lessons from her father, performed in student productions, and played Betsy in Tolstoi's *The Fruits of Enlightenment* directed by Stanislavski. Although her voice was pleasant, it was not sufficiently powerful for a career in opera. During a performance of Tolstoi's play, however, she made such an impression on Ivan Kiselevski, a prominent provincial actor, that he recommended her to the progressive director-entrepreneur, Nikolai Sinelnikov. She signed a contract with Sinelnikov, set off to join his company in Novocherkassk, and at the advanced age of twenty-nine, a time when most actresses were considered past their prime, she began to act professionally.

AN ANTI-HERO OF HER TIME

Although it might legitimately be argued that Fedor Kommissarzhevski's reputation and authority in the theatre community guaranteed his daughter's career, his influence alone cannot explain the enormity of Vera Fedorovna's success or the astonishing rapidity of her ascent. Most of the actresses in this study – Fedotova, Savina, Ermolova, Strepetova, and Brenko – achieved fame during periods of uncertainty, unrest, and transition, but the response to Iavorskaia and Kommissarzhevskaia, both of whom appeared on the very cusp of revolution, was produced by a different spirit. In contrast to Iavorskaia, whose dalliance with liberal politics and avant garde aesthetics propelled her into liminality but not beyond it, Kommissarzhevskaia plunged enthusiastically – and often blindly – into the new ideologies and aesthetics of the late nineteenth and early twentieth centuries. The image of *"zhen-vennost"* associated with her is inseparable from the social context that created it.

Because pre-revolutionary and Soviet theatre historians have written voluminously about Kommissarzhevskaia, the chronology and details of her professional biography are easily accessible. But because her image was so laden with cultural symbolism both during her life and posthumously, she is what semioticians might call a signifier with an unstable signified. During the course of her professional life, as the pressure for sweeping political, social, and cultural reform in Russia increased, Kommissarzhevskaia responded to each new shift in liberal politics and avant garde aesthetics by assimilating it into her own image and work. Following her early death from smallpox while on tour in Tashkent in 1910, pre- and post-Revolutionary eulogists rushed to refashion the actress's image to suit their own ideological agendas – further complicating the task of positioning her ideologically in pre-Revolutionary culture. Nonetheless, Kommissarzhevskaia's image was produced by an identifiable gender ideology and it served the needs of a particular social context.

Vera Fedorovna flourished during the Silver Age, a period marked by contradiction, innovation, and growing political cynicism. Liberal students, artists, and representatives of the progressive intelligentsia were consumed by feelings of alienation and inadequacy. Cultural influences pouring into Russia from the West exacerbated existing tensions between advocates of change and champions of tradition in Moscow and St. Petersburg. Crisis was inevitable, but rather than instituting much needed reforms, the government responded to accelerating antagonism toward the autocracy with a bewildering array of political compromises followed by acts of violent repression. According to Liubov Gurevich, Kommissarzhevskaia was identified with the generation that came of age during the 1890s, a generation marked by anxiety and preoccupation with personal psychology. It was a time of "ideological and artistic uncertainty, of impatient groping for new forms in art and life." There were no firm points of reference or "guiding ideas formulated by some great man of the past or present."[11] Kommissarzhevskaia's success was a natural response to growing social, political, and psychological fragmentation in Russia.[12]

Because she entered the theatre late and died unexpectedly at the age of forty-six, Kommissarzhevskaia's professional life was intense, but relatively brief. Between 1893 and 1896, she traveled the provincial circuit. In 1896, she was hired by the Imperial Aleksandrinskii Theatre where she remained for six years. Finally, between 1902 and 1910, she organized and managed her own theatrical enterprise in St. Petersburg. During the first portion of her career (1893–1902), Kommissarzhevskaia established the stage image of an afflicted adolescent and the reputation of an aesthete; during the second (1902–1910), she expended tremendous energy trying to shed the image and refine the reputation.

Although theatre critic Iuri Beliaev, one of Kommissarzhevskaia's most ardent admirers, tried to pass her off as a provincial phenomenon, her tenure on the circuit was brief and she was not a self-identified provincial actress.[13] Because she worked with two very respectable provincial entrepreneurs and enjoyed enthusiastic support from the local intelligentsia, Vera Fedorovna's experience in the provinces was more fortunate than that of most actresses. But because the predominantly debased tastes of provincial spectators, entrepreneurs, and actors were in contrast to the elevated aesthetic values inculcated by her father, she was not naturally inclined to the provincial repertoire or to life on the provincial circuit.[14] After one season playing second ingenues and vaudeville roles with Sinelnikov, she moved to Konstantin Nezlobin's company in Vilnius, where she occupied the position of first comic and dramatic ingenue. Like most actresses who played the provinces, Kommissarzhevskaia was obligated to perform primarily in commercial rubbish. Nonetheless, the 1894–1895 season at Vilnius was pivotal for two reasons: Kommissarzhevskaia discovered her preferred type – the angst-ridden, alienated adolescent – and she began to cultivate an enthusiastic following among male university students and *kursistki*. Her most effective role was Rosie in Hermann Sudermann's *Battle of the Butterflies* (*Boi babochek*), a popular domestic "coming-of-age" drama that featured a tragic adolescent as its central character.

The action of Sudermann's play can usefully be understood as an adolescent gender rite of passage. Rosie, a young girl who has just begun to explore her own sexuality and understand the implications of "*zhenstvennost*," must accept intense suffering and self-sacrifice as necessary components of a woman's life. Implicit in the play is the conviction that knowledge of self and the possibility of transcendence can be achieved only through affliction, ordeal, and endurance. Among Russian women, the idea that suffering and self-sacrifice are inevitable, necessary, and even desirable aspects of existence was not new. But during the 1890s, it had tremendous appeal for well-educated, idealistic young spectators, many of whom yearned for purpose, direction, and meaningful activity. Although students of both sexes identified strongly with Kommissarzhevskaia's heroines, they had special appeal for young women. The *kursistki*, many of whom sacrificed personal contentment and domestic prosperity for service to higher ideals, were among her most passionate admirers.

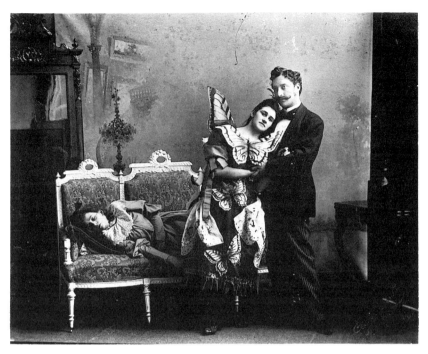

Figure 6 Vera Kommissarzhevskaia in Sudemann's *Battle of the Butterflies*. Courtesy of the Central State Archive of Literature and Art (TsGALI)

Battle of the Butterflies established Kommissarzhevskaia as a major new talent. Rosie not only became her signature role, every role she played subsequently was a variation on Rosie. Kommissarzhevskaia's appeal was based, however, not only on the roles she chose, but on her unique, deeply emotional, "naturalistic" style of acting. Indeed, later commentators often suggest that Vera Fedorovna did naturally what Konstantin Stanislavski developed an entire system to teach less gifted actors to do.[15] In 1895, a Moscow critic who saw Kommissarzhevskaia in Vilnius described the experience: "Spectators are struck first of all by the astonishing simplicity of Kommissarzhevskaia's acting, a simplicity rarely encountered on either provincial or capital stages, with the exception of the Moscow Malyi Theatre. The actress before you is not playing a role; she is a flesh and blood human being. She merges so completely with the person she's playing that she walks, speaks, and feels with the character."[16]

Reports of the new theatrical phenomenon reached the capital cities, and in the summer of 1895, a popular suburban St. Petersburg theatre hired her for the summer season. The following year, her debut on the Aleksandrinskii stage in *Battle of the Butterflies* created a sensation in St. Petersburg.[17]

Although critics were not universally positive, Kommissarzhevskaia's dominant qualities – simplicity, sincerity, spontaneity, and pathos – appealed to sophisticated audiences in St. Petersburg just as they had in the provinces. Long before the first curtain call, enthusiastic spectators and critics began speculating which of the Aleksandrinskii's reigning favorites she would displace.[18] Surely no one who followed internal politics at the Aleksandrinskii Theatre was surprised at the answer, for when the battle lines were finally drawn the principal adversaries turned out to be Kommissarzhevskaia and Savina.

The general contours of this conflict were introduced in Chapter 3: the tacit hierarchy of the Aleksandrinskii Theatre permitted one leading actress at a time and when Kommissarzhevskaia joined the company, Savina, who had already occupied the position for two decades, did not intend to share or relinquish it. A champion of traditional values and commercial expediency, Savina jealously defended her territory from encroachments by younger competitors. The hostility between the two actresses was personal, professional, and ideological. Savina represented the values and ideas of the 1870s and 1880s; Kommissarzhevskaia represented new trends in art, politics, and culture that developed after 1890. The most striking example of the differences between them was the Aleksandrinskii's disastrous production of *The Seagull* in 1896.

There is, perhaps, no greater irony in the history of late nineteenth-century Russian theatre than the original casting of *The Seagull*. Although the selection of the play for production at the Aleksandrinskii did not involve Savina or Kommissarzhevskaia directly, both were deeply implicated in the process of casting. Evtikhi Karpov, the theatre's managing director, asked several leading actors and actresses to read *The Seagull* and one, Elizaveta Levkeeva, was so enthusiastic that she asked Karpov to produce the play for her benefit.[19] Karpov wanted Kommissarzhevskaia for the role of Nina, but Aleksei Suvorin, who represented Chekhov in the negotiations, did not agree. Perhaps because Chekhov's dramaturgy was still a novelty in 1896 and Savina was the reigning star of the Aleksandrinskii, Suvorin wanted to assure the success of his friend's play by casting the now forty-two-year-old actress in the most advantageous, albeit unsuitable, role.

If Savina was excessively egocentric, she was not stupid. After agreeing to play Nina, she did not appear for the first rehearsal, but sent an apologetic note to Suvorin asking him to persuade Chekhov to release her from the obligation. Savina indicated that after rereading the play, she felt Chekhov would be better served by a younger actress and recommended Kommissarzhevskaia for the role. She offered to play Masha, but the role was already assigned.[20] Karpov appealed to Kommissarzhevskaia, who, even though she wanted the role, hesitated to accept Savina's leavings. Nonetheless, she took the script home, reread it, and the following morning agreed to play Nina Zarechnaia.[21] By the third rehearsal, she was "living in the role," and during the first performance, she alone pleased the author, the director, and at least some spectators and critics.[22] According to Karpov, Kommissarzhevskaia succeeded because she was the only member of the cast who understood the new dramaturgy: although the entire cast worked diligently during the brief rehearsal period, except for Vera Fedorovna, none of them had the "right tools" or the "right tone" to realize "Anton Chekhov's delicate, moody play."[23]

Although *Battle of the Butterflies* remained a favorite of Kommissarzhevskaia's devotees, with *The Seagull* she found her genre and strengthened ties with progressives in the Aleksandrinskii audience and in the St. Petersburg theatre community.[24] If the failure of Chekhov's play discouraged the Aleksandrinskii directorate from further forays into modernism, it did not deter Kommissarzhevskaia. The Aleksandrinskii refused to remount *The Seagull*, but Vera Fedorovna was so convinced of the viability of Chekhov's dramaturgy and identified so strongly with Nina Zarechnaia that she insisted upon including the play in her summer touring repertoire. Eventually Zarechnaia and Kommissarzhevskaia were so closely associated in the minds of many spectators, critics, and eulogists that Chekhov's fictional construct and Russia's reigning theatrical princess merged into a single legend of hope for redemption through suffering.

Like most starring actresses, Kommissarzhevskaia tended to eclipse the plays in which she appeared, but her self-selected repertoire was significant because it reflected the social reality of late Imperial Russia. Dissatisfaction with existing conditions and enthusiasm for plays featuring Russia's newest theatrical phenomenon increased proportionately, which suggests that contemporary spectators and at least some critics hungered for forms of drama and theatre that would articulate the feelings of ambivalence, anguish, outrage, fear, and confusion common to a jaded generation of young people and a country on the brink of civil war. The time for Savina's French salon comedies and Ermolova's romantic heroic drama was past; the era of Chekhov's weary anti-heroes had arrived.

During the each phase of her career, Kommissarzhevskaia's preferred repertoire remained consistent. Nina was not a radical departure from her earlier roles and cannot be distinguished in any significant way from Rosie. Both begin as unblemished, sensitive, virginal adolescents who are crushed, or at least immeasurably changed, by confrontations with harsh reality. Oddly, during this period, Kommissarzhevskaia also had tremendous success as Larisa in Ostrovski's *The Dowerless Bride* (*Bespridannitsa*). The play and the role diverged from Vera Fedorovna's usual repertoire: not only is *The Dowerless Bride* coarse domestic realism rather than lyric prose poem, Larisa is distinguished from Rosie and Nina by class, ethnicity, and type. Although Kommissarzhevskaia and Strepetova had little in common, on the basis of her success in *The Dowerless Bride*, one critic suggested that Kommissarzhevskaia would eventually inherit Strepetova's mantle.[25] In Vera Fedorovna's hands, however, Larisa began to sound suspiciously like Nina Zarechnaia, and the author of *The Dowerless Bride* might as well have been Chekhov, Sudermann, or even Ibsen.[26]

According to Beliaev, regardless of their suitability to an individual author's text, three elements were omnipresent in the inner lives of Kommissarzhevskaia's characters: "youth, degradation, and death."[27] Kommissarzhevskaia's preoccupations reflected those of her audience. For that reason, her success with such seemingly disparate characters as Larisa and Nina reveals a great deal about the expectations and inclinations of Russian critics and spectators during the *fin de siècle*. But were they responding to the author's intentions or the actress's reality? Evidence suggests that, for many, the author's construct was indistinguishable from, and subordinate to, Kommissarzhevskaia herself.

For V.V. Rozanov, the most striking feature of Kommissarzhevskaia's life and art was the "overlap of role and reality, of living being and actress." She was not an actress in the same sense as Savina: "Take away Savina's wardrobe, makeup, and roles," Rozanov asked, "and what remains? Just an actress."[28] S. Adrianov, who preferred Kommissarzhevskaia's "lyrical talent" to Savina's "artificial virtuosity," complained that no matter how many roles she played, Savina's reality was hidden from the spectator.[29] Because she brought "her own soul" and "real experiences" onto the stage, Kommissarzhevskaia created an illusion of intimacy that had tremendous appeal for many critics and spectators. I.I. Zabrezhnev added that "Savina's girls were graceful, sympathetic, vital young ladies with great love for life" – but they had no experience of "ennobling suffering" and little inclination to "strive for elusive ideals." In contrast, Kommissarzhevskaia "tears through the conventional cloth of the role and reveals the person, not the actress. All of her roles are illuminated by her own individuality – by the charm of her youth, melancholy, and poetic temperament."[30]

Rozanov spoke for many of Kommissarzhevskaia's admirers when he said that she was not, strictly speaking, an actress. She did not use makeup or elaborate costuming to conceal her reality, her most effective roles were those that allowed her to play herself, and her own physical delicacy was an essential aspect of her appeal.[31] If acting meant the art of transformation, effective mimicry, choreographed gestures, beautiful costumes, contrived sensuality, and feigned emotion, then Kommissarzhevskaia's devotees did not want an actress. The absence of makeup and other marks of feminine artifice gave Vera Fedorovna an aura of pristine pre-sexuality. She was effective precisely because she was perceived as a genuinely tragic individual whose performances were a matter of personal necessity. Rather than a learned skill, her immense powers of expression were divinely inspired. They allowed her to share her authentic emotional anguish with the audience: her pain was their pain.[32]

Kommissarzhevskaia's pain was also Russia's pain. Aleksandr Kugel argued that from the first, Vera Fedorovna was a "sorrowful walking symbol," whose profound existential distress transcended the bounds of prosaic reality.[33] Unhappy from birth, her heroines suffered not from external circumstances, but because suffering was a natural and inevitable consequence of being human and living in Russia during a time of moral, spiritual, and physical decay.[34] Echoing his colleagues, Osip Dymov wrote: "With unusual sensitivity, she caught the rhythm of life, the breath of an epoch. It seemed that our generation empowered her to inspire us. . . . Kommissarzhevskaia's astonishing gifts reflected the aspirations of our country, which was suffocating silently, the confusion of Russian youth with their dream of a more beautiful life."[35] Eternally discordant, impulsive, inspired, and agitated, she embodied modernity.

Both Ermolova and Kommissarzhevskaia served as symbols of inspiration for Russians during times of national distress. But if Kommissarzhevskaia inspired her own generation, it was not by means of classical beauty or romantic-heroic imagery. Embedded within Kommissarzhevskaia's "modernity" was a new gender ideology that required its bearer to project the image of a fragile, ethereal, and rather helpless child. As one reverential critic described her physical appearance, she was "not a beauty in the narrow sense of the word. Fragile, extremely nervous, with a tender, rather childlike profile, her large dark grey eyes often seem to strive upwards. In their expression you feel the secret of spiritual self-knowledge. Her smile is touching and reserved. Her pure, deep, sincere voice charms listeners from the first word she utters." Imbued with "quiet feminine charm," she soars on the "white wings of an angel. Rather than intense joy, her gestures often express sincere tenderness, entreaty, and the helplessness of a dying creature."[36] Another suggested that Kommissarzhevskaia's "charming creatures" inspired deep sympathy in the audience and a desire to "protect them from life's adversities."[37]

Vera Fedorovna was absurd in historical costume dramas; she could not play one-dimensional classical heroines like the Maid of Orleans; and the witty, fashionable, unsympathetic ladies of French salon dramas were equally inaccessible to the somber, rather humorless idol of St. Petersburg's youth culture. Kommissarzhevskaia's brand of "*zhenstvennost*" was personified in the image of Chekhov's ill-starred seagull, Nina Zarechnaia. One historian argued that Zarechnaia was the key to Kommissarzhevskaia herself. Like Nina, Vera Fedorovna came to art through excrutiating personal affliction. For both, suffering opened paths to spiritual freedom and creativity; theatre was not a profession, but a mission, not a career, but a calling.[38] According to one critic, Kommissarzhevskaia and "Chekhov's creation" were not only inseparable, but also represented the collective condition of Russian actresses.[39]

Although reverential critics, spectators, and historians were largely responsible for creating and perpetuating the hyperbolic mythology that surrounded Kommissarzhevskaia, she was complicit in the creation of her own legend. Nadezhda Tiraspolskaia, who performed with Vera Fedorovna in Vilnius, reported one of their conversations about acting. Kommissar-zhevskaia explained that she envied Tiraspolskaia's ability to separate herself emotionally from her characters: "My nature requires me to feel *with* my characters – I don't know how to act any other way. I have to wash each role in the blood of my own heart." Tiraspolskaia added that this was not just empty rhetoric: "Kommissarzhevskaia really did not succeed in roles that were alien to her nature."[40] Nikolai Khodotov, Kommissarzhevskaia's frequent collaborator and constant companion at the Aleksandrinskii Theatre, argued that the intensity of her internal process was unique among Imperial actors. She advised him to apply her method of creating a role to his own process. "Work, work," she wrote: "Take the role and *feel, feel how it would be if this was happening to you*, become one with character, and only after you've immersed yourself in his suffering and joy, confusion and serenity should you remember that you and he are different."[41]

According to Khodotov, each role cost Kommissarzhevskaia tremendous physical and spiritual anguish: "She brought all the truth of her own suffering on stage, all the flutterings of her own fantasy, all her aspirations, doubts, passion, and love for nature and people." Spectators responded so passionately to her because "many of them found answers to their own experiences in hers."[42] Although Kommissarzhevskaia enjoyed nearly universal support among younger spectators, women, especially young women, were particularly responsive to her image and message. If qualities of helplessness and fragility drew male spectators to her, women may have been attracted by her strengths.

During the course of her career, Kommissarzhevskaia earned the sobriquet the "Russian Duse." Because most Russian critics doted on Duse, the comparison was intended to flatter and usually referred to the fact that, like Duse, Kommissarzhevskaia was an actress of little range and great pathos.[43] Iuri Beliaev went a step farther when he identified their "common feminism" as an important similarity. For Beliaev, this "natural feminism" was manifested in the tendency of both actresses to emphasize the most attractive, congenial aspects of their characters' "*zhenstvennost*" – a strategy that encouraged spectators to respond compassionately and "render a verdict of not guilty" on otherwise unsympathetic female characters.[44]

Although there is little evidence that Kommissarzhevskaia was a self-identified feminist, after leaving the Aleksandrinskii in 1902, she began to borrow more heavily from Duse's repertoire. Perhaps because this repertoire included Ibsen, Vera Fedorovna became closely identified in the minds of spectators with the Western European New Woman. Rosie and Nina were joined after 1902 by Nora Helmer (*A Doll's House*) and Hilda Wangel (*The Master Builder*). In addition, although she rarely joined formal movements, Kommissarzhevskaia began to take an active interest in the political life of her country. She associated openly with the liberal left, which often supported women's issues (for example, education reform, equal employment opportun-

Figure 7 Vera Kommissarzhevskaia – the Russian Duse. Courtesy of the Central State Archive of Literature and Art (TsGALI)

ities, suffrage, and property rights) and cultivated the external marks of a progressive woman. Kommissarzhevskaia was fashionable, but her style – elegant in its severity and simplicity – reflected the tastes of the young women of the intelligentsia rather than the doyens of Parisian fashion.[45] Neither Duse nor Kommissarzhevskaia were voluptuous or conventionally beautiful; Duse's mature sensuality was, however, in marked contrast to the passionate, but clearly pre-sexual image cultivated by Kommissarzhevskaia. It is no wonder, then, that the *kursistki* and other sober, socially progressive young women were among Vera Fedorovna's most vocal partisans.

If Kommisssarzhevskaia was not a political feminist, she was perceived by many of her contemporaries as a spokesperson for the New Woman in Russia. Liubov Gurevich, who promoted Ibsen in Russia by publishing his plays in *The Northern Herald*, wrote that Kommissarzhevskaia brought qualities of the "modern woman" into her roles – qualities that the authors themselves may not have wanted.[46] Osip Dymov contended that whenever Kommissarzhevskaia performed, the "spiritual aspect of contemporary women arose." "She bequeathed to us," he continued, "the image of the new woman who reflects all of the most delicate palpitations, possibilities, and experiences of our time." She was the "daughter of the epoch," and when she spoke, it was always about the "impulses of modern women."[47] For Nikolai Efros, Kommissarzhevskaia was not just an actress for new women, but "an actress for all women." Because they "loved Vera Fedorovna most of all," Efros argued, "women were the first to recognize and worship her talent." She was the "singer of their sorrows, the one who expressed their strengths and weaknesses, their tragedy, tears, and disillusionment." She was the "voice of women's collective heart."[48] Although not heroic in the tradition of Ermolova, Kommissarzhevskaia's women had "tremendous reserves of spiritual strength." Perhaps therein lay the secret of their appeal for female spectators. Full of doubt and inner conflict, modern Russian women struggled, like Kommissarzhevskaia's Zarechnaia, to overcome the challenges of a rapidly changing social environment.[49]

Although critics might dismiss the views of her admirers as sentimental, posthumous hyberbole, the fact that Kommissarzhevskaia's detractors also acknowledged the strength of her female following lends credence to the idea that women constituted her principal base of support. Aleksandr Kugel, whose bilious assaults on Kommissarzhevskaia appeared regularly in *Theatre and Art*, complained that she had transformed the Aleksandrinskii Theatre into a children's nursery (*detskii sad*), and that her popularity was based on extreme accessibility rather than art.[50] Arguing that Kommissarzhevskaia's "clarity" compensated for her lack of technique, he accused her of sacrificing the author's text to her own agenda. It was her easy accessibility and "democratic, plebian quality," Kugel concluded caustically, that appealed to "female medical assistants, *gimnazistki*, and *kursistki*," who consider "beautiful manners, a beautiful figure, and a beautiful dress to be the marks of a reactionary." They reserve their admiration for someone who is "awkward, anguished, emotionally shattered, and evokes pity."[51] In other words, these wretched creatures identified with Kommissarzhevskaia because, according to Kugel, she reflected, validated, and even idealized them.

In 1913, in the *European Herald* (*Vestnik evropy*), P.D. Boborykin published a thinly disguised fictional account of Kommissarzhevskaia's career, including the relationship with her obeisant "amazonian admirers."[52] Boborykin's crafty protagonist quickens the passion of her youthful devotees by showering them with gifts. In return, they sit in the audience every evening, applauding wildly each time the object of their adoration appears. Although willing to exploit her female admirers shamelessly, the cynical pragmatist of Boborykin's fiction refuses their friendship: "My amazons are not suitable friends," she insists. "They are too young and too infected with their own passion. No matter what I do or say – it's all wonderful to them. Even when I'm playing poorly, everything is 'divine.' Some of them are really in love. They kiss and embrace me, they throw themselves on their knees and say all sorts of irrational things. There's something perverse in all this."[53] Although there is little evidence that the views of Boborykin's fictional actress correspond to Kommissarzhevskaia's, the fact that this potentially libelous story was published suggests that some critics were deeply disturbed by the relationship between Vera Fedorovna and her female admirers.

ON HER OWN: KOMMISSARZHEVSKAIA AND
THE DRAMATICHESKII THEATRE

For six years, Kommissarzhevskaia struggled to adapt her own aesthetic and ideological convictions to the Aleksandrinskii's, and to flourish in the theatre's intensely competitive, hostile environment. The situation resembled Strepetova's fifteen years earlier: escalating tensions between Savina and Kommissarzhevskaia divided the company into warring camps until eventually the would-be usurper was forced to withdraw. Savina did not, however, succeed in pushing Kommissarzhevskaia into the background to be fired after several years of relative obscurity. Rather, in spite of the directorate's efforts to discourage her, Vera Fedorovna resigned from the Imperial stage voluntarily at the zenith of her popularity.[54]

The situation with Savina was undoubtedly a factor in Kommissarzhevskaia's decision to leave the Aleksandrinskii. According to Khodotov, from the moment Vera Fedorovna joined the theatre, Savina perceived her as a threat. Two aspects of Kommissarzhevskaia's presence were particularly distressing: her success with spectators and the intimate relations she enjoyed with several male colleagues whose devotion to Savina declined as Kommissarzhevskaia's star rose.[55] The relationship between the actresses was reduced to covert sniping. A master of malicious epithets, Savina called Kommissarzhevskaia "a puppet-theatre actress with a face like a fist" and "an inspired milliner"; Kommissarzhevskaia was more restrained, referring to Savina as "a great actress in a trivial business."[56]

Although relations between the two starring actresses were unpleasant, most observers agree that the situation with Savina was neither the principal source of Kommissarzhevskaia's dissatisfaction nor the decisive factor in her departure. Their skirmishes were symptomatic of a more serious disease that afflicted the entire Aleksandrinskii Theatre: ideological and aesthetic stagnation. Although critics responded differently to the issues raised by Kommissarzhevskaia's flight, most acknowledged that, given her personal, aesthetic, and political inclinations, she could not flourish in the discreet, conservative atmosphere of the Aleksandrinskii Theatre.[57] Even Kugel, who preferred Savina's artistry to Kommissarzhevskaia's novelty, argued against the hegemony of any single performer. In spite of her many gifts, Savina's sovereignty had produced a tediously repetitious repertoire.[58]

Kommissarzhevskaia's artistic inclinations and ideological convictions isolated her at the Aleksandrinskii. She was an unapologetic aesthete whose burgeoning interest in Western European avant garde art and literature, fondness for the musings of John Ruskin, and intolerance for commercial

169

vulgarity distinguished her from the vast majority of her colleagues. Historically, the Aleksandrinskii was one of two "exemplary dramatic theatres" in Russia. During the 1870s and 1880s, however, Savina and Krylov transformed it into a commercial enterprise designed to appeal to the shallow tastes of fashionable St. Petersburg society, including the tsar and his sycophants. Khodotov was probably right when he argued that Kommissarzhevskaia's nature rebelled against the constraints of the Imperial Theatre bureacracy: "Her restless spirit," he wrote, "longed to break away to the freedom of a new form of theatre."[59] For Liubov Gurevich, who admired Vera Fedorovna without romanticizing her, Kommissarzhevskaia was one of the few performers of either sex who understood that "real stage art demands broad spiritual horizons and increased erudition."[60]

When she resigned, Kommissarzhevskaia wrote to V.A. Teliakovski, the Aleksandrinskii's managing director, explaining her reasons. First and foremost among them was her desire to perform meaningful work. "I cannot," she declared firmly, "serve a cause if I am not convinced that it is sacred." Refusing Teliakovski's offer to renegotiate her contract, Kommissarzhevskaia argued that the "material side" was irrelevant to a person like herself for whom the entire sense of life resided in "service to art." She concluded: "To fulfill the demands of my artistic individuality is the first and most important duty of my life."[61] Armed with her declaration of creative independence and buoyed by the fanatical devotion of her youthful admirers, Vera Fedorovna abandoned the security of the Imperial stage.

Following her resignation, Kommissarzhevskaia toured Russia for almost two years, gathering the necessary funds for her new project: a theatre of elevated spiritual and ideological content that would reflect current tendencies in progressive art and literature.[62] During this period, she received attractive offers from several prominent theatres, including the Moscow Malyi Theatre, Suvorin's Society for Literature and Art, and the Moscow Art Theatre. She refused them all, even Stanislavski. Given her sense of mission, preferred style of acting, and deeply felt convictions about the sublimity of art, Kommissarzhevskaia should have been a natural for the Moscow Art Theatre. Her response to the MAT's offer suggests why she preferred the more risky path of independent entrepreneurship. Persuaded that excessive subjectivity marred Kommissarzhevskaia's performances, during the negotiations, Stanislavski advised her to begin broadening her repertoire by developing an objective method of creating characters. Already troubled by the MAT actors' apparent subservience, Kommissarzhevskaia saw Stanislavski's advice as further evidence of his "directorial despotism." Having just escaped from the Aleksandrinskii's tyranny, she was in no mood to accept the Moscow Art Theatre's.[63]

Pragmatic admirers and incredulous critics tried to dissuade her from the project. In an article published in 1903 in *Theatre and Art*, Petr Iartsev discussed Kommissarzhevskaia's plans to open a theatre in terms of its inevitable failure. The timing was poor, he argued: new theatres were springing up everywhere, but how could they survive when even stable, well-established institutions were in disarray.[64] Kugel simply dismissed her latest enthusiasm as "risky, unnecessary, and frivolous."[65] Gurevich admired her zeal, but believed that "large scale, practical organizational tasks were beyond Kommissarzhevskaia's natural gifts."[66] The undaunted actress wrote to Chekhov that although friends in St. Petersburg called her plans "nonsense" (*glupost*), she had so much energy and such a vital sense of mission that only death could prevent her from realizing her theatre.[67] Chekhov expressed his reservations about her latest whimsy in a letter to Olga Knipper: "I received a letter from Kommissarzhevskaia; she wants my new play for her private theatre in Petersburg. She is an eccentric. Her theatre will probably last a month and then interest will wane; but I can't tell her that because she's already too deeply involved."[68]

The Dramaticheskii Theatre, which opened in St. Petersburg on September 15, 1904, had two relatively distinct phases. In the first two years, the theatre, called the Dramaticheskii Theatre at the Arcade (*Passazh*), can best be understood as St. Petersburg's answer to the Moscow Art Theatre: the repertoire consisted primarily of socially progressive, realistic plays by foreign and native dramatists and production methods mirrored the MAT's. The second phase began in 1906 when the company moved to a newly renovated theatre on Ofitserkaia Street. The theatre's aesthetic/ideological shift was marked by the presence of Vsevolod Meierhold, a repertoire consisting mainly of symbolist drama, and extreme stylization in production. Because the Dramaticheskii Theatre was, especially during the second phase, at the center of the "theatre crisis" (*krizis teatra*), the relative merits of each phase are difficult to assess.[69] Until recently, Soviet historians regarded the first phase favorably, while dismissing the formalist tendencies of the second as politically reactionary. For Soviet critics, the repertoire at the Arcade, consisting of plays by progressive, ostensibly realist playwrights like Ibsen, Chekhov, and Gorki, provided concrete evidence of Kommissarzhevskaia's revolutionary politics; by emphasizing the symbolist poets, the repertoire at Ofitserskaia marked her unfortunate capitulation to reactionary trends in politics and art. Although the Soviet position has prevailed, it obscures the fact that the Ofitserskaia Street theatre was more aesthetically, if not politically, progressive and interesting.

From the beginning, Kommissarzhevskaia organized the Dramaticheskii Theatre as a shareholding company, but throughout its five-year history she was the principal shareholder.[70] In contrast to Brenko and other entrepreneurs, Kommissarzhevskaia was a starring actress with considerable personal resources and a large, enthusiastic following. Perhaps for that reason, she did not seek support from wealthy philanthropic merchants, but sought to maintain her independence by financing the operation herself: like Virginia Woolf, she had 500 pounds and used it to purchase a room of her own. Like

Duse, Kommissarzhevskaia supported her artistic adventures by touring extensively in Russia and abroad to make up losses incurred during the season.[71] Extant letters suggest that she did not originally want to function as a managing director, but because reliable theatre managers were scarce, Vera Fedorovna assumed an active role in all aspects of management while continuing to act in about one-third of the Dramaticheskii's productions.[72]

During its first two seasons, the theatre's repertoire reflected Kommissarzhevskaia's increased enthusiasm for liberal causes, left-wing politics, and Western European drama. In their rush to refashion Kommissarzhevskaia as a revolutionary icon, Soviet historians may have exaggerated the degree to which she was directly involved in subversive activities; nonetheless, Vera Fedorovna clearly was sympathetic to current reformist and revolutionary tendencies.[73] A progressive voice among the conservatives who dominated the Russian Theatre Society (RTO), she was elected to serve on the regulatory and censorship committees.[74] She frequently arranged philanthropic performances on behalf of unemployed workers and, immediately following the failed revolution of 1905, convened meetings at the Arcade to discuss the theatre community's response to current civil unrest.

In its first two years, the Dramaticheskii Theatre produced thirty-two plays, primarily from the modern repertoire. The most successful productions were of Ibsen's *A Doll's House* and *The Master Builder*, and Gorki's *Summer Folk* and *Children of the Sun*.[75] Reactions from critics were mixed. Although most agreed that Kommissarzhevskaia and her partners maintained high literary and artistic standards and that the authenticity of Dramaticheskii productions rivaled the Moscow Art Theatre's, reactions to the repertoire and the acting company were by no means unanimous. "Zigfrid," a theatre critic for the *St. Peterburg Gazette* (*Sankt Peterburgskie vedomosti*) called the Dramaticheskii "the most interesting theatre in the city, and even Kugel supported it for the first two years.[76] During the first phase, however, many critics responded coldly to Kommissarzhevskaia's enterprise. Dramaticheskii directors were reproached for imitating the MAT's style and repertoire, and Kommissarzhevskaia was often criticized for undertaking roles that were not, in their opinion, suited to her talents. Critical response to the Arcade Theatre was, however, more cautious than savage, and hostility from critics was not the primary source of Kommissarzhevskaia's problems.

The repertoire was, perhaps, her principal obstacle. Having begun the search for suitable material, she quickly discovered how few plays with literary and ideological merit were available. When she did find one, she often had to fight the Moscow Art Theatre for the rights to the script or the censor for permission to produce it.[77] She also discovered that regardless of her private convictions and artistic objectives, audiences regarded her enterprise not as the *Dramaticheskii* theatre, but as *Kommissarzhevskaia's* theatre. For that reason, no matter how interesting or progressive the play, if Kommissarzhevskaia was not featured, ticket sales remained sluggish.[78]

During its first season, the theatre lost 15,000 roubles and attendance figures indicate that only *A Doll's House* consistently drew audiences.[79] In an effort to recoup her losses and earn enough money for the next season, Kommissarzhevskaia set off on a tour of Moscow and the Volga region, but profits were disappointing. Perhaps for that reason, she postponed *Romeo and Juliet*, choosing instead to open the second season with revivals of *The Seagull* and *Uncle Vania*. Response was tepid. The temper of the auditorium had changed: by 1905, the "melancholy poetry" of playwrights like Chekhov and Hauptmann simply did not reflect the public's mood. In addition, the productions were not among the theatre's best. Gurevich suggested that although "neo-realistic drama of mood" suited Kommissarzhevskaia, it was not within the power of the company as a whole.[80] After several attempts to produce "mood" genres, the theatre turned to the decidedly less artistic plays of Maxim Gorki, which excited spectators for different reasons. This desire to appeal to a growing spirit of revolution may also explain why Kommissarzhevskaia chose *The Master Builder* for her next major foray into Ibsen, rather than the more placid *Lady From the Sea*. Perhaps she hoped her animated interpretation of Hilda Wangel would arouse the same kind of spirited response from spectators as Stanislavski's Thomas Stockmann (*An Enemy of the People*) had several years earlier.[81]

Despite the smug conventionality of St. Petersburg audiences and attempts by Stanislavski and Nemirovich to sabotage the repertoire, the Dramaticheskii Theatre might have flourished on a diet of progressive realism if not for an event over which Kommissarzhevskaia had little control: the failed revolution of 1905. Following the uprising, increasingly rigid censorship made it impossible to maintain the current repertoire. First the governor of St. Petersburg ordered Kommissarzhevskaia to expunge Gorki's *Summer Folk*, one of the theatre's most successful productions, from the repertoire. Later, the police and censors prohibited her from producing most of the controversial plays she submitted.[82] She had two options: to begin featuring popular "boulevard" fare, especially non-controversial domestic dramas, light comedies, and vaudevilles, or turn to the artistically innovative, but ostensibly apolitical repertoire favored by the decadents and symbolists. Her decision surely did not surprise anyone who knew her well.

The Dramaticheskii Theatre on Ofitserskaia Street was not simply an extension of the Arcade theatre. Although several of the original actors remained with the company, the Ofitserskaia theatre was created by different people in response to a different social atmosphere. The Arcade theatre was targeted by critics for its imitative repertoire, lack of clear direction, and chaotic approach to theatre management. Although entropy remained a central feature of Kommissarzhevskaia's new enterprise, the Ofitserskaia theatre's artistic objectives were unambiguous. It was to be a "temple of art" (*khram iskusstva*) whose members served a sacred mission: revelation of the eternal mysteries of the soul and the universe through pure art.[83] Kommissarzhevskaia's plan for renovating the theatre's interior reflected her new passion: it called for a "theatre-temple in the ancient style, with white columns and wide benches instead of the usual armchairs."[84] By Kommissarzhevskaia's side, as high priest of the temple, sat the already infamous Vsevolod Meierhold.

Although Russian theatre historians have long been fascinated by Kommissarzhevskaia as a personality and as a standard bearer for the Revolution, only recently have they begun to reevaluate the significance of her theatre on Ofitserskaia Street. As one historian acknowledged in 1981, it marked "the beginning of twentieth century poetic theatre." Because the "theatre crisis" culminated in the policies and practices of the Dramaticheskii Theatre, "its fate and the fate of its creator reflect the complexities of both social and theatrical life during the period."[85] If the Ofitserskaia Street theatre was the most innovative and daring in Russia between 1906 and 1909, it was also the most controversial and reviled. Although critics and historians have tended to focus on Meierhold's activities – usually at Kommissarzhevskaia's expense – without her personal interest and support, and without the considerable resources of her theatre, his ascent might have been delayed indefinitely.

Vera Fedorovna hired Meierhold because she believed absolutely in the new trends in art, literature, and theatre that he professed to represent.[86] Although admirers and detractors alike were dismayed by Kommissarzhevskaia's new direction, Kugel suggested that her sudden enthusiasm for Meierhold was consistent with her character. She was, he contended, easily influenced: someone had only to "throw a small match and she burned like dry brushwood."[87] Kommissarzhevskaia's interest in symbolism was not, however, entirely new: as a producer, she began dabbling with symbolist drama at the Arcade theatre in 1905 and, by her own account, her acting style was always more symbolic than realistic.[88] At the Ofitserskaia theatre, symbolism dominated the repertoire and Kommissarzhevskaia, who had rarely evinced interest in purely formal questions of art, now flung herself passionately into issues of color, line, form, rhythm, and musicality.[89]

Meierhold came to St. Petersburg not because he believed in Kommissarzhevskaia's vision or mission, but because a contract with the Dramaticheskii Theatre was his ticket out of the provinces.[90] Following the debacle with Stanislavski at the First Studio, he took a company of young actors into the provinces where he tried unsuccessfully to persuade provincial spectators of the desirability of pure art and rhythmic stylization. His practices earned him the reputation of a dangerously reckless innovator bent upon destroying the most cherished traditions of realistic (bytovyi) Russian theatre. Although advocates of the avant garde celebrated Kommissarzhevskaia's decision to bring Meierhold to St. Petersburg, conservatives contemplated his arrival with undisguised horror. Cautionary notices about the theatre's intention to produce "decadent" plays appeared in local newspapers and a defamatory interview with Nikolai Arbatov, one of Kommissarzhevskaia's directors, appeared in *Theatre and Art*.[91]

From its inception, the new theatre was troubled. Kommissarzhevskaia struggled daily to mediate conflicts within the company and to defend it from external assaults by critics. During two introductory meetings with the entire company of the Dramaticheskii Theatre, Meierhold stated his intention to "wage war on naturalism, domestic drama, and [theatrical] routine of any sort."[92] The result of his speech was to alienate many of the older actors and divide the company into hostile camps. Although young actors who supported Meierhold's agenda made up two-thirds of the company, among the veterans, only Kommissarzhevskaia, her half-brother Fedor Fedorovich Kommissarzhevski, Petr Iartsev, and Kazimir Bravich sided firmly with Meierhold.[93] Differences of style, experience, artistic principles, and ideological convictions continued to divide the company for the next year and a half.

With Meierhold at the helm, Kommissarzhevskaia renounced the style of theatre upon which her image and reputation were built and committed herself and her company to the largely unexplored realm of post-realist modernism. If the Dramaticheskii Theatre was mildly controversial during its first phase, it became a target for vicious critical reaction during the second. Following Meierhold's first production, a highly stylized interpretation of *Hedda Gabler* with Kommissarzhevskaia in the title role, the storm broke. Liberals and conservatives alike were dismayed by Meierhold's formalism, charging him with intellectual pretension, inaccessibility and, perhaps worst of all, destroying Kommissarzhevskaia's natural charm.[94] A director's and designer's delight, the production was beautiful, cold, and schematic. By emphasizing rhythmic movement, Meierhold reduced the actors to automatons whose "words, cues, and monologues sounded passionless, cold, clear, and rhythmic."[95] The human element was suppressed: heavily influenced by Maeterlinck's call for "static theatre" and "dual dialogue," Meierhold's production bore little resemblance to Ibsen's play.

Most students of Russian theatre history are familiar with the litany of criticism surrounding Meierhold's work; it is not, therefore, necessary to repeat it here. Because Meierhold's reputation preceded him in St. Petersburg, many spectators and critics who attended the opening of *Hedda Gabler* in 1906 also knew the litany – and long before Leon Bakst's stunning front curtain rose, they were prepared to censure the production and its creators. Their outrage was in large part a response to the transformation of Kommissarzhevskaia. From the beginning, Vera Fedorovna was an unlikely choice for Hedda and Meierhold's conception of the character as the "spirit of evil and destruction" emphasized her unsuitability.[96] Like Ermolova, Kommissarzhevskaia tended either to avoid negative characters altogether or make them sympathetic and the strength of her bond with spectators lay precisely in the irresistible feelings of compassion she evoked. Vera

Fedorovna's image of anguished, but eternally irrepressible adolescence had enormous appeal for spectators who responded to her like a daughter or a sister.[97] For that reason, when the object of their devotion appeared on stage as Hedda – wigged, heavily made up, and wearing a seductive, shiny green costume – the audience's displeasure was palpable. Their pristine, pre-sexual teenage icon had been transformed into a malicious, sexually mature adult woman. During the interval, the usual stream of admirers and well-wishers did not flood into Kommissarzhevskaia's dressing room – an ill omen for the production and its star.

Hedda Gabler was a disaster. Although several of Meierhold's productions at the Dramaticheskii Theatre received favorable notices, only one, Maeterlinck's *Sister Beatrice*, featured Kommissarzhevskaia. Perhaps because the text suited his methods and the character suited her individuality, the production was a critical and popular success. Such triumphs were, however, rare, and during the period of Meierhold's residency at the Dramaticheskii Theatre, Kommissarzhevskaia carried the primary responsibility for his novelties and mistakes. She was often in the awkward position having to endorse everything he represented and reject all of the traditions upon which her own fame rested. When Vera Fedorovna stepped forward to defend her controversial director, critics met her with charges of hypocrisy. How, they asked, could she justify Meierhold's presence in her theatre when four years earlier she rejected the Moscow Art Theatre's offer on the basis of Stanislavski's "directorial despotism"? One critic remarked sardonically: "What a metamorphosis (*kakaia metamorfoza*)."[98]

Precisely because her status was unique among Russian actresses, Kommissarzhevskaia's public did not forgive her for what they perceived as a betrayal of sacred trust. Gurevich observed: "Things that the public might have accepted as piquant, diverting novelties from other actresses, especially foreigners, provoked indignation in Kommissarzhevskaia's theatre. . . . Accustomed to playing in an atmosphere of loving attention, she now felt distrust, opposition, and hostility in the auditorium."[99] But what trust had Kommissarzhevskaia betrayed?

Vera Fedorovna occupied a privileged position in the collective imagination of her admirers, but although often compared to Duse, the two actresses were distinct with regard to type. If Duse's women were not voluptuously sensual, they were clearly adult; in contrast, Kommissarzhevskaia's charm was prepubescent. Indeed, her situation following the success of *Battle of the Butterflies* resembled Judy Garland's following *The Wizard of Oz*. Both Kommissarzhevskaia and Garland established the professional image of an artless, pre-sexual adolescent. Typically this pretty (rather than beautiful), essentially benign youngster acquires wisdom "beyond her years" after passing through a spiritual, emotional, or perhaps even physical ordeal. Although Kommissarzhevskaia's Rosie and Garland's Dorothy were produced by particular cultural contexts, the generic type is fundamentally cross-cultural and has strong appeal for sentimental, bourgeois audiences. The challenge for both actresses was to move beyond these beloved adolescents into adult roles. Although the image projected by Kommissarzhevskaia was more fragile and esoteric than the American actress's robust Midwestern teenagers, like Garland, she was so associated with the image of arrested, anguished adolescence that it constrained her development as a mature artist. If Vera Fedorovna had outgrown Rosie and Larisa, her devotees had not – and following each departure from her signature type, critics and spectators stepped up the pressure to revive the old repertoire. Even Sister Beatrice, Kommissarzhevskaia's only successful collaboration with Meierhold and her last significant role, did not satisfy critics who wanted to see the old Vera Fedorovna. Some even preferred the proto-feminist Nora Helmer to the decadent harridans foisted upon her by the villainous Meierhold.[100]

Many progressive critics agreed, however, that *Sister Beatrice* was a victory for both actress and director; those who disliked the production tended to blame Meierhold for its perceived deficiencies. With respect to gender ideology, two aspects of Maeterlinck's play as produced by the Dramaticheskii Theatre are particularly interesting: the rehearsal process and the intensity of Kommissarzhevskaia's identification with the dual role of Beatrice and the Madonna.

With its rhythmic, ritual qualities and long-suffering, sympathetic heroine, *Sister Beatrice* was perfectly suited to both Meierhold and Kommissarzhevskaia. Perhaps, as one actress suggested, Maeterlinck's play should have opened the season, but production was delayed by the censor. When the censor finally released the script, Kommissarzhevskaia, Meierhold and the entire company were ecstatic. As a group, the actresses were particularly enthusiastic because, according to one observer, they saw *Sister Beatrice* as a "woman's play."[101]

Meierhold deferred other projects in order to begin rehearsals immediately. Kommissarzhevskaia set the tone. Both the rehearsal process and the production took place in an atmosphere of "reverential, church-like silence."[102] The attitude of the director, cast, and crew toward the process of preparing *Sister Beatrice* for public presentation reflected Vera Fedorovna's fantasy of a temple of art inhabited by priests and their acolytes. Throughout her career, Kommissarzhevskaia refused the stereotype of a temperamental star and was careful to maintain a modest profile. During rehearsals for *Sister Beatrice*, she went a step farther and strove to exemplify the "new actress" who subordinates her own individuality to the needs of the director, the playwright, and the ensemble. At the first reading, Vera Fedorovna sat with the rest of the actresses listening attentively and obediently to Meierhold's instructions. When she began to read, her intonations were unusually "pure and sublime. In the silence, they sounded like a prayer."[103] The role appealed to Kommissarzhevskaia's taste for mysticism and desire for spiritual transcendence through the medium of performance. According to one admiring actress, when she played Beatrice/Madonna, Kommissarzhevskaia believed absolutely in her transformation. A member of the cast argued that Vera Fedorovna's beatific spirit infected the entire company: "We didn't act," she wrote. "We performed a religious rite on stage. Even backstage, the participants observed the solemn silence appropriate to a place of worship."[104]

In Kommissarzhevskaia's interpretation, Beatrice was "pure of heart, naively childlike, and completely ignorant," and the Madonna was "eternally patient, obedient, and forgiving."[105] Perhaps because Beatrice and the Madonna stirred memories of Rosie and Nina Zarechnaia, many in the audience responded with their former enthusiasm. Beatrice, who achieves grace through the sincerity of her love and the depth of her suffering, marked Kommissarzhevskaia's return to a more familiar – and therefore more acceptable – image of "*zhenstvennost.*" Perhaps because Vera Fedorovna identified so profoundly with the role, her admirers found in it the spontaneity, authentic emotion, and simplicity for which they yearned.[106] The critical and popular success of *Sister Beatrice* encouraged Meierhold and Kommissarzhevskaia to turn for their next collaboration to another Maeterlinck play with many of the same qualities: *Pelleas and Melisande*. It was a misstep that left Kommissarzhevskaia deeply humiliated and cost Meierhold his position at the Dramaticheskii Theatre.

The press attributed the failure of *Pelleas and Melisande* in part to Kommissarzhevskaia. Up to that point, Vera Fedorovna's small stature and youthful face served her well in roles outside her age range. During summer provincial tours, which she undertook annually to meet the theatre's expenses, audiences still responded enthusiastically to her old roles. Well over forty when she agreed to play the youthful Melisande, she had no reason to believe the role was beyond her. Critics quickly disabused her. One pointed out that, even in a gray wig, the actress playing Melisande's mother seemed younger and more attractive than Kommissarzhevskaia.[107] Another wrote: "this is not a production, but some kind of theatrical sadism."[108] According to Kugel, anyone seeing Kommissarzhevskaia for the first time in *Pelleas and Melisande* would leave the theatre with a very poor opinion of a very gifted actress."[109] Having seen Kommissarzhevskaia's theatre in Moscow, Stanislavski allegedly observed: "I paid forty thousand roubles so that [Meierhold's work] wouldn't be shown to the public." A critic added caustically: "If St. Petersburg critics had Stanislavski's money, they would undoubtedly have paid just as much not to see [*Pelleas and Melisande*]."[110]

Criticism of Kommissarzhevskaia's age was both gratuitously cruel and beside the point: the principal source of *Pelleas and Melisande*'s failure and of the general inadequacy of Ofitserskaia productions lay elsewhere. With the possible exception of *Sister Beatrice*, most Dramaticheskii productions were beautiful, but lifeless. If they exemplified an ideal relationship between director and designer, the productions also demonstrated that even enthusiastic, well-intentioned actors were stymied by post-realist texts. This problem predated the Ofitserskaia Street theatre. Kommissarzhevskaia brought a company of some of the most talented individual actors and actresses in Russia to the Arcade, but failed to unify them with respect to style or commitment to a common objective. Many of the same problems plagued the Ofitserskaia theatre. Ironically, Kommissarzhevskaia's own skills were inadequate to the task. In spite of her success with Chekhov and Ibsen and sincere desire to support Meierhold's formalist experiments, Vera Fedorovna was the product of a school that emphasized authentic emotion and the centrality of the actor. Although critics referred to her disparagingly as the "high priestess of Meierholdism," she simply could not adapt her own extremely subjective style to what critics called Meierhold's dehumanized marionette theatre. Nor, finally, could she, in spite of her best intentions, submit to the autocracy of a self-styled master artist.[111]

The Wagnerian concept of the all-powerful regisseur, which prevailed in Russia during the Silver Age, was often manifested in bloody power struggles between starring actresses and directors, especially in the State theatres where actresses like Savina and Ermolova enjoyed considerable authority. Power struggles between actress-entrepreneurs and their directors were also endemic to female-owned private theatres. If the battle between Kommissarzhevskaia and Meierhold received more attention in the press, it was the inevitable result of her status, not the uniqueness of the situation. Although certain management problems were common to all independent entrepreneurs, actor-managers rarely experienced the kind of disruption that plagued actresses. Because most successful male entrepreneurs either acted and directed or renounced acting altogether for the more powerful position of director, there was less conflict of interests and objectives. Actress-managers rarely directed; instead, typically they hired a core of (primarily male) directors and distributed directing assignments among them. Since many of the female entrepreneurs were actresses of considerable stature who had their own firmly established aesthetic ideals as well as ideas about suitable drama and production methods, conflict was inevitable.

With respect to the Dramaticheskii Theatre, Kommissarzhevskaia did not stand passively by while others defined the theatre's objectives and managed her affairs. According to colleagues at the Arcade theatre, even when she was not cast in a production, Vera Fedorovna followed rehearsals zealously and coached other actors. Her letters also reveal that she personally negotiated with playwrights, actors, directors, and the censor.[112] Even her harshest critics acknowledged that Kommissarzhevskaia was absolutely committed to her theatre and that she worked tirelessly to realize and sustain it.[113] Although a gifted, perhaps even visionary actress, she could not function simultaneously as a producer, director, acting coach, conflict mediator, and starring actress. When she began to view productions from the position of a director or critic, not only did her own performances suffer, but she often found herself in conflict with the production's titular director. Interestingly, this conflict of wills and interests did not suggest to her critics that *she* should direct; it simply meant she had no business running a theatre.[114]

Kommissarzhevskaia's apparent inability to manage the *business* of the theatre aggravated an already difficult situation. She often made decisions impulsively, giving the impression that the theatre and its proprietor were unstable, arbitrary, and undependable. She chose controversial plays from the modern repertoire, then seemed surprised when critics attacked and audiences dwindled. She resisted using her "star power" to attract audiences even when it became painfully clear that spectators were more interested in her than the plays. Kommissarzhevskaia also had considerable personal charm, but unlike other female entrepreneurs, she did not use it to entice wealthy patrons. Finally, if she hoped that Meierhold's presence would reverse the theatre's financial decline, she was sorely disappointed.[115] From artistic and ethical points of view, her commitment to the concept and practice of an art theatre was irreproachable; from an economic perspective, however, it was fatal.

Although deeply depressed by the failure of *Pelleas and Melisande*, Kommissarzhevskaia continued to defend Meierhold publicly. Inside the theatre, however, crisis was imminent. During a Moscow tour, Meierhold's critics renewed accusations that he was promoting himself at Vera Fedorovna's expense and destroying her in the process. Her doubts about their continued alliance festered until finally, in the middle of the 1907/08 season, she fired him without warning after a moderately successful production of Fedor Sologub's *The Triumph of Death* (*Pobeda smerti*). Meierhold mounted a legal challenge and a brief, but bitter court battle ensued. Although the court upheld her right to fire him, Kommissarzhevskaia was damaged in the court of public opinion which, ironically, tended to side with the aggrieved director.[116]

FATAL TOURS TO NEW YORK AND TASHKENT

Meierhold's absence did not improve the theatre's fortunes or change its style significantly. Fedor Fedorovich Kommissarzhevski and Nikolai Evreinov, who, following Meierhold's dismissal, assumed directorial responsibilities, continued to mount highly stylized productions of modernist texts. In addition, Vera Fedorovna's growing dependence upon Valeri Briusov, a leading symbolist poet, for professional advice and personal guidance, assured symbolist drama a prominent place in her repertoire. Nonetheless, critics and admirers were hopeful when she returned to a more realistic style in Hamsun's *At the Royal Gates* (*U tsarskikh vrat*) and Ostrovski's *A Wild Woman* (*Dikarka*). Offering thanksgiving to God on high for her resurrection from the dead, one critic expressed his delight that the Kommissarzhevskaia of fifteen years ago had returned: "Give me," he wrote, "my favorite girl, my *dikarka* with the golden curls!"[117]

Because the theatre's financial position remained precarious, Kommissarzhevskaia curtailed the 1907/08 season and, hoping to turn a substantial profit, set off in the spring of 1908 on an American tour. A series of articles in *A Survey of Theatres* (*Obozrenie teatrov*) chronicled the troubled journey. Problems with the Russian press began immediately. Complaining of Kommissarzhevskaia's shabby treatment by critics, I. Osipov argued that January 6, 1908, the day of Vera Fedorovna's departure, should have been treated as a historic moment in Russian theatre. Just as Savina once bore the standard of Russian art into Western Europe, so Kommissarzhevskaia would bear it to America. Instead, ignoring the significance of the occasion, newspapers used it as an opportunity for "careless witticisms and vulgar inferences."[118] Following her arrival in New York, the Russian press focused almost exclusively on the company's repeated failure to attract spectators. According to one anonymous defender, the source of the press's hostility was not her failure in New York, but her failure to buy off powerful "star makers" in St. Petersburg.[119]

In spite of defensive posturing by supporters, from beginning to end, Kommissarzhevskaia's American tour *was* an artistic and financial disaster.[120] Her American producer's first mistake was to book her into Daly's Theatre on Broadway. Not only was it located thirty blocks from the nearest Russian emigré community, but even if Daly's had been closer, ticket prices were beyond the means of most emigrés. These circumstances suggest that Kommissarzhevskaia and her producers did not considered the largely Jewish emigré audience until their losses on Broadway began to mount. They also miscalculated the appeal for American audiences of performances given entirely in Russian and failed take into account competition from Alla Nazimova, who already had a substantial American following and was performing *A Doll's House* in English several blocks away. The Russians were astonished when New York critics compared Kommissarzhevskaia unfavorably to Nazimova, who was undistinguished in her own country.

Beset by a series of minor and major embarrassments, the Dramaticheskii tour dissolved into a comedy of errors. During a performance of *Battle of the Butterflies*, Kommissarzhevskaia found herself in the middle of a dispute over royalties when a representative sent by Sudermann's American agent unexpectedly appeared at the theatre demanding money. After several weeks of losses at Daly's, she moved to the Thalia Theatre in the Bowery where she drew larger audiences, but Yiddish performers loudly protested the presence of non-union Russian performers in their theatre. When she performed at the Lyric Theatre in Brooklyn, police stopped a performance in the middle of the first act because the theatre did not have a license. Although she originally intended to take the company on to Chicago, Boston, New Orleans, and Philadelphia, Kommissarzhevskaia went only as far as Brooklyn, Philadelphia, and New Haven, before returning to New York for several farewell performances.

Shortly before her departure for Paris, the embittered actress expressed her opinion of America to a *New York Times* correspondent. "There is an impression abroad," she remarked, "that Americans do not appreciate the best in art, especially the drama. Everyone warned me, but I did not believe it. I find now that it is for the most part true."[121] In a final interview published in *The Globe*, she complained that Americans were too exhausted from their mercantile activities to appreciate "pure art that stimulates feelings and ideas."[122] Echoing her lament, correspondents in Russia blamed Kommissar-zhevskaia's failure on America's commercialism and its pervasive, albeit false, sense of cultural superiority.[123]

Although not discounting the views of Vera Fedorovna's apologists, her failure to seize the collective imagination of American audiences can surely be attributed in part to the actress herself. Nazimova succeeded in the United States not only because she performed in English, but also because she fashioned an image consistent with commercial gender ideology and American expectations of exotic foreign women.[124] In contrast, Kommissar-zhevskaia not only performed in Russian, but deliberately maintained cultural markers that emphasized her connections with the Russian intelligentsia and the European avant garde.[125] Perhaps for that reason, she offered an image that was intriguing to an educated American elite familiar with European art and culture, but not compelling in the broader commercial context, which required sensuous exoticism from foreign actresses. Descriptions of her in the *New York Times* suggest why Kommissarzhevskaia did not appeal to American consumers of commercial theatre. One reporter wrote: "As she sat by herself in the saloon of the big liner, she seemed a timid, shrinking little woman whose greatest desire was to avoid publicity."[126] Several days later, the *Times* noted that Kommissarzhevskaia was "delicate," "fragile," and "not beautiful in any accepted sense of the word.... To those familiar with the type of Russian actress exemplified by Alla Nazimova ... Mme. Komissarzhevsky [sic] will come as a distinct revelation."[127] The correspondent proceeded to sketch a picture of Vera Fedorovna as a "woman of fine ideas and subtle mentality" whose beauty lay in her simplicity.

Perhaps because Kommissarzhevskaia zealously promoted herself not only as the embodiment of the Russian artistic intelligentsia, but also as a representative of the Russian feudal aristocracy, she seemed remote and alien.[128] American audiences preferred the more accessible Nazimova, who apparently understood their taste for caricature and erotic exoticism. Asked by an American reporter to comment on Nazimova, Kommissarzevskaia, who had never seen her competitor, articulated a decisive difference between them: "I have heard that she has great brilliancy and a great physical charm and power."[129] Photographs of Nazimova confirm the description: Nazimova was a stunningly attractive actress who performed in a wide variety of genres from *Hedda Gabler* to the *Comtesse Coquette*. Her "tantalizing capriciousness" and "audacious sauciness" apparently dazzled American audiences who responded enthusiastically to her image of sophisticated, exotic adult sensuality.[130] In contrast, Kommissarzhevskaia's preferred image was undesirably subdued, mystical, esoteric, and ascetic in an American context. In Russia, her modest appearance and demeanor were proof of her superior artistry, but the very qualities that endeared her to Russians may have been an impediment in the United States. Long before Kommissarzhevskaia's tour, many Russians were persuaded that Americans could not appreciate authentic art; their preference for Nazimova was simply further evidence of American obtuseness.[131]

Although the American tour exacerbated rather than resolved the Dramaticheskii Theatre's financial crisis, Vera Fedorovna and her half-brother, Fedor Fedorovich, returned to Russia to prepare a new season. They opened in Moscow in the fall of 1908 with D'Annunzio's *Francesca da Rimini*, hoping to follow it with Oscar Wilde's controversial *Salome*. Anticipating resistance, Kommissarzhevskaia not only obtained the censor's permission to produce the play well in advance of the opening, but also invited members of the Duma and an assistant to the city governor to attend rehearsals. No ideological or moral objections were originally raised. To the dismay of everyone involved, the censor unexpectedly reversed his decision and prohibited *Salome* on the eve of its opening. Two hours before curtain an officer arrived with an injunction forbidding the performance. The theatre lost 30,000 roubles and, as one observer remarked, the censor's action "killed both the play, and the theatre."[132]

Forced by economic necessity to renounce symbolist drama and formalist production, Kommissarzhevskaia reluctantly resurrected her old repertoire. After the humiliation of *Pelleas and Melisande*, she continued to support stylized productions of decadent and symbolist plays, but rarely performed in them herself. Now, largely due to her presence on stage, the old repertoire succeeded beyond all expectations. Motivated by nostalgia and a desire to see their former idol in her most sympathetic roles, spectators packed the auditorium. Following a production of Sudermann's *Homeland* (*Rodina*), a student leaped onto the stage and read an address extolling Kommissarzhevskaia for bringing Sudermann to Russia. Perhaps she should have been pleased. But the actress who had devoted all of her material, emotional, and spiritual resources to promoting post-realist modernism in Russia could not bear the idea that future generations would remember her for introducing a second-rate realist like Sudermann. After the student's well-intentioned speech, she sat in her dressing room pressing her fingers to her temples and repeating: "Ah, if only they knew, if only they knew."[133]

In 1909, Kommissarzhevskaia resolved to make an extended tour of provincial Russia. In an interview, she explained that the money earned would be used support a new venture: a theatre school in St. Petersburg.[134] Her school would, she argued, be distinguished from all other theatre schools by its unique mission: "This will be a place where people, young souls, will learn to understand and love the truly beautiful and where they will come to God. This is a monumental task, but because I feel God wants it, I've resolved to undertake it. This is my real mission in life."[135] Buoyed by faith in her divinely inspired crusade, Vera Fedorovna set off on her fateful tour.

Early in February 1910, reports reached the capital cities that Kommissar-zhevskaia had fallen seriously ill during a performance of *Battle of the Butterflies* in Tashkent. Physicians diagnosed her with smallpox. Although several members of the company were also stricken, she alone contracted the deadliest strain of the disease. She fell ill on January 28, but improved enough between February 1 and 8 that the local physician began to hope for remission. Then, on February 9 the disease abruptly intensified. Horrific, pussy eruptions broke out on her skin, gangrene infected her blood, and necrosis began to set in.[136] Kommissarzhevskaia lost consciousness and died within a few hours.

Vera Fedorovna's death at age forty-six ensured both her immortality and the inevitable distortion of her life, work, and image. The legend of Kommissarzhevskaia began to take shape when an estimated ten million people gathered at railroad stations where the train bearing her body stopped during its journey from Tashkent to St. Petersburg.[137] In the press, the process of reconsidering Kommissarzhevskaia's life and work and transforming her into a national icon began almost immediately. For weeks after her demise, a flood of eulogies and memoirs written by friends, former colleagues, and remorseful critics filled the pages of newspapers, popular magazines, and theatre journals. For many years, interest in Kommissarzhevskaia did not diminish as new collections of memoirs, letters and tributes stimulated renewed interest in her. This literature is particularly intriguing not only for what it reveals about Kommissarzhevskaia's genuine significance, but also about the process by which celebrity acquires transcendent meaning.

Reevaluation of the Dramaticheskii Theatre's larger signficance was essential to the beatification of Kommissarzhevskaia. Critics who had so recently dismissed as nonsense her aesthetic and spiritual objectives and ridiculed her excesses suddenly experienced an epiphany with respect to the purpose and meaning of her theatre. In a moment of high revisionism, one critic not only insisted on the Dramaticheskii Theatre's "deep revolutionary significance," but compared its founder to Tolstoi."[138] Another complained that theatrical life in St. Petersburg was immeasurably less interesting without the Dramaticheskii Theatre. If Dramaticheskii productions were often "bizarre" and "annoying," he wrote, they always "provided something to argue about, to get excited about."[139] Echoing his colleague, a third cried: "St. Petersburg is empty. The only exciting theatre, the only theatre that drew people, is gone."[140] In a moment of transcendent irony, a fourth thanked Kommissar-zhevskaia for introducing Russians to modernism, a new art which "knew no boundaries of language, territory, government, or everyday life, and which flowered outside linguistics, conventionality, or any external framework."[141]

Soviet historians continued the process of revision by focusing exclusively on the relationship between Kommissarzhevskaia and the political left. One of the most egregious examples is Boris Alpers' contention that even during periods of formalist excess, the Dramaticheskii Theatre enjoyed enthusiastic support from the left.[142]

Kommissarzhevskaia's early death assisted her metamorphosis into a transcendent symbol of Silver Age *"zhenstvennost."* For Russian women, iconic status required intense physical and mental suffering framed by the sustained illusion of unblemished youth. According to one admirer, because Kommissarzhevskaia "died terribly and beautifully," she was an ideal candidate for beatification. Had she waited to die, he continued, "until her teeth were falling out," the transformation could not have been accomplished so smoothly.[143] Death allowed Kommissarzhevskaia, who maintained the facade of youth well past middle age, to remain eternally young in the collective imagination of her devotees; the ravages of age, which devasted so many actresses, touched her briefly. On the eve of her last tour, Vera Fedorovna had already acquired the image of a middle-aged eccentric – a sort of female Don Quixote tilting at windmills. When she returned to St. Petersburg in a coffin, she was once again Chekhov's seagull. All of her failures – Hedda and Melisande, the Meierhold debacle, the humiliating American tour – were erased, and her death from a horribly disfiguring disease was deemphasized. Charming photographs of Rosie, Larisa, Nina, Nora, and Sister Beatrice decorated the margins of published memoirs and eulogies. For a nation rent by internal dissension, Kommissarzhevskaia's death assumed even greater significance. As once critic lamented: "The death of Kommissarzhevskaia is the death of our youth." But Russians should take comfort, he continued: "Kommissarzhevskaia is gone. But there is and always will be a beautiful legend about Kommissarzhevskaia."[144]

THE APOGEE OF THE ACTRESS: FINALE

Among the posthumous tributes to Kommissarzhevskaia, one in particular sounded a disturbing note. In what may have been a moment of poetic hyperbole, Osip Dymov offered *A Doll's House* as a metaphor for the actress's tragic destiny. In a defiant gesture reminiscent of Nora Helmer's, Kommissarzhevskaia left the Aleksandrinskii Theatre, renounced traditional Russian realism, and slammed the door on comfort and security to venture down the still unfamiliar, perilous road of theatrical modernism and independent entrepreneurship. Inevitably, Dymov concluded, her path led straight to Tashkent.[145] Did he intend to imply by this that some horrific fate – for instance, death from smallpox – awaits New Women and independent actresses who transgress the boundaries of social convention and hierarchy? Perhaps not, but given the fate of starring actresses and actress-entrepreneurs after 1910, the temptation to read his metaphor this way is great.

Regardless of Dymov's intention, his metaphor was prophetic: not only was Kommissarzhevskaia the last important actress-entrepreneur in Russia, her death marked the demise of starring actresses. Although several starring actresses from earlier periods survived Vera Fedorovna, by 1910 they were either retired or irrelevant. Skeptics might offer the women of the Moscow Art Theatre or to the Kamernyi Theatre's Alisa Koonen as evidence of the continued authority of actresses. But Stanislavski's and Nemirovich-Danchenko's ensemble credo rendered MAT actresses virtually anonymous; and although exceptionally gifted, Koonen was clearly subordinate to Aleksandr Tairov.

Several factors hastened the demise of powerful actresses and actress-entrepreneurs in Russia, including the rise of modernism, the ascendancy of the omnipotent director, the atmospere of constraint engendered by the First World War, and the triumph of Bolshevism following the October Revolution.

By 1905, the predominance of modernist drama in the repertoires of Imperial and private theatres began to provoke complaints from actresses about the scarcity of suitable or even interesting roles. Starring actresses of Savina's, Ermolova's, and even Kommissarzhevskaia's generation were, first of all, dynamic personalities who imbued each role with their own individuality. For that reason, the dehumanized, generic characters, abstract actions, and rhythmic qualities of the new drama were not hospitable to them. For many, the demand that they subordinate their individuality to an anonymous ensemble made even Ibsen's and Chekhov's dramaturgy seem hostile and inaccessible. Formalist productions, which tended to privilege collaboration between directors and designers rather than actresses and playwrights, were a further source of distress. By reducing starring actresses to an element in the *mise en scène*, the plastic and decorative principles governing formalist production further eroded their status.

Although the "theatre crisis" revolved around the relative merits of *"bytovaia"* and *"uslovnaia"* drama, the rise of the omnipotent master artist further aggravated tensions in the theatre community. Aleksandr Kugel, a vocal opponent of modernism, argued for the centrality of actors and vigorously resisted attempts by directors and designers to displace them.[146] He was particularly critical of Stanislavski, who had, in his opinion, initiated the trend in Russia toward starring directors and designers. Although many critics denounced Meierhold's tyranny, for Kugel, the only distinction between Meierhold and Stanislavski was production style; otherwise their methods were identical. From Kugel's perspective, the omnipotent director proposed by Craig and realized by Stanislavski and Meierhold, was superfluous to the production of aesthetically satisfying theatre. By imposing himself into the production process, the director appropriated the legitimate authority of the leading actress or actor to mediate between the playwright and the audience. In a moment of inspired irony, he asked whether there was any signficiant distinction between Stanislavski and Savina with respect to authority over the repertoire. If playwrights, designers, and actors were once subordinate to the capriciousness of a starring actress, now they were subject to the tyranny of a director. And for Kugel, it was Savina, not Stanislavski, who had a legitimate claim to such power.[147]

Although the Kugel critique relies upon the example of a powerful starring actress and a prominent male director, there is nothing in it to suggest that he intentionally offered the Savina/Stanislavski relationship as a paradigm for gender hierarchy in the Russian theatre. His principal concern was with the general subordination of performers to the arbitrary will of the director. If Kugel carefully circumvented the gender implications of the actress/director relationship, other critics were not so discreet. From a purely theoretical point of view, the "director as master artist" is not a gendered concept. But because the entire infrastructure of Russian society rested on patriarchal and paternalist principles and most Russians assumed openly essentialist attitudes toward sex and gender, this fundamentally hierarchical model could easily be given a gender slant and used to establish the proper relationship between actress and director. P.D. Boborykin's posthumous critique of Kommissarzhevskaia's efforts to manage the affairs of her own theatre reflected widely held views on the proper position of women in the Russian theatre community. According to Boborykin, nature requires that men lead and create, and women follow and submit. Logically, then, Kommissarzhevskaia's ruin was the inevitable consequence of her unnatural desire to lead rather than follow, to create rather than submit to the authority of the creator.[148]

Efforts by directors to wrest power from starring actresses culminated in the battle between Kommissarzhevskaia and Meierhold. Although Meierhold inspired little affection in the St. Petersburg and Moscow theatre communities, his dismissal caused tremendous controversy. Isabella Grinevskaia may have been responding to a paradigm shift when she expressed surprise at the intensity of the reaction. Until recently, she remarked, firing a director would have passed without comment because "the director was the humble servant of the leading actress and the entrepreneur."[149] Critical response to the Kommissarzhevskaia/Meierhold affair indicated a clear shift in the balance of power. If, as Grinevskaia argued in her address to the Women's Congress in 1908, the reign of women in the theatre would last only as long as men tolerated it, the triumph of the director was inevitable.[150] After Kommissarzhevskaia's death, the generation of powerful, independent starring actresses and actress-entrepreneurs who dominated Russian theatre between 1870 and 1910 was replaced by a new generation who accepted their subordinate status in a hierarchy headed by the director.[151] The cult of the starring actress was displaced by the cult of the starring director.

Social and political conditions in Russia after 1910 assisted the displacement of starring actresses. During the First World War and the Revolution, periods of tremendous social stress and material deprivation, "women's themes" and the deification of actresses seemed not only irrelevant, but perverse. In theatre journals, articles about directors, actresses, and the "theatre crisis" were replaced by stories from the front lines of heroic actions performed by actor-soldiers and actress-nurses. In this time of social crisis, individualism, self-gratification, and material excess were deemed unpatriotic; for that reason, critics admonished actresses in St. Petersburg and Moscow to acknowledge the sacrifices of their countrymen by suppressing their individuality and dressing more modestly.

The situation in Russia during and after the Revolution did not favor a resurgence of starring actresses. During the Civil War, continued fighting and political instability kept Russian theatre in limbo. By 1921, the rhetoric and newly formulated policies of the Soviet government rendered impossible any return to pre-Revolutionary conditions. As Spencer Golub suggests, the Soviet state, which introduced the next major shift in gender ideology, "sought to 'defeminize' and detheatricalize men and women, to strip them of all vanity and pretense (code words for individualism) in order to create the appearance of a uniform and a uniformly strong political collective."[152] Strategies for "defeminizing," "detheatricalizing," and "collectivizing" post-Imperial culture created a context in which starring actresses and independent actress-entrepreneurs could not flourish.

As phenomena of late Imperial Russia, the starring actress and the actress-entrepreneur were produced by a particular social context that not only tolerated, but even encouraged Western gender ideology and individualism. Although Russians were often puzzled and distressed by shifts in gender ideology between 1870 and 1910, most still maintained basically essentialist views about the fundamental, necessary – and desirable – distinctions between "*muzhestvennost*" (masculinity) and "*zhenstvennost*" (feminity). Precisely because they reflected the range of "femininities" available to Russian women in an era of transition and social stress, actresses assumed more prominence during the Silver Age than at any other moment in the history of Russian theatre. The reign of the actress was predicated, at least in part, on the instability of gender ideology during the late Imperial period; under the monolithic, state-imposed ideology of anonymous "androgyny" introduced by the Soviets, the *tsarinas* of the Russian theatre disappeared along with the hereditary aristocracy.

NOTES

1 THE APOGEE OF THE ACTRESS

1 John Bowlt, *The Silver Age: Russian Art of the Early Twentieth Century and the "World of Art" Group*, Newtonville, MA: Oriental Research Partners, 1982, p. 6.
2 Max Morol'd, "Otvet na nekotorye voprosy", *Mir iskusstva*, 1899, no. 2, p. 149.
3 Charlotte Rosenthal, "The Silver Age: Highpoint for Women?", in Linda Edmondson (ed.), *Women and Society in Russia and the Soviet Union*, Cambridge: Cambridge University Press, 1992, p. 32.
4 Richard Gordon Thorpe, "The Management of Culture in Revolutionary Russia: The Imperial Theatres and the State, 1897–1928", Ph.D. diss., Princeton University, 1990, p. 7. The "post-reform" era refers to the reforms initiated by Aleksandr II between 1855 and 1881.
5 I.N. Grinevskaia, "Zhenshchina na stsene", *Biblioteka teatra i iskusstva*, 1909, no. 6, pp. 3–24.
6 According to the news media, the elections of 1992 (the "Year of the Woman") were supposed to mark the ascendancy of women in American political life.
7 Grinevskaia, "Zhenshchina na stsene", pp. 16–19.
8 Although Grinevskaia's account is not always consistent with Simon Karlinsky's (*Russian Drama From Its Beginnings to the Age of Pushkin*, Berkeley, CA: University of California Press, 1985), it is confirmed by the comprehensive *Istoriia russkogo dramaticheskogo teatra*, t. 1, Moscow: Iskusstvo, 1977, pp. 91–2.
9 Grinevskaia, "Zhenshchina na stsene", p. 12.
10 Ibid., p. 13.
11 Although ballerinas enjoyed personality cults throughout the nineteenth century, the glorification of dramatic actresses was new after 1870.
12 Barbara Alpern Engel, *Mothers and Daughters of the Intelligentsia in Nineteenth Century Russia*, Cambridge: Cambridge University Press, 1983, p. 7; M.E. Brandova, "O sovremennom polozhenii russkoi zhenshchiny", in *Trudy 1-ogo vserossiiskogo zhenskogo s'ezda pri russkom zhenskom obshchestve v S-Peterburg*, St. Petersburg: n.p., 1909, p. 364. Engel argues that Russian women were more independent because they retained their property rights after marriage and "fulfilled a variety of responsibilities that were vital to maintaining the family's economic and social status." Brandova asked, however, what good these property rights were when men had such absolute authority over women.
13 Barbara Alpern Engel, "Transformation versus Tradition", in Barbara Evans Clements, Barbara Alpern Engel, and Christine D. Worobec (eds), *Russia's Women*, Berkeley, CA: University of California Press, 1991, p. 136.

14 See Louise McReynolds, *The News Under Russia's Old Regime: the Development of a Mass Circulation Press*, Princeton, NJ: Princeton University Press, 1991, and Jeffrey Brooks, *When Russia Learned to Read*, Princeton, NJ: Princeton University Press, 1985.

15 Sidney Monas, "The Twilit Middle Class of Nineteenth-Century Russia", in Edith Clowes, Samuel Kassow, James West (eds), *Between Tsar and People: Educated Society and the Quest for Public Identity in Late Imperial Russia*, Princeton, NJ: Princeton University Press, 1991, pp. 28–37.

16 Literally, *"narod"* means "the people," but because the English term does not do justice to the Russian concept, I prefer to leave it untranslated.

17 Laura Engelstein, *The Keys to Happiness: Sex and the Search for Modernity in Fin-de-Siècle Russia*, Ithica, NY: Cornell University Press, 1992, p. 275.

18 Linda Edmondson, *Feminism in Russia, 1900–17*, Stanford, CA: Stanford University Press, 1984, p. 18; and Engel, "Transformation versus Tradition," p. 138.

19 Barbara Evans Clements, "Introduction: Accommodation, Resistance, Transformation", in *Russia's Women*, p. 9; Engel, "Transformation versus Tradition", pp. 138–9.

20 Clements, "Introduction: Accommodation, Resistance, Transformation", p. 10.

21 For an extensive bibliography of primary literature on the *zhenskii vopros*, see "Ukazatel' literatury zhenskogo voprosa na russkom iazyke", *Severnyi vestnik*, 1887, no. 7, pp. 1–33 and no. 8, pp. 34–56.

22 Edmondson, *Feminism in Russia, 1900–17*, p. 11.

23 Tatiana Shchepkina-Kupernik, *Dni moei zhizni*, Moscow: Federatsiia, 1928, p. 285. Mikhail Shchepkin's granddaughter, Shchepkina-Kupernik, was a prolific author of plays, novels, short stories, and theatrical memoirs.

24 Because neither "femininity" nor "womanliness" adequately conveys the meaning of *"zhenstvennost'"*, I have retained the Russian term.

25 "Zhenshchina i razvitie ei lichnosti", *Zhenskii vestnik*, 1905, no. 7, p. 202.

26 Brandova, "O sovremennom polozhenii russkoi zhenshchiny", p. 361. Brandova adds that this excuse is only trotted out when questions arise about women's access to advantageous, profitable occupations. When women perform heavy physical labor in factories or engage in other undesirable kinds of work, no one mentions *"zhenskaia priroda."* Ironically, however, in the 1890s many second wave feminists resorted to a *"zhenskaia priroda"* argument that emphasized female moral superiority. See, for example, O.N. Klirikova, "Zhenskaia kul'tura", in *Trudy 1-ogo vserossiiskogo zhenskogo s'ezda*, pp. 512–19.

27 Bram Dijkstra, *Idols of Perversity*, New York: Oxford University Press, 1986, p. vii.

28 Linda Edmondson, "Women's Emancipation and Theories of Sexual Difference in Russia, 1850–1917", paper for the conference on "Gender Restructuring – Perestroika in Russian Studies," Helsinki, 1992.

29 I. Astaf'ev, "Psikhicheskii mir zhenshchiny: ego osobennosti, prevoskhodstva i nedostatki", *Russkii vestnik*, 1881, no. 12, part 2, pp. 591–640.

30 "Zhenstvennost' i sinie chulki", in *O zhenshchinakh: mysli starye i novye*, St. Petersburg: n.p., 1886, p. 73.

31 Ibid., p. 75.

32 Ibid., pp. 79–81.

33 S.K. Ispolatova, "Samosoznanie zhenshchiny, kak faktor obnovleniia obshchestvennogo stroia", in *Trudy 1-ogo vserossiskogo zhenskogo s'ezda*, p. 774.

34 Rosenthal, "The Silver Age: Highpoint for Women", p. 35. Bashkirtsev's diary was translated into Russian in 1887.

35 B. Shaikevich, *Ibsen i russkaia kul'tura*, Moscow: Izdatel'stvo Obedinenie "Vishcha Shkola," 1974, p. 70.

36 P. Tverskoi, "Pis'mo iz Ameriki", *Severnyi vestnik*, 1896, no. 2, part II, pp. 49–57. Although the picture drawn by the author of the emancipated American woman is unrealistic, the article suggests how progressive Russians viewed the effects of the women's movement on American culture.

37 "Inostrannye otgoloski", *Zhenskoe delo*, 1899, no. 3, pp. 89–92; Engel, *Mothers and Daughters*, p. 5. The article describes the Russian New Woman's "program" as standing up for rights and justice, struggling against evil, helping the destitute, and encouraging both women and men to pursue higher ideals. According to Engel, the Russian women's movement was distinguished from its Western counterparts because Russian women "derived real satisfaction from living according to the loftiest precepts of their culture, especially because in Russia individual interests remained subordinate to the family or state, and individual self-expression was valued only by a small minority of people."

38 Juliet Blair, "Private Parts in Public Places: The Case of Actresses", in Shirley Ardener (ed.), *Women and Space: Ground Rules and Social Maps*, Oxford: Berg, 1993, p. 206.

39 "Russkie otgoloski", *Zhenskoe delo*, 1899, no. 10, p. 99.

40 "Aktery", *Obozrenie teatrov*, 1908, no. 358, pp. 5–6 and "Aktrisy", *Obozrenie teatrov*, 1908, no. 359, p. 5.

41 P. Nemvrodov, "Pereotsenka teatra", *Teatr i iskusstvo*, 1902, no. 20, p. 391.

42 G.A. Zhernovaia, "Stsenicheskoe voploshchenie zhenskogo ideala v 1880-e gody", in *Russkii teatr i obshchestvennoe dvizhenie*, Leningrad: n.p., 1984, p. 71. Grinevskaia and Aleksandr Kugel', a prominent St. Petersburg critic, also argued that female characters were more numerous and interesting. They attribute this to Savina's influence. See Grinevskaia, "Zhenshchina na stsene", p. 19 and Aleksandr Kugel', "M.G. Savina", in *Teatral'nye portrety*, Leningrad: Iskusstvo, 1967, pp. 144–58.

43 Em. Beskin, "Koroleva zhesta", *Rampa*, 1908, no. 16, pp. 246–8.

44 V. Khabkin, "Sarah divine", *Rampa*, 1909, no. 1, p. 2.

45 Aleksandr Kugel', "Sara Bernar", in *Teatral'nye portrety*, pp. 322–3.

46 Nikolai Efros, "L.B. Iavorskaia", *Kul'tura teatra*, 1921, no. 7–8, p. 63. Efros, an eminent Moscow critic and ardent supporter of the Moscow Art Theatre, wrote a biography of Mariia Ermolova.
    Even today theatre historians are ambivalent about Bernhardt's Russian legacy. Laurence Senelick agrees with Chekhov and other Russian detractors that Bernhardt's influence was baneful; Arthur Gold and Robert Fizdale emphasize her positive influence on other actresses, including her chief rival, Eleonora Duse. See, Laurence Senelick, "Chekhov's Response to Bernhardt", in Eric Salmon (ed.), *Bernhardt and the Theatre of her Time*, Westport, CT: Greenwood Press, 1984, pp. 165–81 and Arthur Gold and Robert Fizdale, *The Divine Sarah*, New York: Vintage Books, 1992.

47 For positive views, see Iv. Ivanov, "Spektakli g-zhi Sary Bernar", *Artist*, 1892, no. 25, pp. 157–64; A. Shvyrov, "Sara Bernar", in *Znamenitye aktery i aktrisy*, St. Petersburg: n.p., 1902, pp. 167–203; Herman Bang, "Sara Bernar v roli Hamleta", *Rampa i zhizn'*, 1911, no. 51, p. 4; "Genial'naia zhenshchina", *Zhenskoe delo*, 1912, no. 19, pp. 21–2.

48 Actress/novelist Mariia Krestovskaia's parable of theatrical life, "Lelia", is instructive with respect to the nature of Bernhardt's influence. In this story, an innocent young woman stricken by the "theatre disease" abandons hearth, husband, and child to become an actress. "Long, red gloves à la Sarah Bernhardt" are the first tangible sign of her corruption. Mariia Krestovskaia, "Lelia", in *Vne zhizn' i ugolki teatral'nogo mirka*, St. Petersburg: A.S. Suvorin, 1889, p. 334.

49 Aleksandr Kugel', "Eleonora Duse", in *Teatral'nye portrety*, p. 311.

50 Ibid., p. 317 and "Eleonora Duse", *Severnyi vestnik*, 1891, no. 8, part II, p. 123.
51 "Sovremennaia zhenshchina na stsene", *Teatral*, 1897, no. 106, pp. 28–9. See also the additional installments in numbers 105, 108, 109, 110, and 114.
52 Ivan Ivanov, "Eleonora Duse", *Artist*, 1891, no. 19, p. 144; A Shvyrov, "Eleonora Duse", in *Znamenitye aktery i aktrisy*, St. Petersburg: n.p., 1902, p. 266.
53 Kugel', "Eleonora Duse", pp. 310, 313, 315.
54 Ibid., pp. 318–19.
55 See A. Volynski, "Kritika", *Severnyi vestnik*, 1896, no. 12, part II, pp. 53–66. According to Volynski, Russian actors and actresses were generally pathetic. After seeing Bernhardt and Duse, he found it painful to sit through performances by the woefully second-rate Russians.
56 Englestein, *Keys to Happiness*, p. 3.
57 McReynolds, *News*, pp. 98–9.
58 "Kharakteristika svetskoi zhenshchiny", in *O zhenshchinakh: mysli starye i novye*, pp. 34, 37.
59 O. Dymov, "Ona na stsene", *Teatr i iskusstvo*, 1905, no. 17, p. 276.
60 Aleksandr Kugel', "Zhenskoe dvizhenie", *Teatr i iskusstvo*, 1897, no. 15, pp. 298–9. Kugel', one of the most powerful voices of the Silver Age, co-founded *Teatr i iskusstvo* with his wife, the actress Zinaida Kholmskaia. For years he was the editor and wrote under the pseudonym "Homo Novus." Although a marvellously witty stylist, he was quite conservative in regard to the Woman Question.
61 Among the nonfiction pieces, see "S akterskogo rynka", *Teatr i iskusstvo*, 1904, no. 9, pp. 188–9; "Zhenshchina na stsene", *Teatral'naia rossia*, 1905, no. 17, pp. 289–91; E. Kliuchareva, "Ob aktrisakh", *Teatral'naia rossia*, 1905, no. 19, pp. 325–7; "Kak oni stali prostitutkami", *Rampa i akter*, 1909, no. 25, pp. 406–10; "Na sud sovesti", *Rampa i zhizn'*, 1910, no. 48, p. 782; "Biuro postom", *Rampa i zhizn'*, 1911, no. 12, pp. 11–12; "Kto vinovat", *Rampa i zhizn'*, 1913, no. 36, pp. 4–5; "Aktrisa i prostitutsiia", *Rampa i zhizn'*, 1913, no. 1, p. 14; "Pis'mo k antrepreneru", *Rampa i zhizn'*, 1915, no. 20, pp. 10–11.

2 THE NINA ZARECHNAIA EPIDEMIC

1 "M.G. Savina", *Artist*, 1890, no. 9, pp. 41–2.
2 "Russkie otgoloski", *Zhenskoe delo*, 1899, no. 10, pp. 93–100.
3 P.N. Arian (ed.), *Pervyi zhenskii kalendar*, St. Petersburg: n.p., 1903, pp. 470–83. The 1904 calendar offers an abbreviated list of positions and salaries (pp. 450–5). According to the editor, labor statistics, especially about women, were difficult to obtain. For that reason, the calendars offer a limited, but nonetheless instructive range of jobs and salaries.
4 "Professional'nye rabotnitsy", *Zhenskii vestnik*, 1909, no. 12, pp. 338–41.
5 Nikolai Urvantsov, "Teatr v stolitsakh i provintsii", *Rampa i zhizn'*, 1909, no. 9, p. 352.
6 A.N. Kremlev, "O zadachakh stsenicheskoi deiatel'nosti zhenshchiny", in *Trudy 1-ogo vserossiiskogo zhenskogo s'ezda*, St. Petersburg: n.p., 1909, pp. 189–94.
7 "Doklad Iulia Vasil'evna Tarlovskoi-Rastorguevoi", *Trudy 1-ogo vserossiiskogo s'ezda stsenicheskikh deiatelei*, St. Petersburg: n.p., 1898, pp. 32–3.
8 "Krizis teatra", *Rampa i zhizn'*, 1911, no. 24, p. 4.
9 "Protokol", *Trudy 1-ogo vserossiiskogo s'ezda stsenicheskikh deiatelei*, p. 112. Tarlovskaia was not, however, blaming women, but rather the conditions that produced moral depravity.
10 Kremlev, "O zadachakh", p. 189; "Rech' A.N. Kremleva", *Trudy 1-ogo vserossiiskogo s'ezda stsenicheskikh deiatelei*, p. 79.

11 "Doklad N.M. Medvedevoi", *Trudy 1-ogo vserossiiskogo s'ezda stsenicheskikh deiatelei*, p. 1. Medvedeva simplified the categories. The provincial theatres could be further subdivided into enterprises, which were organized and managed by theatrical entrepreneurs, and sharing companies (*tovarishchestvo*), in which all of the actors invested. The private companies, which varied widely, included the most unstable, blatantly commercial enterprises as well as art theatres like The Moscow Art Theatre and Kommissarzhevskaia's Dramaticheskii Theatre.

12 Only the Aleksandrinskii and Malyi theatres hired native dramatic actresses. Although the Mikhailovskii occasionally used natives, it specialized in perform-ances in French. The Mariinskii and Bolshoi theatres specialized in opera and ballet. See, Richard Gordon Thorpe, "The Management of Culture in Revolu-tionary Russia: The Imperial Theaters and the State, 1897–1928", Ph.D. diss., Princeton University, 1990.

13 A. Greshnyi, "Polozhenie provintsial'nogo aktera vo vremia debuta na stolichnoi stsene", *Sufler*, 1880, no. 34, p. 1.

14 Mariia Velizarii, *Put' provintsial'noi aktrisy*, Leningrad: Iskusstvo, 1938, p. 115.

15 *Pervyi zhenskii kalendar'*, p. 475. The higher salaries enjoyed by dancers probably reflects the elevated status of the ballet in Russia.

16 The salary figures are from documents located at the Russian State Historical Archive (*dokumenty Rossiiskogo gosudarstvennogo istoricheskogo arkhiva ob artistakh "Serebrianogo veka"*). Wardrobe subsidies were not limited to actresses earning less than 2,000 roubles. Starring actresses often received substantial amounts of money for costumes and actors receiving less than 2,000 were also subsidized.

17 Performing in a colleague's benefit was both an obligation and a professional courtesy. For a popular actress, the need to accommodate her colleagues could considerably increase the number of contractual performances per year.

18 "Neizdannye vospominaniia M.G. Savinoi", in *Teatral'noe nasledstvo*, Moscow: Iskusstvo, 1956, p. 519.

19 A "*tovarishchestvo,*" or sharing company, was distinguished from a traditional theatrical "enterprise" in several ways. All of its members invested an initial sum of money in the organization or signed promissory notes which guaranteed payment by the end of the season. Although "*tovarishchestva*" were usually organized by one or two actors, they were managed democratically: no single authority held absolute power and major roles were distributed by company vote. In general, "*tovarishchestva*" were less stable than theatrical enterprises and when one crashed, the ostensibly democratic structure made it impossible to hold any single person liable. See Velizarii, *Put' provintsial'noi aktrisy*, pp. 119, 127.

20 Gordon, "Management of Culture", p. 28.

21 "Doklad Tarlovksoi-Rastorguevoi", p. 32; Protocol of the Congress, pp. 101, 163–4; and "Doklad N.F. Arbenina", *Trudy 1-ogo vserossiiskogo s'ezda stseni-cheskikhdeiatelci* p. 136.

22 "Doklad Tarlovskoi-Rastorguevoi", p. 32.

23 For two accounts of pre-reform oppression, see "Nov i star", *Ezhegodnik imp. teatrov*, 1910, vypusk III, p. 118; Anastasiia Verbitskaia, *Igo liubvi*, 2 vols. Moscow: n.p., 1916; reprinted Moscow: IPO Poligran, 1993; and "Zapiski L.P. Nikulinoi- Kositskoi", *Russkaia starina*, 1878, no. 1, pp. 64–80; no. 2, pp. 281–304; no. 4, pp. 609–24.

24 S. Svetlov, "S akterskogo rynka", *Teatr i iskusstvo*, 1904, no. 9, p. 189. The "actor's marketplace" refers to the gathering of actors, actresses, and entrepreneurs in Moscow during Lent to negotiate for the coming season's employment.

25 "Zhenshchina na stsene", *Teatral'naia rossia*, 1905, no. 17, p. 290.

26 "Kak oni stali prostitutkami", *Rampa i akter*, 1909, no. 25, pp. 406–7.

27 "Doklad Tarlovskoi-Rastorguevoi", pp. 32–3. Tarlovskaia argues that no matter

how pretty, talented, or conscentious an actress is with respect to her work, without a male "patron" (*pokrovitel'*) to protect her interests, she will not advance.

28 "Za prava zhenshchina-artistki", *Rampa i zhizn'*, 1911, no. 25, p. 2.

29 "Doklad N.F. Arbenina", p. 126.

30 "Na sud sovesti", *Rampa i zhizn'*, 1910, no. 48, p. 782; "Za prava zhenshchina-artistki", p. 2.

31 Kremlev, "O zadachakh", p. 193.

32 S. Svetlov, "Aktery i zhizn", *Teatr i iskusstvo*, 1904, no. 29, p. 536; Augustina Ippoliitovna Izborskaia, "Velikii post", in *Russkii provintsial'nyi teatr*, Leningrad: Iskusstvo, 1937, pp. 141–2. Izborskaia complained that when she and her husband tried to negotiate joint contracts, entrepreneurs responded: "A married ingenue? A married lover? I'm not interested." Entrepreneurs had to be pragmatic, however. If problems arose with one member of the couple in the middle of a season, both would leave. If they played leading roles, his entire enterprise would be jeopardized.

33 Aleksandra Shubert, *Moia zhizn'*, Leningrad, "Academia," 1929, pp. 289–90.

34 Zinaida Kholmskaia, "Iz vospominanii", in *Russkii provintsial'nyi teatr*, pp. 189–201.

35 "Doklad N.F. Arbenina", p. 126.

36 "Kak oni stali prostitutkami", p. 409.

37 Aktrisa, "Pis'mo k antrepreneru", *Rampa i zhizn'*, 1915, no. 20, p. 11.

38 Izborskaia, "Velikii post", pp. 141–56 (quote, p. 154).

39 Svetlov, "Aktery i zhizn'", pp. 536–7. Mariia Krestovskaia's short stories, "Isa" and "Lelia" (in *Vne zhizn' i ugolki teatral'nogo mirka*, St. Petersburg: A.S. Suvorin, 1889), suggest the degree to which actresses were seen as incapable of intimate familial relationships.

40 See "Uchenitsa i professor", *Teatral*, 1897, no. 135, pp. 15–27; K. i O. Kovol'skie, "Neudachnitsa", *Studiia*, 1912, no. 36–7, pp. 5–8

41 "Protocol", *Trudy 1-ogo vserossiiskogo s'ezda stsenicheskikh deiatelei*, pp. 166–7. Regulation number 63 of a standard contract subsumed pregnancy under the category "usual illnesses." Actresses who knew they were pregnant while negotiating for work had to inform the entrepreneur before signing a contract. If he hired her, he could dismiss her when the pregnancy began to show or simply stop her salary until she was "healthy" again. An actress who got pregnant during her term of service could be fired immediately.

42 Evgeniia Garting, "Zhena rezhissera", *Rampa i zhizn'*, 1915, no. 5, pp. 11–12.

43 Evgeniia Garting, "Zhena ego prevoskhoditel'stva", *Rampa i zhizn'*, 1915, no. 11, p. 13.

44 Evgeniia Garting, "Vykhodnaia", *Rampa i zhizn'*, 1915, no. 19, pp. 13–14.

45 Teatral', "Prem'ersha", in *Teatral'nye tipy: vospominaniia rezhissera*, St. Petersburg: n.p., 1889, pp. 3–39.

46 Svetlov, "S akterskogo rynka", p. 189.

47 Velizarii, *Put' provintsial'noi aktrisy*, pp. 110–12.

48 A. N. Voznesenski, "Stsenicheskii dogovor", *Studiia*, 1911, no. 11, p. 5.

49 "Doklad N.F. Arbenina", p. 137. The simpler time to which he alludes is probably pre-1881, the year of Bernhardt's first tour. In 1911, N.S. Vasil'eva claimed that 30 years ago women's costumes consisted of a white muslin dress for ingenue roles and black velvet for heroines. See, N.S. Vasil'eva, "Kak voznikli dramaticheskie kursy", *Ezhegodnik imperatorskikh teatrov*, 1911, vypusk V, p. 2.

50 The Meiningen Theatre, headed by Georg II, Duke of Saxe-Meiningen, was famous for its attention to historical accuracy and detail.

51 Joel Kaplan and Sheila Stowell, *Theatre and Fashion: Oscar Wilde to the Suffragettes*, Cambridge: Cambridge University Press, 1994. Although Kaplan

and Stowell do not address the situation of Russian actresses, their account of the relationship between theatre and the fashion industry at the end of the nineteenth century is useful. Russian theatre was no exception to the trends they describe.

52 I.N. Grinevskaia, "Zhenshchina na stsene", *Biblioteka teatra i iskusstva*, 1909, no. 6, p. 13.
53 "Doklad N.F. Arbenina", p. 136.
54 "Zhenshchina na stsene", p. 290.
55 Grinevskaia, "Zhenshchina na stsene", pp. 14–15.
56 "Kak oni stali prostitutkami", pp. 408–9.
57 Ibid., p. 409.
58 Grinevskaia, "Zhenshchina na stsene", p. 15.
59 Svetlov, "S akterskogo rynka", p. 189.
60 N.I. Aberdukh, "Artisty i tualety", *Rampa i akter*, 1909, no. 27, p. 439.
61 Ibid., p. 440.
62 "Kak oni stali prostitutkami", p. 407; "Doklad N.F. Arbenina", p. 135. According to Arbenin, in rare instances performers could earn up to 800 roubles, but the average salary was 400.
63 "Doklad N.F. Arbenina", p. 135. This discrepancy affected both actors and actresses.
64 Ibid.; Svetlov, "S akterskogo rynka", p. 188. Although most actors worked during the summer, Arbenin argued that their salaries were too low to be considered. Arbenin's figure for an average summer salary was 500 roubles. Svetlov placed it between 75 and 100 roubles a month.
65 "Kak oni stali prostitutkami", p. 408; "Doklad N.F. Arbenin", p. 136.
66 "Kak oni stali prostitutkami", pp. 407–8.
67 "Neizdannye vospominaniia M.G. Savinoi", p. 519; Grinevskaia, "Zhenshchina na stsene", p. 14.
68 "Nechto o 'stsenicheskoi vneshnosti' nashikh artistok", *Teatr i iskusstvo*, 1897, no. 4, pp. 74–5. The author's point is not without merit. But actresses also insisted on flattering gowns because audiences wanted them. In addition, the author's remarks about actors probably reflects gender bias. Actors and actresses were simply governed by different fashion conventions and expectations.
69 Aberdukh, "Artisty i tualety", p. 439.
70 Vasil'eva, "Kak voznikli dramaticheskie kursy", p. 11.
71 N. Smirnova, "O roskoshi i mode", *Rampa i zhizn'*, 1916, no. 18, p. 4.
72 "Protocol", *Trudy vserossiiskogo s'ezda stsenicheskikh deiatelei*, p. 116.
73 Ibid., pp. 163–4.
74 "Otkrytie vserossiikogo zhenskogo s'ezda", *Teatr i iskusstvo*, 1908, no. 49, p. 862.
75 V. Linski, "Stsena i besputstvo", *Teatr i iskusstvo*, 1900, no. 40, pp. 701–3.
76 P.A. Strepetova, *Zhizn' i tvorchestvo tragicheskoi aktrisy*, Leningrad, Iskusstvo, 1959, p. 184. Ironically, Strepetova was married three times.
77 Velizarii, *Put' provintsial'noi aktrisy*, p. 211.
78 Ibid., p. 210. In Kharkov, Shuvalov received 1,000 roubles a month while Velizarii took home 600.
79 Ibid., p. 217.
80 Kholmskaia, "Iz vospominanii", p. 200. So that they would not lose revenue, touring companies frequently packed their belongings after an evening performance, traveled all night, and arrived at their next venue in the morning. This arrangement allowed companies to perform virtually every day.
81 Izborskaia, "Velikii post", p. 142.
82 Aleksandr Kugel', "Eleonora Duse", in *Teatral'nye portrety*, Leningrad, Iskusstvo, 1967, p. 314.
83 Urvantsov, "Teatr v stolitsakh i provintsii", p. 336.

84 Ibid., p. 352. Urvantsov does not define "pornography." It is clear, however, from Mariia Krestovskaia's short story, "Lelia", that the term referred to enormously popular operettas like *Pretty Elena* (*Prekrasnaia Elena*), which were distinguished by the presence of scantily clad actresses dancing the can-can.

85 N. Karabanov, "Teatr v provintsii", *Studiia*, 1912, pp. 1–2.

86 Urvantsov, "Teatr v stolitskakh i provintstii", pp. 352–3. See also "Iz dnevnika teatrala", *Teatral*, 1896, no. 84, pp. 79–84. Urvantsov argues that the problem is not actors, but conditions in the provinces: working under these conditions, Imperial performers would be equally lacking in artistry.

87 The "Protocol" of the *Trudy 1-ogo vserossiiskogo s'ezda stsenicheskikh deiatelei* (p. 105) includes a definition of the "pure art theatre." It must have "serious cultural significance." And because it is a "public institution," the art theatre is "equal to all other public institutions."

88 See, for example, P. Borborykin, "Tvorchestvo aktera", *Iskusstvo*, 1883, no. 2, pp. 14–16.

89 "Iz dnevnika teatrala", *Teatral*, 1896, no. 75, pp. 33–7.

90 G. Arseni, "Chisten'kaia aktrisa", *Teatr i iskusstvo*, 1904, no. 45, p. 799.

91 Ibid. References to "quarter tones," "half tones," and the "half-pause" are ironic. These are the kinds of useless skills taught in theatre courses.

92 Vasil'eva, "Kak voznikli dramaticheskie kursy", p. 1.

93 See, "Zhenshchina na stsene", p. 291. The author called for actresses to start their own union in order to battle "vulgarity, hypocrisy, and backstage filth." Conditions will not change, he argued, until women themselves take action.

94 Strepetova, *Zhizn' i tvorchestvo*, p. 202.

3 MARIIA SAVINA

1 "M.G. Savina", *Zhenskii vestnik*, 1915, no. 10, p. 173.

2 Before the Revolution, only Imperial performers at the top of their field were eligible for this honor. In the post-Revolutionary period, the award was bestowed so freely that it lost significance. See L. Viv'en, "V Aleksandrinskom teatre nakanune revoliutsii", *Zvezda*, 1957, no. 1, p. 181.

3 I. Nikolaev, "Pamiati Marii Gavrilovny Savinoi", *Biblioteka teatr i iskusstvo*, 1915, no. 7, p. 6.

4 Turgenev's name should be familiar. Suvorin, a prominent journalist who founded the conservative newspaper, *The New Times* (*Novoe vremia*), was also a theatre critic, playwright, and founder of the St. Petersburg Society for Art and Literature. Koni was a prominent jurist who also wrote plays.

5 A. Al'tshuller, "M.G. Savina i N.F. Sazonov", in *Piats' rasskazov o znamenitykh akterakh*, Leningrad: Iskusstvo, 1985, p. 100.

6 *M.G. Savina i A. Koni: perepiska, 1883–1915*, Leningrad-Moscow: Iskusstvo, 1938, p. 3.

7 A.F. Koni, "Savina i Turgenev", in *Vospominaniia o pisateliakh*, Lenizdat, 1965, p. 160.

8 *Savina i Koni: perepiska*, p. 3.

9 A.I. Shubert, *Moia zhizn'*, Leningrad: "Academia", 1929, p. 287. Savina was pregnant in 1868, but had a miscarriage. In addition, although her relationship with her birth family was poor, she supported them for years and obtained a position for her father at the Aleksandrinskii as a utility actor.

10 The truth of their salary situation is difficult to locate. According to Shubert, when P.M. Medvedev hired the Savins at the Kazan theatre in 1871, he received 60 roubles a month and she was lucky to get 10. This is not corroborated by M.V.

Karneev, who says Medvedev offered Savina 250 roubles plus four benefits, which was a substantial amount for a young, provincial actress. See Shubert, *Moia zhizn'*, pp. 286–7 and M.V. Karneev, *Dvadtsat' let na imperatorskoi stsene M.G. Savinoi*, St. Petersburg: n.p., 1894, p. 5.

11 A. Alekseev, *Vospominaniia aktera*, Moscow: n.p., 1894, pp. 228–31.

12 Shubert says this occurred during Savina's first season with Medvedev at Saratov and the actress was Stepanova. V.A. Shtein says that the date was 1873, the entrepreneur was P.P. Likhachev, and the actress was Glebova. Whatever the truth of the date and the actress's identity, because many performers worked under non-binding, verbal contracts, mid-season desertion was not unusual. See Shubert, *Moia zhizn'*, p. 287 and V.A. Shtein, "M.G. Savina na stsene Saratovskogo teatra", *Biblioteka teatra i iskusstva*, 1915, no. 9, p. 27.

13 Shtein, "M.G. Savina", p. 22.

14 Savina rehearsed *"pochti pro sebia"* – almost to herself – so that the other actors never knew exactly what she might do in a performance. Savina, who was supremely confident of her interpretive skills, probably did this to avoid unwanted advice from outside observers like directors, critics, and other actors. See V.A. Michurina-Samoilova, *Shest'desiat let v iskusstve*, Leningrad-Moscow: Iskusstvo, 1946, p. 61 for the reference to rehearsals, and Suvorin's and Savina's correspondence for Savina's views on outside interference. The letters are located at the Central Archive of Literature and Art in Moscow.

15 Karneev, *Dvadtsat' let*, p. 10. Rather than auditions, actors were granted "debuts," which were was basically trial performances.

16 "Stsenicheskaia deiatel'nost' M.G. Savinoi v Peterburge", *Teatral'nyi mirok*, 1884, no. 15, p. 4.

17 Homo Novus, "Slovo o Savinoi", *Teatr i iskusstvo*, 1915, no. 37, p. 685.

18 "G-zha Savina i ee benefis", *Artist*, 1892, no. 21, pp. 136–8.

19 Aleksandr Kugel', Introduction to *M. Savina i A. Koni: perepiska, 1883–1915*, p. 6. The Kugel' New Woman does not match the Western paradigm, and although his reference is to a new type of more assertive, independent Russian woman, he does not suggest that Savina introduced the Western model to Russia. Though Savina conducted her personal and professional life like a New Woman, it was later actresses like Kommissarzhevskaia and Iavorskaia who depicted Western New Women on stage.

20 M.G. Svetaeva, *M.G. Savina*, Moscow: Iskusstvo, 1988, pp. 85–93; Aleksandr Kugel', "M.G. Savina", in *Teatral'nye portrety*, Leningrad: Iskusstvo, 1967, p. 147. *"Narodnyi"* is difficult to translate in this context. The allusion is not to characters from folk tales, but from the common or working classes.

21 See Aleksandr Kugel', "Teatral'nye zametki", *Teatr i iskusstvo*, 1904, no. 1, p. 15. "Strictly speaking," Kugel' declared, "[the ingenue] is not characteristic of Russian national theatre." In 1860, one critic argued the coquette was so foreign to Russia that the language did not have a term to describe her. Russians had to borrow the word from France, where the coquette was a native weed. See, Mikhail Mikhailov, "Zhenshchiny: ikh vospitanie i znachenie v sem'e i obshchestve", *Sovremennik*, 1860, no. 3–4, p. 475.

22 Turgenev, who was apparently very much in love with Savina, once said to her: "You are very attractive and very intelligent, which do not often go together." Readers interested in their relationship should see A.F. Koni, "Savina i Turgenev", pp. 157–94, the *Perepiska* cited above, and Svetaeva's biography.

23 A critic in Odessa observed, for example, that Savina made her ingenues so sympathetic and interesting that the public would be very pleased to see more such "abnormal young gentry women" (*anormal'nye baryshni*). "Odessa", *Sufler'*, 1880, no. 39, p. 3.

24 According to Al'tshuller, in 1887, following a benefit performance, Savina joked to Krylov: "For thirteen years you and I have been spoiling the repertoire." I've not found any other evidence that Savina consciously set out to lower the Aleksandrinskii's standards, but she was certainly aware of the criticism and intelligent enough to distinguish garbage. See Al'tshuller, "M.G. Savina i N.F. Sazonov", pp. 90–1.

25 See Ibid., p. 71; Savina's and Suvorin's letters at TsGALI; and "G-zhi Savina i Strepetova", *Sufler'*, 1880, no. 9, pp. 2–3. Suvorin, who admired the populist Strepetova, said some very rude things about Savina. For example, an article in *Novoe vremia* claimed that the empty-headed actress, who had only recently discovered that Shakespeare was dead, had two assets: youth and a pretty face. The author predicted that Savina would disappear the moment she began to show her age.

26 Al'tshuller, "M.G. Savina i N.F. Sazonov", p. 88.

27 Introduction, *Savina i Koni: perepiska*, p. 7; "M.G. Savina", *Teatral'naia gazeta*, 1915, no. 37, pp. 1, 4; and Nikolaev, "Pamiati", p. 19. Because the classics were generally neglected during the 1880s, Savina's attitude was not exceptional. Fashionable spectators responded positively to the Krylov/Potekhin repertoire and critics often preferred it to the other dominant genre, French melodrama. Nikolaev argued that the predominance of "light plays" in the repertoire did not reflect Savina's personal inclinations, but rather the desire of the company and directorate to exploit her success in this genre.

28 *Savina i Koni: perepiska*, pp. 9, 31, 37, 56; Viv'en, "V Aleksandrinskom teatre", p. 181. For some, Savina was the "despot" of the Aleksandrinskii Theatre. Her power increased over time until she was able to negotiate directly with court ministers, influence the repertoire, appoint troupe managers, and invite artists. Although Savina often complained of ill-treatment by the directorate, according to one actor, when she entered a room "literally everyone stood up and no one sat down until she was seated."

29 Nikolai Popov, "Maska Savinoi", *Rampa i zhizn'*, 1915, no. 38, p. 3; Introduction, *Savina i Koni: perepiska*, p. 13. Savina played Ibsen twice (*A Doll's House* and *Ghosts*). Popov observes that, although she was never identified with the "literary camp," intellectually Savina was closer to Ibsen, Turgenev, and Chekhov.

30 *Savina i Koni: perepiska*, p. 89.

31 The first quotation is from a letter dated December 3, 1888; the second is dated December 12, 1888. The Suvorin–Savina correspondence is located at TsGALI.

32 For example, this review of a failure by Potekhin in 1879: "G-zha Savina is surely responsible for the play's success, but she succeeded primarily because the audience loves her, not because the play gave her any material." "Sredi teatral'nykh retsenzentov", *Sufler'*, 1879. Another critic complained that Savina did not use her enormous talents wisely and was satisfied with the immediate gratification of success in popular trash. "G-zha Savina i ee benefis", *Artist*, 1892, no. 21, pp. 136–8. In 1900, Ivan Shcheglov expressed his admiration for her ability to enhance an author's text, but complained that her talent was too often wasted on rubbish. Ivan Shcheglov, "Charodeika russkoi stseny", *Teatr i iskusstvo*, 1900, no. 3, pp. 58–63. Koni politely suggested that Savina "clarified" many of her characters, but "clarified" is, I think, a euphemism for "improved." See *Vospominaniia o pisateliakh*, p. 179.

33 Kugel', "Slovo o Savinoi", p. 685.

34 K.V. Nazareva, "Stsenicheskaia illiuziia", *Dnevnik artista*, 1892, no. 5, pp. 10–28.

35 Letter to Suvorin, October 10, 1896, TsGALI.

36 In 1902, Savina played Arkadina, but without enthusiasm or success. N.N. Khodotov, a young actor mentored by Savina in the late 1890s, observed that she disliked motherly roles and that maternal feelings were foreign to her. See Svetaeva, *M.G. Savina*, pp. 277–81; N.N. Khodotov, *Blizkoe i dalekoe*, Moscow: "Academia", 1932, p. 130.

37 Kugel', Slovo o Savinoi, p. 686.

38 "Gastroli g-zhi Savinoi", *Artist*, 1891, no. 13, pp. 128–31.

39 See, for example, G.A. Zhernovaia, "Stsenicheskoe voploshchenie zhenskogo ideala v 1880-e gody", in *Russkii teatr i obshchestvennoe dvizhenie*, Leningrad, n.p., 1984, pp. 71–87; A.V. Shvyrov, *Znamenitie aktery i aktrisy*, St. Petersburg: n.p., 1902, p. 357; N. Rossov, "Net Savinoi", *Rampa i zhizn'*, 1915, no. 40, p. 5; and Nikolaev, "Pamiati", pp. 9–10.

40 Al'tshuller, "M.G. Savina i N.F. Sazonov", p. 93. Savina visited Tolstoi to obtain his permission to produce *The Power of Darkness* for her benefit. After their initial conversation Tolstoi, who did not particularly admire actresses, said of Savina: "She is apparently a clever, quick-witted woman." This is great praise from one of the era's most notorious misogynists.

41 Svetaeva, *M.G. Savina*, pp. 149–62. Liaisons with male members of the aristocracy were a mixed blessing for actresses. Savina married one of the most notoriously irresponsible womanizers of the era. She apparently wanted this marriage very badly, but the relationship was stormy from beginning to end. After Vsevolozhski gambled away his own fortune and estate, the courts assigned Mariia Gavrilovna legal liability for his debts – which he continued to accumulate and she continued to pay long after they separated.

42 Khodotov, *Blizkoe*, p. 117; "Tsaritsa russkoi stseny", *Rampa i zhizn'*, 1915, no. 38, p. 4.

43 *Savina i Koni: perepiska*, pp. 42–3.

44 Savina usually selected her own costumes. By 1880, the Aleksandinskii directorate had added 3,000 roubles to her salary to be spent strictly on wardrobe. See, "A.F. Koni o Savinoi", *Teatral'naia gazeta*, 1915, no. 51, p. 16 and "M.G. Savina", *Artist*, 1890, no. 9, p. 42. Later, when she was the Aleksandrinskii's reigning prima donna and her yearly salary topped 12,000 roubles, Savina claimed to have spent 7,000 a year on costumes. See, "Neizdannye vospominaniia M.G. Savinoi", in *Teatral'noe nasledstvo*, Moscow: Iskusstvo, 1956, p. 519.

45 *Savina i Koni: perepiska*, p. 17. See also N.V. Drizen, *Sorok let teatra: vospominaniia 1875–1915*, "Prometei," n.d., p. 16. Although the aristocracy did patronize the Aleksandrinskii, the audience was not strictly aristocratic. Because the merchant class had a significant presence in the auditorium, the Aleksandrinskii was nicknamed the "merchant's theatre" (*kupecheskii teatr*).

46 The difference in personal style and fashionableness between Savina and Lidia Iavorskaia, who consciously followed Bernhardt's example, is instructive. Savina was coquettish and self-assured. Her wardrobe, although elegant, was never overstated and always appropriate to the role. In contrast, Iavorskaia was "fantastical and capricious." Her costumes were chosen not on the basis of suitability for the character, but because they were the most expensive examples of the latest Parisian fashions. See, A. Volynski, "Literaturnye zametki: Peterburgskie teatry", *Severnyi vestnik*, 1898, no. 8–9, p. 167. Ironically, although Savina exploited the audience's taste for high fashion, she complained about her role as the Aleksandrinskii's "fashionable attraction." See *Savina i Koni: perepeiska*, p. 41.

47 "Solntse vysokoi komodii", *Rampa i zhizn'*, 1913, no. 28, pp. 2–3; "G-zha Savina i ee benefis", pp. 136–8; "M.G. Savina v Odesse", *Sufler'*, 1880, no. 43, p. 4.

48 Because she toured frequently, Savina also influenced provincial girls and women. The depth of her influence outside the capital can be judged by the fact that, according to the *St. Petersburg Gazette*, all the provincial girls wanted to imitate Mariia Gavrilovna's style. See "Mariia Gavrilovna", *Peterburgskaia gazeta*, 1894, n.v.

49 *Mariia Gavrilovna Savina: gordost' russkogo teatra*, St. Petersburg, n.p., 1900, p. 9.

50 M.G. Savina, *Goresti i skitaniia*, Leningrad, Iskusstvo, 1983, p. 15. Savina, who understood her value as a commodity, wrote: "In Petersburg, I was surrounded by admirers who viewed me as living merchandise; all of them were calculating how to acquire me." Although most actresses were viewed this way, Savina was distinguished by the fact that she not only understood her status, but turned it to her own advantage.

51 Michurina-Samoilova, *Shest'desiat let*, p. 61.

52 Evtikhi Karpov, "M.G. Savina", *Golos minuvshego*, 1916, no. 11, pp. 59–61. Karpov later became the Aleksandrinskii's managing director. One of Karpov's anecdotes suggests Savina's authority. Furious that the actors were still without a set or appropriate props so late in the rehearsal process, she confronted the director and designers while the rest of the cast hung back, letting her take the initiative and the heat. The next day, the set and props appeared.

53 Khodotov, *Blizkoe*, p. 120. Occasionally disingenuous about the extent of her authority, Savina complained to Koni that the Aleksandranskii directorate exploited her shamelessly. Koni reassured her that she was "an eagle in a hen house." See *Savina i Koni: perepiska*, pp. 24–5, 37, 56–7.

54 V.V. Chekhov, "Dve zvezdy russkogo teatra", *Teatr: prilozhenie k zhivopisn. obozren.*, October 1904, p. 112. Interestingly, during an internal search at the Aleksandrinskii for actors to mould into directors, Savina was apparently never considered. See Khodotov, *Blizkoe*, p. 123.

55 "Neizdannye vospominaniia M.G. Savinoi", p. 517. When Meierhold was hired as managing director, he said of her: "Savina? Well, perhaps, but who needs her."

56 Svetaeva, *M.G. Savina*, p. 250.

57 Barbara Alpern Engel, *Mothers and Daughters: Women of the Intelligentsia in Nineteenth Century Russia*, Cambridge: Cambridge University Press, 1983, p. 3.

58 *Mariia Gavrilovna Savina: gordost' russkogo teatra*, p. 10.

59 "Evoliutsiia russkogo aktera", *Teatral'naia gazeta*, 1915, no. 44, p. 12. The author sees Savina as a sort of paradigm for the evolution of the Russian actor. Thanks to her (and other serious actors of her generation), he suggests, the purely commercial side of theatre has been deemphasized and the profession has achieved respectability.

60 Nikolaev, "Pamiati," p. 5.

61 Pavla Vulf, *V starom i novom teatre*, Moscow, Vserossiiskoe Teatral'noe Obshchestvo, 1962, p. 125.

62 Svetaeva, *M.G. Savina*, p. 251. Savina's letters to Suvorin offer confirmation of Savina's tireless efforts on behalf of the RTO.

63 In *Teatral*, 1897, no. 124, there is a photograph of Savina with the inscription "Founder of the Russian Theatrical Society." If Savina didn't single-handedly found the RTO, most acknowledged that she was its guiding spirit. In a full issue devoted to Savina, the editors of *Teatr i iskusstvo* (1915, no. 37, p. 684), noted that "she was not only the chair, but also the true spirit of the Society." She collected more than one million roubles for it. For more information about Savina and the RTO, see Svetaeva, *M.G. Savina*, pp. 250–3; Khodotov, *Blizkoe*, p. 127; "Savina: k godovshchine konchiny", *Rampa i zhizn'*, 1916, no. 36, pp. 3–4; N. Efros,

"Savina", *Zhenskoe delo*, 1915, no. 19, pp. 2–3; "M.G. Savina", *Teatral'naia gazeta*, 1915, no. 37, p. 4.

64 Letter to Suvorin, December 2, 1889, TsGALI.

65 *Trudy pervogo vserossiiskogo s'ezda stsenicheskih deiatelei*, St. Petersburg: n.p., 1898.

66 Svetaeva, *M.G. Savina*, p. 250.

67 V. Nikulin, "K russkomu akterstvu", (pis'mo v redaktsiiu) *Teatr i iskusstvo*, 1915, no. 37, p. 684. Nikulin says, "There were arguments, rumors. Bitter debates took place, but *she* sat there, forever reconciling and calming us, anxiously protecting our Society."

68 *Teatral'naia entsiklopediia*, t.1, Moscow: Sovetskaia Entsiklopediia, 1961, pp. 1038–9; "Ustav Russkogo Teatral'nogo Obshchestva", *Teatral'naia biblioteka*, 1894, no. 42, pp. 109–12; M. Iankovski, "Teatral'naia obshchestvennost' peterburga v 1905–1907 gg.", in *Pervaia russkaia revoliutsiia i teatr*, Moscow: Iskusstvo, 1956, pp. 125–84. According to the *Theatrical Encyclopedia*, the RTO mediated between actors and entrepreneurs. It also organized the First All-Russian Congress of Representatives of the Stage where the "regular contract" (*normal'nyi dogovor*) was worked out and rules and regulations were established with respect to issues of repertoire, aesthetics, and social responsibility. Number 28 in the RTO's published statutes also indicates the RTO's role in mediating labor disputes. Although Iankovski acknowledges Savina's attempt to establish a union for theatre workers, he argues that the RTO was too closely associated with the interests of the autocracy to be effective.

69 "Na povorot", *Rampa i zhizn'*, 1913, no. 19, pp. 3–5.

70 *Teatral'naia gazeta*, 1915, no. 42, p. 1.

71 A. R. Kugel', "Teatral'nye zametki", *Teatr i iskusstvo*, 1899, no. 12, p. 247. Savina was actually not the first. Elizaveta Goreva toured in Berlin before Savina, but according to Kugel', Savina's was the "first really serious attempt to show foreigners Russian actors and the Russian school of dramatic art."

72 This information is appended to a letter from Savina to Suvorin dated January 11, 1892.

73 "Iz memuarov M.G. Savinoi", *Obozrenie teatrov*, 1909, no. 939, p. 17.

74 Ibid., p. 18.

75 Kugel', "Teatral'nye zametki", 1899, no. 12, pp. 247–8.

76 Savina did not take any of Ostrovski's plays to Berlin. Ironically, the German press criticized her for doing obsolete "poison and dagger" plays and avoiding the "modern repertoire." She might have pleased progressive Germans more if she *had* taken an Ostrovski. See "Iz memuarov M.G. Savinoi", *Obozrenie teatrov*, 1910, no. 954, p. 16.

77 Although there were many positive reviews, several German critics said her characters had qualities of "wild, half-asiatic primitiveness," and "characteristic Slavic weakness." One said Savina herself looked Mongolian; another observed that she was most effective in depictions of guile and cunning. None of this would have pleased Mariia Gavrilovna, whose reputation in Russia was primarily for brilliant comedy. See Svetaeva, *M.G. Savina*, pp. 232–8.

78 "Iz memuarov M.G. Savinoi", *Obozrenie teatrov*, 1910, no. 950, p. 16.

79 "Iz memuarov M.G. Savinoi", *Obozrenie teatrov*, 1910, no. 966, pp. 10–11. This "bean counting" makes Savina look petty, but it should be remembered that she published this diary in 1909/10 at a time when she was losing her grip on the spectators and critics.

80 A.R. Kugel', "Teatral'nye zametki", *Teatr i iskusstvo*, 1899, no. 10, pp. 209–10.

81 *Teatral'nyi mirok*, 1884, no. 15, p. 4; Introduction to *Savina i Koni: perepiska*,

p. 15. The Introduction suggests that the situation in the Aleksandrinskii was particularly "anti-artistic and unhealthy" in this regard.

82 See Shubert, *Moia Zhizn'*, pp. 261–94; "G-zhi Savina i Strepetova", pp. 2–3; Al'tshuller, "M.G. Savina i N.F. Sazonov", p. 85; and Kugel', "Teatral'nye zametki", 1899, no. 10, p. 210. The *Sufler'* article clearly demonstrates how critics took sides. *Novoe vremia* supported Strepetova by making rude remarks about Savina, while *Sufler'* attacked Strepetova. In this instance, the critic suggests that Strepetova's entire repertoire consists of two roles and that improved working conditions (at the Aleksandrinskii) will not improve her acting. Al'tshuller confirms that Suvorin tried to make an idol of Strepetova at Savina's expense. Kugel' himself was guilty of fanning the flames between Savina, whom he admired, and Kommissarzhevskaia, whom he considered a charlatan.

83 "Gastroli g-zhi Savinoi", pp. 128–31.

84 *Teatral'nyi mirok*, 1884, no. 15, pp. 2–5 and "Mariia Gavrilovna", *Peterburgskaia gazeta*, 1894.

85 Al'tshuller, "M.G. Savina i N.F. Sazonov", p. 87; Khodotov, *Blizkoe*, p. 161; Nikolaev, "Pamiati", pp. 13–15.

86 Khodotov, *Blizkoe*, p. 161. Several critics echo this point of view, including V.V. Chekhov, "Dve zvezdy", pp. 110–15 and Nikolaev, "Pamiati", p. 15.

87 Chekhov, "Dve zvezdy", p. 111.

88 "Tsaritsa russkoi stseny", *Rampa i zhizn'*, 1915, no. 38, p. 4.

89 "A.F. Koni o Savinoi", p. 16. The translation is mine, but the sentiments belong to Koni.

90 Vulf, *V starom*, p. 120; Michurina-Samoilova, *Shest'desiat let*, pp. 61–94. Michurina-Samoilova's anecdotes confirm that Savina blew hot and cold with younger actresses.

91 Volynski, "Literaturnye zametki", p. 174.

92 In the 1870s and 1880s, Savina's progressive impulses received little encouragment. The censor kept her from producing Tolstoi's *Power of Darkness* and when she produced *A Doll's House* in 1884, critics rebuked her for making them sit through a deadly play with no relevance to Russian life. But times changed. When Kommissarzhevskaia played Nora after 1900, critics saw it as a mark of her progressive spirit.

93 "Beseda s M.G. Savinoi", *Teatral'naia rossia*, 1905, no. 41, pp. 1218–20.

94 *Savina i Koni: perepiska*, p. 86.

95 Ibid., p. 91.

96 Kugel', "Slovo o Savinoi," p. 688.

97 M.G. Savina, "Otvety na voprosy", TsGALI. Savina had little patience with either the technicians of the MAT or performers who relied primarily on inspiration. She observed wryly: "If all actors played by means of inspiration and really experienced their roles, the world would be deluged with homes for the spiritually deranged."

98 "Neizdannye vospominaniia", p. 521.

99 Viv'en, "V Aleksandrinskom teatre", pp. 181–2.

100 "Neizdannye vospominaniia", p. 522. Although this remark has vestiges of racist imperialism, in this context Savina may simply have used strong language to express her disdain for the "alien" modernists who were displacing her. On the other hand, racist imperialism certainly was not unknown in Russia.

101 See Svetaeva, *M.G. Savina*, p. 303. Svetaeva's term, "collaborate" (*sotrudnichestvo*), is appropriate. Savina would have been more comfortable "collaborating" with Meierhold than being directed by him. "Collaboration" suggests a relationship of equals rather than the usual subordinate position of actresses.

4 AN UNEASY ALLIANCE

1 Boris Alpers, *Akterskoe iskusstvo v Rossii*, Moscow: Iskusstvo, 1945, pp. 40–1. According to Alpers, their relationship was really quite hostile, but the animosity was well concealed. A few primary sources hint at problems between them, but the kind of open warfare that characterized Savina's relationships with other actresses was largely absent. If Ermolova and Fedotova were relatively tolerant of each other in public, their partisans were not. When the actresses performed together, the parterre was divided into two camps. An ovation addressed to Fedotova provoked whistles from Ermolova's supporters and vice versa. The partisanship turned dangerous when a fanatical admirer of Ermolova's stationed himself outside the Malyi with a revolver. Fortunately, he was disarmed before he had an opportunity to shoot Fedotova. This story is repeated in several sources, including "Glikeriia Fedotova", *Vestnik rabotnikov iskusstv*, 1925, no. 4, p. 7; "Pervye shagi velikoi artistki (iz vospominanii ob M.N. Ermolovoi)", *Teatr i iskusstvo*, 1907, no. 12, pp. 203–4.

2 "Pis'ma o Moskovskikh teatrakh", *Delo*, 1886, no. 3–4, pp. 115–22. Until 1886, most Malyi actresses were products of the Malyi's own training program.

3 N.S. Vasil'eva, "Kak voznikli dramaticheskie kursy", *Ezhegodnik imperator-skikh teatrov*, 1911, vypusk 5, p. 5.

4 G.N. Fedotova, "Vospominaniia iunosti i pis'ma", in *Malyi teatr*, t.1, Moscow, Vserossiiskoe Teatral'noe Obshchestvo, 1978, p. 240.

5 "G.N. Fedotova", *Russkie vedomosti*, 1887, no. 23, 1.24; A. Shvyrov, *Znamenitye aktery i aktrisy*, St. Petersburg: n.p., 1902, p. 321. Because the theatre apparently kept a larger number of actors in the regular company, male students were not needed for small roles at the Malyi. But because the supply of salaried secondary actresses was much smaller, the directorate recruited female students. According to Shvyrov, secondary male roles were considered important, so regular company members played them; secondary female roles, however, were unimportant and could be given to students.

6 Aleksandra Asenkova's memoirs suggest the debased status of the dramatic theatre. As a student at the Aleksandrinskii in the early nineteenth century, Asenkova used every trick at her disposal to avoid being reassigned to the drama courses. See Aleksandra Asenkova, "Kartiny proshedshego: zapiski russkoi artistki", *Teatral'nyi i muzykal'nyi vestnik*, 1857, no. 50, pp. 709–13. Asenkova's memoirs were serialized in nos. 36, 37, 39, 42, 44, 46, 49, 50, and 51.

7 Fedotova, "Vospominaniia", p. 239; Nikolai Efros, "Iz detskikh i otrocheskikh vospominanii G.N. Fedotovoi", *Galereia stsenicheskikh deiatelei*, t.2, Moscow, Izdanic zhumala *Rampa i zhizn*, n.d., p. 35. Most of the students were from theatrical families. One or both of their parents would have been employed by the theatre. Orphaned at birth (1846), Fedotova was adopted by a local landowner, Madame Pozdniakova, and sent to Moscow. Fedotova's benefactress subsidized her ward's education until her death in the late 1850s. Fedotova confessed in her memoirs that she had no particular desire to be an actress, but simply wanted to attend the theatre school to be close to her best friend, who had transferred there. The school accepted her, but as a member of the provincial gentry, she was distinguished from the daughters of actors, dancers, prompters, and other theatrical personnel, who constituted the majority of the students.

8 Fedotova, "Vospominaniia", p. 245. Her enthusiasm for ballet was considerably dampened after one of her classmates caught fire during a performance (she was dancing too close to the gas lights) and died in great agony two days later.

9 Ibid., p. 246.

10 A.I. Urusov, "Moskovskii teatr i g-zha Pozdniakova", in *Stat'i ego o teatre, o literature i ob iskusstve*, t.1, Moscow: n.p., 1907, p. 37. Although Urusov and other critics praised Fedotova for these qualities in the 1860s and 1870s, later observers complained that she was excessively mannered and declamatory. No one noticed, however, until more "natural" actresses like Ermolova, Savina, and Strepetova appeared in the 1870s.

11 Konstantin Stanislavski, *Moia zhizn' v iskusstve*, Moscow: Iskusstvo, 1954, p. 67.

12 Fedotova, "Vospominaniia", p. 246.

13 Nikolai Efros, "Mariia Nikolaevna Ermolova", *Ezhegodnik imp. teatrov*, 1895–6, pp. 427–8.

14 Nikolai Arbenin, "M.N. Ermolova", *Teatr i iskusstvo*, 1905, no. 5, p. 71.

15 "Slovno legenda", *Teatral'naia zhizn'*, 1978, no. 14, p. 20.

16 Vladimir Nemirovich-Danchenko, *Rozhdenie teatra*, Moscow: n.p., 1989, p. 289.

17 Efros, "Ermolova", p. 430.

18 Shvyrov, *Znamenitye*, p. 333; Efros, "Ermolova", p. 427; "Stroki iz dnevnika", *Teatral'naia zhizn'*, 1978, no. 14, p. 18. Ermolova's relationship to Samarin is difficult to sort out. He and her father were good friends and, according to the article in *Teatral'naia zhizn'*, Samarin not only paid Ermolova's tuition at the Malyi school, but also subsidized the education of one of her sisters at a *gimnaziia*. Efros, however, says that children of Malyi employees could attend the theatre school for free.

19 Efros, "Ermolova", p. 431.

20 "Stroki iz dnevnika", p. 18.

21 Efros, "Ermolova", pp. 433–4. Efros observed: "That's life backstage.... They are merciless."

22 Shvyrov, *Znamenitye*, p. 324; P. Nevezhin, "G.N. Fedotova", *Teatr i iskusstvo*, 1912, no. 1, p. 7. Nevezhin suggests that the directorate was motivated by profit. Talented newcomers could not generate the box office enjoyed by established stars.

23 N.V. Drizen, "K istorii odnogo talanta", *Istoricheskii vestnik*, 1907, no. 3, p. 915.

24 Nevezhin, "G.N. Fedotova", p. 7.

25 "M.N. Ermolova: k 40-letiiu stsenicheskoi deiatel'nosti", *Teatr i iskusstvo*, 1910, no. 5, p. 102; "Moskovskii fel'eton", *Novoe vremia*, February 3, 1890; Shvyrov, *Znamenitye*, p. 336; "Pervye shagi velikoi artistki", p. 204; Nemirovich-Danchenko, *Rozhdenie teatra*, p. 290; M.N. Ermolova, "Dnevnik i pis'ma", in *Malyi teatr*, pp. 316–29. Fedotova may have conspired to suppress Ermolova. Shvyrov talks of backstage intrigue; *Novoe vremia* blames the "backstage hierarchy;" and the author of "Pervye shagi velikoi artistki" claims: "In backstage language, M.N. Ermolova was 'impeded' (*zatirali*) and G.N. Fedotova organized the intrigue against her." Nemirovich-Danchenko suggests that conspiracy theories against Ermolova were greatly exaggerated, but given Fedotova's relationship with the MAT, his objectivity is dubious. Ermolova's own diary indicates that she envied Fedotova and desperately wanted several of her roles, but there is nothing about alleged intrigues.

26 Alpers, *Akterskoe iskusstvo*, pp. 20–50; Nemirovich-Danchenko, *Rozhdenie teatra*, pp. 290–322. Although he regarded Shchepkin as an ideal combination of craft and inspiration, Alpers had little use for Shchepkin clones who mastered his technique, but had none of his spirit. Actors like Samarin, who emerged from the "cult of craft" (*kul't masterstva*), did not appreciate Ermolova because she was an artist first and a craftsperson second. In contrast, Fedotova was an enormously skilled craftsperson who lacked the inspiration of a true artist.

Interestingly, although Ermolova had no direct contact with Shchepkin, Nemiro-vich suggests that she, rather than Fedotova, carried on the Shchepkin heritage. Ermolova led the "truth on stage" movement, while Fedotova carried on the traditions of French melodrama.

27 A.I. Urusov, "Moskovskii teatr i g-zha Pozdniakova", in *Stat'i*, t. 1, pp. 34–5; "Gastroli g-zhi Savinoi", *Artist*, 1891, no. 13, pp. 128–31; A.S. Suvorin, "G-zhi Savina i Ermolova", *Novoe vremia*, 1891, n.d., n.p.; "Pis'ma o Moskovskikh teatrakh", *Delo*, 1886, no. 3–4, p. 116; "Teatr i musyka", *Severnyi vestnik*, 1891, no. 1, p. 113; A.R. Kugel', "M.N. Ermolova", in *Teatral'nye portrety*, Leningrad: Iskusstvo, 1967, p. 121. There were also a few lonely voices like Aleksandr Kugel's, for whom actresses like Ermolova and Fedotova were "too Moscow," which meant they were too bourgeois, too virtuous, and too modest. These critics were, however, in the minority.

28 "Temperament" should not be confused with "temperamental." In the Russian context, "temperament" was a very desirable quality. For performers, tempera-ment was the ability to feel deeply and express one's feelings passionately on stage.

29 V. Ermilov, "Vestalka stseny-khrama", *Studiia*, 1912, no. 15, p. 5.

30 A.I. Urusov, "Letopis' Malogo teatra", in *Stat'i*, t. 1, p. 104.

31 The *domostroi* is discussed more fully in Chapter 5.

32 Urusov, "Letopis Malogo teatra", in *Stat'i*, t.1, p. 107.

33 Linda Edmondson, *Feminism in Russia, 1900–17*, Stanford, CA: Stanford University Press, 1984, p. 11.

34 Fedotova, "Vospominaniia", p. 265; I. Popov, "Glikeriia Nikolaevna Fedotova", *Zhenskoe delo*, 1912, no. 2, p. 3; Nemirovich-Danchenko, *Rozhdenie teatra*, p. 284. Shchepkin, for example, avoided Ostrovski's plays. Fedotova, who was only seventeen when the Malyi assigned her to play Katerina, was not pleased: "Nobody asked me whether I could [play the role] or not, or even whether I wanted to play it," she wrote. Later, according to Nemirovich-Danchenko, no director could compel her to play a role against her will.

35 "G.N. Fedotova", *Russkie vedomosti*, January 24, 1887. Fedotova was successful with *bytovaia* roles in Moscow because she brought a "tinge of populism" (*narodnost'*) to her characterizations. Compare this to Strepetova's approach described in Chapter 5.

36 Ibid. *Romeo and Juliet* was a disaster primarily because Fedotova did not have suitable actor for Romeo. She asked a Malyi actress named (ironically) Savina to play the role, but the scheme apparently did not impress the critics or the public.

37 Ibid. See also, Shvyrov, *Znamenitye*, pp. 327–8; 'G.N. Fedotova i N.A. Nikulina', *Artist*, 1892, no. 20, p. 91.

38 "Glikeriia Fedotova", *Vestnik rabotnikov iskusstv*, 1925, no. 4, p. 7. The play, produced in 1892, was *The Vikings at Helgeland* (*Severnye bogatyri*). Although the author claims Fedotova was the first in Russia to play Ibsen, this is clearly not accurate. Savina produced *A Doll's House* in 1884.

39 Georg Goian, *Glikeriia Fedotova*, Moscow: Iskusstvo, 1948, p. 290. Fedotova understood that, in Russia, comic actresses garnered less respect and status than dramatic actresses. Savina, who was also a natural comedienne, confronted similar prejudices. Perhaps for that reason, she too felt compelled to play dramatic roles.

40 Nevezhin, "G.N. Fedotova", p. 7.

41 See, for example Nevezhin, "G.N. Fedotova", p. 9; A. Kizeveter, *Teatr*, Moscow: n.p., 1922, p. 91; Shvyrov, *Znamenitye*, p. 331; Urusov, "Moskovskii teatr i g-zha Pozdniakova", *Stat'i*, t.1, p. 45; Goian, *Fedotova*, p. 295; Ermilov, "Vestalka", p. 5; Alpers, *Akterskoe iskusstvo*, pp. 20–50.

42 Alpers, *Akterskoe iskusstvo*, p. 50. Alpers, who wrote from a Soviet perspective, did not intend this as a compliment. What he and other Soviet critics objected to about Savina and Fedotova was the absence of a clear ideological identity: "They thought little," Alpers argued, "about what exactly their technique was serving." Soviet critics generally preferred actresses like Ermolova and Vera Kommissar-zhevskaia, whose ideological inclinations were unambiguously leftist.

43 "Iz dnevnik teatrala", *Teatral*, 1896, no. 84, pp. 79–84. Fedotova "condescended shamelessly" to provincial performers. Her elitism and intolerance was in marked contrast to Savina's great sympathy, which was engendered by her own experiences on the provincial circuit.

44 Goian, *Fedotova*, p. 300.

45 Ibid., pp. 300–3.

46 Kizeveter, *Teatr*, p. 91. Many critics commented on this aspect of Fedotova's performance. See also, "Dnevnik Moskogo teatrala", *Iskusstvo*, 1883, no. 7, p. 77; "Moskva (dnevnik teatrala)", *Iskusstvo*, 1883, no. 47, p. 590; and Nevezhin, "G.N. Fedotova", p. 9.

47 A. Bazhenov, "Benefis g-zhi Fedotovoi-Pozdniakovoi", in *Sochinenie i perevody*, t.1, Moscow: n.p., 1869, pp. 353–8. Several reviews of Fedotova's performances are included in this collection. See also, "Eshche p'esa Shekspira na nashei stsene", pp. 526–31 and "Benefis g-zhi Fedotovoi", pp. 701–9. Bazhenov, who con-sistently praised Fedotova for her good taste in literature, was sympathetic to her desire to take risks and play roles outside her type. But he asked whether she should do this at Shakespeare's expense.

48 Quoted in Goian, *Fedotova*, p. 310. The anonymous author of "G.N. Fedotova i N.A. Nikulina" (p. 91) suggests, however, that Fedotova refused roles that did not yield to her analysis.

49 Kizeveter, *Teatr*, p. 88.

50 Alpers, *Akterskoe iskusstvo*, pp. 39, 50.

51 Vlas Doroshevich, "20 let tomu nazad – stat'ia V.M. Doroshevich", in *Galereia stsenicheskikh deiatelei*, p. 58.

52 A. Amfiteatrov, "Mariia Nikolaevna Ermolova", in *Kontury*, St. Petersburg: n.p., 1906, p. 37.

53 Doroshevich, "20 let tomu nazad", p. 60.

54 Inessa Rodinova, "Drugaia Ermolova ili velikaia molchal'nitsa", *Teatral'naia zhizn'*, 1992, no. 6, pp. 24–5 and No. 7, pp. 22–3; A. Rostislavov, "Studencheskaia madonna", *Teatr i iskusstvo*, 1910, no. 6, pp. 131; N. Rossov, "Doch' Apollona", *Teatr i iskusstvo*, 1910, no. 12, p. 252. "*Molchal'nitsa*" has an ecclesiastical connotation. The term designates one who has taken a vow of silence.

55 Efros, "Ermolova", pp. 441–7; Drizen, "K istorii", pp. 917–20.

56 Drizen, "K istorii", p. 920. Not all critics are so severe, but most do acknowledge that, unlike Fedotova, Ermolova could only play "*po dushe*" – that is, roles close to her "in spirit." She did not characterize, but always played herself. See also Amfiteatrov, "Mariia Nikolaevna Ermolova", p. 232; Alpers, *Akterskoe iskusstvo*, pp. 20–28; and Evdokiia Turchaninova, *Evdokiia Dmitrievna Turchaninova: sbornik stat'ei*, Moscow: Iskusstvo, 1959, p. 96.

57 M.N. Ermolova, "Dnevnik i pis'ma", pp. 316–28. Whether by accident or intention, Ermolova apparently destroyed most of her personal archive. These few pages from her school notebook and a few letters preserved by friends and relatives constitute the personal archive.

58 Efros, "Ermolova", p. 442.

59 A. Pazhitnov, *A.P. Lenski*, Moscow: n.p., 1988, p. 62; Aleksandr Kugel', "M.N. Ermolova", in *Teatral'nye portrety*, p. 119. Long after she overcame her physical

clumsiness and developed a reputation for grace and plasticity, Aleksandr Kugel' still complained that she was too "masculine" and did not have the "soft, undulating lines" appropriate to women.

60 Efros, "Ermolova", p. 441.

61 Ibid., pp. 442–3; Amfiteatrov, "Mariia Nikolaevna Ermolova", pp. 232–3. Amfiteatrov offers a particularly interesting comparison between Savina and Ermolova. Savina was a "graceful, naturally joyful fairy" on stage. Ermolova was a "gloomy, awkward thistle," who had to work diligently to become a fairy.

62 Efros, "Ermolova", p. 440; Drizen, "K istorii", pp. 917–18.

63 Drizen, "K istorii", pp. 917–18. Drizen hints that Ermolova "paid" for her involvment with radical students, but his precise meaning is deliberately ambiguous. Efros, who was afraid that her work would become flat and monotonous, warned of the aesthetic consequences of ideological idealism.

64 Doroshevich, "20 let tomu nazad", p. 54.

65 Ermolova, "Dnevnik i pis'ma", pp. 331–57. Shubinski was actually a member of the hereditary aristocracy. Although he clearly influenced Ermolova's personal, professional, and intellectual development, the letters are disturbing. She was terribly afraid of this enlightened, godlike man and he did little to dispel her doubts about her own worthiness. Although she read everything he recommended (even tomes on international law), he frequently used her lack of formal education as an excuse to postpone their marriage. In one letter, she explains that although she is "crippled and diseased," her association with him has had a curative effect (342). In another, she writes: "Intellectually and morally, I always feel so much lower than you" (345). They did finally marry, but it was not a particularly happy union.

66 Drizen, "K istorii", pp. 917–19. The friend who suggested *Fuente Ovejuna* was S.A. Iur'ev, who had just translated several plays by de Vega.

67 Efros, "Ermolova", p. 444.

68 Amfiteatrov, "Mariia Nikolaevna Ermolova", p. 38; Iuri Sobolev, "Aktrisa tragedii", Sovremennyi teatr, 1928, no. 12, p. 238; Turchaninova, *Turchaninova*, p. 98. Although it drew full houses, the censors recognized *Fuente Ovejuna's* subversive potential and removed it. Turchaninova confirms that the authorities were concerned about the production: the first performance provoked a demonstration and police were stationed in the theatre for the second.

69 Efros, "Ermolova", p. 445; Doroshevich, "20 let tomu nazad", p. 52; Drizen, "K istorii", p. 920.

70 Efros, "Ermolova", p. 445.

71 Boris Alpers, "Ob Ostrovskom", *Teatr*, 1972, no. 9, p. 75; "Slovno legenda", p. 20.

72 "Slovno legenda", p. 20.

73 "Pis'ma M.N. Ermolovoi", in *Teatral'noe nasledstvo*, Moscow: Iskusstvo, 1956, pp. 412–413.

74 Turchaninova, *Turchaninova*, pp. 98–9; A. Shtein, *Friedrich Schiller: stat'i i materialy*, Moscow: n.p., 1966, p. 174; "Orleanskaia deva", *Iskusstvo*, 1884, no. 56, p. 786.

75 Pavel Veinberg, "M.N. Ermolova", *Teatral'naia rossiia*, 1905, no. 7, p. 94; "Slovno legenda", p. 20.

76 "Slovno legenda", p. 20; Turchaninova, *Turchaninova*, p. 96. Turchaninova says that Ermolova was so effective as Joan that the audience called her out sixty-four times after one performance.

77 Nemirovich-Danchenko, *Rozhdenie teatra*, p. 291.

78 Ivan Ivanov, 'Sovremennoe obozrenie', *Artist*, 1893, no. 26, p. 157. Ivanov, for

example, criticized Ermolova's interpretation of Schiller's Mary Stuart because she emphasized the queen rather than the woman. She eliminated the feminine qualities that made Mary so attractive.

79 Amfiteatrov, "Mariia Nikolaevna Ermolova", p. 38.
80 Rostislavov, "Studencheskaia madonna", p. 131.
81 Rossov, "Doch' Apollona", p. 252. Rossov met Ermolova backstage; when she spoke to him, it was like the Maid, "secret and chaste as the Madonna, had descended to him from the sky itself."
82 Doroshevich, "20 let tomu nazad", pp. 56–8.
83 Aleksandr Kugel', "O temperamente", in *Utverzhdenie teatra*, Leningrad, Izdatel'stvo zhurnala *Teatr i iskusstvo*, n.d., pp. 136–43. Kugel', who did not particularly care for Nemirovich's and Stanislavski's innovations, suggests that the MAT is a theatre without temperament.
84 Nemirovich-Danchenko, *Rozhdenie teatra*, pp. 290–1. Essays documenting Ermolova's "stunning temperament abound. See also, Sobolev, "Aktrisa tragedii", pp. 238–9; Turchaninova, *Turchaninova*, p. 99; Amfiteatrov, "Mariia Nikolaevna Ermolova, p. 42; and N.I. Storozhenko, "Iz vospominanii o M.N. Ermolovoi", *Teatr i iskusstvo*, 1907, no. 11, pp. 192–3.
85 Although no one equaled Ermolova's temperament, when she was having a bad night, she often mumbled and was inaudible. In *Teatral'nye portrety* (pp. 121–2), Kugel' relates an anecdote about a friend who dropped into Ermolova's dressing room between acts and found the actress "crying bitterly with her head against the wall." Apparently she could not find the appropriate mood. Kugel' was astonished that a woman who had been the "idol of Moscow" for many years could "cry like a child" because her performance was off.
86 G.A. Zhernovaia, "Stsenicheskoe voploshchenie zhenskogo ideala v 1880-e gody", in *Russkii teatr i obshchestvennoe dvizhenie*, Leningrad: n.p., 1984, p. 73.
87 Drizen, "K istorii", p. 921. Drizen wrote of Ermolova's Western characters: "Having grasped the images, she imbued them with Russian spirit.... Ermolova understood their modes of protest, their motives, and their reasoning, but she had to embody them in images native to her own element. The wives of Decembrists, nurses, village teachers."
88 Zhernovaia, "Stsenicheskoe voploshchenie", p. 75.
89 Tatiana Shchepkina-Kupernik, *Ermolova*, Moscow: VTO, 1940; reprint Moscow Iskusstvo, 1983, p. 157. For example, A.P. Lenski tried to persuade Ermolova to play Hedda Gabler. She refused, saying that she could not possibly play such a "completely perverted" woman. Another friend suggested she play Nora, but Ermolova refused because Nora abandons her children.
90 Shvyrov, *Znamenitye*, p. 338; Kugel', "M.N. Ermolova", in *Teatral'nye portrety*, pp. 122–4.
91 "Sovremennoe obozrenie", *Teatral'*, 1896, no. 83, pp. 94–5. The play was *Dishonorable People (Beschestnye)*.
92 Iu. Rybakova, "Talanty i poklonniki Savinoi i Ermolovoi", in *Traditsii stsenicheskogo realizma*, Leningrad: Ministerstvo Kul'tury RSFSR, 1980, p. 161.
93 Shchepkina-Kupernik, *Ermolova*, p. 123.
94 Doroshevich, "20 let tomu nazad", p. 59.
95 Ibid., p. 58. Doroshevich suggests that Ermolova's natural inclination for tragedy had to find an outlet somewhere in the modern repertoire. For that reason, "she often saw a deeply suffering soul even where there wasn't one."
96 Kugel', "M.N. Ermolova", in *Teatral'nye portrety*, pp. 124–9. Ermolova was distinguished from "neurasthentics" like Polina Strepetova because her suffering was always elegaic, never clinical or pathological.

97 Nikolai Efros, "M.N. Ermolova", *Zhenskoe delo*, 1910, no. 4, pp. 2–4. According to Efros: "What Turgenev did for women in the novel, Ermolova did for women on stage." In regard to Efros's crack about "feminist tendentiousness," like most critics of his generation, Efros refused to place his favorite actresses in a feminist framework. It is possible, however, that, influenced by her sister, A.N. Sheremetevskaia, Ermolova was consciously feminist in her choice of roles. Sheremetevskaia was a teacher and vocal advocate of women's rights in Russia. She taught natural science in a woman's *gimnaziia* and in the Lubianskii women's courses, and championed higher education and equal rights for women. The Lubianskii courses were the first in Russia to offer women the same program of classical education taught in men's *gimnaziia*. Because the sisters enjoyed a long and intimate relationship, there is reason to believe Sheremetevskaia influenced Ermolova. See also, Ermolova, "Dnevnik i pis'ma", pp. 317–18.

98 Nemirovich-Danchenko, *Rozhdenie teatra*, pp. 293–4.

99 "Slovo", *Teatral'naia zhizn'*, 1990, no. 9, p. 15.

100 See Barbara Heldt's *Terrible Perfection: Women and Russian Literature* (Bloomington, IN, Indiana University Press, 1987) for an analysis of the idealization of women in Russian literature. Heldt, who dates the "feminization of virtue from the eighteenth century, observes that: "The Russian heroine is generally taken as a marvelous given of nature, a being in whom not only her own and her family's future, but the future hope of Russia resides."

101 Rodinova, "Drugaia Ermolova", no. 6, p. 25 and no. 7, p. 23; Shchepkina-Kupernik, *Ermolova*, pp. 131–2; Kugel', "M.N. Ermolova", in *Teatral'nye portrety*, p. 128; Amfiteatrov, "Mariia Nikolaevna Ermolova", p. 39. Photographs of Fedotova suggest a modest wardrobe. Ermolova apparently had little fashion sense. For years Sophia Smirnova-Sazonova kept a diary in which she described the actress's trips to St. Petersburg. On one occasion Ermolova came to dinner wearing 2,000-rouble earrings and a "worthless boa made of plucked feathers." Smirnova also suggests a discrepancy between Ermolova's elevated stage image and her private behavior: "Ermolova is beautiful on stage," she remarked, "but at home she stubs cigarettes out on her boot." According to Shchepkina-Kupernik, early in her career, Ermolova was indifferent to stage costume and wore whatever the costumer gave her. Although never a "fashionable attraction" like Savina, she eventually took a more active interest in her costumes. Off stage, Kugel' suggests that Ermolova always dressed uniquely according to her own tastes (*po-ermolovskii*). With respect to lifestyle, Amfiteatrov says that Ermolova behaved like an actress who "respects herself." That is, she did not give interviews, promote herself, or encourage interest in her private life.

102 Doroshevich, "20 let tomu nazad", p. 53. According to Doroshevich, the Malyi became an "extension of the university."

103 Amfiteatrov, "Mariia Nikolaevna Ermolva", p. 43.

104 Barbara Alpern Engel, "Transformation Versus Tradition", in Barbara Evans Clements, Barbara Alpern Engel, Christine D. Worobec (eds), *Russia's Women*, Berkeley, CA: University of California Press, 1991, p. 139.

105 Fedotova, "Vospominaniia", pp. 283–5. Fedotova's request was very unusual. Fearing that the directorate would replace them before they returned, some actresses even refused vacations .

106 Ibid., p. 285.

107 Kugel', "O temperamente", pp. 140–1.

108 Drizen, "K istorii", p. 921.

109 "Pis'ma M.N. Ermolovoi", p. 418. Interestingly, in spite of attempts by critics

and spectators to establish a competitive relationship between them, Savina and Ermolova were quite friendly, corresponded frequently, and were hospitable when they toured in each other's cities.

110 G. Malinovskii, "Stranichka iz zhizni M.N. Ermolovoi", *Teatr*, 1990, no. 9, p. 106.

5 *NARODNICHESTVO*, NATIONALISM AND NEURASTHENIA

1 P.A. Strepeptova, *Zhizn' i tvorchestvo tragicheskoi aktrisy*, Leningrad: Iskusstvo, 1959, p. 99. This volume includes both P. Ben'iash's biography of Strepetova and her own autobiography, *Minuvshie dni*. In subsequent citations, I will specify when the reference is to Ben'iash.

2 Ibid., p. 36. In Ben'iash.

3 G.A. Zhernovaia, "Stsenicheskoe voploshchenie zhenskogo ideala v 1880-e gody", in *Russkii teatr i obshchestvennoe dvizhenie*, Leningrad: n.p., 1984, p. 79.

4 Unless otherwise indicated, the basic facts of Strepetova's biography are taken from P. Ben'iash's book-length introduction to Strepetova's memoirs (*Minuvshie dni*) and from the memoirs themselves.

5 From her earliest years Strepetova's family called her Polina, which she used as her stage name.

6 Strepetova, *Zhizn'*, p. 127.

7 Ibid., p. 132. She argued that the "principle of moral dissipation reigned" in the debauched environment of the theatre and that "everything good inevitably perished" there. This attitude, especially among gentry women, was not exceptional.

8 Ibid., pp. 6–7. In Ben'iash.

9 Ibid., p. 125. In *Minuvshie dni*, Strepetova described several hallucinatory experiences, including one in which she imagined that her doll, whom she had struck a few moments earlier, fixed her with her porcelain eyes and threatened to strangle her. Such an active imagination may have enhanced her later reputation not only for trance-like performances, but for a tendency toward neurasthenia. See also, V.N. Davydov, *Rasskaz o proshlom*, Moscow: "Academia", 1937, p. 225. (Two editions of Davydov's memoirs are cited in this chapter. Subsequent citations indicate whether the data is from the 1937 or the 1962 edition of the text.) In his memoir, Davydov tells of the actor, Nikitin, who refused to act with her because "she does not listen to her partner, talks to herself, ruins the verse . . . and never softens her tone."

10 Strepetova, *Zhizn'*, p. 8. In Ben'iash.

11 Although Strepetova's parents were not peasants, they were clearly "*iz naroda*" (from the people). For that reason, the social conventions governing peasant communities help to clarify Strepetova's position in her family and her desire to live independently at a such a young age. According to Christine Worobec: "Girls were generally poor investments for their parents. They departed from the household when they reached adolescence, just at a point when their labors became a significant element in the household economy. At best girls could bring honor upon their families through good marital matches. Sons, on the other hand, were more coveted as future providers and perpetuators of the family through the male line." Strepetova's voluntary exodus was consistent with peasant convention, the only difference being that she left to work rather

than to marry. See Christine Worobec, *Peasant Russia: Family and Community in the Post Emancipation Period*, Princeton: Princeton University Press, 1991, p. 209.

12 Strepetova, *Zhizn'*, p. 195.

13 "P.A. Strepetova (nekrolog)", *Ezhegodnik imperatorskikh teatrov*, prilozhenie, 1903–4, p. 100; N. Sever, *Letopis' teatra imeni F. Volkova*, Iaroslav: n.p., 1973, p. 52; and Strepetova, *Zhizn'*, p. 147; "Vospominaniia A.M. Pazukhina", in *Galereia stsenicheskikh deiatelei*, t. 1, Moscow: Izdanie zhurnala *Rampa i zhizn'*, 1915, p. 19. The quotation is from Sever. According to him, Strepetova was lucky to get any salary: when parents were in a company, their children served free of charge when a child was needed for a role.

14 "P.A. Strepetova (nekrolog)", p. 101; K. Kolosov, "P.A. Strepetova", *Teatr i iskusstvo*, 1903, no. 42, p. 772; Strepetova, *Zhizn'*, p. 10. According to Ben'iash, Medvedev – who was trained at the Moscow Malyi Theatre and had a reputation for both commerical and aesthetic perspicacity – first met Strepetova two years earlier, but wasn't impressed by what he saw: an "uncombed, unwashed, unattractive woman in worn down shoes." Still, he offered her 75 roubles a month, which in spite of Medvedev's considerable reputation, she refused. Ben'iash says that she finally joined the troupe when Medvedev agreed to 75 roubles per performance.

15 A.I. Urusov, *Stat'i ego, pis'ma ego, vospominaniia o nem*, t. 1, Moscow: n.p., 1907, p. 299. Technically, club theatres were still amateur in the 1870s. According to Urusov, the "Popular People's Theatre" (*Obshchedostupnyi narodnyi teatr*) was the "first important attempt to create a private theatre."

16 V.N. Davydov, *Rasskaz*, 1937 edition, p. 174. Davydov, who cared little for Strepetova, wrote that, at the beginning, Strepetova had to "eat off the same plate" as her colleagues, but later made her disdain for operettas and other popular genres eminently clear.

17 Strepetova, *Zhizn'*, p. 45. In Ben'iash. "Serious Russian realism" refers to plays by men like Ostrovski and Pisem'ski. According to Ben'iash, Strepetova transformed sentimental family drama into high tragedy: "the suffering of Russian women and their protest against the terrible conditions of life, expressed with the utmost inner dramatism and simplicity, achieved the force of a summons to revolution."

18 Urusov, *Stat'i*, t. 1, p. 328.

19 Victor Terras (ed.), *Handbook of Russian Literature*, New Haven, CT, Yale University Press, 1985, p. 340.

20 Urusov, *Stat'i*, t. 1, pp. 334–5; Strepetova, *Zhizn'*, p. 12. In Ben'iash.

21 Urusov, *Stat'i*, t.1, pp. 334–35. Even without additional modifiers, the term "*baba*" carries negative connotations. Literally a peasant wife, "*baba*" suggests an ill-bred, lower class, shrewish, and possibly promiscuous woman.

22 N.A. Selivanov, "Godovshchina", *Teatr i iskusstvo*, 1913, no. 44, p. 882.

23 Urusov, *Stat'i*, t. 1, p. 333. Urusov's account of Strepetova's performance is intriguing. His emphasis on each departure from Pisem'ski's stage directions suggests that it was unusual for actresses to assume an independent interpretive role. Since Urusov was not an actor himself, it is unclear whether his description is naive, idiosyncratic, or reflects genuine changes in actresses' authority. Certainly other starring actresses, especially Savina and Kommissarzhevskaia, took liberties with authors' texts, and were often extolled by critics for improving them.

24 Davydov, *Rasskaz*, 1937 edition, pp. 172, 249–50; Strepetova, *Zhizn'*, 28. In

Ben'iash. This was Strepetova's second marriage. Her first was to the actor, Mikhail Strel'ski, a handsome womanizer, who was physically abusive. Strepetova, who had one child by Strel'ski, left him after a particularly violent scene. Davydov mentions having to protect a pregnant Strepetova when Strel'ski attacked her with a heavy object.

25 V.M. Doroshevich, "P.A. Strepetova", in *Izbrannye rasskazy i ocherki*, Moscow: Moskovskii Rabochii, 1962, p. 101.
26 Ibid., p. 103.
27 Andrzej Walicki, *A History of Russian Thought from the Enlightenment to Marxism*, trans. Hilda Andrews-Rusiecka, Stanford, CA: Stanford University Press, 1979, p. 222.
28 Ibid.
29 Ibid., p. 92.
30 Ibid., p. 223.
31 Ibid., pp. 228–9. A central irony was that the movement consisted mostly of students and the intelligentsia. Distrustful Russian peasants often turned these "town-bred intellectuals" over to the police.
32 A. Ia. Al'tshuller (ed.), *Ocherki istorii russkoi teatral'noi kritiki, vtoraia polovina XIX veka*, Leningrad: Iskusstvo, 1976, p. 119.
33 Aleksandr Kugel', "Iz zapisnoi knizhki", *Teatr i iskusstvo*, 1903, no. 42, p. 776.
34 Davydov, *Rasskaz*, 1937 edition, pp. 249–50.
35 Ibid., p. 224.
36 Ibid., p. 226.
37 V.A. Michurina-Samoilova, *Polveka na stsene Aleksandrinskogo teatra*, Leningrad-Moscow, Iskusstvo, 1935, p. 63; Urusov, *Stat'i*, t.1, p. 300. Michurnina-Samoilova's remark was not motivated by ill-will. Her memoir suggests that she liked Strepetova offstage, admired her talent, and preferred her to Savina in virtually every respect.
38 "P.A. Strepetova – vospominaniia A.M. Pazukhina", p. 19. Pazukhin adds that when she was a young woman, she was so transformed on stage as to be almost beautiful.
39 Urusov, *Stat'i*, t.1, p. 305. For Urusov, the fact that she did not cover her face with makeup or affect frivolous glibness was an asset, not a liability.
40 Zinaida Kholmskaia, "Memuary dvukh aktrisy", *Teatr i iskusstvo*, 1904, no. 23, p. 442.
41 Kugel', "Iz zapisnoi knizhki", p. 776.
42 Ibid.
43 Davydov, *Rasskaz*, 1937 edition, p. 220.
44 Al'tshuller (ed.), *Ocherki*, p. 204.
45 Ibid., p. 205.
46 "P.A. Strepetova – vospominaniia Sergei Iablanovskogo", in *Galereia stsenicheskikh deiatelei*, p. 23; "Pis'ma I.E. Repin k P.A. Strepetovoi", in *Teatral'noe nasledstvo*, Moscow: Iskusstvo, 1956, pp. 402–4.
47 Strepetova, *Zhizn'*, pp. 58–9. In Ben'iash. This is Ben'iash's point of view and therefore typically Soviet. Readers must remember that the Soviets had a tendency to demonize conservatives like Suvorin.
48 Al'tshuller, *Ocherki*, p. 180.
49 Strepetova, *Zhizn'*, p. 66. In Ben'iash.
50 Ibid., p. 79. Her views were not, however, extraordinary. Another actor gave a rabidly antisemitic address at the congress in 1897. See "Doklad N.S. Vekhtera", in *Trudy 1-ogo vserossiiskogo s'ezda stsenicheskikh deiatelei*, St. Petersburg: n.p., 1898, pp. 159–65.

51 Kugel', 'Iz zapisnoi knizhki,' p. 776. Although *"raskol'nitsa"* means "dissenter," it is not clear whether Kugel' is alluding to the Orthodox Old Believers or using the term generically. Strepetova was deeply religious, but this is the only reference I've found to her being a member of the Old Believer sect.

52 See Worobec, *Peasant Russia*, p. 175. "The patriarchal Russian peasant family was but a microcosm of a hierarchical social order that extended from God to his representative on earth, the *"batiushka"* (little father) tsar to all other fathers."

53 B. Shoikevich, *Ibsen i russkaia kul'tura*, n.p, 1974, p. 70; Selivanov, "Godovshchina", p. 882.

54 Doroshevich, "P.A. Strepetova", p. 103.

55 For a recent edition of the "Domostroi" (translated into modern Russian) see V.V. Kolesov (ed.), *Domostroi*, Moscow: Sovetskaia rossiia, 1990.

56 Ibid., p. 146.

57 Ibid., p. 155.

58 Worobec, *Peasant Russia*, p. 185.

59 Doroshevich, "P.A. Strepetova", p. 104.

60 "P.A. Strepetova – vospominaniia Sergei Iablonovskogo", p. 24.

61 Urusov, *Stat'i*, t.1, p. 312.

62 Selivanov, "Godovshchina", p. 882.

63 Urusov, *Stat'i*, t.1, p. 299. Urusov actually preferred her to Fedotova in *"bytovaia"* roles because Fedotova, a product of the Imperial school with no life experience in the provinces, was too "mannered."

64 Selivanov, "Godovshchina", p. 882. Selivanov wrote: "God, how we hated Savina and worshipped Strepetova, even though we didn't know either personally. . . . For us, Savina was like a member of the Black Hundreds and Strepetova represented the opposition."

65 Vladimir Nemirovich-Danchenko, "Teatr i shkola", *Artist*, 1894, no. 42, pp. 136–54; "Pis'ma o Moskovskikh teatrakh", *Delo*, 1886, no. 3–4, pp. 116–19. Generally speaking Imperial theatres did not welcome provincial performers. In this period, the Aleksandrinskii hired more provincials than the Malyi, but prejudice permeated both theatres.

66 Strepetova, *Zhizn'*, pp. 30 and 50. Ben'iash quotes a remark published in *Russkii mir* that just as connoisseurs of art rejected paintings depicting "louts who picked their noses," so the Aleksandrinskii connoisseurs rejected Strepetova's art.

67 A.N. Ostrovski, *Vsia zhizn' – teatru*, Moscow: n.p., 1989, p. 263.

68 Urusov, *Stat'i*, t.1, p. 295.

69 "P.A. Strepetova – vospominaniia Sergei Iablonovskogo", p. 22.

70 Ibid., p. 26.

71 I. Petrovskaia, *Teatr i zritel' provintsial'noi rossii*, Leningrad, Iskusstvo, 1979, p. 205. Although both played the *"bytovaia"* repertoire, the sub-genre in which each specialized was virtually inaccessible to the other. This was a class issue. Savina specialized in Western influenced *"bytovaia"* drama, which reflected the urban gentry and aristocracy. Strepetova played a *"bytovaia"* repertoire that depicted the peasant and merchant classes. Each made forays into the other's repertoire, but neither had much success when she did.

72 Ibid.

73 "P.A. Strepetova: neskol'ko slov k portretu artistki", *Teatral'nyi mirok*, 1884, no. 8, p. 1.

74 Ibid.

75 "P.A. Strepetova – vospominaniia Sergei Iablonovskogo, p. 22.

76 Petrovskaia, *Teatr i zritel'*, p. 211; K. Kolosov, "P.A. Strepetova", *Teatr i iskusstvo*, 1903, no. 42, p. 773. Petrovskaia explains that actors succeeded with neurasthenics because the range of men's experience was much greater. "Women suffered only for themselves or their children. Men, who participated in social life, suffered disorders (*neustroistvo*) on a broader plane." This is a modern, rather than contemporaneous point of view, however. Kolosov notes that in *Darkness and Light*, a popular melodrama, critics agreed that Strepetova's portrayal of insanity was both astonishingly artistic and disturbingly real.

77 "P.A. Strepetova – vospominaniia Sergei Iablonovskogo, p. 21.

78 Petrovskaia, *Teatr i zritel'*, p. 209.

79 Strepetova, *Zhizn'*, p. 89. In Ben'iash.

80 Ibid.

81 Davydov, *Rasskaz*, 1962 edition, p. 149.

82 Strepetova, *Zhizn'*, p. 62 (In Ben'iash); V. Viren, "Narodnyi talant", *Teatral'naia zhizn'*, 1975, no. 19, p. 31. Early in his career, Nemirovich called Strepetova a genius, which seems odd in view of his later demands for historical accuracy and culturally specific detail. Arguing that Strepetova's characters embodied universal feelings, Nemirovich advised spectators to let go of national differences so that they could enjoy Strepetova in the European repertoire.

83 Al'tshuller, *Ocherki*, p. 180.

84 Strepetova, *Zhizn'*, p. 49. In Ben'iash.

85 Urusov, *Stat'i*, t.1, p. 304. He argued that Strepetova could not effect spectators so profoundly if her acting was simply a "pathological phenomenon." Her performances had a feeling of "measure" and "delicacy," which could only be achieved by a combination of art and inspiration. He also offers a fascinating Darwinian argument. Strepetova's facial flexibility was the product of heredity: a particular grouping of facial muscles allowed her greater physical expressiveness than the ordinary person!

86 Strepetova, *Zhizn'*, p. 57. In Ben'iash.

87 "P.A. Strepetova – vospominaniia Sergei Iablonovskogo", p. 26.

88 Ibid., p. 25.

89 A.G., "Iz vospominanii o P.A. Strepetovoi", *Istoricheskii vestnik*, February 1904, pp. 547–63.

90 See Strepetova, *Zhizn'*, pp. 87–8 (in Ben'iash); A.G., "Iz vospominanii o P.A. Strepetovoi", pp. 547–63; M. Nesterov, "P.A. Strepetova", in *Davnie dni*, Moscow: n.p., 1959, pp. 239–40; and A.S. Suvorin, *Dnevnik*, Moscow: Novosti, 1992, p. 21. This husband, Sasha Pogodin, was half her age and extremely jealous. Accounts of their marriage and his suicide differ. Some argued that Strepetova pursued her career at the expense of Pogodin's happiness. When she refused to accompany him to Moscow, he shot himself and she discovered the body. According to Nesterov, Pogodin was so insanely (and unjustifiably) jealous that he could not bear to see her kiss another man on stage. According to Suvorin, Strepetova was still very much attached to Pisarev – which turned up the heat of Pogodin's jealousy. One thing, at least, is certain: Stepetova tended to put the theatre ahead of her husbands.

91 A.G., "Iz vospominanii o P.A. Strepetovoi", pp. 552–3.

92 Ibid., p. 554.

93 The Aleksandrinskii directorate hired her again in 1899, but she stayed for only half a season.

94 A.N. Ostrovski, *O literature i teatre*, Moscow, Sovremenik, 1986, pp. 322–3; Strepetova, *Zhizn'*, p. 74 (in Ben'iash); *P.A. Strepetova: Vospominaniia i pis'ma*, Moscow-Leningrad: "Academiia", 1934, pp. 438–9. Ostrovski also tried to get

Strepetova transferred to the Malyi theatre where he felt she would find more sympathy, but the plan failed. In a letter to Ostrovski, Strepetova hints that Fedotova's opposition may have hindered her transfer to the Malyi.

95 "Novaia p'esa A.N. Ostrovskogo, *Bez viny vinovatye*", *Teatral'nyi mirok*, 1884, no. 5, p. 4.

96 "P.A. Strepetova (nekrolog)", p. 102 and Ostrovski, *Vsia zhizn' – teatru*, p. 263.

97 Doroshevich, "P.A. Strepetova", p. 104; E. Polkova, *Teatr L'va Tolstogo*, Moscow: n.p., 1978, pp. 95–8. The quotation in full is: "Matriona was a simple Russian woman whom the darkness transformed into a 'village lady Macbeth.'" She was, in other words, a logical development of the roles Strepetova played as young woman – a provincial "*baba*" turned ugly and dangerous by the rigors of village existence. Polkova points out that Tolstoi never actually saw Strepetova in the role.

98 Evtikhi Karpov, "A.S. Suvorin i osnovanie Teatra Literaturno Artisticheskogo kruzhka", *Istoricheskii vestnik*, 1914, no. 9, pp. 873–902. The following anecdote is Karpov's.

99 Viren, "Narodnyi talant", p. 31. During her tenure at the Aleksadrinskii, Strepetova was the idol of the "*raznochints*, students, and *kursistky*." (A "*raznochinets*" was an intellectual not of gentle birth; "*kursistky*" were female university students.)

100 Kolosov, "P.A. Strepetova", p. 773 In Ben'iash; Strepetova, *Zhizn'*, pp. 94–7.

101 See, for example Urusov, *Stat'i*, t. 1, p. 343; Kugel', "Iz zapisnoi knizhki", p. 776; Kolosov, "P.A. Strepetova", p. 773; Strepetova, *Zhizn'*, p. 99 (In Ben'iash); T. Pavlova, "Repin i Strepetova", *Teatr*, 1970, no. 8, p. 133; "Teatral'nyi kalendar: P.A. Strepetova", *Teatr*, 1953, no. 10, p. 171.

102 Kholmskaia, "Memuary dvukh aktrisy", p. 443.

103 "Khronika", *Teatr i iskusstvo*, 1903, no. 42, p. 765.

104 Davydov, *Rasskaz*, 1962 edition, pp. 223–4.

6 ENTER THE ACTRESS-ENTREPRENEUR

1 Richard Gordon Thorpe, "The Management of Culture in Revolutionary Russia: The Imperial Theatres and the State, 1897–1928", Ph.D. diss., Princeton University, 1990, p. 20. Initiated during Catherine's reign, the monopoly was formalized in the nineteenth century. In 1827, a statute gave the Direction of the Imperial Theaters the right to regulate and restrict theatrical life in St. Petersburg and Moscow. During the 1830s and 1840s, this right was extended to a monopoly in both capitals. In 1856 and 1862, the monopoly was formalized.

2 Actress-managers were not the only entrepreneurial women in the theatre; Elizaveta Nikolaevna Rassokhina established the first theatrical agency in Russia in 1892. Until 1896, Rassokhina's was the only commercial agency in Russia. The agency mediated contracts between performers and entrepreneurs and later began organizing companies and tours for Russian and foreign stars. It was also the central broker in Russia for tickets to theatre events, circuses, concerts, exhibitions, lectures, and philanthropic performances. Rassokhina's archive is located at the Central State Archive of Literature and Art (TsGALI). The information is from *Pervoe teatral'noe agenstvo dlia Rossii i zagranitsy E.N. Rassokhinoi, 1892–1918.*

3 In a paper given at the Conference on Women in Russia (Bath, 1992), Catriona Kelly suggested that during the nineteenth century, the number of independent women merchants in Russia increased. Although there is no concrete evidence

that they set an example for female theatrical entrepreneurs, it is tempting to hypothesize a relationship.

4 Julie Holledge, *Innocent Flowers: Women in the Edwardian Theatre*, London: Virago Press, 1981, p. 162.

5 "Russkaia dramaticheskaia stsena", *Vestnik evropy*, 1871, n.v., p. 389.

6 A.I. Urusov, "Teatr: zametki i vpechatleniia", in *A.I. Urusov: Stat'i ego, pis'ma ego, vospominaniia o nem*, Moscow: n.p., 1907, pp. 230–3.

7 E.G. Kholodov (ed.), *Istoriia russkogo dramaticheskogo teatra*, t. 5, Moscow: Iskusstvo, 1980, pp. 232–52; A.N. Ostrovski, "Klubnye stseny, chastnye teatry, i liubitelskie spektakli", in *Polnoe sobranie sochinenii*, t. 10, Moscow: Iskusstvo, 1978, pp. 114–25. Interest in these activities was widespread. Attempts in Moscow to establish alternatives to the Imperial system began in 1861 with the Amateur Circle of Dramatic Art (*Kruzhok liubitelei dramaticheskogo iskusstva*) and the Krasnovorot Theatre. Ostrovski opened the Artistic Circle (*Articheskii kruzhok*) in 1865, and during the 1870s, several club theatres flourished. The professional writers and critics who led the pre-reform amateur groups were usually more interested in providing a forum for new plays than in exploring new production methods. They also emphasized the art rather than the business of theatre, and many prominent actresses, including Savina and Strepetova, were introduced to audiences in the capitals through the club theatres.

8 Urusov, "Zametki i vpechatleniia", p. 232.

9 Ibid., pp. 235–6; Baron N.V. Drizen, "Monopoliia teatral'nikh zrelishch", *Istoricheskii vestnik*, 1902, no. 9, p. 954.

10 D.I. Zolotnitski, "Strashnaia sila teatra . . ." in *Russkii teatr i dramaturgiia kontsa XIX veka*, Leningrad: n.p., 1983, p. 106. The topographical designation "Theatre near the Pushkin Monument" was a popular, although informal name used by audiences, critics, and the theatre community to refer to Brenko's theatre because it was located near a new statue of Pushkin erected on June 6, 1880. Since the statue was considerably more famous than Brenko, it was probably convenient to have Pushkin's name associated with the theatre, if only by an accident of geography.

11 Iuri Iur'ev, *Zapiski*, Leningrad: Iskusstvo, 1938, p. 66.

12 "A.A. Brenko i 'Rabochii teatr'", *Rampa i zhizn'*, 1915, no. 37, p. 11; G.A. Khaichenko, *Russkii narodnyi teatr kontsa XIX – nachala XX veka*, Moscow: Nauka, 1975, pp. 230–3. She started by giving lessons in diction, declamation, and makeup to workers at no cost. Their first production was *The Storm*, which, according to *Rampa i zhizn'*, was as good as anything produced in a "real dramatic studio." Stanislavski, who was present at this production, greeted Brenko as a "pioneer of democratic theatre."

13 *Istoriia*, p. 253, and A.A. Brenko, "Avtobiografiia 1", p. 3. I will be citing two sets of manuscript memoirs in this chapter, both of which are located at the Bakhrushin Museum (*Gosudarstvennyi tsentral'nyi muzei imeni A.A. Bakhrushina*) in Moscow. One set, a fourteen page typescript, will be designated "Avtobiografiia 1"; the other, a 300-page handwritten manuscript, will be designated "Avtobiografiia 2", but all page citations will be from the typescript copy in my collection. The first focuses on Brenko's efforts to establish the Pushkin Theatre; the second is mostly concerned with her efforts to rescue it from unscrupulous colleagues.

14 Brenko, "Avtobiografiia 1", p. 3.

15 R. Vitenzon, *Anna Brenko*, Leningrad, Iskusstvo, 1985, p. 18.

16 Brenko, "Avtobiografiia 1", pp. 1–2.

17 "Dvadtsatipiatiletie stolichnykh chastnykh teatrov", *Teatral'naia rossiia*, 1905, no. 39, p. 1172.

18 Brenko, "Avtobiografiia 1", p. 6.

19 Ibid., p. 4.

20 Em. Beksin, "Svetlyi put", *Zhizn' iskusstva*, 1924, no. 42, p. 4.

21 According to several sources, Brenko not only graduated from the Malyi's theatre school, she was also the first actress to attend the "higher women's courses" (*vyshie zhenskie kursy*) offered by the University in St. Petersburg. See, *Teatral'naia entsiklopediia*, t. 1, Moscow, Sovetskaia Entsiklopediia, 1961, p. 694; *Istoriia*, t. 5, pp. 253–8; and S.S. Danilov, *Ocherki po istorii russkogo dramaticheskogo teatra*, Moscow: Iskusstvo, 1948, p. 423. Vitenzon, challenges the fact of her higher education by offering an elaborate proof that she could not have been in St. Petersburg at this time. With respect to radical politics, a notorious "revolutionary" with subversive pamphlets hanging out of his pockets loitered around the Pushkin Theatre with several of the actors, but whether Brenko herself engaged in revolutionary politics during this period is less certain. See V.A. Giliarovski, *Liudi teatra*, Moscow: Moskovskii Rabochii, 1960, p. 421.

22 Brenko's theatre was "*obshchedostupnyi*" rather than "*narodnyi.*" The latter was for the "people"; the former was a moderately priced, "popular" theatre that could attract a broader cross-section of the population. For a useful account of the genuine people's and worker's theatres that arose in the 1890s, see Gary Thurston, "The Impact of Russian Popular Theatre, 1886–1915", *Journal of Modern History*, 1983, no. 55, pp. 237–67.

23 Zolotnitski, "Strashnaia sila", p. 108.

24 V. Maslikh, "Pamiati A.A. Brenko", *Teatr*, 1966, no. 4, p. 107; B.A. Shchetinin, "F.A. Korsh i ego teatr", *Istoricheskii vestnik*, 1907, no. 10, p. 171. Shchetinin wrote that getting the sponsorship of the Society for Christian Assistance was a "cunning" move on Brenko's part.

25 Brenko, "Avtobiografiia 1", p. 4.

26 "Dvadtsatipiatiletie stolichnykh chastnykh teatrov", p. 1172. Having had no experience in the provinces, Brenko had little knowledge of the quality of provincial actors.

27 Brenko, "Avtobiografiia 1", p. 4; "Dvadtsatipiatiletie stolichnykh chastnykh teatrov", p. 1172. Brenko obtained permission under the name of her maid's brother and paid him 25 roubles a month for the use of his name. Because she was still an actress at the Malyi Theatre, she was afraid to have a permit under her own name, but she did retain power of attorney.

28 Shchetinin, "F.A. Korsh", p. 171; "Dvadtsatipiatiletie stolichnykh chastnykh teatrov", p. 1172.

29 Brenko, "Avtobiografiia 1", p. 7.

30 "Dvadtsatipiatiletie stolichnykh chastnykh teatrov", p. 1172.

31 Giliarovski, *Liudi*, p. 422; A. Glama-Meshcherskaia, *Vospominaniia*, Moscow, Iskusstvo, 1937, p. 170.

32 A.V. Anisimov, *Teatry Moskvy: vremia i arkhitektura*, Moscow: Moskovskii Rabochii, 1984, p. 75.

33 Urusov, "Zametki i vpechatleniia", pp. 238–9; Giliarovski, *Liudi*, p. 423.

34 Urusov, "Zametki i vpechatleniia", p. 239; Glama-Meshcherskaia, *Vospominaniia*, p. 132. The first impression was overwhelming because, like most provincial performers, Glama was accustomed to being treated like refuse by directors and entrepreneurs.

35 Giliarovski, *Liudi*, p. 423.

36 "Dvadtsatipiatiletie stolichnykh chastnykh teatrov", p. 1172. See also, Glama-Meshcherskaia, *Vospominaniia*, p. 132. Glama came to the theatre as a young, virtually unknown provincial actress. Although she does not mention an actual salary figure for her first contract, Brenko's offer was so substantial that she apparently she saw no necessity to negotiate. Later, without even asking for an increase, Glama received a substantial raise. The fact that she was Pisarev's second wife may have contributed to her good fortunes, but many contemporaneous commentators refer to Brenko's generous nature.

37 Glama-Meshcherskaia, *Vospominaniia*, p. 132.

38 *Istoriia russkogo dramaticheskogo teatra*, t. 5, p. 255. "Along with solving problems with the repertoire, the theatre's leadership had to unite this motley group of provincial actors into a unified, creative collective, to teach them to work systematically and inventively, and to achieve 'artistic discipline.' If the Pushkin Theatre did not completely solve the problems, it took the first steps."

39 Strepetova's debut did, however, create a stir in Moscow. Fedotova's admirers were particularly offended when Strepetova's devotees dared to compare their idol to the great Fedotova. "Pervyi chastnyi teatr v stolitse", *Teatr i iskusstvo*, 1905, no. 36, p. 577.

40 A.I. Urusov, *Stat'i ego, pis'ma ego, vospominaniia o nem*, pp. 240, 468.

41 Glama-Meshcherskaia, *Vospominaniia*, p. 164; 'Dvadtsat' piat' let nazad', *Teatr i iskusstvo*, 1905, no. 37, p. 592.

42 Zolotnitski, "Strashnaia sila", p. 108.

43 Brenko, "Avtobiografiia 1", p. 7; Brenko, "Avtobiografiia 2", p. 3; Vitenzon, *Anna Brenko*, p. 103. Early in the venture, Pisarev was Brenko's real collaborator. Andreev-Burlak was a talented actor, but whether he took his administrative role seriously is doubtful. An irresponsible alcoholic who rarely memorized his lines, he was also an incorrigible gossip who eventually stirred up trouble among the actors. Brenko relates a telling incident. Andreev-Burlak was supposed to work with the architect, Chichagov, and assist the builders, but more often than not, they "went hunting," leaving Brenko "to work alone with the foreman." Vitenzon recalls that Andreev-Burlak hired far too many actors (the company included fifty). He had many friends among provincial actors and brought anyone with a hard luck story into the Pushkin company.

44 Glama-Meshcherskaia, *Vospominaniia*, pp. 132, 167. The "long run" was not established in Russia until after the turn of the century. The Imperial theatres maintained enormous repertoires which included not only full-length plays, but one-acts, vaudevilles, and all kinds of brief, comic sketches. Although plays stayed in the repertoire for years, consecutive performances were unusual.

45 Nikolai Sinel'nikov (1855–1939) was a progressive provincial director. Interestingly, the extended rehearsals instituted by the MAT were controversial within the company. Nemirovich was extremely impatient with Stanislavski's desire to rehearse indefinitely. When Stanislavski worked at the Society for Art and Literature, twenty rehearsals were considered "thorough preparation." Brenko was at least as thorough. For an excellent account of the MAT, its practices and predecessors, see Jean Benedetti, *Stanislavski: A Biography*, New York: Routledge, 1988.

46 Marie Wilton (Mrs. Bancroft), a British actress who managed the Prince of Wales Theatre between 1865 and 1879, helped establish Tom Robertson's "cup and saucer" realism in England.

47 Vitenzon, *Anna Brenko*, p. 51; "Avtobiografiia 2", p. 5. Brenko described a production for which she designed and sewed the costumes based on historical data: "Beginning with the marvelous scenery and ending with buttons and finger rings, everything was true to the epoch."

48 Quoted in Vitenzon, *Anna Brenko*, p. 52.
49 Laurence Senelick, "Russia, 1812–1898", in *National Theatre in Northern and Eastern Europe, 1746–1900*, Cambridge: Cambridge University Press, 1991, p. 359. According to Senelick, "In practice, the Russian *'regisseur'* was a glorified stage manager, who had to deal with the day-to-day tasks that were beneath the attention of a bureaucratic administrator.... As in Central Europe, the term eventually came to be applied to the stage director, so that the two functions, total artistic control and physical *mise-en-scène*, became invested in one individual."
50 "Avtobiografiia 2", p. 10. Trained at the Malyi Theatre, Aleksandr Fedotov enjoyed a substantial reputation as an actor/director. Because he also had a reputation for treating actors harshly, not all of them were pleased when he arrived to oversee the second season.
51 Iur'ev, *Zapiski*, p. 64. Iur'ev's rhetorical flourishes remind us that his memoirs were published under Stalin. Although information from books and articles published during this period is not necessarily false, one must be careful to separate fact from ideological bias.
52 Brenko, "Avtobiografiia 2", p. 10.
53 Urusov, "Zametki i vpechatleniia", pp. 240–1; *Istoriia*, t. 6, pp. 510–16.
54 *Istoriia*, vol. 5, p. 257; Brenko, "Avtobiografiia 2", p. 15. Brenko sent free tickets to the schools for Sunday matinees. Complaining that Moliere's and Gogol's plays were "immoral," some teachers returned the tickets. Brenko was baffled; she had specifically chosen native and foreign classics with the goal of introducing children to great literature.
55 Quoted in A. Ia. Al'tshuller (ed.), *Ocherki istorii russkoi teatral'noi kritiki*, Leningrad, Iskusstvo, 1976, pp. 293, 297.
56 Ibid., p. 118.
57 Urusov, *Stat'i, pis'ma, vospominaniia o nem*, pp. 240–1, 468–9.
58 Ostrovski, *Polnoe sobranie sochinenii*, p. 124; Zolotnitski, "Strashnaia sila", p. 107.
59 Glama-Meshcherskaia, *Vospominaniia*, p. 163.
60 Giliarovski, *Liudi*, pp. 418–25.
61 Anisimov, *Teatry Moskvy*, p. 76.
62 Maslikh, "Pamiati", p. 108.
63 Glama-Meshcherskaia, *Vospominaniia*, p. 174.
64 Brenko, "Avtobiografiia 2", p. 17.
65 P.A. Kanshin, "Pis'ma o Moskovskikh teatrakh", *Delo*, 1886, no. 3–4, pp. 119–20.
66 Shchetinin, "F.A. Korsh", p. 171.
67 "Dvadtsat' piat' let tomu nazad", p. 592; "Iubilei A.A. Brenko", *Teatral'naia gazeta*, 1915, no. 37, pp. 5–6.
68 Brenko, "Avtobiografiia 2"; *Sovremennyi liud*, Moscow: Obshchestvo russkikh dramaticheskikh pisatelei, 1883. Published as a handwritten manuscript, the play appeared under Brenko's married name, A.A. Levenson. Much of the plot and many of the characters are based on Brenko's experiences at the Pushkin.
69 Brenko, "Avtobiografiia 2", p. 4. For most of the performers, the tsar's death was a financial tragedy. According to Brenko, their reaction was simultaneously sad, amusing, and childish. One exclaimed: "If only I had known [that the tsar would be assassinated] I wouldn't have had a fur coat sewn for my wife!" Having frittered away their money, most were penniless during the period of mourning.

70 Ibid.

71 Ibid., pp. 20–1. Brenko wrote: "Because I did not want my theatre lowered to the level of a fairground spectacle (*balagannoe zrelishche*), I refused to produce the rubbish favored by provincial actors. They were only interested in gratifying their own vanity and did not understand my concerns. A play could be right off the fairground, but if it had one advantageous role, the actor would be offended if I refused to produce it." Distressed by Brenko's refusal to produce her favorite benefit play, one actress threatened to thrash her. The woman complained to Pisarev, who accused Brenko of exploiting the performers and suppressing their talents. Finally, Brenko allowed the production, but when she saw the can-can and heard the gypsy music, she covered her ears and ran out of the theatre. She could not bear to see the Pushkin so debased. See also "Pis'ma o Moskovskikh teatrov", p. 120. Although Kanshin's point of view is tinged with Moscow chauvinism, he confirms Brenko's description: the actors were "villainous, petty, vain, undisciplined, and completely unsuited to Moscow."

72 Ibid., pp. 16–17. Many years later, when the critic, Sokolova, and Brenko became friendly, Sokolova admitted that Korsh gave her an expensive bracelet in exchange for writing whatever he asked.

73 "Dvadtsatipiatiletie stolichnykh chastnykh teatrov", p. 1173.

74 "Material' dlia istorii russkogo teatra: iz vospominanii F.A. Budrina", *Vestnik evropy*, 1901, no. 10, pp. 576–600. Budrin wrote his memoir in 1883. His account of the mismanagement of the Imperial theatres, especially under Baron Kister, helps to explain the increasing pressure for repeal of the monopoly and for general theatrical reform.

75 "Dvadtsatipiatiletie stolichnykh chastnykh teatrov", p. 1172; Brenko, "Avtobiografiia 2", p. 6; and Ostrovski, *Polnoe sobranoe sochinenii*, p. 28.

76 Brenko, "Avtobiografiia 2", p. 7. In view of Brenko's progressive reputation and later political activism, this letter is ironic. In essence, it said that "in such confused times, people are preoccupied with all sorts of political ideas; this theatre is desirable and necessary because it will provide distraction from these ideas."

77 Brenko, "Avtobiografiia 2", p. 12.

78 Zolotnitski, "Strashnaia sila", p. 109; Glama-Meshcherskaia, *Vospominaniia*, p. 244.

79 A "jubilee" is an anniversary marking years of service to the Russian theatre. Before 1917, they were high-priced benefit performances at which the object of celebration received expensive presents, immoderate ovations, and enough bouquets to traumatize an asthmatic.

80 "Dvadtsatipiatiletie stolichnykh chastnykh teatrov", p. 1173.

81 "Iubilei A.A. Brenko", p. 6.

82 "A.A. Brenko i 'rabochii teatr'", p. 11.

83 *Istoriia*, t. 6, p. 67; "Sovremennoe obozrenie", *Artist*, 1890, no. 7, pp. 125–6.

84 "Mariia Moritsovna Abramova", *Dnevnik artista*, 1892, no. 4, p. 27. The "anonymous friend" and author of this article was probably her common-law husband, Vladimir Ivanovich Manotskov, who wrote: "She seemed less like an actress than anyone in her literary circle.... There wasn't the slightest trace of the theatre's demoralizing influence in her personality." (31)

85 "Mariia Moritsovna Abramova", p. 30; Ksenia Kuprina, "Dorogi", *Teatral'naia zhizn'*, 1964, no. 22, p. 30.

86 "Mariia Moritsovna Abramova", p. 31.

87 Kuprina, "Dorogi", p. 30.

88 *Teatral'naia entsiklopediia*, t. 1, p. 30.

89 "Teatr g-zhi Abramovoi", *Artist*, 1889, no. 4, p. 127.

90 "Sovremennoe obozrenie", p. 126.

91 Ivan Ivanov, "Teatr g-zhi Abramovoi", *Artist*, 1890, no. 6, p. 124. The play (*The Wood Demon*) was panned. According to Ivanov, if Chekhov wants to put real life on stage, he should first consider that no one wants to see it. "We want," Ivanov wrote, "extraordinary occurrences."

92 *Artist*, no. 4, p. 128; "Teatr g-zhi Abramovoi", *Artist*, 1890, no. 5, pp. 142–6. What is the point of producing good plays, the critic asks, when the actors are too careless and indifferent to make anything of the material?

93 "Mariia Moritsovna Abramova", p. 31.

94 Henry Weldon, "Inostranets o Gorevoi (pis'mo iz Berlin)", *Teatral'nyi mirok*, 1886, no. 4, p. 3; "Berlin", *Teatral'nyi mirok*, 1886, no. 2, p. 1; "Berlinskiia gastroli E.N. Gorevoi", *Teatral'nyi mirok*, 1886, no. 3, p. 2; "Russkoe iskusstvo za granitsei: E.N. Goreva", *Teatral'nyi mirok*, 1886, no. 5, pp. 3–4; Aleksandr Pleshcheev, "Teatral'naia beseda", *Teatral'nyi mirok*, 1886, no. 10, p. 2. Pleshcheev's nationalist rhetoric is particularly interesting. Extolling Goreva for carrying the banner of Russian art abroad, he calls her German tour a "heroic deed dear to the hearts of all Russians." The anonymous author of "Russkoe iskusstvo za granitsei" calls her Russia's "little Peter the Great." She even received an invitation to perform in New York. Curiously, Goreva toured without a Russian company. In Berlin and Leipzig, she acted in Russian while the rest of the cast spoke German.

95 A.R. Kugel', "E.N. Goreva", in *Teatral'nye portrety*, Leningrad, Iskusstvo, 1967, pp. 190–1. Kugel' notes that Goreva made the old men's tongues hang out. She was a "marvelous woman with a charming voice," but not much more.

96 "E.N. Goreva (nekrolog)", *Rampa i zhizn'*, 1917, no. 29–30, p. 12; "Tekushchiia novosti", *Teatr i zhizn'*, 1888, no. 169, pp. 1–2; N. Rossov, "Pamiati Gorevoi", *Teatral'naia gazeta*, 1917, no. 34–35, pp. 8–10. Goreva finally won a contract with the Aleksandrinskii in the 1890s because someone with authority "ordered" the Imperial directorate to hire her. The Aleksandrinskii, however, "starved her out" by keeping her unoccupied. She resigned after playing only three roles during the year.

97 Glama-Meshcherskaia, *Vospominaniia*, p. 234.

98 Ibid., p. 236; Mariia Velizarii, *Put' provintsial'noi aktrisy*, Leningrad, Iskusstvo, 1938, p. 88; Elizaveta Goreva, "Iz moei avtobiografii", *Teatr i iskusstvo*, 1917, no. 10–11, p. 196. Although Glama is circumspect, she implies that Goreva and Karpenko had a lesbian relationship. Claiming that Goreva "regarded her male admirers scornfully," Glama alludes to the "rumors, legends, and gossip" surrounding her (234). She also observes that "Goreva was too smart and had experienced too many hard knocks not to understand her milieu and her own isolation within it." In the excerpt from her autobiography, Goreva calls Karpenko the "faithful companion" (*vernaia sputnitsa*) who never deserted her.

99 Kugel', "E.N. Goreva." p. 193; Velizarii, *Put'*, pp. 87, 104; Glama-Meshcherskaia, *Vospominaniia*, pp. 253–4. Glama was offered a five-year contract with a guaranteed payment of 30,000 roubles to be deposited directly into her bank. Velizarii got 200 roubles a month and a nominal benefit without any haggling. During the second season, several actors received as much as 1200 roubles a month.

100 "Teatr g-zhi Gorevoi", *Artist*, 1889, no. 2, pp. 85–103. The reviews are of *The Misanthrope*, *Don Carlos*, an unnamed play by Alphonse Dode, K.V.

Nazar'eva's *Uneasy Happiness* (*Trevozhnoe schast'e*), and *A Friend for Life* (*Podruga zhizni*), which was first published in *The Woman's Bulletin* (*Zhenskii vestnik*). Whether Goreva produced plays by women as a political statement is uncertain. Nazar'eva, for example, was a prolific playwright who also got productions at the Imperial theatres.

101 *Artist*, 1889, no. 2, p. 86 and "Teatr g-zhi Gorevoi", *Artist*, 1890, no. 4, p. 119.

102 *Teatral'naia entsiklopediia*, t. 2, p. 74. For the encyclopedia's compilers, "financial mismanagement" was a permanent feature of woman-managed enterprises.

103 "Teatr g-zhi Gorevoi", *Artist*, 1890, no. 4, p. 137.

104 "Sovremennoe obozrenie", *Artist*, 1890, no. 7, pp. 125–6; "Dramaticheskii teatr g-zhi Gorevoi", *Artist*, 1890, no. 10, pp. 138–9; "Dramaticheskii teatr g-zhi Gorevoi", *Artist*, 1890, no. 11, p. 150; "Dramaticheskii teatr g-zhi Gorevoi", *Artist*, 1891, no. 12, p. 157. Critics complained that scenery and costumes took precedence over inner content, and classic plays had been supplanted by popular trash. Rather than setting high artistic standards, she relied on "coarse effects" and "vulgar tricks" to attract audiences.

105 *Artist*, no. 2, p. 89 and no. 4, p. 136.

106 *Artist*, no. 7, p. 126.

107 *Artist*, no. 10, p. 138.

108 *Artist*, 1890, no. 11, p. 150; *Artist*, 1891, no. 12, p. 157.

109 Glama-Meshcherskaia, *Vospominaniia*, p. 255; Goreva, "Iz moei avtobiografii", p. 195; "E.N. Goreva", *Teatr i iskusstvo*, 1917, no. 28–9, p. 489. The excerpt from Goreva's autobiography indicates a loss of 25,000 roubles. The figure in *Teatr i iskusstvo*'s obituary is 250,000 roubles.

110 "Pervyi chastnyi teatr v stolitse", *Teatr i iskusstvo*, 1905, no. 36, p. 576.

111 Elizaveta Shabel'skaia, *Vekseliia antreprenershi*, St. Petersburg: n.p., 1907. For general information on Shabel'skaia, I am also indebted to the *Dictionary of Russian Women Writers*, Marina Ledkovsky, Charlotte Rosenthal, and Mary Zirin (eds), Westport, CN: Greenwood Press, 1994, pp. 566–8. In the memoir, Shabel'skaia implies that Kovalevski was both her backer and her lover.

112 Shabel'skaia, *Vekseliia*, p. 3.

113 Ibid., p. 5.

114 The clear implication in Shabel'skaia's memoir is that most of her financial backing came from current and past lovers. She passes off this slander as the product of "evil tongues," but it would not be the first time a woman traded sexual favors for money.

115 Boborykin, Goreva's literary manager/artistic director, expressed his views on actress-entrepreneurs in a story entitled "Tuda! tuda!", *Vestnik evropy*, 1913, no. 8, pp. 5–70. In his opinion, nature did not endow women with creativity or management skills.

116 I. Grinevskaia, "Zhenshchina na stsene", *Biblioteka teatra i iskusstva*, 1909, no. 6, p. 18.

7 LIDIA IAVORSKAIA

1 Although Madonna has access to a range of media that nineteenth-century actresses could not imagine, the mass-circulation press was a nineteenth-century phenomenon that helped make Sarah Bernhardt one of the first international superstars. In Russia, mass-circulation newspapers became popular in the 1860s. Because these newspapers tended to pander to the prurient interests of their readers, it is probably not coincidental that the rise of starring actresses parallels

the rise of this industry. Nothing sells more papers than scandalous revelations about prominent entertainers. For information about the mass-circulation press in Russia and its attitude toward Bernhardt, see Louise McReynolds, *The News Under Russia's Old Regime: The Development of a Mass-Circulation Press*, Princeton: Princeton University Press, 1991.

2 Tatiana Shchepkina-Kupernik, "N.S. Butova i L.B. Iavorskaia", unpublished memoir, Moscow: TsGALI, p. 3.

3 N. Negorev, "Zametki", *Teatr i isskustvo*, 1902, no. 26 pp. 495–6.

4 Nikolai Efros, "L.B. Iavorskaia", *Kultura teatra*, 1921, no. 7–8, p. 65, I. Petrovskaia, "Kononovskii zal. Novyi teatr," in *Teatral'nyi Peterburg*, St. Petersburg: Rossiiskii Institut Istorii Isskustv, 1994, pp. 216–21.

5 Tatiana Shchepkina-Kupernik, *Dni moei zhizni*, Moscow: Federatsiia, 1928, pp. 285–6.

6 Iuri Beliaev, *L.B. Iavorskaia*, Nahi Artistki, vypuskz, 1900, p. 4.

7 See *Ezhegodnik imperatorskikh teatrov*, 1892–3, p. 369; Iuri Iur'ev, *Zapiski*, t. 2, Leningrad-Moscow: Iskusstvo, 1945, p. 352; Shchepkina-Kupernik, *Dni moei zhizni*, p. 275. A notice in the *Ezhegodnik* indicates that Iavorskaia's examination piece was quite successful.

8 *L.B. Iavorskaia: biograficheskiie svedeniia*, author's collection. This collection of interviews and newspaper clippings was apparently part of Iavorskaia's promotional package. Of particular interest is the refashioning of the Aleksandrinskii's rejection. Claiming that she abandoned St. Petersburg for Paris because studying theatre abroad was essential to an authentic artist, she transformed necessity into choice.

9 Shchepkina, "Butova i Iavorskaia", p. 8; see also Iur'ev, *Zapiski*, p. 463, and Aleksandr Kugel', "Iz moikh vospominanii", *Zhizn' iskusstva*, 1924, no. 33, pp. 8–9.

10 Shchepkina-Kupernik, "Butova i Iavorskaia", p. 9. In *Dni moei zhizni*, Shchepkina called the Korsh a "theatre for digestion" because it specialized in mindless nonsense (p. 274). Early reviews of Iavorskaia's work suggest that the Korsh Theatre had declined since its founding in 1882. For example, in a review of *Trudovoi khlebe* (*Artist* no. 10, pp. 23–5), the critic complains of careless production values, unprepared actors, and lack of unity: "All the actors play any way they want to and often their knowledge of the text is shaky." (p. 23) In a review of *Teshcha* (*Artist*, no. 31, 1893, p. 163), another critic complains about the blandness of Korsh's repertoire and the fact that he does not support new playwrights.

11 A. Ia. Al'tshuller, "Tip vo vsiakom sluchae liubopytnyi", in *Chekhoviana*, Moscow: Nauka, 1990, pp. 142–3, 146. In contrast to critics who charged that Iavorskaia was lazy and undisciplined, Shchepkina claimed that Lidia Boris-ovna rehearsed constantly, read huge quantities of plays, and spent all of her free time at the theatre. Iavorskaia herself wrote: "Sometimes I'm bored, but art compels me to forget and forgive. I forget myself in the theatre. I study . . . I try not to miss anything interesting." According to Shchepkina, a "light flirtation" developed between Chekhov and Iavorskaia. Claiming that she was a "timid debutante" who needed a famous playwright to stimulate public interest, she asked him for a play for her first benefit at the Korsh. He turned her down, and instead she turned to Sofia Kovalevskaia, who gave her the heretofore unproduced *A Struggle for Happiness* (*Bor'ba za schast'e*), with which Iavorskaia had unexpected critical success. Interestingly, Chekhov later gave her *The Seagull* (*Chaika*), which she read with a group of friends at her salon. Unimpressed by the play and indifferent to the role of Nina, she took no steps to produce it.

12 Ibid., p. 146. He is alluding to her French schooling.

13 Shchepkina, *Dni moei zhizni*, pp. 276–82. Although at the pinnacle of her popularity in Moscow, her colleagues, especially the actresses, disliked her so intensely and mocked her so mercilessly that working at the Korsh became unbearable. Shchepkina also suggests that Iavorskaia was desperate to prove herself in the Aleksandrinskii Theatre's home town. Therefore the temptation to move to St. Petersburg and shove her stardom in faces of those who had rejected her was too great. Her move to St. Petersburg, where critics responded to her with undisguised hostility, proved to be fatal. One can only wonder if her legacy might have been different had she remained in Moscow.

14 A.R. Kugel', "Teatr Lit. Art. Kruzhka", *Teatr i iskusstvo*, 1898, no. 19, pp. 353–4.

15 Evtikhi Karpov, "A.S. Suvorin i osnovanie teatra literaturno-articheskogo kruzhka", *Istoricheskii vestnik*, 1914, no. 8, pp. 452–3, 461.

16 Evtikhi Karpov, "A.S. Suvorin i osnovanie teatra literaturno-articheskogo kruzhka", *Istoricheskii vestnik*, 1914, no. 9, pp. 900–1. According to Suvorin, the play was without any significant content: "Some fool sits on a foolish island. Some other fools arrive at this island on a foolish boat, the devil knows why. Then, later, the fools [on the boat] leave and the fool [on the island] stays. That's it."

17 Kugel', "Teatr Lit. Art. Kruzhka", p. 353.

18 Efros, "L.B. Iavorskaia", p. 64; Negorev, "Zametki", p. 495.

19 Kugel', "Vospominanii", no. 33, p. 8.

20 Although male members of the aristocracy often "kept" starring actresses, marriage was a very different matter. Iavorskaia and Bariatinski, however, formed a working partnership; together, they founded the ill-starred *Northern Courier* (*Severnyi kur'er*), and Iavorskaia regularly produced her husband's plays at the Novyi Theatre. They did, however, divorce in 1917. Iavorskaia's marriage may have been an attempt to compete with Savina, who was also married to a prince. Because she blamed Savina for keeping her out of the Aleksandrinskii, Iavorskaia was both envious of and angry at St. Petersburg's most influential starring actress.

21 "Suvorin i ego teatr", *Teatral'naia gazeta*, 1915, no. 39, pp. 8–9; Kugel', "Vospominanii", no. 33, p. 8. Kugel' says Suvorin was a *parvenu* and therefore vulnerable to Iavorskaia's charms: "Iavorskaia, whose uncle was a former minister, belonged to the *beau monde* and, as an actress, she imitated it brilliantly. . . . Suvorin, who quite justifiably saw no discernible talent or artistic truth in Iavorskaia, nonetheless quickly dismissed his own biases and voluntarily gave her free reign."

22 Kugel', "Vospominanii", no. 33, p. 9; A.S. Suvorin, *Dnevnik A.S. Suvorin*, Moscow-Petrograd: Izdatel'stvo L.D. Frenkel', 1923, pp. 169–266. Two of Suvorin's actresses were competing with him on literary grounds; Zinaida Kholmskaia (with Aleksandr Kugel') had just founded *Theatre and Art. The Smugglers* was the work of S.K. Litvin-Efron, a journalist for the conservative *Russian Herald* (*Russkii vestnik*), and Victor Krylov – the same Victor Krylov who wrote enormously popular potboilers for Savina.

23 Kugel' claims that he ignored the ban and wrote about it anyway, but if he did, the articles are not available. Negorev and Vladimir Linski, however, both published articles on the performance in *Teatr i iskusstvo*. Negorev confirms that the production provoked an unprecedented riot, while Linski focuses on the complete absence of artistic and literary merit in the play. See, N. Negorev, "Khronika", *Teatr i iskusstvo*, 1900, no. 48, p. 867, and V. Linski, "Kontra-

bandisty", *Teatr i iskusstvo*, 1901, no. 3, pp. 54–6. The ban apparently did not extend to Suvorin's own decidedly antisemitic newspaper, *Novoe vremia*. On November 24, the production was mentioned briefly. In contrast to other sources, this article claims that the disturbance consisted of a little whistling, a few catcalls, and an occasional piece of rotten fruit tossed at the stage. The author further claims that the actors finished the performance. *Novoe vremia* is the only source that downplays the violence; given the newspaper's ideological bias and Suvorin's intimacy with ministers and state bureaucrats of all sorts, this treatment is hardly surprising. On November 25, *Novoe vremia* published another article entitled "Sowers of Antisemitism" (*Seiateli antisemitizma*) in which the Jews themselves are blamed for fanning the flames of antisemitism by staging demonstrations like the one at the opening of *The Smugglers*. See, "Teatr i muzyka", *Novoe vremia*, November 24, 1900, p. 4; S.N. Syroshiatninov-Sigma, "Seiateli antisemitizma", *Novoe vremia*, 25 November, 1900, p. 3.

24 B.A. Gorin-Goriainov, *Aktery: iz vospominanii*, Leningrad-Moscow: Iskusstvo, 1947, p. 80. The order in which the play was offered to Suvorin and the Imperial theatres is not certain. Gorin-Goriainov claims that it was offered to Suvorin first while Linski (cited above) suggests that the authors asked Suvorin only after the Imperial directorate turned it down. Because Krylov wrote regularly for the Imperial theatres and Linski's article was published immediately following the event, his account is more likely.

25 Ibid.; *Zhurnal zasedaniia direktsii literaturno-khudozhestvennogo obshchestva, December 6, 1900*, manuscript, Moscow: TsGALI. The *Zhurnal* is a particularly invaluable source of information about the theatre riot and its consequences. It includes the minutes of the Society's meeting, statements by the director, Evtikhi Karpov, and several of the actors, and a petition from the actors demanding that Iavorskaia be fired.

26 Attempting to persuade the public that *Sons of Israel* and *The Smugglers* were different plays, Suvorin placed the following notice in *The New Times*: "It has been reported in a certain newspaper [probably *The Northern Courier*] that the Society for Art and Literature is producing Krylov's and Efron's *Sons of Israel*. This is not true. The play being produced is Krylov's and Efron's *The Smugglers*, which deals with the morals of Russian Jews who live on the Western border and engage in smuggling. The Society accepted the play under this title, which reflects its contents exactly." "Teatr i musyka", *Novoe Vremia*, November 16, 1900, p. 4.

27 P.P. Gnedich, *Kniga zhizni: vospominaniia, 1855–1918*, Leningrad: Priboi, 1929, p. 257.

28 Gorin-Goriainov, *Aktery*, p. 85. It is ironic that when Suvorin first proposed to produce the play two years earlier, several of the Society's actors refused their roles, but Iavorskaia was not among them. A cynic might even suggest that her refusal to participate in the later production was motivated more by a desire to get Suvorin's goat than to exercise her right to express deeply felt political convictions.

29 Kugel', "Vospominanii", no. 33, p. 9.

30 Suvorin, who studiously avoided all emotionally charged confrontations, had already disappeared to Moscow. He lived to regret this action, which resulted in the death of his brother-in-law, A.P. Kolomnin. Kolomnin, who was left in charge of the theatre, was so distressed by the riot that he died suddenly the next day.

31 Gorin-Goriainov, *Aktery*, p. 90.

32 Ibid. and *Zhurnal Zasedaniia*.

33 See Aleksandr Kugel', "Iz moikh vospominanii", *Zhizn' iskusstva*, 1924, no. 38, p. 6. According to Kugel', the police themselves provoked the riot: "It would have been simpler to stop the performance and clear the auditorium [the actors attempted several times to continue it on police orders]. Instead, a dual performance took place; by dragging demonstrators out, the police themselves created much of the furor – that is, they did things that created the noise and scandal necessary for a demonstration." With respect to arrests, the number was between one and six hundred.

34 *Zhurnal zasedaniia*, p. 2.

35 Ibid., pp. 2, 6; Gorin-Goriainov, *Aktery*, p. 93. Gorin-Goriainov suggests that the actors who signed the petition had "black spots on their consciences." Most of them agreed in principle with Iavorskaia's action, but did not want to be implicated in a conspiracy theory. They had families and could not afford political protest, so they allowed her to be sacrificed. They comforted themselves with the thought that "because she was wealthy and could afford the luxury of open protest, Iavorskaia would survive somehow."

36 It is ironic that Iavorskaia was fired for breach of contract since, like many starring performers, she worked on the basis of a verbal rather than a written contract. The Society's directorate deftly maneuvered around that minor obstacle by censuring her for doing what surely *would* have been a breach of contract if a contract had ever been written, signed, and sealed. The particulars of her "hearing" are in the *Zhurnal zasedaniia* and Suvorin's *Diary*. The whole story of the *The Smuggler*'s scandal will probably never be clear, and Kugel' suggests in his memoirs that Russian antisemitism was a powder keg waiting for a match: Iavorskaia happened to be the unlucky one who threw it. There is, however, evidence to suggest that, exhausted by Iavorskaia's demands and journalistic escapades, Suvorin wanted a pretext to fire her and close down *The Northern Courier*. By scapegoating her in this affair, he achieved both. Interestingly, shortly after Iavorskaia left, a fire broke out at the Society for Art and Literature. In the *Diary*, Suvorin implies that she set it in retaliation for her dismissal, but his charge was never confirmed (266).

37 Negorev, "Zametki", p. 495.

38 Shchpekina-Kupernik, "Butova i Iavorskaia", pp. 16–17.

39 Ibid., p. 17. Stanislavski was particularly hostile to Iavorskaia. For his opinion of her, see Konstantin Stanislavski, "Pis'ma k zhene", in *O Stanislavskom*, Moscow: VTO, 1948, p. 73.

40 P. Iartsev, "Litso teatra", *Teatr i iskusstvo*, 1904, no. 16, p. 323 and Petrovskaia, "Kononovski zal. Novyi teatr," pp. 216–21. Iartsev offers a surprisingly positive description of the Novyi Theatre. The theatre was established, he wrote, "by an actress who achieved tremendous popularity among people who have a poorly developed taste for art, but enjoy a certain influence on the street." Nonetheless, he argued, the theatre would have perished long ago if not for its marvelous repertoire: "Even though the acting company is poor, you can still see plays by Ibsen, Maeterlinck, and D'Annuncio there. No one knows how the theatre was conceived or planned, but its repertoire is fresh and substantial." Critics often praised the attention to detail shown by directors and designers; extant reviews of Novyi productions suggest that most were in the Meiningen style. See "*Vlast' t'my*", *Teatr i iskusstvo*, 1902, no. 39, p. 699; "*Antonii i Kleopatra*", *Teatr i iskusstvo*, 1903, no. 89, p. 707. If Iavorskaia was not personally responsible for designing and directing Novyi productions, surely she deserves credit for seeking out and hiring creative directors and designers.

41 "Uchastie peterburgskikh teatrov v obshchei politicheskoi zabastokov", *Teatral'naia rossiia*, 1905, no. 44–5, p. 1269. On January 9, 1905, tsarist troops fired into a group of unarmed workers who were marching peacefully on the Winter Palace in St. Petersburg. This day, known as Bloody Sunday, marks the beginning of the 1905 revolution. In response to the massacre, strikes broke out all over Russia. Many theatres wanted to demonstrate their solidarity with striking workers by canceling performances. In St. Petersburg, representatives from all the theatres met to discuss the advisability of joining the strike. The Imperial theatres declined to participate, but many others, including Iavorskaia's and Kommissarzhevskaia's, did cancel performances.

42 N.F. Skarskaia and P.P. Gaideburov, *Na stsene i v zhizni*, Moscow: Iskusstvo, 1959, p. 272.

43 Shchepkina-Kupernik, "Butova i Iavorskaia", p. 2 and Efros, "L.B. Iavorskaia", p. 63.

44 See, for example, the review of "*Chad zhizni*", *Artist*, 1893, no. 31, p. 168.

45 "*Trudovoi khlebe*", *Artist*, 1893, no. 10, p. 24. The critic went on to note that everything about her – her beautiful face, expressive eyes, and the pleasant timber of her voice – predicts a successful career.

46 "*Twelfth Night* i *Teshcha*", *Artist*, 1893, no. 31, pp. 162–3.

47 "*Dama S Kameliiani*", *Artist*, 1894, no. 34, pp. 244–6. The reviewer notes that scenes involving repentance were difficult for Iavorskaia and that she was a bit too healthy in the final act.

48 "*Madame Sans-Gêne*", *Artist*, 1894, no. 42, p. 237. The author also concluded that heroic roles requiring strength and "temperament" were not really within Iavorskaia's range. He advised her to stick to the ingenues of light French comedy.

49 "Ekzamenatsionnye spektakli shkoly peterburgskikh imperatorskikh teatrov", *Artist*, 1893, no. 28, p. 172. For references to her artistic potential, see *Chekhoviana*, p. 147. E.B. Krasnianski, *Vstrechi v puti: stranitsy vospominanii*, Moscow: VTO, 1967, p. 24.

50 By her third year with the Korsh, critics were encouraging her to settle on a type. In a review of Rostand's *The Romantics*, one critic observed that although she had played everything from grand coquettes to purely lyrical roles to straight dramatic, she should stick to "delicate, but not particularly deep French comedy." "*Romantiki*", *Artist*, 1895, no. 45, p. 210.

51 Krasnianski, *Vstrechi*, p. 24. For example, playing with your back to the audience was still considered a mistaken piece of naturalism, but Iavorskaia, who was famous for her "boldness" on stage, didn't allow obsolete conventions to stop her. Although this innovation pleased the public, according to Krasnianski she did it not to advance the cause of realistic acting, but because she had a very attractive back.

52 "*Uriel Akost*", *Artist*, 1895, no. 46, p. 151.

53 There are many reviews and anecdotes about Iavorskaia's eccentricities and onstage antics. Among the most entertaining are Mariia Velizarii, *Put' provintsial'noi aktrisy*, Leningrad: Iskusstvo, 1938, pp. 216–28; A. Ia. Al'tshuller (ed.), *Vera Fedorovna Komissarzhevskaia: pis'ma aktrisy, vospominaniia o nei, materialy*, Leningrad-Moscow: Iskusstvo, 1964, p. 155; M.S. Narokov, *Biografiia moego pokoleniia: teatral'nye memuary*, Moscow: VTO, 1956; and Shchepkina's and Skarskaia's memoirs. Velizarii's anecdotes about Iavorskaia's improvisations are particularly amusing: "Apparently she didn't care about playwrights' texts because during performances, she tried to extend her most effective scenes by improvisation. It would finally reach the height

of absurdity when Iavorskaia herself lost thread of a scene and muddled all of us who were on stage with her." St. Petersburg critics slammed Iavorskaia even when she was not in a Novyi production. One wrote: "Madame Iavorskaia did not perform [in *Na dvore vo fligel*] because there was no suitable role for her in the play. I regard this as one of the play's merits." See *"Na dvore vo fligel"*, *Teatr i iskusstvo*, 1902, no. 52, p. 1008.

54 Shchepkina acknowledged the problems at the Novyi, but categorically denied that Iavorskaia drank heavily. She claimed that if Iavorskaia's performances suffered during this period, it was because her every waking hour was consumed by the exigencies of theatre management.

55 Narokov, *Biografiia*, p. 119.

56 London playbills and undated articles and reviews from the London *Times* are located in Iavorskaia's archive at TsGALI.

57 Russia enjoyed both a Golden Age (the age of Pushkin) and a Silver Age (the age of modernism). Strictly speaking, the period in question was the Silver Age of literature and art. Because developments in theatre were not particularly significant during the Golden Age, it is legitimate to suggest that, the Silver Age of art and literature was a "golden age" for Russian drama and theatrical production.

58 Many of these issues were discussed at length in chapters one and two. For points of view expressed by critics see Aleksandr Kugel', "Zhenskoe dvizhenie", *Teatr i iskusstvo*, 1897, no. 15, pp. 298–9; O. Dymov, "Ona na stsene", *Teatr i iskusstvo*, 1905, no. 17, pp. 276–8; "Bez predvaritel'noi tsenzury", *Teatr i iskusstvo*, 1905, no. 32, n.p. For actresses' points of view, see "Doklad Iu. V. Tarlovskoi-Rastorguevoi", in *Trudy 1-ogo vserossiiskogo s'ezda stsenicheskikh deiatlei*, St. Petersburg: n.p., 1898, pp. 32–3; I.N. Grinevskaia, "Zhenshchina na stsene", *Biblioteka teatra i iskusstva*, 1909, no. 6, pp. 3–24; and A.N. Kremlev, "O zadachakh stsenicheskoi deiatel'nosti zhenshchiny", in *Trudy 1-ogo vserossiiskogo zhenskogo s'ezda*, St. Petersburg: n.p., 1909, pp. 189–94.

59 See, for example, E. Shabel'skaia, "Dramaticheskiia shkoly i dramaticheskaia shkola", *Teatr i iskusstvo*, 1897, no. 45, pp. 807–9; E. Shabel'skaia, "Vragi russkogo teatra", *Teatr i iskusstvo*, 1898, no. 2, pp. 35–8; Sergei Sutugin, "Talant i tekhnika", *Teatr i iskusstvo*, 1904, no. 19, pp. 376–7. In 1898, Iuri Ozarovski published twelve installments devoted to the question of theatre education. Interested readers should see *Teatr i iskusstvo*, 1898, nos. 34, 35, 36, 37, 38, 40, 43, 45, 47, 50, 51, and 52.

60 Shchepkina-Kupernik, "Butova i Iavorskaia", p. 20, and for an example of critical response to Iavorskaia's costume excesses, see *"Lady from the Sea"*, *Teatr i Iskusstvo*, 1903, no. 5, pp. 114–15. Iavorskaia was passionate about costumes and her productions were pretexts for displaying the latest Parisian fashions. An exemplary model of the actress as "clothes horse," Iavorskaia came under particularly heavy criticism for her emphasis on fashionable dress.

61 See, for example Aleksandr Kugel', "Dobrye nravy i nravstvennost'", *Teatr i iskusstvo*, 1899, no. 4, pp. 73–4; a three-part series by V. Linski, "Stsena i besputstvo", *Teatr i iskusstvo*, 1900, no. 38, pp. 660–1, no. 40, pp. 701–3, no. 48, pp. 862–4; M. Zel'dovich, "Zhenskaia dobrodetel' i stsena", *Teatr i iskusstvo*, 1904, no. 34, pp. 623–5; G. Arseni, "Chisten'kaia aktrisa", *Teatr i iskusstvo*, 1904, no. 45, pp. 799–800; "S akterskogo rynka", *Teatr i iskusstvo*, 1904, no. 9, p. 188; "O moral'nom vlianii teatra", *Teatr i iskusstvo*, 1905, no. 26, pp. 419–20; "Zhenshchina na stsene", *Teatral'naia rossiia*, 1905, no. 17, pp. 289–91; E. Kliuchareva, "Ob aktrisakh", *Teatral'naia rossiia*, 1905, no. 19,

pp. 325–7. Many of the articles target actresses because in theatre, as in society, women were held responsible for the moral development and stature of the community. Actresses themselves used the notion of theatre as a tool of moral instruction and social progress as a justification for equal rights. A.N. Kremlev ("O zadachakh stenicheskoi deiatel'nosti zhenshchiny", 192) suggests that women are by nature better suited than men to clean up the theatre and make it a genuine instrument of cultural enlightenment. Tarlovskaia-Rastorgueva argues that women will transform theatre into a "temple of art" (*khram iskusstva*) because only women love the theatre selflessly and wholeheartedly (33).

62 Kugel', "Dobrye nravy i nravstvennost'", p. 73.
63 See especially Linski's "Stsena i besputstvo" (cited above). A similar three-part series of articles appeared in 1904. See S. Svetlov, "Aktery i zhizn'", *Teatr i iskusstvo*, 1904, no. 26, pp. 489–90, no. 29, pp. 536–7, no. 30, pp. 552–3.
64 I take "bougeois" to mean "middle class" and refer interested readers to Edith W. Clowes, Samuel D. Kassow, and James L. West (eds), *Between Tsar and People: Educated Society and the Quest for Public Identity in Late Imperial Russia*, Princeton: Princeton University Press, 1991. I am not arguing that Russia actually had a large, influential middle class (although that small percentage of the population would have been most likely to support and be involved in theatre); more important is the fact many Russians *aspired* to a Western European bourgeois lifestyle and theatre was implicated in, and often used the rhetoric of, what I have termed "bourgeoisification." See also Laura Engelstein, *Sex and the Search for Modernity in Fin-de-Siècle Russia*, Ithaca, NY: Cornell University Press, 1992, for a discussion of Russian response to the importation of bourgeois Western European sexual ideology.
65 Shchepkina-Kupernik, "Butova i Iavorskaia", pp. 13–14.
66 Ibid., p. 7. Iavorskaia had other "unfeminine" traits: "One of the most original ... was her complete fearlessness, the complete absence of any timidity or fearfulness.... In those moments when my heart froze and my teeth chattered ... she still had her vacant look and was genuinely undisturbed and happy" (20). "*Rusalka*" is usually translated as "mermaid," but the English term does not do justice to the Russian concept. A *rusalka* is one of the undead. Perhaps the most famous and fearful figures of Russian folklore, *rusalki* are women who drown themselves after getting pregnant outside of wedlock. They are very beautiful, often have extremely large breasts, and exude sexuality. Their considerable physical charms are employed to lure men to their deaths – usually by drowning. For a brief, very informative essay on *rusalki*, see Natalie K. Moyle, "Mermaids (*Rusalki*) and Russian Beliefs About Women", in Anna Lisa Crone and Catherine V. Chvany (eds), *New Studies in Russian Language and Literature*, Columbus, OH: Slavica Publishers, 1986, pp. 221–38.
67 Shchepkina-Kupernik, "Butova i Iavorskaia", p. 10.
68 Ibid., p. 20. According to Shchepkina, Iavorskaia was amoral rather than immoral.
69 Kugel', "Zhenskoe dvizhenie", pp. 298–9.
70 "*Zhenshchina nauki*" is literally "woman of science," but "female scholar" seemed a bit less awkward. See V. Linski, "Stsena i besputstvo", part 2, p. 702.
71 V. Linski, "Novaia zhenshchina", *Teatr i iskusstvo*, 1903, no. 7, pp. 154–6, no. 8, pp. 176–8, no. 9, pp. 197–8. The quotation is found in part 2, p. 176. Of course, not all critics and publications condemned the New Woman. During the 1880s and 1890s, several respectable, progressive literary journals, including *The European Herald* (*Vestnik evropy*) and *The Northern Herald*

(*Severnyi vestnik*), (the latter was published, I might add, by a woman, Liubov Gurevich, who did much to introduce Russians to Ibsen), published many positive articles on the New Woman and the Woman Question. For some reason, theatre journals seemed to be particularly reactionary with respect to these issues.

72 Efros, "L.B. Iavorskaia", p. 64.

73 Kugel', "Vospominanii", no. 33, p. 8. He compares her to the egomaniacal Mariia Savina, who could not carry on a conversation because she suffered from a complete inability to listen to what others had to say. In contrast, Iavorskaia was quite an accomplished listener – at least in retrospect.

74 For examples of Iavorskaia's erasure, see S.S. Danilov, "Revoliutsiia 1905–1907 godov i russkii teatr", *Teatr*, 1955, no. 7, pp. 116–26; *Istoriia russkogo dramaticheskogo teatra*, t. 7, Moscow: Iskusstvo, 1987. Even more revealing is a letter (preserved at TsGALI) addressed to a certain Z. Dal'tsev. The letter, which dates from 1950, is from an author to his editor. Apparently he was writing a history of progressive pre-Revolutionary theatres, made the mistake including Iavorskaia and the Novyi Theatre in his survey, and found it expedient to recant. Attempting to mollify his editor, he wrote: "When seeking their predecessors in pre-revolutionary theatre, Soviet theatre artists can ignore Iavorskaia's Novyi Theatre." Iavorskaia and the Novyi Theatre have finally been rehabilitated by I. Petrovskaia in the recently published *Teatral' nyi Peterburg* (see note 4).

8 LITTLE GIRL LOST

1 Aleksandr Kugel', "V.F. Komissarzhevskaia", in *Teatral'nye portrety*, Moscow: Iskusstvo, 1967, p. 162. See also Spencer Golub, *The Recurrence of Fate: Theatre and Memory in Twentieth-Century Russia*, Iowa City: University of Iowa Press, 1994, pp. 38–69. Although Golub is occasionally careless with the facts of Kommissarzhevskaia's career and his discussion of her as a *femme fragile* is reductive, his general analysis of actresses and female iconicity during the Silver Age is useful.

2 N.F. Skarskaia and P.P. Gaideburov, *Na stsene i v zhizni*, Moscow: Iskusstvo, 1959, p. 105. Nadezhda Skarskaia was one of Kommissarzhevskaia's sisters.

3 Vera and Nadezhda were actresses. Olga, a sculptor, settled in Paris. The only boy, Grisha, died as a child. Fedor Petrovich had at least two more sons by his second wife. The most famous, Fedor Fedorovich (Theodore) Kommissarzhevski, worked with Vera at the Dramaticheskii Theatre. Following the Revolution, he settled in London.

4 E.T. Karpov, *Vera Fedorovna Komissarzhevskaia: biograficheskii ocherk*, n.p., 1916, p. 174; Skarskaia, *Na stsene*, p. 133.

5 Liubov Gurevich, "Na putiakh obnovleniia teatra", in *Pamiati Very Fedorovny Kommissarzhevskoi*, St. Petersburg: Izdanie Peredvizhnogo teatra P.P. Gaideburova i N.F. Skarskoi, 1911, p. 174.

6 Ibid., p. 174; Karpov, "Komissarzhevskaia", pp. 2–3.

7 Skarskaia, *Na stsene*, p. 140. The most bitter irony was that Mariia Shul'gina took the blame for the divorce on herself. By law, Kommissarzhevski could not remarry in the church unless his first wife would confess to infidelity. Although *he* was the guilty party, Shul'gina agreed to accuse herself so that he could remarry.

8 Karpov, *Komissarzhevskaia*, p. 5.

9 Skarskaia, *Na stsene*, pp. 144–6; Karpov, "Komissarzhevskaia", p. 6. All of Kommissarzhevskaia's biographers mention this marriage, but because Soviet

historians rarely discuss the salacious aspects of their subject's private life, most pass it over with little comment other than the marriage failed and Kommissarzhevskaia was traumatized by it. Skarskaia is more frank. Apparently Murav'ev was an abusive womanizer. He initiated an adulterous liaison with Skarskaia herself, who became pregnant. Skarskaia lived with Murav'ev until he tried to kill her and their child. She escaped with the help of local villagers.

10 A. Al'tshuller, "Primer vdokhnovennogo sluzheniia narodu", *Zvezda*, 1960, no. 2, p. 173.

11 Gurevich, "Na putiakh", p. 172.

12 Osip Dymov, "V.F. Kommissarzhevskaia (k godovshchine so dnia smerti)", *Obozrenie teatrov*, 1911, no. 1316, p. 12.

13 Iuri Beliaev, *V.F. Kommissarzhevskaia*, Nashi Artistki, vypusk 1, 1900, p. 5. Beliaev wrote: "She came to us from the remote provinces like a poor, wandering princess, without friends, without publicity, a 'bride without a dowry' (*bespridannitsa*) in the fullest sense of the word."

14 *Vera Fedorovna Komissarzhevskaia: pis'ma aktrisy, vospominaniia o nei, materialy*, A.Ia. Al'tshuller (ed.), Leningrad-Moscow: Iskusstvo, 1964, pp. 32–4. Although the provincial theatre environment was fundamentally anti-aesthetic, Kommissarzhevskaia did not single out provincial theatre and actors; she was simply repulsed by anti-aestheticism wherever she found it. One of her most famous letters (to N.P. Roshchin-Insarov) suggests how offensive typical provincial theatre must have been for her. In the letter, she berates Roshchin-Insarov for his vulgarity and inability to cultivate and maintain a sense of the beautiful. Complaining that he knows nothing of the spiritual life, she warns that he will die as an artist without it.

15 See, for example Liubov Gurevich, "Pamiati V.F. Kommissarzhevskoi", *Rech'*, 1910, no. 49; Gurevich, "Na putiakh", p. 177; and Al'tshuller, "Primer vdokhnovennogo sluzheniia narodu", p. 175. If this is true, it is ironic that she subsequently rejected an invitation to join the Moscow Art Theatre because she felt Stanislavski's style and method were incompatible with her own.

16 "Zametki teatrala: starorusskii teatr", *Teatral*, 1895, no. 33, p. 128.

17 K.V. Bravich, "Pervye shagi V.F. Kommissarzhevskoi", *Rampa*, 1908, no. 5, p. 78. She was invited to join for the 1894–5 season. Unsure of her own abilities, she turned the offer down and went voluntarily to the provinces for more experience.

18 "Sovremennoe obozrenie", *Teatral*, 1896, no. 66, pp. 26–7. Kommissarzhevskaia's debut was a "real theatical event." The house was sold out. The auditorium was filled not only with the usual first nighters, but with performers from all of the St. Petersburg theatres. The critic praises Kommissarzhevskaia for her "artistic simplicity" and for not seeming to "act." He also tries to discourage talk about "displacement." "People should not," he argued, "be talking about competition between the young actress and other St. Petersburg favorites, but about the addition of an important new force to our theatre, a force that will enliven and freshen the St. Petersburg stage."

19 Evtikhi Karpov, "Istoriia pervogo predstavleniia *Chaika* na stsene Aleksandrinskogo teatra 17 oktiabria 1896", *Rampa i zhizn'*, 1909, no. 3, pp. 252–4.

20 Unpublished letters of Mariia Savina and Aleksei Suvorin, TsGALI.

21 Karpov, "Istoriia", p. 254.

22 A.P. Chekhov, *Polnoe sobranie sochinenii i pisem*, t. 6, Moscow: Nauka, 1978,

pp. 519–23 and 568–9. Chekhov, who attended several rehearsals, was pleased with Kommissarzhevskaia's Nina. Although the first production was such a failure that no one in the cast received overwhelmingly positive responses, she was encouraged enough to produce the play on her own and pursue Chekhov independently.

23 Karpov, "Istoriia", p. 254. If it had been a typical Krylov comedy, the actors could have pulled it off with nine rehearsals. But they did not have the skills to deal with an unfamiliar genre or the time to develop them. Karpov's account contradicts critics who charged that Aleksandrinskii actors were lazy and careless with *The Seagull* because they did not like Chekhov's dramaturgy. See, for example "Peterburgskie pis'ma", *Teatral*, 1896, no. 95, pp. 75–82. This critic says that in twenty years of attending the Aleksandrinskii he has never witnessed such a dismal failure. He holds the audience responsible for their inability to respond appropriately to challenging material and the actors for their carelessness and inability to perform as an ensemble. He also notes that the play was badly cast: in his opinion, Savina should have played Arkadina.

24 Beliaev, *Kommissarzhevskaia*, p. 9. Kommissarzhevskaia was at her best in "small elegaic prose poems like *The Seagull*."

25 I.I. Zabrezhnev, *V.F. Kommissarzhevskaia: vpechatleniia*, St. Petersburg, n.p., 1898, p. 15.

26 Beliaev, *Kommissarzhevskaia*, p. 10; Ia. A. Aleksandrov, *Chaika russkoi stseny: teatral'no – literaturnye ocherki*, Kazan: n.p., 1914, p. 12. According to Beliaev, Ostrovski's Larisa is sharp, arrogant, and unsympathetic. In Kommissarzhevskaia's interpretation, this "turbulent gypsy" becomes a "white seagull who doesn't reach the shore and dies on the cliffs." The gypsy sensibility is absent and the image is drawn in "soft, sincere colors." Aleksandrov observed how strange it was to see Kommissarzhevskaia, "a new, sensitive, multi-dimensional actress in the primitive plays of Ostrovski."

27 Beliaev, *Kommissarzhevskaia*, p. 14.

28 V.V. Rozanov, "Pamiati V.F. Kommissarzhevskoi", in *Sredi khudozhnikov*, St. Petersburg: n.p., 1914, p. 323.

29 Adrianov, "Pamiati Kommissarzhevskoi", p. 430.

30 Zabrezhnev, "V.F. Kommissarzhevskaia", pp. 4–5.

31 Rozanov, "Pamiati", pp. 322–7; Kommissarzhevskaia, *Pis'ma aktrisky*, p. 153; Chekhov, *Polnoe sobranoe sochinenii*, t. 8, p. 8. Kommissarzhevskaia suffered from what Chekhov calls "women's illnesses." Although his description suggests what is now called severe premenstrual syndrome, the precise nature of her illness is not clear. Her own letters indicate that she took arsenic injections, which were sometimes used to treat venereal disease.

32 Beliaev, *Kommissarzhevskaia*, pp. 6, 12; Rozanov, "Pamiati", p. 326; Kugel', "V.F. Komissarzhevskaia", p. 162. According to Beliaev, no one else so accurately represented "the diseased soul of our difficult times." He continued: "She has very little stage experience – and, thank God because [her lack of experience] keeps her original and allows her to spread her wings." Her natural charm and creativity "keep her on the summit where talent is not touched by the disease of self-deception and does not pander to the debased tastes of the crowd." Rozanov wrote that Kommissarzhevskaia's tragic soul resonated with Russia's. She appealed to a pervasive sense of personal inadequacy among Russians, many of whom sensed what was possible and necessary, but were unable to accomplish it. Kugel' wrote that Kommissarzhevskaia's expressions of intense physical and spiritual pain had tremendous appeal for average spectators.

33 Kugel', "V.F. Komissarzhevskaia", p. 166.

34 Fedor Steppun, "V.F. Komissarzhevskaia i M.N. Ermolova", *Russkaia mysl'*, 1913, no. 34, pp. 27–8. Steppun's example is from *The Dowerless Bride*. The protagonist, Larisa, suffers because she is caught between two men; she's married to one and loves the other. In Komissarzhevskaia's interpretation, Larisa's mystical inner conflict takes precedence over the mundane reality of a triangular romance. Her melancholy is universal angst, a perpetual feature of the human condition. What should be a concrete realistic play becomes the sort of dual dialogue proposed by Maeterlinck. See also Chapter 7 in Golub's *The Recurrence of Fate* for an illuminating discussion of the Russian "love of suffering." (p. 175) Komissarzhevskaia's stage image is consistent with Russian "Hamletism" described by Golub.

35 Dymov, "V.F. Komissarzhevskaia", p. 12.

36 Zabrezhnev, "V.F. Komissarzhevskaia", pp. 14–15; Beliaev, *Komissarzhevskaia*, p. 24; Aleksandrov, *Chaika russkoi stseny*, p. 10. Beliaev echoes Zabrezhnev: Komissarzhevskaia was "small, with a delicate, agile figure. Her movements are sharp and impulsive.... Her face and smile are childlike. But her eyes contrast sharply with her general expression. One might say that Komissarzhevskaia is her eyes." Aleksandrov wrote: "Komissarzhevskaia was not considered beautiful, but I did not know a more beautiful woman's face ... her face was illuminated by inner beauty." See also D. Musina, "Tonal'noe iskusstvo Komissarzhevskoi", *Biblioteka teatra i iskusstva*, 1913, no. 2, pp. 2–5 and no. 3, pp. 3–6 for a discussion of Komissarzhevskaia's voice.

37 Boris Alpers, "Komissarzhevskaia", *Teatr*, 1964. no. 11, p. 51. Komissarzhevskaia's image also corresponds to the "cult of invalidism" described by Bram Dikstra in *Idols of Perversity*, New York, Oxford University Press, 1986, pp. 25–63.

38 Ibid.

39 "Chaika russkoi stseny", *Rampa i zhizn'*, 1911, no. 6, p. 3. Like Komissarzhavskaia, Nina Zarechnaia is a "trembling, homeless girl, a persecuted, exhausted wayfarer [who] embodies the tragic fate of the Russian actress."

40 N. Tiraspol'skaia, *Iz proshlogo russkoi stseny*, Moscow: VTO, 1950, p. 54.

41 Komissarzhevskaia, *Pis'ma aktrisy*, p. 124. The emphasis is Komissarzhevskaia's.

42 N.N. Khodotov, *Blizkoe – Dalekoe*, Leningrad-Moscow: Iskusstvo, 1962, pp. 126–7. Interestingly, this is exactly what Kugel' disliked about Komissarzhevskaia. From his perspective, spectators were not making the necessary distintion between art and sentimentality. See A.R. Kugel', "Zametki", *Teatr i iskusstvo*, 1914, no. 6, p. 137. See also Musina, "Tonal'noe iskusstvo Komissarzhevskoi", no. 3, p. 6. Although Komissarzhevskaia gave the impression of complete spontaneity and emotional authenticity, she was quite capable of suppressing the "flame of her soul" during rehearsals while she searched for the most effective rhythms and intonations. Unlike Strepetova, whose trance-like performances lacked self-restraint, Komissarzhevskaia paid close attention to the author's text and the other actors.

43 Beliaev, *Komissarzhevskaia*, p. 6; Steppun, "Komissarzhevskaia i Ermolova", p. 29. Some critics found Duse and Komissarzhevskaia monotonous. For others, this monotony was a factor of the dramaturgy and the times, not the actresses. Beliaev wrote: "To say that Komissarzhevskaia is monotonous is to recognize her as our best modern actress, one whose gifts reflect all the signs of our times." Steppun takes her monotony to the level of mysterium

by suggesting that the subject of the mystical life is by its very nature general rather than particular: it is the "Name of God." See also Susan Bassnett, "Eleonora Duse", in John Stokes, Michael R. Booth, and Susan Bassnett, *Bernhardt, Terry, Duse: The Actress in her Time*, Cambridge: Cambridge University Press, 1988, pp. 119–70. The parallels between Kommissarzhevskaia and Duse are striking and probably not coincidental. It is ironic that critics angrily berated Iavorskaia for imitating Bernhardt, but saw Kommissarzhevskaia's borrowings from Duse as evidence of her elevated spirituality and refined artistic palate.

44 Beliaev, *Kommissarzhevskaia*, pp. 9–10. Beliaev's remarks about Kommissarzhevskaia's alleged "feminism" predate her turn toward the Western repertoire, when the association might more logically be made.

45 Alpers, "Komissarzhevskaia", p. 45. Her image harmonized perfectly with the *kursistki* painted by Repin, Russia's most accomplished nineteenth-century realist painter.

46 Liubov Gurevich, "Pamiati V.F. Kommissarzhevskoi", n.p. Although "her most cherished beliefs and hopes were shattered," Kommissarzhevskaia's modern woman was still "indomitable;" although "helpess and broken," she was "not reconciled." All of her characters had a note of "grief and suppressed protest." She had little success with "strong, whole women," women whose souls "resound with one consistent, powerful motive."

47 Dymov, "Kommissarzhevskaia", pp. 12–13.

48 Nikolai Efros, "Kommissarzhevskaia", *Zhenskoe delo*, 1910, no. 7, pp. 4–5.

49 Alpers, "Komissarzhevskaia", p. 51.

50 A.R. Kugel', "Teatral'nye zametki", *Teatr i iskusstvo*, 1899, no. 10, p. 210 and "Teatral'nye zametki", *Teatr i iskusstvo*, 1898, no. 4, pp. 786–8.

51 Kugel', "Zametki", no. 10, p. 210.

52 P.D. Boborykin, "Tuda! tuda! (ispoved' artistki)", *Vestnik evropy*, 1913, no. 8, pp. 5–70; V. Botsianovski, "Nov i star", *Ezhegodnik imperatorskogo teatrov*, 1913, vypusk VII, pp. 103–10.

53 Boborykin, "Tuda! tuda!", pp. 16–17.

54 S. Durylin, "Zritel' Kommissarzhevskoi". Clippings file, Bakhrustin Museum. Reduced box office receipts at the Aleksandrinskii forced the directorate to acknowledge that it was not the theatre's conservative repertoire or core company of established favorites that drew spectators – it was Kommissarzhevskaia. See also, "Po povodu 'ukhoda' g-zhi Kommissarzhevskoi", *Teatr i iskusstvo*, 1902, no. 31, pp. 581–2. Rumors of Kommissarzhevskaia's imminent departure circulated for months, but the Aleksandrinskii directorate claimed she was obligated to finish her two-year contract. As it turned out, there was no contract. The author asks how it is possible that an actress who carries half the theatre's repertoire could be working without a contract!

55 Khodotov, *Blizkoe-dalekoe*, pp. 90, 285.

56 Ibid., p. 114. The "trivial business" refers to Savina's self-selected repertoire of plays by hacks like Krylov.

57 See, for example, Gurevich, "Pamiati", n.p.; Gurevich, 'Na putiakh', pp. 177–8; Bravich, "Pervye shagi V.F. Kommissarzhevskoi", p. 78; Karpov, *Kommissarzhevskaia*, p. 9; Al'tshuller, "Primer", p. 175

58 A.R. Kugel', "Teatral'nye zametki," 1899, no. 10, p. 210.

59 Khodotov, *Blizkoe-dalekoe*, p. 115. The final straw was the Aleksandrinskii's refusal to produce *Daughter of the People* (*Doch' naroda*), a new version of the Joan of Arc legend, for Kommissarzhevskaia. Instead, they insisted she do Schiller's *The Maid of Orleans*. Although Kommissarzhevskaia acknowl-

edged that *Daughter of the People* was not a landmark of great literature, it was, she argued, better suited to her talents and to her audience than Schiller's obsolete romanticism.

60 Gurevich, "Na putiakh", p. 175. According to Gurevich, She was also too "childish, unbalanced, disturbed, and trusting" ("typically female" characteristics) to realize her convictions in practice. Indeed, those qualities that so charmed Khodotov – her impressionability, impatience with existing conditions, and tendency to act impulsively – were also, in Gurevich's eyes, her greatest liabilities.

61 Kommissarzhevskaia, *Pis'ma aktrisy*, p. 119.

62 Gurevich, 'Na putiakh", p. 180. See also Kommissarzhevskaia, *Pis'ma aktrisy*, pp. 31–178. Her letters provide ample evidence of her convictions about art, theatre, ideology and the artist's mission.

63 Gurevich, "Na putiakh", p. 179; Khodotov, *Blizkoe-dalekoe*, pp. 100–1; Kommissarzhevskaia, *Pis'ma aktrisy*, p. 116, 136; D. Talnikov, *Kommissarzhevskaia*, Moscow-Leningrad: Iskusstvo, 1939, p. 207. Kommissarzhevskaia's major conditions were: 1) at least five interesting roles per season; 2) a salary of not less than 10,000 roubles a year. Their subsequent correspondence suggests that Stanislavski considered these terms outrageous. According to Khodotov, Kommissarzhevskaia knew that her style of acting was not suited to the MAT. She was a starring actress who relied on inspiration, personality, and a strikingly rich voice. Although aware of her limited range, she had no apparent desire to study the methods being developed by Stanislavski.

64 Petr Iartsev, "Litso teatra", *Teatr i iskusstvo*, 1904, no. 16, p. 322. Iartsev later joined her directing staff.

65 Kugel', *Portrety*, p. 165.

66 Gurevich, "Na putiakh", p. 180.

67 Kommissarzhevskaia, *Pis'ma aktrisy*, pp. 129–30.

68 A.P. Chekhov, *Pis'ma*, t. 11, Moscow: Nauka, 1982, pp. 133–4.

69 A.R. Kugel', "Teatral'nye zametki", *Teatr i iskusstvo*, 1907, no. 46, pp. 764–6; A.R. Kugel', "Teatral'nye zametki", *Teatr i iskusstvo*, 1907, no. 48, pp. 804–06; A.R. Kugel', "Teatral'nye zametki", *Teatr i iskusstvo*, 1907, no. 49, pp. 827–9. In 1908, the editors of *Teatr i iskusstvo* published a three-part series entitled "Krizis teatra", (see nos. 17, 18, and 20). Much of the debate was in response to two books published during the period. One, *A Book About the New Theatre* (*Kniga o novom teatre*) included essays by advocates of symbolism; the other, *The Theatre Crisis* (*Krizis teatra*) included essays by the opposition. The "theatre crisis" was the conflict that arose between partisans of "*uslovnyi*" and "*bytovyi*" theatre. "*Bytovyi*" was domestic drama produced in a recognizably realistic setting. Best translated as "conventional" (in the sense of theatre that makes deliberate use of theatrical conventions), "*uslovnyi*" was associated primarily with symbolism, decadence, and other abstract movements.

70 Kommissarzhevskaia, *Pis'ma aktrisy*, p. 156. Her partners included K.V. Bravich, N. Arbatov, A.L. Volynski, N.A. Popov, and her half brother, F.F. Kommissarzhevski.

71 "Iz pisem, dnevnikov i zametok K.V. Bravicha", *Maski*, 1912, no. 2, p. 7; Bassnett, "Duse", p. 156. Kommissarzhevskaia did not articulate her reasons for avoiding wealthy patrons. Perhaps she was simply emulating Duse. Perhaps she wanted to be a New Woman offstage as well as on. Leonid Andreev suggested in 1909 that Kommissarzhevskaia's theatre would have

survived if she'd found a Savva Morozov, but perhaps she knew of the unhappy relationship at the MAT between Stanislavski, Nemirovich, and their wealthy patron. Her critics argued that she chose to be self-supporting because she was too impractical, impulsive, and naive to grasp the financial implications independent entrepreneurship.

72 Kommissarzhevskaia, *Pis'ma aktrisy*, pp. 120–54.
73 Gurevich, "Na putiakh", p. 180. Before the 1905 uprising, Kommissar-zhevskaia's sympathy for the "courageous people" who spoke out against injustice increased. Gurevich met her several times at the "Union of Unions" (*Soiuz soiuzov*), which was organized by various professions: "She was the only one there from the world of actors." She wore a simple black dress with a white collar and sat there "silent and pale" with an "extremely serious" expression and an "almost childish reverence for the proceedings." She even gave a speech at one meeting. Some post-Revolutionary accounts of Kommissarzhevskaia's activities are probably true, but given the Soviet tendency to revise historical data and romanticize cultural icons, it is difficult to separate fact from fiction. See, for example, N. Zelov, "V nei bylo mnogo solntsa", *Teatral'naia zhizn'*, 1964, no. 21, p. 21; A.M. Kollontai, "Molodezh' zvala ee solntsem", in *Vera Fedorovna Komissarzhevskaia: pis'ma aktrisy, vospominaniia o nei, materialy*, pp. 248–51; Al'tshuller, "Primer", pp. 173–7.
74 M. Iankovski, "Teatral'naia obshchestvennost' Peterburga v 1905–1907", in *Pervaia russkaia revolutsiia i teatr: stat'i i materialy*, Moscow: Iskusstvo, 1956, p. 148.
75 V. Maslikh, "Trudy i dni dramaticheskogo teatra", Author's collection.
76 Zigfrid, reviews of "No. 13" and "Master", *Sankt Peterburgskie vedomosti*, December 17, 1904, p. 3.
77 Kommissarzhevskaia, *Pis'ma aktrisy*, pp. 137, 139, 141–4, 146, 148–9. In order to discourage competition, Stanislavski and Nemirovich required authors to sign exclusive contracts with the MAT. With respect to Kommissarzhevskaia, this was a deliberate attempt to withhold scripts that the MAT intended to produce. Accusing her of "stealing our productions," Stanislavski justified the MAT's actions by claiming that their lucrative St. Petersburg tours must be protected from competition. See the editor's note on page 381.
78 M. Prygunov, "Teatr V.F. Komissarzhevskoi", in *Sbornik pamiati V.F. Komissarzhevskoi*, Gosudarstvennoe Izdatel'stvo Khudozhestvennoi Literatury, 1931, p. 156.
79 Maslikh, "Trudy i dni", pp. 153–7.
80 Gurevich, "Na putiakh", p. 182. Gurevich added: "Periods of social unrest and political revolution are not propitious for authentic artistry."
81 Ibid.
82 Al'tshuller, "Primer", pp. 176–7. Al'tshuller includes a list of the prohibited plays.
83 "Na iubilee V.F. Kommissarzhevskoi", Author's collection. In the words of her acting company, concluding a contract with Kommissarzhevskaia's theatre was like taking a "great monastic vow."
84 Aleksandrov, "Chaika russkoi stseny", p. 15. Because the benches did not accommodate enough paying spectators, they were replaced by conventional seating.
85 E. Ia. Dubnova, "Iz istorii dramaticheskogo teatra V.F. Komissarzhevskoi", in *Pamiatniki kul'tury, novye otkrytiia*, Leningrad: Nauka, 1981, p. 184.
86 V.E. Meierhold, *Perepiska, 1896–1939*, Moscow: Iskusstvo, 1976, p. 61. Already a controversial figure before Stanislavski brought him into the First

Studio, by 1906 Meierhold's name had come to represent everything new and dangerous in the theatre. Fairly or not, he was particularly associated in the minds of conservatives with decadence and symbolism. See also Bassnett, "Eleonora Duse", p. 128. The working relationship between Kommissarzhevskaia and Meierhold bore a striking resemblance to Duse's and D'Annunzio's. It is tempting to speculate that Kommissarzhevskaia consciously emulated Duse when she hired Meierhold.

87 Kugel', *Portrety*, p. 169.

88 "V.F. Kommissarzhevskaia o svoem teatre i ego novykh putiakh", *Obozrenie teatrov*, 1907, no. 69, p. 6. She claimed that individual characters were always less interesting to her than the universal image of an "eternal woman's soul." For some critics, her inability to create a wide range of closely observed, realistic characters was a liability. For others who saw in Kommissarzhevskaia the symbol of an epoch, it was her strength. From either point of view, her style was far too human for Meierhold's productions.

89 A useful article in English on Kommissarzhevskaia's relationship with the symbolist poets is Laurence Senelick, "Vera Kommissarzhevskaya: The Actress as Symbolist Eidolon", *Theatre Journal*, December 1980, pp. 475–87.

90 Meierhold, *Perepiska*, p. 64. Meierhold's letters to Kommissarzhevskaia and to his first wife, Olga, reveal his attitude. In one letter to Olga, he writes honestly about his objectives. He explains that the Dramaticheskii Theatre is a mess and that it cannot be saved. He intends to spend only one season there pursuing an agenda he and Diaghilev had worked out several years earlier, but which they had not had the resources to realize.

91 Ibid., p. 76. Arbatov was a conservative director of the Moscow Art Theatre persuasion.

92 V.P. Verigina, *Vospominaniia*, Leningrad: Iskusstvo, 1974, p. 84. Verigina was one of Meierhold's actresses. Her memoirs provide an intimate, if rather tendentious, view of the internal dynamics of the Ofitserskaia street theatre.

93 Aleksandr D'iakonov, "Dramaticheskii teatr V.F. Komissarzhevskoi, ch. II, teatr na Ofitserskoi", in *Pamiatniki kul'tury, novye otkrytiia*, Leningrad: Iskusstvo, 1981, p. 186; Verigina, *Vospominaniia*, p. 85. Bravich was the theatre's leading actor.

94 "Gazety o teatre V.F. Kommissarzhevskoi", *Obozrenie teatrov*, 1906, no. 3, pp. 5–8. "Never," the author wrote, "have the newspapers been so unanimously negative." One critic left feeling he had been in an "enemy camp." Another noted sarcastically that Meierhold and Kommissarzhevskaia did not go far enough with *Hedda*. They should have rejected domestic realism completely and dressed the characters in chitons. "Friends of new art," another declared, "do not want your passè decadent theatre." See also, Zigfrid, "Otkrytie teatra V.F. Kommissarzhevskoi", *Sankt Peterburgskie vedomosti*, November 12, 1906, p. 2. Zigfrid asks whether it was Hedda or Kommissarzhevskaia who had committed suicide during the production. Apparently, Meierhold was quite satisfied with *Hedda*. In a letter to Olga, he remarked that rehearsals were going well. He liked working with actors who could take direction and was especially impressed by Kommissarzhevskaia's attentiveness. In general, he felt that the company was very satisfied with him. See Meierhold, *Perepiska*, p. 77.

95 D'iakonov, "Dramaticheskii teatr V.F. Komissarzhevskoi", p. 190.

96 Ibid., p. 191; Verigina, *Vospominaniia*, p. 90. Verigina observed that "there was not a grain of Hedda Gabler in Kommissarzhevskaia." Nora Helmer and Hilda Wangel were within her natural range; Hedda was not.

97 Iuri Beliaev, *Mel'pomena*, St. Petersburg: A.S. Suvorin, n.d., p. 148.
98 "Paki i paki o teatre V.F. Kommissarzhevskoi", *Obozrenie teatrov*, 1906, no. 11, p. 6.
99 Gurevich, "Na putiakh", p. 185; D'iakonov, "Dramaticheskii teatr V.F. Komissarzhevskoi", p. 195.
100 "*Sestra Beatrisa* v teatre V.F. Kommissarzhevskoi", *Obozrenie teatrov*, 1906, no. 14, pp. 5–8. One remarked about *Sister Beatrice*: "I think the real beauty is still to come. It will appear one fine morning when, having awoken from her hypnotic stupor, Madame Kommissarzhevskaia will boot all of these hysterical directors and unemployed artists out the door – and announce *The Dowerless Bride*. Another observed: "The theatre has devoted itself to the death of realistic drama, but what is really happening is the death of Kommissarzhevskaia's talent. See also, Iuri Beliaev, "Apofeoz Kommissarzhevskoi", *Rampa i zhizn'*, 1910, no. 12, pp. 189–91; "*Nora*", *Novosti*, 19 September 1904, p. 4; Iu. Rybakova, *Komissarzhevskaia*, Leningrad: Iskusstvo, 1971, p. 108. Beliaev argued that Kommissarzhevskaia was at her best in adolescent roles and that her most productive years were those she spent at the Aleksandrinskii. The review of *A Doll's House* suggests that Kommissarzhevskaia's Nora, an "unspoiled, carefree half-woman, half-child," worked for the first two acts, but not the third, which required more maturity. Rybakova quotes Kugel', who contended that Kommissarzhevskaia's "dollies" (*kukolki*) were charming, but she should not have presumed to go beyond them.
101 Verigina, *Vospominaniia*, p. 91; D'iakonov, "Dramaticheskii teatr V.F. Kommissarzhevskoi", p. 194. Actresses constituted the overwhelming majority in the company, which was unusual given the scarcity of women's roles in the symbolist/decadent repertoire. D'iakonov does not suggest that *Sister Beatrice* is a "woman's play" conceptually. Rather because it requires a large female cast, the play offers unprecedented opportunities for the enthusiastic group of young actress who serve in the theatre.
102 D'iakonov, "Dramaticheskii teatr V.F. Komissarzhevskoi", p. 199.
103 Ibid.
104 Ibid., p. 200; Verigina, *Vospominaniia*, p. 92.
105 D'iakonov, "Dramaticheskii teatr V.F. Komissarzhevskoi", p. 201.
106 See Kommissarzhevskaia, *Pis'ma aktrisy*, pp. 168–74. Kommissarzhevskaia's identification with roles occasionally turned pathological. In letters to Valeri Briusov, written during the theatre's most troubled times in 1907 and 1908, she frequently signed herself "Beatrice."
107 "*Pelleas i Melisanda* v teatre V.F. Kommissarzhevskoi", *Obozrenie teatrov*, 1907, no. 16, p. 17.
108 I. Osipov, "V.F. Kommissarzhevskoi", *Obozrenie teatrov*, 1907, no. 217, p. 12.
109 "*Pelleas i Melisanda*", p. 16.
110 Ibid. The reference to Stanislavski's 40,000 roubles is not explained in the article. Perhaps that is the amount he spent on Meierhold's experiments at the First Studio before cancelling the whole venture.
111 "V.F. Kommissarzhevskaia o svoem teatre i ego novykh putiakh", p. 5. See also, Bassnett, "Eleonora Duse", pp. 128 and 165. The parallels between Kommissarzhevskaia/Meierhold and Duse/D'Annunzio, and later Duse/Craig, are striking. Like the Duse/D'Annunzio collaboration, the Kommissarzhevskaia/Meierhold collaboration was based on a misjudgment. And, in spite of her theoretical arguments for a new theatre, like Duse, Kommissarzhevskaia did not know how to go about creating one.

112 Gurevich, "Na putiakh", p. 181; Kommissarzhevskaia, *Pis'ma aktrisy*, pp. 31–178.

113 Kugel', "V.F. Komissarzhevskaia", *Portrety*, p. 170. "Each year, tired, tormented, overstrained, she 'sold herself' by touring with plays like *Dikarka*." Kommissarzhevskaia did this in order to pay the bills for a "business that may have been necessary to someone, but not to her."

114 A.R. Kugel', "Teatral'nye zametki", 1908, no. 37, p. 643.

115 Meierhold, *Perepiska*, p. 61. With respect to the commercial viability of his work, Meierhold's letter indicates that he had no intention of modifying his agenda in order to assure the theatre's continued survival.

116 Verigina, *Vospominaniia*, p. 122; Isabella Grinevskaia, "Chem on byl vreden", *Obozrenie teatrov*, 1907, no. 253, pp. 12–13; Zigfrid, "Na chto on byl nuzhen", *Obozrenie teatrov*, 1907, no. 25, pp. 13–14; Petr Pil'ski, "Stolby", *Teatr i iskusstvo*, 1907, no. 46, pp. 762–3; Petr Pil'ski, "Stolby", *Teatr i iskusstvo*, no. 47, pp. 778–80. *Teatr i iskusstvo* also published several untitled notices about the firing. See 1907, no. 51, p. 852, and 1907, no. 52, p. 875. Kommissarzhevskaia, who was developing a reputation for losing or firing directors without sufficient cause, dismissed him in the middle of the season. Pil'ski noted: "Whatever you think about Meierhold, one thing is clear; Kommissarzhevskaia treats her directors worse than we treat our servants, for even lackeys aren't fired without warning."

117 N. Shebuev, "Ne mogu molchat", *Obozrenie teatrov*, 1908, no. 535, p. 8; A.R. Kugel', "Dramaticheskii teatr", *Teatr i iskusstvo*, 1908, no. 40, pp. 687–8. Shebuev says she's healthier, younger, and more energetic. Is it a miracle cure of some sort? No, he cries, she's gotten rid of Meierhold! The review by Kugel' is of the Hamsun play.

118 I. Osipov, "K otezdu V.F. Kommissarzhevskoi", *Obozrenie teatrov*, 1908, no. 299, pp. 15–16. Many saw the trip as purely mercenary; her objective, critics claimed, was self-promotion, not art. Although this was probably true, the intolerance in Russia, especially within the intelligentsia, for self-promotion and commercial success was so great that critics would have castigated a self-styled aesthete like Kommissarzhevskaia for demonstrating commercial savvy or acknowledging profit as a motive. For a useful discussion of Russian views on Western commercialism, see Valery Semenovsky, "America as a Russian Idea", in Laurence Senelick (ed.), *Wandering Stars: Russian Emigré Theatre, 1905–1940*, Iowa City, IA: University of Iowa Press, 1992, pp. 196–204.

119 "O 'provale' V.F. Kommissarzhevskoi v Amerike", *Obozrenie teatrov*, 1908, no. 306, p. 5.

120 See, "New Russian Actress Comes to Play Here", *New York Times*, February 27, 1908; "Russia's Foremost Actress Won't Talk about the Situation at Home but is Most Communicative About Her Ideas on the Drama", *New York Times*, March 1, 1908; "Russian Actress Appears as Nora", *New York Times*, March 3, 1908; "Russian Actress in Play by Sudermann", *New York Times*, March 6, 1908; "Demand Royalty on a Play", *New York Times*, March 10, 1908; "Actors Locked out at Thalia Theatre", *New York Times*, March 22, 1908; "Stop Komisarzhevsky" (*sic*), *New York Times*, March 24, 1908; "Enthusiastic Adieu for Komisarchevsky" (*sic*), *New York Times*, April 20, 1908.

121 "Calls Us Artless", *New York Times*, April 4, 1908.

122 *A.N. Ostrovski: Literaturnoe nasledstvo, novye materialy i issledovaniia*, kn. 2, Moscow: Nauka, 1974, p. 335.

123 "Vesti o V.F. Kommissarzhevskoi", *Obozrenie teatrov*, 1908, no. 378, pp. 3–4; "Pravda o poezdke Kommissarzhevskoi", *Obozrenie teatrov*, 1908, no. 380, p. 4. For an introduction to anti-Americanism in Russia, see also Semenovsky, "America as a Russian Idea", p. 197. In the collective imagination of Russians, "America stands for the decline of Europe, the hell of a civilization beyond the bounds of spirituality."

124 This is, perhaps, an oversimplification of Nazimova's dual identity in America. After emigrating in 1905, she not only enjoyed a lucrative film career as a *femme fatale*, but also performed in art theatres like Eva le Galliene's Civic Repertory Theatre. Because film reached a wider audience, however, her film image was more familiar to Americans.

125 "Russia's Foremost Actress", p. 10. In response to the interviewer, Kommissarzhevskaia proclaimed emphatically: "I do not expect to play here in the English language and I have no intention of becoming an American actress."

126 "New Russian Actress Comes to Play Here", p. 7.

127 "Russia's Foremost Actress", p. 10.

128 Kommissarzhevskaia's producers tried to capitalize on the alleged American weakness for titles by promoting her as the Countess Murav'ev.

129 "Russia's Foremost Actress", p. 10.

130 "Madame Nazimova on Tour in Repertoire of Classic Plays After Two Seasons in New York City", author's collection. The remarks are attributed to Adolph Klauber, a critic for the *New York Times*.

131 F. Kommissarzhevski, "Poezdka v Ameriku", in Evt. Karpov (ed.), *Sbornik pamiati V.F. Kommissarzhevskoi*, St. Petersburg: n.p., 1911, pp. 250–61; "Iz pisem K.V. Bravich", p. 32–3. Kommissarzhevski and Bravich blamed the tour's failure on the mental laziness of American spectators and their preference for vaudeville and "similar rubbish." See also "Russian Actress Appears as Nora". This *New York Times* critic wrote that whatever Kommissarzhevskaia's claims to consideration might be, they did not include "the attractiveness of a brilliant and magnetic personality."

132 "Peterburgskie pis'ma", *Rampa*, 1908, no. 11, p. 179.

133 Gurevich, "Na putiakh", p. 191.

134 "V.F. Kommissarzhevskaia o sebe", *Obozrenie teatrov*, 1909, no. 839, pp. 7–8.

135 I. Johnson, "Kommissarzhevskoi", *Maski*, 1913–14, no. 5, pp. 7–8.

136 *Rech'*, 1910, no. 41, n.p.

137 Dymov, "V.F. Kommissarzhevskaia", p. 11.

138 M. Iur'ev, "10-ogo fevralia", *Rampa i zhizn'*, 1912, no. 7, p. 5.

139 Zigfrid, "Pamiati V.F. Kommissarzhevskaia", *Obozrenie teatrov*, 1911, no. 1316, p. 14.

140 S. Adrianov, "Pamiati Very Fedorovny Kommruissarzherskoi", *Vestnik Evropy*, 1910, no. 3, p. 436.

141 Dymov, "V.F. Kommissarzhevskaia", p. 14.

142 Alpers, "Komissarzhevskaia", pp. 56–7. The political left must be distinguished from the artistic avant-garde. Seen in relation to other performers, Kommissarzhevskaia was a political activist with decidedly leftist sympathies, but she was a liberal, not a revolutionary in Lenin's terms. The political left supported her productions of Gorki at the Arcade, but their enthusiasm cooled considerably during the Ofitserskaia period. For a typically Soviet perspective on theatrical left during the 1905 revolution, see Iankovski, "Teatral'naia obshchestvennost' Peterburga", pp. 127–184. For a con-

temporaneous opinion of Kommissarzhevskaia and the political left, see "Novyi vklad na 'iskaniia' teatra V.F. Kommissarzhevskoi", *Obozrenie teatrov*, 1907, no. 47, pp. 5–8. According to Lunacharski, her theatre encouraged the bourgeois spectator to "sit in a soft armchair while a splendid picture of a tranquil, intoxicating fairytale unfolds before him." If the intelligentsia preferred theatres like Kommissarzhevskaia's, Lunacharski wrote, their commitment to revolution must be very weak indeed.

143 Rozanov, "Pamiati", p. 326.
144 Dymov, "V.F. Kommissarzhevskaia", p. 14.
145 Ibid., p. 13.
146 Among other articles by Kugel', see "Rezhisser", in *Utverzhdenie teatra*, Leningrad: Izdatel'stvo zhurnala *Teatr i iskusstvo*, n.d., pp. 41–59; "Teatral'nye zametki", *Teatr i iskusstvo*, 1907, no. 46, pp. 764–6; "Teatral'nye zametki", *Teatr i iskusstvo*, 1907, no. 48, pp. 804–6; and "Teatral'nye zametki", *Teatr i iskusstvo*, 1907, no. 49, pp. 827–9.
147 Kugel', "Rezhisser", p. 43.
148 Boborykin, "Tuda! tuda!" See especially pp. 20, 38, 42,45, 55, 56, 60, and 70.
149 Grinevskaia, "Chem on byl vreden", p. 12.
150 Isabella Grinevskaia, "Zhenshchina na stsene", *Biblioteka teatra i iskusstva*, 1909, no. 6, pp. 16–17.
151 Until the 1920s when directors like Mariia Knebel' and Seraphima Birman emerged from the Moscow Art Theatre studios, women rarely directed.
152 Spencer Golub, *The Recurrence of Fate*, p. 79.

SELECT BIBLIOGRAPHY

BOOKS AND PAMPHLETS

Abalkin, N. (ed.), *Malyi teatr, 1824–1974*, t. 1, Moscow: VTO, 1978.

Aleksandrov, A., *Chaika russkoi stseny: teatral'no – literaturnye ocherki*, Kazan: n.p., 1914.

Alekseev, A., *Vospominaniia aktera*, Moscow: n.p., 1894.

Alpers, B., *Akterskoe iskusstvo v rossii*, Moscow: Iskusstvo, 1945.

Al'tshuller, A. (ed.), *Vera Fedorovna Komissarzhevskaia: pis'ma aktrisy, vospominaniia o nei, materialy*, Leningrad-Moscow: Iskusstvo, 1964.

—— *Ocherki istorii russkoi teatral'noi kritiki, vtoraia polovina XIX veka*, Leningrad: Iskusstvo, 1976.

—— *Piats' rasskazov o znamenitykh akterakh*, Leningrad: Iskusstvo, 1985.

Amfiteatrov, A., *Kontury*, St. Petersburg: n.p., 1906.

Anisimov, A.V., *Teatry Moskvy: vremia i arkhitektura*, Moscow: Moskovskii Rabochii, 1984.

Arian, P.N. (ed.), *Pervyi zhenskii kalendar*, St. Petersburg: n.p., 1903.

—— *Pervyi zhenskii kalendar*, St. Petersburg: n.p., 1904.

Bazhenov, A., *Sochinenie i perevody*, t. 1, Moscow: n.p., 1869.

Beliaev, I., *Mel'pomena*, St. Petersburg: A.S. Suvorin, n.d.

Benedetti, J., *Stanislavski: A Biography*, New York: Routledge, 1988.

Bowlt, J., *The Silver Age: Russian Art of the Early Twentieth Century and the "World of Art" Group*, Newtonville, MA: Oriental Research Partners, 1982.

Brenko, A.A., *Avtobiografiia*, unpublished manuscript, Moscow, Bakhrushin Museum.

—— *Sovremennyi liud*, Moscow: Obshchestvo russkikh dramaticheskikh pisatelei, 1883.

Brooks, J., *When Russia Learned to Read*, Princeton, NJ: Princeton University Press, 1985.

Chekhov, A.P., *Pis'ma*, t. 11, Moscow: Nauka, 1982.

—— *Polnoe sobranie sochinenii i pisem*, t. 6–9, Moscow: Nauka, 1978.

Clowes, E., S. Kassow, and J. West (eds), *Between Tsar and People: Educated Society and the Quest for Public Identity in Late Imperial Russia*, Princeton, NJ: Princeton University Press, 1991.

Danilov, S.S., *Ocherki po istorii russkogo dramaticheskogo teatra*, Moscow: Iskusstvo, 1948.

Davydov, V.N., *Rasskaz o proshlom*, Moscow: "Academia", 1937.

Dikstra, B., *Idols of Perversity*, New York: Oxford University Press, 1986.

Doroshevich, V.M., *Izbrannye rasskazy i ocherki*, Moscow: Moskovskii Rabochii, 1962.

Drizen, N.V., *Sorok let teatra: vospominaniia 1875–1915*, "Prometei," n.d.

Edmondson, L., *Feminism in Russia, 1900–17*, Stanford, CA: Stanford University Press, 1984.

Engel, B., *Mothers and Daughters of the Intelligentsia in Nineteenth-Century Russia*, Cambridge: Cambridge University Press, 1983.

Engelstein, L., *The Keys to Happiness: Sex and the Search for Modernity in Fin-de-Siècle Russia*, Princeton, NJ: Princeton University Press, 1992.

Giliarovski, V.A., *Liudi teatra*, Moscow: Moskovskii Rabochii, 1960.

Glama-Meshcherskaia, A., *Vospominaniia*, Moscow: Iskusstvo, 1937.

Gnedich, P., *Kniga zhizni': vospominaniia, 1855–1918*, Leningrad, Priboi, 1929.

Goian, G., *Glikeriia Fedotova*, Moscow: Iskusstvo, 1948.

Gold, A. and R. Fizdale, *The Divine Sarah*, New York: Vintage Books, 1992.

Golub, S., *The Recurrence of Fate: Theatre and Memory in Twentieth-Century Russia*, Iowa City: University of Iowa Press, 1994.

Gorin-Goriainov, B.A., *Aktery: iz vospominanii*, Leningrad-Moscow: Iskusstvo, 1947.

Heldt, Barbara, *Terrible Perfection: Women and Russian Literature*, Bloomington, IN: Indiana University Press, 1987.

Holledge, J., *Innocent Flowers: Women in the Edwardian Theatre*, London: Virago Press, 1981.

Istoriia russkogo dramaticheskogo teatra, t. 1, Moscow: Iskusstvo, 1977.

Istoriia russkogo dramaticheskogo teatra, t. 5, Moscow: Iskusstvo, 1980.

Istoriia russkogo dramaticheskogo teatra, t. 6, Moscow: Iskusstvo, 1982.

Istoriia russkogo dramaticheskogo teatra, t. 7, Moscow: Iskusstvo, 1987.

Iur'ev, I., *Zapiski*, Leningrad: Iskusstvo, 1938.

Kaichenko, G.A., *Russkii narodnyi teatr kontsa XIX – nachala XX veka*, Moscow: Nauka, 1975.

Kaplan, J. and S. Stowell, *Theatre and Fashion: Oscar Wilde to the Suffragettes*, Cambridge: Cambridge University Press, 1994.

Karlinsky, S., *Russian Drama and Theatre from its Beginnings to the Age of Pushkin*, Berkeley, CA: University of California Press, 1985.

Karneev, M.V., *Dvadtsat' let na imperatorskoi stsene M.G. Savinoi*, St. Petersburg: n.p. 1894.

Karpov, E. (ed.), *Sbornik pamiati V.F. Kommissarzhevskoi*, St. Petersburg: n.p., 1911.

Khodotov, N., *Blizkoe i dalekoe*, Moscow: "Academia", 1932.

Kizeveter, A., *Teatr*, Moscow: n.p., 1922.

Kolesov, V.V. (ed.), *Domostroi*, Moscow: Sovetskaia rossiia, 1990.

Koni, A.F., *Vospominaniia o pisateliakh*, Lenizdat, 1965.

Krasnianski, K.B., *Vstrechi v puti: stranitsy vospominanii*, Moscow: VTO, 1967.

Krestovskaia, M., *Vne zhizn' i ugolki teatral'nogo mirka*, St. Petersburg: A.S. Suvorin, 1889.

Kugel', A., *Teatral'nye portrety*, Leningrad: Iskusstvo, 1967.

—— *Utverzhdenie teatra*, Leningrad: Izdatel'stvo zhurnala *Teatr i iskusstvo*, n.d.

L.B. Iavorskaia: biograficheskie svedeniia, Lenin Library.

Ledkovsky, M., C. Rosenthal, and M. Zirin (eds), *Dictionary of Russian Women Writers*, Westport, CN: Greenwood Press, 1994.

M.G. Savina i A. Koni: perepiska, 1883–1915, Leningrad-Moscow: Iskusstvo, 1938.

Mariia Gavrilovna Savina: gordost' russkogo teatra, St. Petersburg, n.p., 1900.

McReynolds, L., *The News under Russia's Old Regime: The Development of a Mass Circulation Press*, Princeton, NJ: Princeton University Press, 1991.

Meierhold, V., *Perepiska, 1896–1939*, Moscow: Iskusstvo, 1976.

Michurina-Samoilova, V.A., *Shest'desiat let v iskusstve*, Leningrad-Moscow: Iskusstvo, 1946.

Narokov, M.S., *Biografiia moego pokoleniia: teatral'nye memuary*, Moscow: VTO, 1956.

Nemirovich-Danchenko, V., *Rozhdenie teatra*, Moscow: n.p., 1989.

Nesterov, M., *Davnie dni*, Moscow: n.p., 1959.

Ostrovski, A.N., *Literaturnoe nasledstvo, novye materialy i issledovaniia*, kn. 2, Moscow: Nauka, 1974.

—— *Polnoe sobranie sochinenii*, t. 10, Moscow: Iskusstvo, 1978.

—— *O literature i teatre*, Moscow: Sovremenik, 1986.

—— *Vsia zhizn' – teatru*, Moscow: n.p., 1989.

Pazhitnov, A., *A.P. Lenski*, Moscow: n.p., 1988.

Petrovskaia, I., *Teatral 'nyi Peterburg*, St. Petersburg: Rossiiskii Institut Isskusstv, 1994.

—— *Teatr i zritel' provintsial'noi rossii*, Leningrad: Iskusstvo, 1979.

Polkova, E., *Teatr L'va Tolstogo*, Moscow: n.p., 1978.

Rybakova, I., *Komissarzhevskaia*, Leningrad: Iskusstvo, 1971.

Savina, M.G., *Goresti i skitaniia*, Leningrad: Iskusstvo, 1983.

Sbornik pamiati V.F. Komissarzhevskoi, Gosudarstvennoe Izdatel'stvo Khudozhestvennoi Literatury, 1931.

Senelick, L. (ed.), *National Theatre in Northern and Eastern Europe, 1746–1900*, Cambridge: Cambridge University Press, 1991.

—— (ed.), *Wandering Stars: Russian Emigré Theatre, 1905–1940*, Iowa City, IA: University of Iowa Press, 1992.

Sever, N., *Letopis' teatra imeni Volkova*, Iaroslav: n.p., 1973.

Shabel'skaia, E., *Vekselia antreprenershi*, St. Petersburg: n.p., 1907.

Shaikevich, B., *Ibsen i russkaia kul'tura*, Moscow: Izdatel'stvo Obedinenie "Vishcha Shkola," 1974.

Shchepkina-Kupernik, T., *Dni moei zhizni*, Moscow: Federatsiia, 1928.

—— *Ermolova*, Moscow: VTO, 1940; reprinted Moscow: Iskusstvo, 1983.

Shtein, A., *Friedrich Schiller: stat'i i materialy*, Moscow: n.p., 1966.

Shubert, A., *Moia zhizn'*, Leningrad: "Academia", 1929.

Shvyrov, A., *Znamenitye aktery i aktrisy*, St. Petersburg: n.p., 1902.

Skarskaia, N.F. and P.P. Gaideburov, *Na stsene i v zhizni*, Moscow: Iskusstvo, 1959.

Stanislavski, K., *Moia zhizn' v iskusstve*, Moscow: Iskusstvo, 1954.

Stokes, J., M. Booth, and S. Bassnett, *Bernhardt, Terry, Duse: The Actress in her Time*, Cambridge: Cambridge University Press, 1988.

Strepetova, P.A., *Vospominaniia i pis'ma*, Moscow-Leningrad: "Academia", 1934.

—— *Zhizn' i tvorchestvo tragicheskoi aktrisy*, Leningrad: Iskusstvo, 1959.

Suvorin, A.S., *Dnevnik*, Moscow: Novosti, 1992.

Svetaeva, M.G., *M.G. Savina*, Moscow: Iskusstvo, 1988.

Talnikov, D., *Kommissarzhevskaia*, Moscow-Leningrad: Iskusstvo, 1939.

Terras, V., *Handbook of Russian Literature*, New Haven, CT: Yale University Press, 1985.

Thorpe, R., "The Management of Culture in Revolutionary Russia: The Imperial Theatre and the State, 1897–1928", unpublished Ph.D. diss., Princeton University, 1990.

Tiraspol'skaia, N., *Iz proshlogo russkoi stseny*, Moscow: VTO, 1950.

Trudy 1-ogo vserossiiskogo s'ezda stsenicheskikh deiatelei, St. Petersburg: n.p., 1898.

Trudy 1-ogo vserossiiskogo zhenskogo s'ezda, St. Petersburg: n.p., 1909.

Turchaninova, E., *Evdokiia Dmitrievna Turchaninova: sbornik stat'ei*, Moscow: Iskusstvo, 1959.

Urusov, A.I., *Stat'i ego o teatre, o literature i ob iskusstve*, t. 1–3, Moscow: n.p., 1907.

Velizarii, M., *Put' provintsial'noi aktrisy*, Leningrad: Iskusstvo, 1938.

Verbitskaia, A., *Igo liubvi*, 2 vols., Moscow: n.p., 1916; reprinted Moscow: IPO Poligran, 1993.

Verigina, V., *Vospominaniia*, Leningrad: Iskusstvo, 1974.

Vitenzon, R., *Anna Brenko*, Leningrad: Iskusstvo, 1985.

Vulf, P., *V starom i novom teatre*, Moscow: VTO, 1962.

Walicki, A., *A History of Russian Thought from the Enlightenment to Marxism*, trans. Hilda Andrews-Rusiecka, Stanford, CA: Stanford University Press, 1979.

Worobec, C., *Peasant Russia: Family and Community in the Post Emancipation Period*, Princeton, NJ: Princeton University Press, 1991.

Zabrezhnev, I.I., *V.F. Kommissarzhevskaia: vpechatleniia*, St. Petersburg: n.p., 1898.

Zhurnal zasedaniia Direktsii Literaturno-Khudozhestvennogo Obshchestva, December 6, 1900, unpublished manuscript, Moscow: TsGALI.

ARTICLES AND REVIEWS

"A.A. Brenko i 'Rabochii teatr' ", *Rampa i zhizn'*, 1915, no. 37, p. 11.

"A.F. Koni o Savinoi", *Teatral'naia gazeta*, 1915, no. 51, p. 16.

A.G., "Iz vospominanii o P.A. Strepetovoi", *Istoricheskii vestnik*, 1904, no. 2, pp. 547–63.

Aberdukh, N.I. and A. Murski, "Artisty i tualeti', *Rampa i akter*", 1909, no. 27, pp. 439–40.

"Actors Locked Out at Thalia Theatre", *New York Times*, March 22, 1908.

Adrianov, S., "Pamiati Very Fedorovny Kommissarzhevskoi", *Vestnik evropy*, 1910, no. 3, pp. 430–6.

"Aktery", *Obozrenie teatrov*, 1908, no. 358, pp. 5–6.

Aktrisa, "Pis'mo k antrepreneru", *Rampa i zhizn'*, 1915, no. 20, p. 11.

"Aktrisa i prostitutsiia", *Rampa i zhizn'*, 1913, no. 1, p. 14.

"Aktrisy", *Obozrenie teatrov*, 1908, no. 359, p. 5.

Alpers, B., "Komissarzhevskaia", *Teatr*, 1964, no. 11, pp. 43–54.

—— "Ob Ostrovskom", *Teatr*, 1972, no. 9, pp. 73–96.

Al'tshuller, A., "Primer vdokhnovennogo sluzheniia narodu", *Zvezda*, 1960, no. 2, pp. 173–7.

—— "Tip vo vsiakom sluchae liubopytnyi", in *Chekhoviana*, Moscow, Nauka, 1990, pp. 140–51.

"*Antonii i Kleopatra*", *Teatr i iskusstvo*, 1903, no. 89, p. 707.

Arbenin, N.F., "Doklad N.F. Arbenina", in *Trudy 1-ogo vserossiiskogo s'ezda stsenicheskikh deiatelei*, St. Petersburg: n.p., 1898, pp. 120–152.

—— "M.N. Ermolova", *Teatr i iskusstvo*, 1905, no. 5, pp. 71–4.

Arseni, G., "Chisten'kaia aktrisa", *Teatr i iskusstvo*, 1904, no. 45, pp. 799–800.

Asenkova, A., "Kartiny proshedshego: zapiski russkoi artistki", *Teatral'nyi i muzykal'nyi vestnik*, 1857, no. 50, pp. 709–13.

Astaf'ev, I., "Psikhicheskii mir zhenshchiny: ego osobennosti, prevoskhodstva i nedostaki", *Russkii vestnik*, 1881, no. 12, part II, pp. 591–640.

Bang, H., "Sara Bernar v roli Hamleta", *Rampa i zhizn'*, 1911, no. 51, p. 4.

Beliaev, I., "V.F. Kommissarzhevskaia", *Nashi artistki*, vypusk 1, 1900.

—— "L.B. Iavorskaia", *Nashi artistki*, vypusk 2, 1900.

—— "Apofeoz Kommissarzhevskoi", *Rampa i zhizn'*, 1910, no. 12, pp. 189–91.

"Berlin", *Teatral'nyi mirok*, 1886, no. 2, p. 1.

"Berlinskiia gastroli E.N. Gorevoi", *Teatral'nyi mirok*, 1886, no. 3, p. 2.

"Beseda s M.G. Savinoi", *Teatral'naia rossiia*, 1905, no. 41, pp. 1218–20.

Beskin, E., "Koroleva zhesta", *Rampa*, 1908, no. 16, pp. 246–8.

—— "Svetlyi put", *Zhizn' iskusstva*, 1924, no. 42, pp. 4–5.

"Bez predvaritel'noi tsenzury", *Teatr i iskusstvo*, 1905, no. 32, n.p.

"Biuro postom", *Rampa i zhizn'*, 1911, no. 12, pp. 11–12.

Blair, J., "Private Parts in Public Places: The Case of Actresses", in Shirley Ardener (ed.), *Women and Space: Ground Rules and Social Maps*, Oxford: Berg, 1993, pp. 200–21.

Borborykin, P., "Tvorchestvo aktera", *Iskusstvo*, 1883, no. 2, pp. 14–16.

—— "Tuda! Tuda!", *Vestnik evropy*, 1913, no. 8, pp. 5–70.

Botsianovski, V., "Nov i star", *Ezhegodnik imperatorskikh teatrov*, 1913, vypusk VII, pp. 103–10.

Brandova, M.E., "O sovremennom polozhenii russkoi zhenshchiny", in *Trudy 1-ogo vserossiiskogo zhenskogo s'ezda*, St. Petersburg: n.p., 1909, pp. 359–67.

Bravich, K.V., "Pervye shagi V.F. Kommissarzhevskoi", *Rampa*, 1908, no. 5, p. 78.

Budrin, F.A., "Material dlia istorii russkogo teatra: iz vospominanii F.A. Budrina", *Vestnik evropy*, 1901, no. 10, pp. 576–600.

"Calls Us Artless", *New York Times*, April 4, 1908.

"Chaika russkoi stseny", *Rampa i zhizn'*, 1911, no. 6, pp. 3–4.

Chekhov, V.V., "Dve zvezdy russkogo teatra", *Teatr: prilozhenie k zhivopisn. obozren.*, October 1904, pp. 110–15.

Clements, B., "Introduction: Accommodation, Resistance, Transformation", in Barbara Evans Clements, Barbara Alpern Engel, and Christine D. Worobec (eds), *Russia's Women*, Berkeley, CA: University of California Press, 1991, pp. 1–13.

"Dama s kameliiami", *Artist*, 1894, no. 34, pp. 244–6.

Danilov, S.S., "Revoliutsiia 1905–1907 godov i russkii teatr", *Teatr*, 1955, no. 7, pp. 116–26.

"Demand Royalty on a Play", *New York Times*, March 10, 1908.

D'iakonov, A., "Dramaticheskii teatr V.F. Komissarzhevskoi, ch. II, teatr na Ofitserskoi", in *Pamiatniki kul'tury, novye otkrytiia*, Leningrad: Iskusstvo, 1981, pp. 186–210.

"Dnevnik Moskogo teatrala", *Iskusstvo*, 1883, no. 7, p. 77.

Doroshevich, V., "20 let tomu nazad", in *Galereia stsenicheskikh deiatelei*, t. 2, Moscow, Izdanie zhurnala *Rampa i zhizn'*, n.d., pp. 50–60.

"Dramaticheskii teatr g-zhi Gorevoi", *Artist*, 1890, no. 10, pp. 138–9.

"Dramaticheskii teatr g-zhi Gorevoi", *Artist*, 1890, no. 11, p. 150.

"Dramaticheskii teatr g-zhi Gorevoi", *Artist*, 1891, no. 12, p. 157.

Drizen, N.V., "K istorii odnogo talanta", *Istoricheskii vestnik*, 1907, no. 3, pp. 902–21.

Dubnova, E., "Iz istorii dramaticheskogo teatra V.F. Komissarzhevskoi", in *Pamiatniki kul'tury, novye otkrytiia*, Leningrad-Moscow, 1981, pp. 183–6.

Durylin. S., "Zritel' Komissarzhevskoi", clippings file, Bakhrushin Museum.

"Dvatdtsat' piat' let nazad", *Teatr i iskusstvo*, 1905, no. 37, p. 592.

"Dvadtsatipiatiletie stolichnykh chastnykh teatrov", *Teatral'naia rossiia*, 1905, no. 39, pp. 1172–3.

Dymov, O., "Ona na stsene", *Teatr i iskusstvo*, 1905, no. 17, pp. 276–8.

—— "V.F. Kommissarzhevskaia (k godovshchine so dnia smerti)", *Obozrenie teatrov*, 1911, no. 1316, pp. 11–14.

"E.N. Goreva", *Teatr i iskusstvo*, 1917, no. 28–9, p. 489.

"E.N. Goreva (nekrolog)", *Rampa i zhizn'*, 1917, no. 29–30, p. 12.

Edmondson, L., "Women's Emancipation and Theories of Sexual Difference in Russia", paper for the conference on "Gender Restructuring – Perestroika in Russian Studies," Helsinki, 1992.

Efros, N., "Mariia Nikolaevna Ermolova", *Ezhegodnik imperatorskikh teatrov*, 1895–6, pp. 426–47.

—— "M.N. Ermolova", *Zhenskoe delo*, 1910, no. 4, pp. 2–4.

—— "Kommissarzhevskaia", *Zhenskoe delo*, 1910, no. 7, pp. 2–5.

—— "Savina", *Zhenskoe delo*, 1915, no. 19, pp. 2–3.

—— "L.B. Iavorskaia", *Kul'tura teatra*, 1921, no. 7–8, pp. 63–5.

—— "Iz detskikh i otrocheskikh vospominanii G.N. Fedotovoi", in *Galereia stsenicheskikh deiatelei*, t. 2, Moscow, Izdanie zhurnala *Rampa i zhizn'*, n.d., pp. 32–45.

"Ekzamenatsionnye spektakli shkoly peterburgskikh imperatorskikh teatrov", *Artist*, 1893, no. 28, p. 172.

"Eleonora Duse", *Severnyi vestnik*, 1891, no. 8, part II, pp. 117–35.

Engel, B., "Transformation versus Tradition", in Barbara Evans Clements, Barbara Alpern Engel, and Christine D. Worobec (eds), *Russia's Women*, Berkeley, CA: University of California Press, 1991, pp. 135–47.

"Enthusiastic Adieu for Komisarchevsky", *New York Times*, April 20, 1908.

Ermilov, V., "Vestalka stseny-khrama", *Studiia*, 1912, no. 15, p. 5.

"Evolutsiia russkogo aktera", *Teatral'naia gazeta*, 1915, no. 44, pp. 11–12.

"G.N. Fedotova", *Russkie vedomosti*, 1887, no. 23, 1.24.

"G.N. Fedotova i N.A. Nikulina", *Artist*, 1892, no. 20, pp. 90–2.

Garting, E., "Zhena rezhissera", *Rampa i zhizn'*, 1915, no. 5, pp. 11–12.

—— "Zhena ego prevoskhoditel'stva", *Rampa i zhizn'*, 1915, no. 11, p. 13.

—— "Vykhodnaia", *Rampa i zhizn'*, 1915, no. 19, pp. 13–14.

"Gastroli g-zhi Savinoi", *Artist*, 1891, no. 13, pp. 128–31.

"Gazety o teatre V.F. Kommissarzhevskoi", *Obozrenie teatrov*, 1906, no. 3, pp. 5–8.

"Genial'naia zhenshchina", *Zhenskoe delo*, 1912, no. 19, pp. 21–2.

"Glikeriia Fedotova", *Vestnik rabotnikov iskusstv*, 1925, no. 7, p. 7.

Goreva, E.N., "Iz moei avtobiogafii", *Teatr i iskusstvo*, 1917, no. 10–11, pp. 194–6.

Greshnyi, A., "Polozhenie provintsial'nogo aktera vo vremia debuta na stolichnoi stsene", *Sufler'*, 1880, no. 34, p. 1; no. 35, pp. 1–2; no. 36, pp. 2–3; no. 37. p. 2; no. 38, p. 2; no. 39. pp. 1–2.

Grinevskaia, I.N., "Chem on byl vreden", *Obozrenie teatrov*, 1907, no. 253, pp. 12–13.

—— "Zhenshchina na stsene", *Biblioteka teatra i iskusstva*, 1909, no. 6, pp. 3–24.

Gurevich, Liubov, "Pamiati V.F. Kommissarzhevskoi", *Rech'*, 1910, no. 49, n.p.

—— "Na putiakh obnovleniia teatra", in *Pamiati Very Fedorovny Kommissarzhevskoi*, St. Petersburg: Izdanie Peredvizhnogo teatra P.P. Gaideburov i N.F. Skarskaia, 1911, pp. 171–94.

"G-zha Savina i ee benefis", *Artist*, 1892, no. 21, pp. 136–8.

"G-zhi Savina i Strepetova", *Sufler'*, 1880, no. 9, pp. 2–3.

Iankovski, M., "Teatral'naia obshchestvennost' peterburga v 1905–1907 gg.", in *Pervaia russkaia revoliutsiia i teatr: stat'i i materialy*, Moscow: Iskusstvo, 1956, pp. 125–84.

Iartsev, P., "Litso teatra", *Teatr i iskusstvo*, 1904, no. 16, pp. 323–4.

"Inostrannye otgoloski", *Zhenskoe delo*, 1899, no. 3, pp. 89–92.

Ispolatova, S.K., "Samosoznanie zhenshchiny, kak faktor obnovleniia obshchestvennogo stroia", in *Trudy 1-ogo vserossiiskogo zhenskogo s'ezda*, St. Petersburg: n.p., 1909, pp. 771–9.

"Iubilei, A.A. Brenko", *Teatral'naia gazeta*, 1915, no. 37, pp. 5–6.

Iur'ev, M., "10-ogo fevralia", *Rampa i zhizn'*, 1912, no. 7, pp. 4–6.

Ivanov, I., "Teatr g-zhi Abramovoi", *Artist*, 1890, no. 6, pp. 124–5.

—— "Spektakli g-zhi Sary Bernar", *Artist*, 1892, no. 25, pp. 157–64.

—— "Sovremennoe obozrenie", *Artist*, 1893, no. 26, pp. 157–8.

"Iz dnevnika teatrala", *Teatral*, 1896, no. 75, pp. 33–7.

"Iz dnevnika teatrala", *Teatral*, 1896, no. 84, pp. 79–84.

"Iz memuarov M.G. Savinoi", *Obozrenie teatrov*, 1909, no. 939, pp. 17–19; no. 949, pp. 15–16.

"Iz memuarov M.G. Savinoi", *Obozrenie teatrov*, 1910, no. 950, pp. 16–17; no. 952, pp. 13–14; no. 954, pp. 16–17; no. 966, pp. 9–11; no. 987, pp. 15; no. 989, pp. 15–16.

"Iz pisem, dnevnikov i zametok K.V. Bravicha", *Maski*, 1912, no. 2, pp. 1–8.

Izborskaia, A.I., "Velikii post", in *Russkii provintsial'nyi teatr*, Leningrad: Iskusstvo, 1937, pp. 141–56.

"Izvestnye aktery ob izuchenii roli", *Biblioteka teatra i iskusstva*, 1914, no. 2, pp. 44–58.

Johnson, I., "Kommissarzhevskaia", *Maski*, 1913–14, no. 5, pp. 1–8.

"Kak oni stali prostitutkami", *Rampa i akter*, 1909, no. 25, pp. 406–10.

Karabanov, N., "Teatr v provintsii", *Studiia*, 1912, no. 24, pp. 1–3.

Karpov, E., "Istoriia pervogo predstavleniia *Chaika* na stsene Aleksandrinskogo teatra 17 oktiabria 1896", *Rampa i zhizn'*, 1909, no. 3, pp. 252–4.

—— "A.S. Suvorin i osnovanie Teatra Literaturno Artisticheskogo kruzhka", *Istoricheskii vestnik*, 1914, no. 8, pp. 449–70; no. 9, pp. 873–902.

—— "M.G. Savina", *Golos minuvshego*, 1916, no. 11, pp. 29–61.

—— "Vera Fedorovna Komissarzhevskaia: biograficheskii ocherk", clippings file, New York Public Library.

Kanshin, P.A., "Pis'ma o Moskovskikh teatrakh", *Delo*, 1886, no. 3–4, pp. 119–20.

Khabkin, V., "Sarah divine", *Rampa*, 1909, no. 1, pp. 2–3.

"Kharakteristika svetskoi zhenshchiny", in *O zhenshchinakh: mysli starye i novye*, St. Petersburg: n.p., 1886, pp. 23–46.

Kholmskaia, Z., "Memuary dvukh aktrisy", *Teatr i iskusstvo*, 1904, no. 23, pp. 442–3.

—— "Iz vospominanii", in *Russkii provintsial'nyi teatr*, Leningrad: Iskusstvo, 1937, pp. 189–201.

"Khronika", *Teatr i iskusstvo*, 1903, no. 42, p. 765.

Klirikova, O.N., "Zhenskaia kul'tura", in *Trudy 1-ogo vserossiiskogo zhenskogo s'ezda*, St. Petersburg: n.p., 1909, pp. 512–19.

Kliuchareva, E., "Ob aktrisakh", *Teatral'naia rossiia*, 1905, no. 19, pp. 325–7.

Kolosov, K., "P.A. Strepetova", *Teatr i iskusstvo*, 1903, no. 42, pp. 771–3.

Kosorotov, A., "Krizis teatra", *Teatr i iskusstvo*, 1908, no. 17, pp. 310–13; no. 18, pp. 327–8; no. 20, pp. 358–61.

Koval'skie, K. and O., "Neudachnitsa", *Studiia*, 1912, no. 36–7, pp. 5–8.

Kremlev, A.N., "O zadachakh stsenicheskoi deiatel'nosti zhenshchiny", in *Trudy 1-ogo vserossiiskogo zhenskogo s'ezda*, St. Petersburg: n.p., 1909, pp. 189–94.

"Krizis teatra", *Rampa i zhizn'*, 1911, no. 24, pp. 4–5.

"Kto vinovat", *Rampa i zhizn'*, 1913, no. 36, pp. 4–5.

Kugel", A., "Zhenskoe dvizhenie", *Teatr i iskusstvo*, 1897, no. 15, pp. 298–9.

—— "Teatral'nye zametki", *Teatr i iskusstvo*, 1898, no. 4, pp. 786–8.

—— "Teatr Lit. Art. Kruzhka", *Teatr i iskusstvo*, 1898, no, 19, pp. 353–4.

—— "Teatral'nye zametki", *Teatr i iskusstvo*, 1899, no. 10, pp. 209–10.

—— "Dobrye nravy i nravstvennost", *Teatr i iskusstvo*, 1899, no. 4, pp. 73–4.

—— "Teatral'nye zametki", *Teatr i iskusstvo*, 1899, no. 10, pp. 209–10.

—— "Teatral'nye zametki", *Teatr i iskusstvo*, 1899, no. 12, pp. 247–8.

—— "Iz zapisnoi knizhki", *Teatr i iskusstvo*, 1903, no. 42, pp. 776–7.

—— "Teatral'nye zametki", *Teatr i iskusstvo*, 1904, no. 1, p. 15.

—— "Teatral'nye zametki", *Teatr i iskusstvo*, 1907, no. 46, pp. 764–6.

—— "Teatral'nye zametki", *Teatr i iskusstvo*, 1907, no. 48, pp. 804–6.

—— "Teatral'nye zametki", *Teatr i iskusstvo*, 1907, no. 49, pp. 827–9.

—— "Teatral'nye zametki", *Teatr i iskusstvo*, 1908, no. 37, p. 643.

—— "Dramaticheskii teatr", *Teatr i iskusstvo*, 1908, no. 40, pp. 687–8.

—— "Zametki", *Teatr i iskusstvo*, 1914, no. 6, pp. 136–8.

—— "Slovo o Savinoi", *Teatr i iskusstvo*, 1915, no. 37, pp. 685–90.

—— "Iz moikh vospominanii", *Zhizn" iskusstva*, 1924, no. 33, pp. 8–9; no. 38, pp. 6–7.

Kuprina, K., "Dorogi", *Teatral'naia zhizn'*, 1964, no. 22, pp. 30–1.

Linski, V., "Stsena i besputstvo", *Teatr i iskusstvo*, 1900, no. 38, pp. 660–2; no. 40, pp. 701–03; no. 48, pp. 862–4.

—— "*Kontrabandisty*", *Teatr i iskusstvo*, 1901, no. 3, pp. 54–6.

—— "Novaia zhenshchina", *Teatr i iskusstvo*, 1903, no. 7, pp. 154–6; no. 8, pp. 176–8; no. 9, pp. 197–8.

"M.G. Savina", *Artist*, 1890, no. 9, pp. 41–2.

"M.G. Savina", *Teatral'naia gazeta*, 1915, no. 37, pp. 1 and 4.

"M.G. Savina", *Teatral'nyi mirok*, 1884, no. 15, pp. 2–5.

"M.G. Savina", *Zhenskii vestnik*, 1915, no. 10, p. 173.

"M.N. Ermolova: k 40-letiiu stsenicheskoi deiatel'nosti", *Teatr i iskusstvo*, 1910, no. 5, pp. 101–3.

"Madame Sans-Gêne", *Artist*, 1894, no. 42, pp. 232–7.

Malinovski, G., "Stranichka iz zhizni M.N. Ermolovoi", *Teatr*, 1990, no. 9, pp. 105–6.

"Mariia Gavrilovna", *Peterburgskaia gazeta*, 1894, n.v.

"Mariia Moritsovna Abramova", *Dnevnik artista*, 1892, no. 4, pp. 26–32.

Maslikh, V., "Pamiati A.A. Brenko", *Teatr*, 1966, no. 4, pp. 107–9.

Medvedeva, N.M., "Doklad N.M. Medvedevoi", *Trudy 1-ogo vserossiiskogo s'ezda stsenicheskikh deiatelei*, St. Petersburg: n.p., 1898, pp. 1–5.

Mikhailov, M., "Zhenshchiny: ikh vospitanie i znachenie v sem'e i obshchestve", *Sovremennik*, 1860, no. 3–4, pp. 473–500.

Monas, S., "The Twilit Middle Class of Nineteenth-Century Russia", in Edith Clowes, Samuel Kassow, and James West (eds), *Between Tsar and People: Educated Society and the Quest for Public Identity in Late Imperial Russia*, Princeton: NJ, Princeton University Press, 1991, pp. 28–37.

Morol'd, M., "Otvet na nekotorye voprosy", *Mir iskusstva*, 1899, no. 2, pp. 145–55.

"Moskovskii fel'eton", *Novoe vremia*, February 3, 1890.

"Moskva (dnevnik teatrala)", *Iskusstvo*, 1883, no. 47, pp. 589–90.

Moyle, N., "Mermaids (*Rusalki*) and Russian Beliefs About Women", in Anna Lisa Crone and Catherine V. Chvany (eds), *New Studies in Russian Language and Literature*, Columbus, OH: Slavica Publishers, 1986, pp. 221–38.

Musina, D., "Tonal'noe iskusstvo V.F. Kommissarzhevskoi", *Biblioteka teatra i iskusstva*, 1913, no. 2, pp. 2–5; no. 3, pp. 3–6.

"*Na dvore vo fligel*", *Teatr i iskusstvo*, 1902, no. 52, p. 1008.

"Na iubilee V.F. Kommissarzhevskoi", clippings file, Bakhrushin Museum.

"Na povorot", *Rampa i zhizn'*, 1913, no. 19, pp. 3–5.

"Na sud sovesti", *Rampa i zhizn'*, 1910, no. 48, pp. 782.

Nazareva, K.V., "Stsenicheskaia illiuziia", *Dnevnik artista*, 1892, no. 5, pp. 10–28.

Negorev, N., "Khronika", *Teatr i iskusstvo*, 1900, no. 48, p. 867.

—— "Zametki", *Teatr i iskusstvo*, 1902, no. 26, pp. 495–6.

Nemirovich-Danchenko, V., "Teatr i shkola", *Artist*, 1894, no. 42, pp. 136–54.

Nemvrodov, P., "Pereotsenka teatra", *Teatr i iskusstvo*, 1902, no. 18, pp. 358–60; no. 20, pp. 390–2; no. 21, pp. 406–8.

"Nechto o 'stsenicheskoi vnestnosti' nashikh artistok", *Teatr i iskusstvo*, 1897, no. 4, pp. 74–5.

Nevezhin, P., "G.N. Fedotova", *Teatr i iskusstvo*, 1912, no. 1, pp. 7–8.

"New Russian Actress Comes Here to Play", *New York Times*, February 27, 1908.

Nikolaev, I., "Pamiati Marii Gavrilovny Savinoi", *Biblioteka teatra i iskusstva*, 1915, no. 10, pp. 3–22.

Nikulin, V., "K russkomy akterstvu", (pis'mo v redaktsiiu) *Teatr i iskusstvo*, 1915, no. 37, p. 684.

Nikulina-Kositskaia, L.P., "Zapiski", *Russkaia starina*, 1878, no. 1, pp. 64–80; no. 2, pp. 281–304; no. 4, pp. 609–24.

"*Nora*", *Novosti*, September 19, 1904, p. 4.

"Nov i star", *Ezhegodnik imperatorskikh teatrov*, 1910, vypusk III, p. 118.

"Novaia p'esa A.N. Ostrovskogo, *Bez viny vinovatye*", *Teatral'nyi mirok*, 1884, no. 5, pp. 4–5.

"Novyi vklad na 'iskaniia' teatra V.F. Kommissarzhevskoi", *Obozrenie teatrov*, 1907, no. 47, pp. 5–8.

"O moral'nom vlianii teatra", *Teatr i iskusstvo*, 1905, no. 26, pp. 419–20.

"O 'provale' V.F. Kommissarzhevskoi v Amerike", *Obozrenie teatrov*, 1908, no. 306, p. 5.

"Odessa", *Sufler'*, 1880, no. 39, p. 3.

"Orleanskaia deva", *Iskusstvo*, 1884, no. 56, p. 786.

Osipov, I., "K otezdu V.F. Kommissarzhevskoi", *Obozrenie teatrov*, 1908, no. 299, pp. 15–16.

"Otkrytie vserossiiskogo zhenskogo s'ezda", *Teatr i iskusstvo*, 1908, no. 49, p. 862.

"P.A. Strepetova (nekrolog)", *Ezhegodnik imperatorskikh teatrov*, prilozhenie, 1903–4, pp. 100–4.

"P.A. Strepetova: neskol'ko slov k portretu artistki", *Teatral'nyi mirok*, 1884, no. 8, pp. 1–2.

"P.A. Strepetova – vospominaniia Sergei Iablonovskogo", in *Galereia stsenicheskikh deiatelei*, t.1, Moscow, Izdanie zhurnala *Rampa i zhizn'*, 1915, pp. 20–6.

"Paki i paki o teatre V.F. Kommissarzhevskoi", 1906, no. 11, pp. 5–6.

Pavlova, T., "Repin i Strepetova", *Teatr*, 1970, no. 8, pp. 131–3.

"*Pelleas i Melisanda* v teatre V.F. Kommissarzhevskoi", *Obozrenie teatrov*, 1907, no. 16, pp. 16–17.

"Pervye shagi velikoi artistki (iz vospominanii ob M.N. Ermolovoi)", *Teatr i iskusstvo*, 1907, no. 12, pp. 203–4.

"Pervyi chastnyi teatr v stolitse", *Teatr i iskusstvo*, 1905, no. 36, pp. 576–7.

"Peterburgskie pis'ma", *Rampa*, 1908, no. 11, pp. 178–9.

"Peterburgskie pis'ma", *Teatral*, 1896, no. 95, pp. 75–82.

Pil'ski, Petr, "Stolby", *Teatr i iskusstvo*, 1907, no. 46, pp. 762–3; no. 47, pp. 778–80.

"Pis'ma M.N. Ermolovoi", in *Teatral'noe nasledstvo*, Moscow: Iskusstvo, 1956, pp. 410–26.

"Pis'ma o Moskovskikh teatrakh", *Delo*, 1886, no. 3–4, pp. 115–22.

"Pis'mo k antrepreneru", *Rampa i zhizn'*, 1915, no. 20, pp. 10–11.

Pleshcheev, A., "Teatral'naia beseda", *Teatral'nyi mirok*, 1886, no. 10, p. 2.

"Po povodu 'ukhoda' g-zhi Kommissarzhevskoi", *Teatr i iskusstvo*, 1902, no. 31, pp. 581–2.

Popov, I., "Glikeriia Nikolaevna Fedotova", *Zhenskoe delo*, 1912, no. 2, pp. 2–5.

Popov, N., "Maska Savinoi", *Rampa i zhizn'*, 1915, no. 38, p. 3.

"Pravda o poezdke Kommissarzhevskoi", *Obozrenie teatrov*, 1908, no. 380, p. 4.

"Professional'nye rabotnitsy", *Zhenskii vestnik*, 1909, no. 12, pp. 338–41.

Rodinova, I., "Drugaia Ermolova ili velikaia molchal'nitsa", *Teatral'naia zhizn'*, 1992, no.6, pp. 24–5; no. 7, pp. 22–3.

"*Romantiki*", *Artist*, 1895, no. 45, pp. 207–11.

Rosenthal, C., "The Silver Age: Highpoint for Women?" in Linda Edmondson (ed.), *Women and Society in Russia and the Soviet Union*, Cambridge: Cambridge University Press, 1992, pp. 32–47.

Rossov, N., "Doch' Apollona", *Teatr i iskusstvo*, 1910, no. 12, pp. 251–3.

—— "Net Savinoi", *Rampa i zhizn'*, 1915, no. 40, pp. 5–7; no. 41, pp. 4–7.

—— "Pamiati Gorevoi", *Teatral'naia gazeta*, 1917, no. 34–5, pp. 8–10.

Rostislavov, A., "Studencheskaia madonna", *Teatr i iskusstvo*, 1910, no. 6, pp. 130–2.

Rozanov, V.V., "Pamiati V.F. Kommissarzhevskoi", in *Sredi khudozhnikkov*, St. Petersburg: n.p., 1914, pp. 322–7.

"Russian Actress Appears as Nora", *New York Times*, March 3, 1908.

"Russian Actress in Play by Sudermann", *New York Times*, March 6, 1908.

"Russia's Foremost Actress Won't Talk About the Situation at Home but is Most Communicative About Her Ideas on the Drama", *New York Times*, March 1, 1908.

"Russkaia dramaticheskaia stsena", *Vestnik evropy*, 1871, n.v., pp. 383–403.

"Russkie otgoloski", *Zhenskoe delo*, 1899, no. 10, pp. 93–100.

"Russkoe iskusstvo za granitsei: E.N. Goreva", *Teatral'nyi mirok*, 1886, no. 5, pp. 3–4.

Rybakova, I., "Talanty i poklonniki Savinoi i Ermolovoi", in *Traditsii stsenicheskogo realizma*, Leningrad: Ministerstvo Kul'tury RSFSR, 1980, pp. 160–88.

"Savina: k godovshchine konchiny", *Rampa i zhizn'*, 1916, no. 36, pp. 3–4.

Savina, M.G., "Otvety na voprosy", clippings file, TsGALI.

—— "Neizdannye vospominaniia", in *Teatral'noe nasledstvo*, Moscow: Iskusstvo, 1956, pp. 517–23.

Selivanov, N.A., "Godovshchina", *Teatr i iskusstvo*, 1913, no. 44, pp. 881–2.

Senelick, L., "Vera Kommissarzhevskaia: The Actress as Symbolist Eidolon", *Theatre Journal*, December 1980, pp. 475–87.

—— "Chekhov's Response to Bernhardt", in Eric Salmon (ed.), *Bernhardt and the Theatre of Her Time*, Westport, CT: Greenwood Press, 1984, pp. 165–81.

"*Sestra Beatrisa* v teatre V.F. Kommissarzhevskoi", *Obozrenie teatrov*, 1906, no. 14, pp. 5–8.

Shabel'skaia, E., "Dramaticheskiia shkoly i dramaticheskaia shkola", *Teatr i iskusstvo*, 1897, no. 45, pp. 807–9.

—— "Vragi russkogo teatra", *Teatr i iskusstvo*, 1898, no. 2, pp. 35–8.

Shcheglov, I., "Charodeika russkoi stseny", *Teatr i iskusstvo*, 1900, no. 3, pp. 58–63.

Shchepkina-Kupernik, T., "N.S. Butova i L.B. Iavorskaia", unpublished memoir, Moscow: TsGALI.

Shchetinin, B.A., "F.A. Korsh i ego teatr", *Istoricheskii vestnik*, 1907, no. 10, pp. 169–79.

Shebuev, N., "Ne mogu molchat'", *Obozrenie teatrov*, 1908, no. 535, pp. 7–8.

Shtein, V.A., "M.G. Savina na stsene Saratovskogo teatra", *Biblioteka teatra i iskusstvo*, 1915, no. 9, pp. 20–31.

"Slovno legenda", *Teatral'naia zhizn'*, 1978, no. 14, p. 20.

Smirnova, N., "O roskoshi i mode", *Rampa i zhizn'*, 1916, no. 18, pp. 3–4.

Sobolev, I., "Aktrisa tragedii", *Sovremennyi teatr*, 1928, no. 12, pp. 238–9.

"Solntse vysokoi komodii", *Rampa i zhizn'*, 1913, no. 28, pp. 2–3.

"Sovremennoe obozrenie", *Artist*, 1890, no. 7, pp. 125–6.

"Sovremennoe obozrenie", *Teatral*, 1896, no. 66, pp. 26–9.

"Sovremennoe obozrenie", *Teatral*, 1896, no. 83, pp. 90–9.

"Sredi teatral'nykh retsenzentov", *Sufler'*, 1879.

Stanislavski, K., "Pis'ma k zhene", in *O Stanislavskom*, Moscow: VTO, 1948, p. 73.

Steppun, F., "V.F. Kommissarzhevskaia i M.N. Ermolova", *Russkaia mysl'*, 1913, no. 34, pp. 25–9.

"Stop Komisarzhevsky", *New York Times*, March 24, 1908.

Storozhenko, N.I., "Iz vospominanii o M.N. Ermolovoi", *Teatr i iskusstvo*, 1907, no. 11, pp. 192–3.

"Stroki iz dnevnika", *Teatral'naia zhizn'*, 1978, no. 14, pp. 18–19.

"Stsenicheskaia deiatel'nost' M.G. Savinoi v Peterburge", *Teatral'nyi mirok*, 1884, no. 15, p. 4.

Sutugin, S., "Talant i tekhnika", *Teatr i iskusstvo*, 1904, no. 19, pp. 376–7.

Suvorin, A.S., "G-zhi Savina i Ermolova", *Novoe vremia*, 1891, n.d.

"Suvorin i ego teatr", *Teatral'naia gazeta*, 1915, no. 39, pp. 8–9.

Svetlov, S., "S akterskogo rynka", *Teatr i iskusstvo*, 1904, no. 9, pp. 188–9.

—— "Aktery i zhizn'", *Teatr i iskusstvo*, 1904, no. 26, pp. 489–90; no. 29, pp. 536–7; no. 30, pp. 552–3.

Syroshiatninov-Sigma, S.N., "Seiateli antisemitizma", *Novoe vremia*, November 25, 1900, p. 3.

Tarlovskaia-Rastorgueva, I.V., "Doklad Iulia Vasil'evna Tarlovskaia-Rastorgueva", in *Trudy 1-ogo vserossiiskogo s'ezda stsenicheskikh deiatelei*, St. Petersburg: n.p., 1898, pp. 32–5.

"Teatr g-zhi Abramovoi", *Artist*, 1889, no. 4, pp. 127–33.

"Teatr g-zhi Abramovoi", *Artist*, 1890, no. 5, pp. 142–6.

"Teatr g-zhi Gorevoi", *Artist*, 1889, no. 2, pp. 85–103.

"Teatr g-zhi Gorevoi", *Artist*, 1890, no. 4, pp. 134–8.

"Teatr i musyka", *Novoe vremia*, November 16, 1900, p. 4.

"Teatr i musyka", *Novoe vremia*, November 24, 1900, p. 4.

"Teatr i musyka", *Severnyi vestnik*, 1891, no. 1, pp. 113–24.

Teatral, "Prem'ersha", in *Teatral'nye tipy: vospominaniia rezhissera*, St. Petersburg: n.p., 1889, pp. 3–39.

"Teatral'nyi kalendar: P.A. Strepetova", *Teatr*, 1953, no. 10, pp. 170–1.

"Tekushchiia novosti", *Teatr i zhizn'*, 1888, no. 169, pp. 1–2.

"*Teshcha*", *Artist*, 1893, no. 31, p. 163.

Thurston, G., "The Impact of Russian Popular Theatre, 1886–1915", *Journal of Modern History*, 1983, no. 55, pp. 237–67.

"*Trudovoi khlebe*", *Artist*, 1893, no. 10, pp. 23–5.

"Tsaritsa russkoi stseny", *Rampa i zhizn'*, 1915, no. 38, pp. 4–5.

Tverskoi, P., "Pis'mo iz Ameriki," *Severnyi vestnik*, 1896, no. 2, part II, pp. 49–57.

"Uchastie peterburgskikh teatrov v obshchei politicheskoi zabastokov", *Teatral'naia rossiia*, 1905, no. 44–45, pp. 1269–70.

"Uchenitsa i professor", *Teatral*, 1897, no. 135, pp. 15–27.

"Ukazatel' literatury zhenskogo voprosa na russkom iazyke", *Severnyi vestnik*, 1887, no. 7, pp. 1–33; no. 8, pp. 34–56.

"*Uriel Akost*", *Artist*, 1895, no. 46, pp. 147–52.

Urvantsov, N., "Teatr v stolitsakh i provintsii", *Rampa i zhizn'*, 1909, no. 8, pp. 336–8; no. 9, pp. 352–4; no. 10, pp. 369–71.

"Ustav russkogo teatral'nogo obshchestva", *Teatral'naia biblioteka*, 1894, no. 42, pp. 109–12.

"V.F. Kommissarzhevskaia o sebe", *Obozrenie teatrov*, 1909, no. 839, pp. 7–8.

"V.F. Kommissarzhevskaia o svoem teatre i ego novykh putiakh", *Obozrenie teatrov*, 1907, no. 69, pp. 5–8.

Vasil'eva, N.S., "Kak voznikli dramaticheskie kursy", *Ezhegodnik imperatorskikh teatrov*, 1911, vypusk V, pp. 1–11.

Veinberg, P., "M.N. Ermolova", *Teatral'naia rossiia*, 1905, no. 7, pp. 93–4.

"Vesti o V.F. Kommissarzhevskoi", *Obozrenie teatrov*, 1908, no. 378, pp. 3–4.

Viren, V., "Narodnyi talant", *Teatral'naia zhizn'*, 1975, no. 19, pp. 30–1.

Viv'en, L., "V Aleksandrinskom teatre nakanune revolutsii", *Zvezda*, 1957, no. 1, pp. 180–94.

"*Vlast' t'my*", *Teatr i iskusstvo*, 1902, no. 39, pp. 699–700.

Volynski, A., "Kritika", *Severnyi vestnik*, 1896, no. 12, part II, pp. 53–66.

—— "Literaturnye zametki: Peterburgskie teatry", *Severnyi vestnik*, 1898, no. 8–9, pp. 156–81.

"Vospominaniia A.M. Pazukhina", in *Galereia stsenicheskikh deiatelei*, t. 1, Moscow, Izdanie zhurnala *Rampa i zhizn'*, 1915, pp. 17–26.

Voznesenski, A.N., "Stsenicheskii dogovor", *Studiia*, 1911, no. 11, pp. 4–5.

Weldon, Henry, "Inostranets o Gorevoi (pis'mo iz Berlin)", *Teatral'nyi mirok*, 1886, no. 4, p. 3.

"Za prava zhenshchina-artistki", *Rampa i zhizn'*, 1911, no. 25, pp. 2–3.

"Zametki teatrala: starorusskii teatr", *Teatral*, 1895, no. 33, pp. 126–30.

Zel'dovich, M., "Zhenskaia dobrodetel' i stsena", *Teatr i iskusstvo*, 1904, no. 34, pp. 623–5.

Zelov, N., "V nei bylo mnogo solntsa", *Teatral'naia zhizn'*, 1964, no. 21, p. 21.

"Zhenshchina i razvitie ei lichnosti", *Zhenskii vestnik*, 1905, no. 7, pp. 202–5.

"Zhenshchina na stsene", *Teatral'naia rossia*, 1905, no. 17, pp. 289–91.

"*Zhenshchina s moria*", *Teatr i iskusstvo*, 1903, no. 5, pp. 114–15.

"Zhenstvennost' i sinie chulki", in *O zhenshchinakh: mysli starye i novye*, St. Petersburg: n.p., 1886, pp. 68–89.

Zhernovaia, G.A., "Stenicheskoe voploshchenie zhenskogo ideala v 1880-e gody", in *Russkii teatr i obshchestvennoe dvizhenie*, Leningrad: n.p., 1984, pp. 71–86.

Zigfrid, "*No. 13 i Master*", *Sankt Peterburgskie vedomosti*, December 17, 1904, p. 3.

—— "Otkrytie teatra V.F. Kommissarzhevskoi", *Sankt Peterburgskie vedomosti*, November 12, 1906, p. 2.

—— "Na chto on byl nuzhen", *Obozrenie teatrov*, 1907, no. 251, pp. 13–14.

—— "Pamiati V.F. Kommissarzhevskoi", *Obozrenie teatrov*, 1911, no. 1316, pp. 14–15.

Zolotnitski, D.I., "Strashnaia sila teatra", in *Russkii teatr i dramaturgiia kontsa XIX veka*, Leningrad: n.p., 1983, pp. 104–11.

INDEX